Inscription and Rebellion

Studies in German Literature, Linguistics, and Culture

Inscription and Rebellion

Illness and the Symptomatic Body in East German Literature

Sonja E. Klocke

Rochester, New York

Copyright © 2015 Sonja E. Klocke

All Rights Reserved. Except as permitted under current legislation,
no part of this work may be photocopied, stored in a retrieval system,
published, performed in public, adapted, broadcast, transmitted,
recorded, or reproduced in any form or by any means,
without the prior permission of the copyright owner.

First published 2015 by Camden House
Reprinted in paperback 2019

Camden House is an imprint of Boydell & Brewer Inc.
668 Mt. Hope Avenue, Rochester, NY 14620, USA
www.camden-house.com
and of Boydell & Brewer Limited
PO Box 9, Woodbridge, Suffolk IP12 3DF, UK
www.boydellandbrewer.com

Paperback ISBN-13: 978-1-64014-055-4
Paperback ISBN-10: 1-64014-055-7
Hardcover ISBN-13: 978-1-57113-933-7
Hardcover ISBN-10: 1-57113-933-8

Library of Congress Cataloging-in-Publication Data

Names: Klocke, Sonja E., author.
Title: Inscription and rebellion : illness and the symptomatic body in East German literature / Sonja E. Klocke.
Description: Rochester, New York : Camden House, [2015] | Series: Studies in German literature, linguistics, and culture | Includes bibliographical references and index.
Identifiers: LCCN 2015021722| ISBN 9781571139337 (hardcover : alk. paper) | ISBN 1571139338 (hardcover : alk. paper)
Subjects: LCSH: German literature—Germany (East)—History and criticism. | Diseases in literature. | Medical care in literature.
Classification: LCC PT3710.D57 K56 2015 | DDC 830.9/356109431—dc23 LC record available at http://lccn.loc.gov/2015021722

This publication is printed on acid-free paper.
Printed in the United States of America.

Meinen Eltern

Contents

Acknowledgments	ix
Introduction	1
1: Disease, Death, and Desire Pre-1989: Christa Wolf's Symptomatic GDR Bodies	34
2: Christa Wolf's Goodbye to Socialism?: Illness, Healing, and Faith since 1990	72
3: Retrospective Imagination in Post-GDR Literature: Gender, Violence, and Politics in Medical Discourses	114
4: Haunted in Post-Wall Germany: Sickness, Symptomatic Bodies, and the Specters of the GDR	155
Conclusion	188
Glossary	197
Bibliography	199
Index	233

Acknowledgments

THIS BOOK HAS GROWN over the course of several years. Many colleagues, mentors, friends, and family members shaped and encouraged it. Thanks go first to the Department of German at the University of Wisconsin-Madison for advocating a teaching release I received in spring 2014, and to the University of Wisconsin-Madison Graduate School with funding from the Wisconsin Alumni Research Foundation for supporting this project with summer funding in 2013 and 2014. Earlier stages of my research were sponsored by an Andrew W. Mellon Foundation Grant for Faculty Career Enhancement at Knox College, which allowed me to conduct research in the spring and summer of 2010.

I am fortunate to belong to the vibrant and collegial Department of German at the University of Wisconsin–Madison. I owe particular gratitude to Sabine Gross and Marc Silberman for guiding me through the publication process, and for offering advice, inspiration, and feedback at various stages of the project. Both of them, together with my colleagues and friends from different paths of life, Julie Allen, Claudia Breger, Kate Brooks, Claudia Kost, Peter Paul Schwarz, Jeff Simpson, Jill Suzanne Smith, and Faye Stewart, supported me by reading, discussing, and commenting on various portions of the manuscript, fellowship applications, or publishing materials. All of them provided invaluable feedback, sound advice, encouragement for my project, and generously shared their knowledge. Claudia Breger supervised my dissertation, parts of which laid the groundwork for this book. Over the course of many years, she has continued to be an inspiring mentor and friend. Claudia Kost listened to and commented on various stages of the project on a weekly basis. I cherish our Sunday-night dinners on Skype. My project also benefitted from discussions with numerous friends and colleagues in the Coalition of Women in German. I would not want to miss being part of this network. I am grateful to my wonderful friend and incredibly gifted colleague in the UW-Madison Art Department, Gerit Grimm, for allowing me to use a photograph of one of her ceramic sculptures for the cover of this book. Jim Walker and his staff at Camden House were wonderful to work with. In particular, I thank Jim for his enthusiastic reception of my topic from the first time we made contact. I am also grateful to the anonymous reviewers for their helpful suggestions and advice.

Parts of chapter 3 appeared in *Glossen* 26 (December 2007) under the title "Lost in Transition: 'Unfinished Women,' Insanity, and

Deviant Bodies as Locus of Memory in the No Man's Land of Thomas Brussig's *Wie es leuchtet*," and in *Germanistik in Ireland: Jahrbuch der/Yearbook of the Association of Third-Level Teachers of German in Ireland* 5 (2010) under the title "Die frohe Botschaft der Kathrin Schmidt?—Transsexuality, Racism, and Feminist Historiography in *Die Gunnar-Lennefsen-Expedition* (1998)." An earlier version of some topics addressed in chapter 4 was published in *Emerging German Novelists*, edited by Lyn Marven and Stuart Taberner (Camden House, 2011) under the title "A Woman's Quest for Agency: Kathrin Schmidt, *Du stirbst nicht* (2009)." Both journals and Camden House have kindly granted permission to republish this material.

Words cannot express how grateful I am for my family: the repeated expressions of interest from my nephew, Timi, cheered me on; and especially the ongoing encouragement from my parents, Ellen and Hans-Joachim Klocke, has been a tremendous support, especially in the final stages of this project. I dedicate this book to them.

Introduction

IN THE 2003 MOVIE *Good Bye, Lenin!*, the staunch socialist Christiane Kerner witnesses East Berlin's *Volkspolizei* (people's police) ruthlessly clubbing peaceful demonstrators during the celebrations marking the fortieth anniversary of the founding of the German Democratic Republic (GDR) in October 1989.[1] When she discovers her teenage son Alex among the predominantly young people demanding freedom of the press and the right to travel without restrictions, Christiane suffers a near-fatal heart attack, falls into a coma, and is hospitalized. When she awakens eight months later, the Berlin Wall has fallen, and the new furniture and appliances in the family's apartment signal the changes in society. The doctors warn Alex that any anxiety could kill her, prompting him to protect his mother from the historical transformations by reconstructing the GDR in and also as her sickroom. Christiane's death three days after German unification (October 3, 1990) and the dispersal of her ashes in the wind correlate with the end of the East German socialist state. Alex highlights this idea at the end of the film: "Das Land, das meine Mutter verließ, war ein Land, an das sie geglaubt hatte. . . . Ein Land, das in meiner Erinnerung immer mit meiner Mutter verbunden sein wird." (The country my mother left was a country she believed in. . . . A country that in my memory will always be linked with my mother.)[2] Alex's final words link the grief over his mother's death with the demise of the socialist state she believed in. They leave the audience with an opportunity to mourn the GDR, which symbolically comes to an end when the mother's body vanishes into thin air. When Alex emphasizes the role memory plays in connecting the GDR with Christiane, he points to the female character's function as a reminder of cultural, political, and historical memory. The son remembers the GDR through his mother, assigning her a commemorative function that suggests to the audience how history from below is an addition and a challenge to hegemonic historiography.[3]

This film became the biggest commercial success of any German film since the fall of the Berlin Wall. It won numerous European awards, circulated internationally, and was nominated for a Golden Globe for Best Foreign Language Film. It brings together several topics: the (final days of the) GDR and its state authorities' brutal exercise of power; a gendered body reacting physically and submitting to medical treatment in a GDR hospital; and the cultural, political, and historical memory of the GDR linked to an ailing female body. These topics are also crucial in a significant number of East German literary texts. Their convergence forms the core of the prose works analyzed in this book. This includes GDR as well as post-GDR texts written by authors who lived in and portray the GDR, published both before and after October 1990.[4]

The conspicuous existence of post-1989 texts focusing on the GDR and the noted convergence of topics in East German literature raise several questions. First, why does the GDR remain a persistent topic, well into the twenty-first century? After all, *Good Bye, Lenin!* is not a singular phenomenon but one of many popular texts that revolve around, remember, and often creatively re-imagine the GDR.[5] Second, what is the significance of ill, female (both cis- and transgender) bodies and of GDR medical institutions at the center of many texts focusing on the GDR and its demise?[6] And finally, to what extent is this convergence of illness, gender, bodies, and the (socialist) state a literary convention that is specific to East German literature? If this custom proliferated in GDR literature, how did it develop after unification?

To explore these questions, this book offers a dual approach. In the first part, it examines prose texts by Christa Wolf (1929–2011), the GDR's most prominent writer, who ideologically and emotionally identified with the socialist state. Emphasizing the importance of her portrayal of ill female bodies and the healthcare system, the first two chapters demonstrate how Wolf mobilized her work to expose imperfections and inconsistencies of the socialist state through representations of illness inscribed on female characters who are subjected to male-dominated medical institutions. Chapter 1 concentrates on the author's pre-unification texts and particularly on *Nachdenken über Christa T.* (1968; *The Quest for Christa T.*, 1970), which highlights the female body marked by psychosomatic ailments and fatal disease in order to expose the obstacles Wolf discerned in advancing the socialist state.[7] The protagonist's physical reaction to political events of the 1950s and 1960s is illness and death. Read with a focus on the body as it relates to its socio-political environment, the text reveals the author's ongoing belief in the future of socialism. Chapter 2 discusses developments in Wolf's writing strategies after the fall of the Wall. For example, *Leibhaftig* (2002; *In the Flesh*, 2005) focuses more centrally and dramatically on the ill female body than any other of Wolf's novels. Reading it in conjunction with *Stadt der Engel oder The Overcoat of Dr. Freud* (2010; *City of Angels, Or the Overcoat of Dr. Freud*, 2013) reveals the extent to which bodies serve as symbolic spaces where political conflicts and the individual's struggles play themselves out in Wolf's oeuvre, both pre- and post-unification. This comparative approach further uncovers how Wolf negotiates societal problems and discourses surrounding the memory of the GDR through medical discourses after the historical turning point of 1989.

The second half of this study traces the ways in which Wolf's representations of ill female bodies and of the GDR healthcare system have inspired the literary production of writers who were raised in the GDR, were shaped by its political system, and who have published either predominantly or exclusively after 1989.[8] Discourses on bodies as well as the medical system, including the genetic and pharmaceutical research conducted on patients in the GDR as retrospectively imagined in Kerstin Hensel's *Lärchenau* (Lärchenau, 2008), Kathrin Schmidt's *Die Gunnar-Lennefsen-Expedition* (The Gunnar-Lennefsen-Expedition, 1998), and Thomas Brussig's *Wie es leuchtet* (How It Shines, 2004), are the topics of chapter 3. Chapter 4 explores Antje Rávic Strubel's *Sturz der Tage in die Nacht* (When Days Plunge into Night, 2012), Kathrin Schmidt's *Du stirbst nicht* (You Are Not Going to Die, 2009), and again Kerstin Hensel's *Lärchenau*. These post-GDR novels use bodies and medical discourses to reveal vestiges of the GDR lingering in unified Germany. In a manner reminiscent of Christa Wolf's writing style, the GDR, and sometimes even the fascist German past, emerge as overshadowing contemporary East German lives as expressed in the characters' suffering. Here bodies that are preoccupied with—and often plagued by—their GDR past provide readers with a sense of the lived experiences of GDR citizens; experiences that—in the manner of a history from below—give voice to those previously marginalized in a way that can add to, and challenge, hegemonic historiography.

The close readings offered in chapters 3 and 4 illustrate how these younger post-GDR authors playfully engage with Wolf's oeuvre and writing style and implicitly or explicitly refer to her use of ill bodies and the depiction of medical institutions. Both the novels that retrospectively imagine the GDR—explored in chapter 3—and the fictional texts that portray suffering characters haunted by their GDR past—probed in chapter 4—disclose the underlying propinquity of Christa Wolf and her works. Through this comparative look at individual post-GDR prose texts, we can see how even in very recent fiction that may not initially seem concerned with the GDR, the socialist state uncannily surfaces in medical discourses or is signaled by bodies suffering from illness. This study thus maps a genealogy of an East German literary convention: indicating, criticizing, and rebelling against political and social norms and constraints is depicted in specific instances, states, and manifestations of the body within the operations of a healthcare system. It is a poetic practice that has not only continued, but proven fertile in generating portraits of the GDR, its demise and its wholesale subsumption by the FRG, as well as the loss of utopian energy in post-GDR fiction. In order to render the significance of ill bodies in East German prose fiction visible, this study establishes a conceptual framework in which research investigating the GDR medical system—a system shaped by Marxist-Leninist thought—and scholarship on the significance of the female body for conceptions of the nation and German history intersect.

"Health Is a Valuable Asset of the State": The Idiosyncrasies of the GDR Healthcare System

German studies scholarship has pointed to the proliferation of fictional discourses about illness and health—predominantly, but not exclusively, in East German literature—in the aftermath of the so-called *Wende* of 1989/90, and explained the phenomemon as a means to express threats to the social body after the fall of the Wall.[9] This observation, while accurate, overlooks the fact that depictions of illness and bodies in medical institutions were already abundant in GDR literature before the fall of the Wall; and they continue to play a vital role in post-GDR fiction written in the twenty-first century.[10] Given the profusion of discourses of pathology in East German literature dealing with the idiosyncrasies of the political situation both before and after unification, it might seem surprising that scholarship has largely neglected to focus on the links between illness, medical institutions, and history.[11] Yet the disregard for the portrayal of the GDR medical system and its patients pre- and post-unification may partially be explained by the lack of serious and unbiased scholarly work on the specificity of the quotidian reality in GDR medical institutions. Such research would have to build on archival material as much as on the testimony of contemporary witnesses whose individual experiences, taken in their entirety, could illuminate the complex processes at work in medical institutions as well as these institutions' cooperation with individual stakeholders. While serious attempts to expand such research have been made in the last few years and continue to be made, scholarship on the subject is clearly still in its fledging stages.[12]

In *The People's State*, Mary Fulbrook points out that in the GDR, "as everywhere, the very physical existence of people—their births, the pattern of their illnesses, the manner and timing of their deaths—cannot be disentangled from the circumstances in which they lived" (90). Without doubt, the political, social, and also the GDR medical system was different from that of all other German-speaking countries; and while the GDR as a political entity has ceased to exist, the cultural aspects persist, including a medical culture influenced by and medical staff trained in accordance with Marxist-Leninist thought.[13] Precisely because of this link between illness and politics, medical discourses that surface in GDR and post-GDR literature produced by writers who experienced the GDR medical system first-hand can be enlightening. I therefore place depictions not only of diseased female (both cis- and transgender) bodies, but also of the healthcare system in East German literature into dialogue with the available medical-historical research. Additionally, I investigate the link between the medical system and surveillance by the Stasi.[14] This approach demonstrates East German literature's capacity to function as a reservoir of knowledge about everyday culture in the

GDR which can contribute to writing a GDR history that challenges dominant narratives.

Michel Foucault's work on the emergence of medical institutions since the eighteenth century informs our understanding of how governments increasingly control medical institutions and therapeutic spaces. The latter were linked with other state institutions such as prisons or courts in order to enforce norms resulting from medical "truth" and contingent on culture and history.[15] Considering the medical realm as part of a larger power network is essential in the case of the GDR, which built and later consolidated various state institutions along the lines of Marxist-Leninist ideology. As early as 1946, people's health and access to free medical care for everyone in the Soviet Occupied Zone were of official concern, and the Soviet Military Administration began developing a nationalized healthcare system. The overall concept was based on healthcare policies propagated by the German labor movement prior to the "Third Reich" and the Soviet model. Lenin's idea that health presented "ein wertvolles Staatseigentum" (a valuable asset of the state) linked healthcare with the state's interest in utilizing each citizen's productivity for the building of socialism.[16] From the start, however, improving citizens' health was also seen as an aspect of "democratization." For many people, the new socialist system constituted a significant improvement regarding access to healthcare. At the same time, the ideological emphasis on the collective implied that the individual was to be physically incorporated into the socialist state. In other words, the individual bodies came to be regarded as the property of the GDR and thus as representative of, even capable of standing in symbolically for the state and its socialist values.

Since symbolic and physical appropriation could not be detached from each other, the body's perfect semiotic performance depended on its state of physical health—which had to be controlled and regulated by a variety of state institutions, particularly the medical system. Since the 1950s, the widely circulated slogan "die beste Prophylaxe ist der Sozialismus" (the best prophylaxis is socialism) accordingly points to the significance of prevention, both on the medical and the social level.[17] Again, overcoming social difference clearly included eliminating health disparities caused by class difference.[18] At the same time, the individual had no chance to opt out: since the body was deemed both a possession and a metonymic representation of the socialist state, failure to participate in preventive programs would have been tantamount to an attack on state property.

To enforce this conception of the socialist body as a public asset whose health had to be assured, the government attempted to anchor the medical system ideologically by placing reliable members of the ruling *Sozialistische Einheitspartei Deutschlands* (SED, Socialist Unity Party of Germany) in significant new positions in the public health sector and particularly in university hospitals.[19] Both the facilities and the medical staff were integrated into the centralized state-run system and became subject to a socialist professional ethics that emphasized each doctor's responsibility towards society over patient care.[20] Several university reforms, the first introduced as early as 1946, ensured that degree programs in medicine were adapted accordingly by incorporating new compulsory classes in areas including the humanities, Marxism-Leninism, and political economy.

Compared with these swift modifications, the infiltration of the medical system by Stasi informants began later, in the second half of the 1950s, after Erich Mielke assumed office as Minister for State Security in November 1957.[21] While his predecessor Ernst Wollweber had focused on Stasi activities outside the GDR, Mielke considered domestic affairs more significant. The medical system came into focus because of the high number of physicians and nurses who left the GDR before the Wall was built in 1961, which resulted in a dramatic shortage of physicians and nursing staff and placed a strain on remaining coworkers.[22] While the Wall mitigated the crisis in the healthcare system as the number of physicians leaving the GDR decreased after 1961, the situation worsened again in the 1970s when more employees took advantage of relaxed travel restrictions for professionals in the Honecker years and left for the West. Consequently, Stasi infiltration in medical institutions, particularly in hospitals, increased steadily in subsequent years: the aim was less to gather information about patients than to gain knowledge about physicians planning to leave the country illegally.[23] A 1976 order issued by the Ministry for State Security also cast Stasi officers in the somewhat surprising role of mediating between hospitals and doctors, and later between physicians and the SED. They participated in finding solutions for conflicts that doctors, in particular, had to face in their quotidian life in GDR hospitals (Süß, *Pm*, 234).

GDR law placed a great deal of power in the hands of physicians—power that could easily be directed against individual patients' interests. The GDR-specific doctor-patient relationship in particular, in which there was no legal contract between a patient and a doctor, meant that the responsibility for balancing the protection of a patient's individual health and the greater good of the community rested entirely with the physician. In this context, the physician Susanne Hahn highlights the major difference between the GDR's *Betreuungsverhältnis* (medical care relationship) and legal practice in the Federal Republic of Germany (FRG):

> Während in der BRD der ärztliche Eingriff im Strafrecht... als Körperverletzung galt und bis heute gilt, die nur durch die Einwilligung des Patienten exkulpiert werden kann, war der indizierte und lege artis durchgeführte ärztliche Eingriff in der DDR prinzipiell eine Heilbehandlung.

[While in the FRG a medical intervention has been and still is considered an infliction of bodily harm in criminal law, which can only be suspended by means of a patient's consent, a prescribed medical intervention deemed necessary and carried out according to standard practice was, as a matter of principle, considered therapy in the GDR.][24]

GDR law left decisions regarding a prescribed therapy exclusively to the physician. While the medical staff tried to persuade patients to agree to compulsory examinations and, if applicable, to treatment, patients knew they were obligated to follow doctors' orders either way. As "socialist personalities" firmly committed to the advancement of socialism, it was incumbent upon patients to cooperate since individual health and the health of the community—in analogy to personal and societal interests—were considered one entity.[25] Accordingly, patients had to participate in any measure supporting the *Volksgesundheit* (community health), such as preventative personal hygiene, vaccination campaigns, and medical screenings.[26]

This centralized approach proved most successful in healthcare technology assessment and in combating cancer. The GDR established a World Health Organization-certified Comprehensive Cancer Center, which positioned the socialist state as an international leader in cancer prevention, but which was dismantled in the unification process.[27] While protecting one's health ceased to be a private matter, and notions of individual choice and doctor-patient confidentiality were considered secondary to the health of the entire population, the individual benefitted from the overall success of preventative care.[28] On the downside, these measures implied state control, which extended to fields tangentially related to the medical sphere. Since the protection of individuals' health was an effort of society at large, power exercised in healthcare was tightly linked with the judicial system and social welfare, and often also included the support received from a working person's collective.[29] In other words, while GDR citizens benefitted from the healthcare system in a supposedly classless society, these benefits simultaneously demanded compliance with the needs and goals of GDR society at large.

Class differences emerged primarily in terms of privilege when the socialist state encountered glitches that presented obstacles to its goal of providing adequate healthcare services to everyone. While in the FRG and other capitalist countries the economic situation of the patient is the main factor in determining privilege in the healthcare system, in the supposedly classless society of the GDR the system of privilege was largely a function of politics.[30] Members of the government, political cadres, high-ranking military officers, veterans of the "antifascist struggle," and representatives of the wider socialist elite—including members of the cultural intelligentsia—were treated in special hospitals that were substantially better equipped with supplies and medical technology.[31] Yet, since the semiotic function of every citizen's physical body for the state depended on its health, all regular hospitals did not as a rule differentiate among patients admitted.[32] While socialist countries, too, needed to make decisions regarding the availability of specialized care for specific patients, the GDR was generally interested in providing all citizens—who, after all, formed the collective—with the best care the state could possibly afford to ensure the well-being of its assets, or: the bodies that also served as the metonymic representation of the GDR. In other words, if those bodies became ill, they temporarily escaped the state's control in what amounted to a form of rebellion. In these instances the impairment of the body's semiotic performance doubled as damage to state resources.

Symptomatic Bodies as a Form of Rebellion and Corporeal Memory

As indicated earlier, this book's point of departure—the convergence of illness, gender, representations of the body, and the (socialist) state in the discursive field of East German fiction—raises questions of literary conventions, politics, and historiography. When tackling these concerns and themes, the physicality of the body and the significance of corporeal memory for understanding and interpreting the past inevitably move to the forefront. Sigrid Weigel asserted that memory discourses in Western traditions developed a tendency to downplay corporeal memory, not least of all as a result of the significance assigned to psychoanalytical models deemed capable of dealing with the past in order to incorporate it into the present and the future.[33] Without aiming to slight the importance of psychoanalytical approaches, I emphasize the corporeal dimension of lived experience. As I will demonstrate in what follows, the knowledge embodied in what I call the *symptomatic body* comes to the fore as a powerful socioaesthetic construct in East German literature. The symptomatic body in these fictional worlds is identified as female by the society in which it moves; historical and political events leave their traces on the character's flesh and/or psyche, where they appear as physical and/or psychological illness.

The symptoms range from headaches, fevers, and blindness to severe depression and loss of speech. Sometimes, sickness opens up possibilities for temporary escape from uncomfortable circumstances or psychic conflicts; at other times, physical symptoms serve as warning signs that allow a fictional character to prepare for outside threats. Scars on the body indicate violent experiences during surgery or imprisonment; they can even be deciphered as a tattooed number burned into the flesh in a Nazi concentration camp. The fictional characters who endure the various physical and psychological wounds largely understand the opportunities inherent in their suffering: supported by their symptoms, these bodies gain access to previously hidden memories and to knowledge of the past. When the historical learning process materializes in a visible inscription on the flesh, these bodies become mnemonic sites. While the fictional characters analyzed in this study take up very different positions vis-à-vis the social reality that triggers their symptoms, their bodies all produce insight into or increased awareness of a political situation and often greater cognizance of their individual entanglement in political affairs. Symptomatic bodies placed in specific historical circumstances—such as revolutions or wars—invite us to read them as allegories for the body politic: a character's health is then turned into a seismograph of the state of the country. A severely ill character might mirror a state struggling for survival: disease thus indicates social problems and criticizes political norms. A character's physical breakdown might challenge the ideology at the core of a portrayed state; a patient's survival, in turn, can signal victory and possibly confirm an ideology.

While the prototype is the cis-gender female body marked by illness, the spectrum of symptomatic bodies also includes transgender and transsexual female bodies as well as persons with intersexual bodies who choose to identify as female.[34] Of particular interest in these literary texts are cis- and transgender, transsexual, and intersexual females who are forced to submit to a healthcare provider because the diegetic social world in which they move considers this necessary. This can, for example, affect pregnant women as well as transsexual persons forced to undergo surgery. Both the depicted medical systems and the traces left on the body as a consequence of their therapeutic interventions speak to the power of the socio-political forces at work in the examined prose texts. Understood in this manner as a socioaesthetic construct in literature and a locus of cultural inscriptions,[35] symptomatic bodies can be analyzed with regard to their aptitude to resist, display, or reinforce structures of domination in the displayed fictional worlds.

Simone Barck's claim that GDR fiction is a more illuminating source of knowledge about GDR society than scholarly publications by historians includes the medical realm and medical historiography.[36] This is particularly true since in the GDR, discussions surrounding problematic topics—such as, for example, questions regarding ethics in the medical field—tended to take place in small circles, not in public forums supported by the media. Since the GDR mass media merely broadcast experts' decisions, much of the reflection about illness and patients in medical institutions in the GDR that became available to the general public was conveyed through literature and film.³⁷ As a result, GDR fiction presents a remarkable archive of information about daily life and issues debated in GDR society. Texts that depict symptomatic bodies and the healthcare system reveal cultural and ideological discourses in medical institutions as well as norms governing GDR society. This includes, but is by no means limited to, the signifiers for pathology, since GDR citizens clearly understood the medical system as a part of society that reflected both the problems and the standards governing their GDR world at large.³⁸ Especially because they are engendered and socialized in their particular cultural and political environment, bodies privy to the social experience of the GDR reveal both that society's particular norms and the desire to challenge and even escape those norms.

As the locus of political and cultural inscription as well as a means of responding to historical events, the symptomatic body plays a key role in the challenges to hegemonic GDR history presented by and in the prose texts investigated here—a history that is understood as encompassing both the official narratives propagated by the GDR government and the discourses about the GDR that circulate in unified Germany. As various historians and German Studies scholars have established, East German history has been predominantly constructed in ways that reinforce the image of the GDR as a dictatorship. This favored historiography promotes the development and preservation of a collective memory of the GDR along the lines of what Martin Sabrow has identified as the *Diktaturgedächtnis* (memory of the GDR as a dictatorship).³⁹ This memory discourse focuses exclusively on the antagonism between perpetrator and victim and on the oppressive character of the SED regime and the Stasi vis-à-vis the opposition's courage in 1989/90. It is grounded in the FRG's early founding narrative which collapsed the atrocities of the Nazi regime and Communist rule in the rhetoric of totalitarianism to justify the supremacy of the West German model of democracy.⁴⁰ Accordingly, discourses along the lines of the *Diktaturgedächtnis* exclusively interpret the GDR as an *Unrechtsstaat* (unconstitutional state; literally, a state in which the rule of law did not exist) or, influenced by the resurgence of the totalitarian paradigm, as a dictatorship comparable to Nazi Germany.⁴¹ Modes of interpreting the GDR along the lines of the *Diktaturgedächtnis* dominate the media, official discourse, school textbooks, state-funded museums and memorials, and public commemorations in the Berlin Republic. They overshadow memories of the GDR that follow what has been termed the *Arrangementgedächtnis* (memory of accommodation) and the *Fortschrittsgedächtnis* (memory of progress).⁴² The former focuses on quotidian life in the GDR and emphasizes the complexity of lived experiences of GDR citizens, while the latter adheres to socialist ideals and insists on socialism's legitimacy as an alternative to capitalism. These two forms of memory largely comprise the communicative memory of the majority of former GDR citizens, which differs from the images propagated by the media as well as official memory.

This divergence points to a deep-seated lack of consensus about what the GDR was and how it should be remembered, and about what its place in national history and its significance for the construction of German national identity should be. The predominantly negative image of the GDR conveyed in discourses based on *Diktaturgedächtnis* devalues GDR biographies by staging East Germans as fundamentally different and deficient. It confirms the East-West division and the hegemony of West German elites. Yet the ongoing production and reception of literary works and films that revolve around and remember the GDR, as mentioned at the outset of this introduction, indicates a strong desire on the part of authors and filmmakers to influence collective views of the GDR. If their contributions disturb the *Diktaturgedächtnis*, their engagement may lead to a more nuanced understanding of the GDR. One of the aims of this study, then, is to reveal how the fictional texts under investigation and their representations of the historical reality of the GDR participate in promoting a particular image of the GDR; an image that may contribute to shaping the collective memory of the socialist country. Allowing us to read their embodied knowledge, symptomatic bodies can tell the untold stories of daily life as influenced by political events. If, for example, the body and its performance challenge the hegemonic social norms valid in the GDR society portrayed, such bodily acts need to be understood as rebellious. Whether they buttress notions of the *Diktaturgedächtnis* must be determined by careful analysis. After all, fictional texts may refrain from assuming a monolithic perspective and allow for a more contradictory image of the GDR by presenting, for example, a variety of individuals and diverging subject positions. Other symptomatic bodies may serve to affirm the depicted social and political environment in which an individual moves, and may consequently support interpretations of the GDR along the lines of the *Arrangementgedächtnis* or even the *Fortschrittsgedächtnis*. In other words, symptomatic bodies, which emerge as a site of social experience as well as potential resistance to political and social constraints and standards, are inherently political.

As stated before, the proliferation of symptomatic bodies and GDR-specific medical discourses in East German literature written before and after 1989 is conspicuous. Since this practice of defying social norms and indicating political upheaval continues after German unification, GDR literature can hardly be said to have ended in 1990. Yet the plurality of diverging, at times contradictory, ideas of what constitutes GDR literature is astonishing. The following overview of developments in East German literature is aimed in particular at readers who are not German Studies experts. It also provides the background for my understanding of GDR and post-GDR literature.

Authors and Literature in the GDR

Positioned at the Cold War front, the two German states each developed master narratives, complemented by a biased image of their respective counterpart, to support their respective claims that they had drawn the right conclusions from the catastrophe of National Socialist rule. While Western propaganda collapsed Nazi terror and Communist dictatorship into the rhetoric of totalitarianism, the SED claimed that the GDR presented the only alternative to capitalism and National Socialism. The latter was considered an outgrowth of the imperialist capitalist system, a view that was vindicated by the FRG's "strong personal ties with the Third Reich," as Thomas Ahbe notes in "Competing Master Narratives" (222). These continuities in personnel led the GDR to declare the capitalist West the exclusive successor of National Socialism, while they positioned themselves as legitimate heir to the antifascist resistance to Nazi rule.[43] In other words, the SED legitimated its claims to power through the discourse of antifascism.

This ideological division was replicated in the cultural sphere. Jan Assmann's *Das kulturelle Gedächtnis* (1992; *Cultural Memory and Early Civilization*, 2011) suggests that authors in all cultures participate in constructing the cultural memory fundamental for perpetuating a group identity (54). Yet GDR authorities took a noteworthy path by interfering in their writers' social function. From the start, the government supported its authors, many of whom were survivors of Nazi concentration camps or returning exiles—with the expectation that they imbue their literature with partisan political meaning. Since writers like Willi Bredel, Otto Gotsche, Anna Seghers, or Stefan Heym identified with the country, its ideology, and the underlying ideals, their writings reflected the attendant values and norms privileged by the state. Early GDR literature thus served as an effective means of educating citizens and of convincing them of the legitimacy of the socialist state. With their *Aufbauliteratur* (literature of socialist construction), these writers helped define GDR identity by developing modes of writing that engaged the GDR's founding narrative of antifascism by celebrating the Communist martyrdom of heroes of the antifascist resistance alongside the liberation by the Red Army. These early texts presented everyone who accepted the Soviet offer of redemption in the shape of socialist reeducation with the opportunity to associate discursively with either resistance or victimhood to National Socialism.

In *Post-Fascist Fantasies*, Julia Hell has examined the underlying model in detail. She reads the early GDR texts of *Aufbauliteratur* as "*foundational narratives of antifascism*."[44] They create fictional surrogate families organized around ideal communists who assume the role of symbolic parental figures whom the sons and daughters in the narrative can admire, and with whom young readers are solicited to identify (*PFF*,

107). Under fascist torture, the antifascist heroes suffered indescribable pain, which is inscribed in the body and at the same time leads to purification. This brought Hell to describe this "body-in-pain" (*PFF*, 33)—with reference to Slavoj Žižek—as "the *sublime body* of the communist hero of antifascism," and as an asexual, "*post-fascist body*" (*PFF*, 19; italics in original). Hell traces how "in these novels, sexuality is defined as that part of subjectivity which links the subject to its fascist past, and the new [Communist] subject comes about as a result of the erasure of its material body, its sexual body" (*PFF*, 19). Accordingly, fascism is linked with sexuality and juxtaposed against communism, which is in turn linked with antifascism; with the antifascist, sublime und suffering body; with the absence of a sexual body; and with purity. The foundational GDR texts of *Aufbauliteratur*, their manner of narrating social relations as family relations and of placing suffering bodies center stage proved influential for the next generation of writers, those who were teenagers in 1945: the imaginary antifascist parental figures of *Aufbauliteratur* could take the place of their biological parents.

One of the writers influenced by early GDR literature, Christa Wolf, became the central figure of a generation of authors that emerged in the 1960s and had to position themselves vis-à-vis the "parent generation" of exiles and communist resistance fighters.[45] This generation, often identified today as "1929ers,"[46] was influenced by three decisive events: the experience of National Socialism and World War II as children and adolescents; the construction of the Berlin Wall in 1961, which led to a more relaxed political atmosphere and societal modernization after the pressure of constant direct confrontation with the West had ceased;[47] and the experience of the infamous Eleventh Plenum of the Central Committee of the ruling SED in 1965, also known as the *Kahlschlag-Plenum* (clean-sweep plenum). At this party event, Erich Honecker, who later became the General Secretary of the Central Committee of the SED (1971–89), announced that skepticism and the development of socialism were mutually incompatible. His words officially put an end to any tendencies that he and his comrades associated with liberalism and the West, and justified the banning of numerous films and books. Honecker insisted on the artists' commitment to a partisan approach to political and aesthetic evaluations of GDR reality; an approach that supported SED politics at all times.[48] When Christa Wolf spoke out against such demands, her status as potential member of the Central Committee of the SED was upended, but she became the canonical GDR writer. She was nationally and internationally celebrated and influential for decades, not least of all because her texts contravened Honecker's orders in their ongoing struggle to negotiate notions of freedom and democratization in socialist society.[49]

After the Eleventh Plenum, dissenting intellectuals such as Christa Wolf, Heiner Müller, and Volker Braun faced a quandary: because of the ties of the FRG elite to the fascist German past, the West did not present an alternative for most of them, which meant they could only advocate reforms of the GDR from within.[50] Convinced of the socialist ideals and often with ties to the administration, these loyal dissidents were still considered oppositional by the government.[51] They were kept under Stasi surveillance because they understood their prominent position as an obligation to pinpoint socialist values largely ignored in quotidian life, and to reflect on GDR society in the absence of a critical media presence. When this first generation of writers who came of age in the socialist state emerged in the 1960s, Germany saw the beginning of a discrete GDR literature. It developed both thematic and stylistic specificities, which, starting in 1967, were also acknowledged in the FRG as characteristic of a socialist literature.[52] In their fiction, authors like Christa Wolf negotiated societal controversies and cautiously took up official and unofficial discourses prevalent in society. And readers in the GDR, aware that books constituted the prime public space where differences of opinion were articulated, developed their competence in uncovering the relevant arguments.[53] Fictional discourses could therefore, in return, feed the societal discourses upon which they were built, a cycle that explains the constantly growing social significance of literature and of authors in the GDR.

By the 1970s, readers in the FRG, in contrast, lacked the knowledge about relevant societal discourses and quotidian life in the GDR, and were apparently largely unable to grasp the significance of these texts. In a letter to Lew Kopelew from 1973, Christa Wolf, for example, comments on West German reviews of *Nachdenken über Christa T.* She explains their superficiality and shallowness with the critics' ignorance about the essence of GDR life, particularly about the individual's conflictedness that arises from the experienced discrepancy between socialist ideals and the realities of daily life in socialism.[54] Similarly, in his preface to the 1974 edition of the West German standard work on GDR literature, Konrad Franke insists that Germans' shared history and language only give the appearance of a common ground shared by the literatures of the two German states.[55] Franke thus clearly contradicts West German claims that German cultural identity prevails over political changes affecting the nation. The political detachment on the national level, which started with the building of the Berlin Wall in 1961 and culminated in the second revision of the GDR constitution in 1974, is therefore reflected in literary history.[56] These developments in the political and the cultural spheres indicate that East German literature written since the 1960s, in particular, provides a unique window onto the empirical realities of life in the GDR. These narratives merit attention on the aesthetic and political levels: they develop specific and intriguing poetic strategies; moreover, they counter official GDR discourses and challenge hegemonic myths about the GDR that formed after unification. This study is situated at the intersection of both levels as it concentrates on the poetic strategy of depicting symptomatic bodies in literature written after 1961: since the power structures underlying lived GDR reality are inscribed in these bodies, and since they reflect—and often participate in creating—the discourses that were most relevant in GDR society, in reading them we can identify how writers were coping with their everyday experiences by expressing political support or social critique.

Abjecting the Other

The increasing separation of the two German literatures as well as the two German states culminated in two distinctly formed subject identities. Subject formation, according to Judith Butler's *Bodies That Matter*, relies on "the simultaneous production of a domain of abject beings, those who are not yet 'subjects,' but who form the constitutive outside to the domain of the subject. . . . In this sense, then, the subject is constituted through the force of exclusion and abjection, one which produces a constitutive outside to the subject, an abjected outside, which is, after all, 'inside' the subject as its own founding repudiation" (3). If we understand that the two German states functioned as each other's "constitutive outside," then their "subject formation" emerges as relying precisely on abjecting the very parts the respective Other embraced in all realms of quotidian life. Dichotomies such as socialism/capitalism, planned economy/market economy, or community/individual represent values and norms that found their way into the respective literatures. Yet at the same time, the abjected outside remained inside the respective Other. It surfaced as influence on the other state, for example in the FRG's attempts to effect improvements in the social realm (e.g., by allocating resources for more comprehensive child care and by ensuring access to affordable if not free healthcare), or the GDR's constant efforts to raise the standard of living and improve the supply of consumer goods ranging from coffee to TVs.[57] Over forty years, the two German states developed distinct national identities that simultaneously separated and linked them.

Yet neither the FRG nor the GDR were, of course, homogenous, inclusive communities. Notwithstanding national discourses of inner unity, both German states featured internal hierarchies that developed—not unlike other nations—on the basis of categories such as gender, race, class, and sexuality. Yet the two German states each displayed additional, idiosyncratic features that were diametrically opposed to the other's norms: favored values such as solidarity versus self-interest, community versus individual freedom, the desire to belong to the working class versus the desire to belong to the middle class, or adherence to the party line—the most important factor in the GDR—versus economic status.[58] With the so-called *Wende* and unification, which from a Western point of view established 1989/90 as the historical moment that marked the end of the Cold War and conclusively settled the anticipated failure of socialism, GDR-specific hierarchies and the values on which they were determined became null and void.[59] In the most recent German social organization, a new signifier for defining internal hierarchies came into play and cemented West German supremacy: East/West German, aligned with the gender categories female/male respectively.[60]

In the mass media, a discourse developed that brought together nationalism and gender. It frequently featured colonial imagery of an undiscovered exotic terrain to be conquered, and often pejoratively "feminized" and "infantilized" the "colony" and its people, East Germany and East Germans. The constructed female Other yielded two main narratives, in both literature and film. Unification was either celebrated in the allegory of the heterosexual couple consisting of a naïve, weak, East German "bride" dependent on the protection of a robust, assertive, and male West; or, pointing to the violence involved in the unification process, the West was portrayed as subjugating and even raping a supposedly wild, alien East that was allegedly closer to nature.[61] Effectively, both narratives supported a modified new pattern of subject formation via abjecting the Other in continuation of the process identified above as already functioning for both the GDR and the FRG: now the two categories "East German" (as opposed to "West German") and "female" (as opposed to "male") were relegated to the realm of the abject, while the category "West German," formerly considered the abject in the GDR, was promoted to signify the new norm next to "male"—a norm that was now supposedly also applicable to GDR citizens. East Germans could become West German subjects in unified Germany, provided they were willing to accept that the West had acquired what Kersten Sven Roth termed "*Normal-Null-Status*" (standard-zero-status): the West acquired a normativity that encompassed the fields of economy, culture, language, politics, and history in the East-West opposition.[62]

Yet the massive economic problems and high unemployment rates in the "new states" in the East quickly contributed to the creation of a new kind of post-GDR identity that the citizens of the bygone socialist state fashioned into a defiant act of resistance to the hegemony of the new FRG. Ulrich Mählert, for instance, in his *Kleine Geschichte der DDR*, cites the popularity of GDR music and products, though now produced by West German companies, and the practice of traveling with a GDR passport, which was still valid until 1995 (8). In the face of major social and economic transformations, many East Germans did not remember life before 1989 along the lines of the *Diktaturgedächtnis*, which characterized the image of the perished state in the media and shaped people's imagination in the West. It was predominantly West Germans who subscribed to the model of "two German dictatorships" which aimed at equating the unparalleled crimes committed by the NS regime with the anti-capitalist and collectivist class-war ideology of the GDR.[63] This led to further societal polarization: while the West largely dismissed East Germans' claim to a distinctive identity as incomprehensible *Ostalgie* (nostalgia for the East), this trend to self-identify as former GDR citizen has persisted in social strata of post-unification Germany, albeit without the power to effectively challenge West German hegemony. Despite the geographical and political incorporation of the GDR into the national boundaries of the FRG on October 3, 1990, West Germans continue to create their identity through a distorted perception and representation of East Germans, who remain the unknown Other, the abject in this hegemonic narrative.[64]

East German Literature in Unified Germany: Towards a New Terminology

Unsurprisingly, this abjection of the GDR within the new FRG extended to the official literary scene, where it was acted out in the so-called *deutsch-deutscher Literaturstreit* (German-German debate on literature) starting in 1990.[65] Triggered by West German media reactions to Christa Wolf's novella *Was bleibt* (1990; "What Remains," 1995), a menacing press campaign evolved that was first directed at Wolf, and subsequently extended more generally to intellectuals who had allegedly stabilized the GDR regime. When it expanded to include all politically engaged literature, including West German fiction and its putative *Gesinnungsästhetik* (aesthetics of political conviction), the debate's true motivation came to light: the campaign aimed to put an end to critical, political literature in unified Germany and to appropriate the authority to interpret (literary) history for the future, as Ulrich Greiner, one of the most influential literary critics in Germany and head of the culture section of *Die Zeit* in 1990, eventually admitted.[66]

For GDR literature, the consequences of this endeavor to diminish the significance of fiction that carried political content was particularly grave. Given the absence of critical media in the GDR, literature and film had long served as the venue where sensitive social topics were aired, which resulted in a fundamentally political literature. A campaign directed against critical literature therefore affected the flow of first-hand accounts of GDR citizens' lived experiences in the socialist German state and debates surrounding the issues that most affected their lives. Demeaning cultural products that originated in the GDR results in the loss of the cultural values and norms preserved in these memory media for present and future generations.[67] The strategy underlying the so-called *Literaturstreit* thus turns out to present another variation of the model of subject formation via abjection of the Other. Within this framework, the campaign Greiner revealed as aiming to terminate critical, political literature can be understood as an operation that relegates the categories "intellectual," "political," and "critically engaged" to the realm of the abject—the very realm we have identified as occupied by the categories "East German" and "female." After this attack against politically engaged literature, the ultimate abject reads like the personification of GDR intellectuals, and particularly female writers like Christa Wolf.[68]

The so-called *Literaturstreit* also affected scholarly discussions in Germany. Often, GDR writers and their texts appear as the Other to FRG writers and their oeuvre, and sometimes the former even occupy the sphere of the abject. Looking back at the forty years from 1949 to 1989, some Germanists ignore the existence of GDR literature altogether. Eliminating the political background, the authors' socialization, and the specificity of the socialist background of production, they subsume it under West German literature, relegate it to the literatures of the German-speaking countries in general, or consider it a regional literature.[69] Yet the crucial significance of narrative fiction for GDR citizens as the one domain where relevant societal issues could be enunciated and where (literary) means were developed that could challenge the hegemony of dominant norms and discourses, highlights why the term "GDR literature" cannot be reduced to a regional phenomenon.[70]

Even approaches that treat GDR literature as an autonomous phenomenon often continue either to exclusively parse the (loyal or critical) authors' politics or to solely focus on the aesthetic value of the works at the expense of acknowledging how texts negotiate political and social context. In an attempt to "rescue" GDR literature, Wolfgang Emmerich, for example, dedicates both his *Kleine Literaturgeschichte der DDR* and the volume *Die andere deutsche Literatur* to the aesthetic legacy of the GDR in literature. Other scholarly works, such as Astrid Köhler's aptly titled monograph *Brückenschläge: DDR-Autoren vor und nach der Wiedervereinigung* (Bridgings: GDR Authors Before and After Reunification, 2007) and Holger Helbig's *Weiterschreiben: Zur DDR-Literatur nach dem Ende der DDR* (Writing Further: On GDR Literature After the End of the GDR, 2007), demonstrate how writers build bridges from their GDR texts to those composed after 1989. Similarly, edited volumes such as Janine Ludwig and Mirijam Meuser's *Literatur ohne Land?* (Literature Without a Country, 2009) and David Clarke and Axel Goodbody's *The Self in Transition* (2012) assert continuities in GDR authors' writing styles beyond the historical caesura of 1989/90. Yet few critics focus on literary traditions that originate in the GDR and persist in post-GDR literature. Heinz Ludwig Arnold and Iris Radisch, for example, attribute specific East German writing styles to writers who started writing after 1989.[71]

In acknowledging the significance of the particular socialization that so strongly shaped GDR authors and their texts, I first insist on the specificity of a distinct GDR literature prior to 1990. I also challenge the notion that this literature ceased to exist with unification, coming to a sudden demise overnight on October 3, 1990. To this end, I propose a new terminology, since the categories frequently applied in US scholarship elide the political significance of the socialization of those raised in the GDR. Typically, "East German" is used to designate writers and the works they published in the GDR—a practice that retrospectively denies the existence of the socialist state. "Eastern German" is employed to label the authors of the five new German states who acceded to the FRG in October, 1990 and the texts they composed—irrespective of whether or not these writers already published in the GDR.[72] "Eastern German" is a geographic term that, while it might enable individuals to acknowledge their geographic origins, omits the social, cultural, and ideological aspects of being socialized in the GDR. Christa Wolf might serve as an example: for an author who has the protagonist of her 2010 novel *Stadt der Engel oder The Overcoat of Dr. Freud* insist on entering the UNITED STATES with her GDR passport in 1993, the term "Eastern German" seems inadequate because it ignores the political dimension of her life and work.

Given that both communal and literary or cultural socialization in the socialist German state influenced those who commenced writing in the GDR, this study proposes a double reconceptualization. To this end, throughout this study, the term "GDR literature" signifies—without an arbitrary expiration date—the oeuvre of authors who lived and published their works in the GDR.[73] Correspondingly, "post-GDR literature" refers to texts published after 1989 by authors who grew up in the GDR and were shaped by the experience of quotidian life in socialism and the country's literary conventions. These "post-GDR writers" often deal with the GDR and its specters in their fictional texts. They gained more recognition and predominantly published their prose texts after 1989, like Kerstin Hensel or Kathrin Schmidt,[74] or began publishing after the fall of the Wall, as for example Thomas Brussig or Antje Rávic Strubel. For lack of more suitable terms that would capture the political dimension, the expression "East German writer" includes both GDR authors and post-GDR authors, and "East German literature" serves as an umbrella term to encompass both categories: "GDR literature" and "post-GDR literature."[75]

Contradicting any predictions and claims of the end of GDR literature, Astrid Köhler's *Brückenschläge* is one of the few monographs to uncover continuing aesthetic and thematic trajectories in the oeuvre of GDR authors in unified Germany. Not least of all because she demonstrates that features such as the focus on social outsiders and the quest for individual identity and subjectivity can be traced back to early

Aufbauliteratur, Köhler highlights the distinctiveness of GDR literature pre- and post-unification (227). She identifies two topics she considers emblematic: critical reflections on hegemonic history, and an investigation of the relationship between the individual and society (215). Köhler finds that GDR fiction is concerned particularly with the foundational structures of history—structures that constantly repeat themselves, independent of a specific ruling ideology. Authors tackle the complexity and the contradictions inherent in history by retelling it from a variety of perspectives in literature (213–17). Emphasizing that the two topics she considers distinctive for GDR literature cannot be separated, Köhler highlights the ways in which individuals negotiate society's demands to adjust by defying political, ideological, and cultural dogmas. She shows that the two dominant themes often converge on bodies where they play out in physical and psychological illness that emerges as one of the markers for an individual's marginalization (225).

Christa Wolf's protagonists—Christa T. as well as the nameless patient portrayed in *Leibhaftig*—suffer both physically and psychologically from the discrepancy between their idealistic belief in humanist, socialist ideals and the realities of life in quotidian socialism. Their bodies are discursively linked to the fascist past, and moreover react physically to political events in the GDR. Similarly, various symptomatic bodies in Kathrin Schmidt's *Die Gunnar-Lennefsen-Expedition* and *Du stirbst nicht*, and in Antje Rávic Strubel's *Sturz der Tage in die Nacht*, delimit the symbolic space where controversies between the individual and society, often represented by state institutions, are acted out. Thomas Brussig's *Wie es leuchtet* and Kerstin Hensel's *Lärchenau* specifically place bodies in a medical domain that raises disconcerting questions about the legitimacy of genetic and pharmaceutical research conducted on patients in the GDR. In short, these cis- and transgender female, male-to-female transsexual, and female-identified intersexual bodies possess a political and historical dimension. Leslie Adelson, in *Making Bodies, Making History*, asserts the necessity "to contemplate the body as a secret of history" and "history as an even better-kept secret of the body" (1). If we concur with her assessment and transfer it to the specific East German context, then we will understand how an analysis of the symptomatic body in East German literature can support an understanding of (East) German history.

The Symptomatic Body and the Nation

Like Leslie Adelson, Sigrid Weigel underscores the significance of the female body for "storing" memory and historical information. In *Bilder des kulturellen Gedächtnisses* (Images of Cultural Memory, 1994), Weigel describes what she terms the "Symptomkörper" (symptom-body) as a "Matrix für die Erinnerungssymbole des Verdrängten" (matrix for the memory symbols of everything suppressed), a body which therefore must be "read" in order to decipher its "lettering" (16). When we read on the flesh the inscriptions left by history, politics, and subjectivities—specified along the lines of gender, race, and class—we are dealing with the heterogeneity of the body and the manifold and potentially contradictory positionalities of an individual's experience. Yet the body is not simply an inert surface awaiting inscription from specific relations of power. Rather, it can also claim a voice and agency through symptoms such as, for example, illness—and emerge as a symptomatic body. Indeed, illness—the very embodiment of the transgression of norms, of something menacing such as a physically invasive virus—challenges the structure of any society.

In *Gender Trouble*, Judith Butler emphasizes the threat implied in the proximity of the body and society, which are both regulated in analogous ways. She further insists that the idea of the body emblematizing society is not merely based on metaphor or analogy; it is synecdochal: "If the body is synecdochal for the social system *per se*, . . . then any kind of unregulated permeability constitutes a site of pollution and endangerment" (168). Recalling that Lenin considered health a valuable public asset in socialist society which had to be protected at all costs, we realize that he not only emphasizes the linkage between symbolic and physical appropriation; he also implies that an ailing, out-of-control physique is more than just sick flesh. Belonging to the socialist state for which it stands symbolically and which it *is* synecdochally, a body thus inscribed by illness signals socio-political crisis. It can challenge traditional beliefs about history and social structures that surface in established notions of gender, sex, race, class, and health, all of which are usually constructed as binary oppositions.[76]

Since the female body is understood as the "Other" to the (white male) norm and imagined as "natural" in occidental convention, its representations are particularly suitable for challenging norms and established dichotomies.[77] In *Making Bodies, Making History*, Leslie Adelson established the axiom that "the relationship between the material world and its discursive signification is contested on and through the signified and signifying ground of women's bodies" (xiii). Motivated by women's cultural, biological, and symbolic significance in reproducing nations, female bodies have traditionally been favored for allegorical and symbolic depictions of the body politic.[78] Such feminization of the nation is not uncommon, and Germany, as Patricia Herminghouse and Magda Mueller argue in their introduction to *Gender and Germanness*, has a long history of representing the nation as the figure Germania. The political body, exclusively available as an imagined utopia, acquired particular efficacy for an imagined unity in the territorially fragmented German states of the late eighteenth and nineteenth centuries.[79] Yet despite the central positioning of the female body in national iconography, feminist scholarship has underscored just how marginal a role women occupy when it comes to participating in the actual implementation of national identity. As a heterosexual male construct connected to patriarchal hierarchies and norms, the concept of the nation assigns men the role of protectors of the homeland and women the role of biological, cultural, and symbolic reproducers and representatives of purity.[80]

In her groundbreaking work, *The Body in Pain*, Elaine Scarry insists that "the body is political" (110). She also observes that "at particular moments when there is within a society a crisis of belief—that is, when some central idea or ideology or cultural construct has ceased to elicit a population's belief either because it is manifestly fictitious or because it has for some reason been divested of ordinary forms of substantiation—the sheer material factualness of the human body will be borrowed to lend that cultural construct the aura of 'realness' and 'certainty'" (14). For Scarry, then, the politics of portraying a body inevitably signal societal crisis and the loss of idea(l)s, and simultaneously indicate the attempt to confirm the endangered ideology by stressing the presumed materiality of an idea. We can infer accordingly that while the incarnation of the nation in a robust male body aims at reaffirming its potentially discredited strength and ability to defend its *Heimat* (homeland), the representation via a healthy female body corroborates a nation's virtue, its claim to eternal biological, cultural, and symbolic procreation, and hence its endurance, especially in times of anxiety.

In a historical framework in which women seem to "innately" reproduce as well as embody the healthy nation, the symptomatic body—declared by Judith Butler to be synecdochal for the social system per se—not only emblematically points to perturbations in the social and cultural order but also physically embodies them. The implied threat to the nation can be symbolically reversed when the symptomatic body is successfully restored to health, which signifies the substantiation of the ideology in question. Within the category of the symptomatic body, depictions of those outside the male/female binary can similarly be considered a threat. Deviant within the "obligatory frame of reproductive heterosexuality,"[81] they are unable (symbolically and actually) to reproduce the nation. When such transgender, transsexual, or intersexual characters are portrayed as sick or seeking medical help, they serve as an even more pronounced marker for a troubled nation than the prototype of the symptomatic body, the ailing cis-gender female body. After all, such doubly-Othered bodies violate the norms for both health and gender. Not least of all because the institutionalization of medicine coincided with an increasingly heteronormative order in the nineteenth century, bodies defying a specific society's hegemonic norms for health and illness as well as those challenging its heteronormative model came under scrutiny from medical professionals. Since the gender-ambiguous body has historically been pathologized and branded deviant,[82] it lends itself to subversive representations of the troubled nation.

Symptomatic bodies outside the male/female binary may further possess privileged, embodied knowledge inaccessible to other subject positions. Accordingly, this study devotes particular attention to symptomatic bodies that are defined, accepted, and categorized as effeminate by the society imagined in the literary texts under discussion, as well as to symptomatic bodies which perform "femininity": that is, bodies that are gender-ambiguous, transgender, transsexual, or intersexual. These bodies, after all, are already pathologized, which might be further complicated by attempts to alter their sex by means of hormone therapies and sex operations. Pathologized per se, they had to be regarded as a challenge for the socialist state under the obligation to turn them into healthy, valuable public property, so to speak. Such thought-provoking bodies—presented in literature, Othered in multiple ways—are inherently subversive. Particularly in literature written in the context of a socialist society and a socialist medical system, these symptomatic bodies are suited for indicating political and social upheaval and for challenging hegemonic ideologies and historiography.

Notes

[1] Wolfgang Becker, dir., *Good Bye, Lenin!* (2003).

[2] Lichtenberg, "Screenplay *Good Bye, Lenin!*," 131. To make this study accessible to readers without knowledge of German, I have supplemented citations from primary German-language texts with my own English translations in the following format: "German original text" (English translation; page number). Where a published translation of a text is available, quotes appear in the following format: "German original text" (page number in German original: published English translation; page number in English translation). The same system is used to translate German terminology, which is supplemented by a glossary at the end of the book. All texts are referred to by their original language title. On the first mention of a book, an English translation in parentheses and styled in roman follows the original title: *German Original Title* (English Translation, publication date of the German original). If a published English translation of a book is available, it appears in the following format: *German Original Title* (publication date of German original; *English Translation*, publication date of English translation).

[3] The British historian Edward Palmer Thompson famously employed the term "history from below" in an article in the *Times Literary Supplement* in 1966 to draw attention to historical narratives that account for historical events from the point of view of common people.

[4] I will clarify my terminology later, but wish to explain here that I use "GDR literature" for fiction written by authors who started publishing in the GDR. "Post-GDR literature" refers to fiction composed by authors who were raised in the GDR but whose works were published predominantly after October 1990. "East German literature" serves as an umbrella term.

⁵ Blockbusters like Florian Henckel von Donnersmarck's Oscar-winning *Das Leben der Anderen* (2006; *The Lives of Others*, 2007), trendy TV series like *Weißensee* (2010–15, dir. Friedemann Fromm), and bestsellers such as Uwe Tellkamp's award-winning *Der Turm* (2008; *The Tower*, 2014)—also adapted for film—find large audiences inside and outside Germany. Lutz Seiler's *Kruso* (2014) won the prestigious German Book Prize in 2014 for its portrayal of the last months of the GDR. As the award evidences, the GDR still plays a vital role in East German writers' production and more generally in German cultural and historical memory.

⁶ The term cisgender denotes individuals whose experience of their own gender corresponds to the biological sex they were assigned at birth. It complements transgender, which refers to individuals whose experience of their own gender does not conform unambiguously to the biological sex they were assigned at birth. Both cisgender and transgender are entirely independent of sexual orientation.

⁷ This point could, albeit to a lesser extent, be made for *Kindheitsmuster* (1976; *Patterns of Childhood*, 1980), *Kassandra* (1983; *Cassandra*, 1984), and *Sommerstück* (Summer Play, 1989).

⁸ In *Brückenschläge*, Köhler identified Christa Wolf as the most significant point of reference for established GDR writers as well as for younger East German authors such as Kerstin Hensel (228).

⁹ Brüns, *Nach dem Mauerfall*, 96. In *Writing the New Berlin*, Gerstenberger offers an excellent analysis of the (pathological) body in and after the unification process in Berlin literature (52–76). The predominance of pathological discourses in East German literature is often attributed to profound changes and upheaval in all aspects of East German life and culture. In the Western part of the new FRG, however, continuities played a major role. In literature, this is often reflected in a thematic return to Germany's National Socialist past, rather than a focus on more recent developments in German history like the fall of the Wall and German unification. See Fischer and Roberts, *Schreiben nach der Wende*, xiv; Schmitz, "Return of the Past," 272.

¹⁰ In *Rifts in Time and in the Self*, Dueck observes the proliferation of disease in GDR literature, yet limits the phenomenon to female writers (158). However, displaying bodies suffering from disease is not merely a mode of feminist writing, nor is it exclusively attributable to female writers. Examples of depictions of illness and/or the medical realm by female and male GDR writers include the following (the list is by no means exhaustive): Jurek Becker, *Schlaflose Tage* (1978); Thomas Brasch, *Vor den Vätern sterben die Söhne* (1977); Volker Braun, *Die Übergangsgesellschaft* (1987) and *Unvollendete Geschichte* (1990); Werner Bräunig, *Rummelplatz* (2007); Marianne Bruns, *Szenenwechsel* (1982); Brigitte Burmeister, *Anders oder Vom Aufenthalt in der Fremde* (1988); Hanns Cibulka, *Swantow* (1982); Roswitha Geppert, *Die Last, die du nicht trägst* (1978); Günter Görlich, *Eine Anzeige in der Zeitung* (1978); Paul Gratzik, *Kohlenkutte* (1982); Werner Heiduczek, *Tod am Meer* (1977); Christoph Hein, *Der fremde Freund* (1982; *The Distant Lover*, 1989) and *Horns Ende* (1985); Monika Helmecke, *Klopfzeichen* (1979); Stefan Heym, *Collin* (1979; *Collin*, 1980); Helga Königsdorf, *Respektloser Umgang* (1986), *Ungelegener Befund* (1990); Monika Maron, *Flugasche* (1981; *Flight of Ashes*, 1986); *Überläuferin* (1986; *The Defector*, 1986); Brigitte Martin, *Nach Freude anstehen* (1981); Irmtraud Morgner,

Leben und Abenteuer der Trobadora Beatriz (1974; *The Life and Adventures of Trobadora Beatrice*, 2000) and *Amanda* (1983); Brigitte Reimann, *Franziska Linkerhand* (1974); Winfried Völlger, *Das Windhahnsyndrom* (1983); Maxie Wander, *Leben wär' eine prima Alternative* (1979). Examples of twenty-first century post-GDR prose texts that engage in medical discourses and/or depict illness or medical realms include, for example: Sibylle Berg, *Vielen Dank für das Leben* (2012; *Thank you for This Life*, 2014); Marion Brasch, *Ab jetzt ist Ruhe* (2012); Jenny Erpenbeck, *Heimsuchung* (2007; *Visitation*, 2010); Julia Franck, *Lagerfeuer* (2003) and *Rücken an Rücken* (2011; *Back to Back*, 2013); Annett Gröschner, *Moskauer Eis* (2000) and *Walpurgistag* (2011); Kerstin Hensel, *Im Spinnhaus* (2003); André Kubiczek, *Der Genosse, die Prinzessin und ihr lieber Herr Sohn* (2012); Eugen Ruge, *In Zeiten des abnehmenden Lichts* (2011; *In Times of Fading Light*, 2013); Judith Schalansky, *Der Hals der Giraffe* (2011; *The Giraffe's Neck*, 2014); Julia Schoch, *Mit der Geschwindigkeit des Sommers* (2009); Torsten Schulz, *Nilowsky* (2013); Uwe Tellkamp, *Der Turm*; Judith Zander, *Dinge, die wir heute sagten* (2010).

[11] Even very recent publications that focus on the link between the ill body, medicine, and literature do not specifically consider GDR literature and the GDR medical system. See, for example, Käser and Schappach, *Krank geschrieben*. The contributions in Erdbrügger and Krause's edited volume *Leibesvisitationen*, which analyze the body as an object of political interest in socialist and post-socialist cultures and literatures, also neglect to consider the specificity of medical systems in socialist countries.

[12] The volume *Medizinische Ethik in der DDR*, co-edited by Bettin and Gadebusch Bondio, presents an outstanding collection of essays on GDR-specific ethics and medicine. The editors emphasize the lack of research and scholarly publications on the medical field in socialist countries and point to recent attempts to fill the gap at the institutional level at the universities in Greifswald, Erlangen, Tübingen, and Ulm. Bettin and Gadebusch Bondio, "An Stelle einer Einleitung," 8. Few GDR histories contain even one chapter on healthcare: Bollinger and Vilmar, *Die DDR war anders*; Fischer et al., *Gegen den Zeitgeist*; Fulbrook, *People's State*; Fulbrook and Port, *Becoming East German*. A volume recently edited by Ahbe, Hofmann, and Stiehler entitled *Redefreiheit* (Freedom of Speech) contains transcripts of all public debates that took place in Leipzig in the fall of 1989. It also includes a chapter on problems in the healthcare system, which points to the awareness of the topic in the GDR. Research that developed in response to allegations against GDR medical institutions includes Rosemarie Stein's *Die Charité 1945–1992*; Süß's *Politisch mißbraucht?*; Weil's *Zielgruppe Ärzteschaft*.

[13] Bettin and Gadebusch Bondio, "An Stelle einer Einleitung," 13.

[14] The Ministerium für Staatssicherheit (Ministry for State Security) is often referred to as the Staatssicherheit (State Security), the MfS, or simply the Stasi. My translation of Stasi-related terminology follows the English translation of Jens Gieseke's *DDR-Staatssicherheit/GDR State Security*, published by the Federal Commissioner for the Records of the State Security Service of the former German Democratic Republic.

[15] Foucault, *Discipline and Punish*, 144; *History of Sexuality*, 25.

[16] Hans Stein, "Gemeinsame Ansätze in Prävention," 244. Hockerts, "Grundlinien und soziale Folgen," talks about each citizen's obligation to strive for health (526).

[17] Thießen, "Vorsorge als Ordnung des Sozialen," 415.

[18] Weil, *Zielgruppe Ärzteschaft*, 11–12; Wagner, "Polikliniken—ein gesundheitspolitisches Modell," 236. With the revised GDR constitution of 1968, article 35, paragraph 2, every GDR citizen was given the right to protection of their health and labor power. See Ernst, '*Die beste Prophylaxe*'; Günther, "Das Arztrecht in der DDR," 86; Schleiermacher and Schagen, "Rekonstruktion und Innovation (1949–1961)," 213; Seifert, *Gesundheit staatlich verordnet*, 348 (hereafter cited as *GSV*).

[19] This practice apparently never stopped. In *Redefreiheit*, Ahbe, Hofmann and Stiehler quote several doctors, some of them members of the SED, who lament, with strong applause from the citizens of Leipzig present, a "selbstmörderische Kaderpolitik" (suicidal cadre politics; 538). Allegedly, by 1989 this resulted in leadership positions in medicine predominantly staffed on the basis of membership in the party or the military, not on expertise, to the detriment of medical education (538, 542–43, 553, 558).

[20] Bettin and Gadebusch Bondio, "An Stelle einer Einleitung," 7.

[21] Gieseke, *GDR State Security*, 108.

[22] The effects are documented in early Stasi files that Süß cites in her study, which presents the first thorough investigation of links between the Stasi and the medical institutions in the GDR. Süß, *Politisch mißbraucht?*, 124 (hereafter cited as *Pm*). In *Redefreiheit*, Ahbe, Hofmann and Stiehler quote Christian Tauchnitz, physician at a Lutheran hospital, who explains that from the mid-1950s until 1961 physicians did not receive their certificates confirming that they passed their state exams, presumably in a (failed) attempt to prevent them from leaving the GDR for the FRG (539).

[23] Süß, *Pm*, 142–43, 151–52, 157–68; Weil, "Ärzte als inoffizielle Mitarbeiter," A1594.

[24] Susanne Hahn, "Ethische Fragen und Problemlösungen," in Bettin and Gadebusch Bondio, 73–85; here, 75 (hereafter cited as "EF"). Günther, "Das Arztrecht in der DDR," considers this specific doctor-patient relationship unique in history (87). See Günther, "Patientenschutz," 161; Seifert, *GSV*, 168, 304; Wagner, "Polikliniken—ein gesundheitspolitisches Modell," 234. The *Bundesgerichtshof* (Federal Court of Justice) in the FRG considers a medical intervention, including a successful intervention carried out according to standard practice, as fulfilling the legal criteria for assault and battery according to §223 *Strafgesetzbuch* (StGB, Criminal Code). A patient's consent to treatment is therefore indispensable, with the exception of an emergency operation performed when the patient is unconscious and therefore unable to provide consent. See BGH judgment BGHSt 11.

[25] Seifert, *GSV*, 353; Günther, "Das Arztrecht in der DDR," 89. On the ideal of the "socialist personality" and the efforts of the GDR educational system to implement the ideal in society, see Angela Brock, "Producing the 'Socialist

Personality'?" On the failure to create uniform "socialist personalities," see Fulbrook, "Living through the GDR," 218.

26 Seifert states that engagement in prophylaxis is part of the socialist personality because it is linked to societal progress, and deduces from the GDR's civil law both the medical profession's and the patient's obligation to emphasize and practice prophylaxis (Seifert, *GSV*, 35, 202, 268, 275). See Ernst, *'Die beste Prophylaxe'*; Schleiermacher and Schagen, "Rekonstruktion und Innovation (1949–1961)," 213; Thießen, "Vorsorge als Ordnung des Sozialen."

27 Tanneberger, "Ethik in der medizinischen Forschung," 52–55.

28 *Der Spiegel* reported that in 1972, the number of new infections with tuberculosis was five times higher in the FRG than in the GDR, which benefitted from its preemptive measures. "Das Geschäft mit der Krankheit," 55.

29 Seifert, *GSV*, 61–62, 64, 305; Günther, "Das Arztrecht in der DDR," 90.

30 On social inequalities and patterns of stratification, see Fulbrook, *People's State*, 19.

31 The existence of such special hospitals was debated in fall 1989. In *Redefreiheit*, Ahbe, Hofmann and Stiehler quote Roland Rogos, Deputy Principal for Medicine, who demands that all citizens who fall ill receive the same care they would in a special hospital reserved for the socialist elite (541). Beate Zimmermann, a physician at the Karl-Marx-University, similarly lamented the two-tier medical system and demanded to know who determined which hospital received priority status (551). Hahn, "EF" (76–77) and Wiesner, "Zur Gesundheitslage der beiden Bevölkerungsteile DDR und BRD" (24) emphasize the high death rate due to inappropriate therapy in hospitals that were not among the privileged ones.

32 Fulbrook, *People's State*, 95, 113; Hahn, "EF," 76, 82. In "Polikliniken—ein gesundheitspolitisches Modell," Wagner reports that after unification, the majority of former GDR citizens considered the GDR healthcare system superior to the FRG system because the quality of care they received was not driven by physicians' financial interests (240).

33 Weigel, *Bilder des kulturellen Gedächtnisses*, 49–50. See Scarry, *Body in Pain*, 1–45.

34 My understanding of the prototype as the most central member of a category (here: cis-gender females), which also allows for other related members (here: transgender females, transsexual females, and intersexual individuals who choose to identify as female) to be included follows Rosch, "Cognitive Representation of Semantic Categories."

35 When I use the terms "inscription" or "inscribed," I refer to Foucault's notion of the body. In "Nietzsche, Genealogy, History," he calls the body the "surface of the inscription of events" (356). He understands it as shaped by various disciplines (*Discipline and Punish*), discourses, and practices (*History of Sexuality*, vol. I). In other words, bodies become the text which is written upon them. They are sites of concrete political struggle, "totally imprinted by history and the process of history's destruction of the body"—and we can read the traces conflicting forces have left on the bodies' surfaces ("Nietzsche, Genealogy, History," 357). The notion of an all-encompassing power network simultaneously allows for resistance

to power and for the development of counter-discourses and subversive practices. Feminists, like Butler in "Foucault and the Paradox," have taken issue with his notion of the inscribed body, claiming that Foucault assumes a pre-inscriptive body prior to such cultural marking. Others, like McLaren in *Feminism, Foucault, and Embodied Subjectivity*, have demonstrated how Foucault's notion of the body and power can be harnessed for a feminist understanding of the body as an effect of power and as a source of resistance.

[36] Barck, "Fragmentarisches zur Literatur," 315. See Bridge, *Women's Writing and Historiography*, 10.

[37] Hahn, "EF," 77. In *Rifts in Time and in the Self*, Dueck similarly emphasizes that "in a society in which potent political and social messages were transmitted by fiction, the fates of characters in novels can be read as a thermometer of societal health" (112).

[38] In *Redefreiheit*, Ahbe, Hofmann and Stiehler quote Dieter Lohmann, Medical Director of the city hospital in Leipzig, and Rudolf Weiner, Medical Director of the district hospital St. Georg. In their contributions, which met with strong approval by the audience, both Lohmann and Weiner emphasize that the healthcare system must be considered as integral part of society, which means its trials and tribulations reflect the grievances of society at large (526, 531).

[39] Sabrow, "Die DDR erinnern," 16, 18–19; Meyen, *"Wir haben freier gelebt,"* 13, 25–26.

[40] Clarke and Wölfel, "Remembering the German Democratic Republic," 15; Jarausch, "Die Zukunft der ostdeutschen Vergangenheit," 83–84; Vollnhals and Weber, *Der Schein der Normalität*, 9–10; Wippermann, *Dämonisierung durch Vergleich*; Großbölting, "Die DDR im vereinten Deutschland," Pearce, "An Unequal Balance," 180. In *Facing the Nazi Past*, Niven has pointed to the troubling equation of victimhood in commemorations for the victims of National Socialism and Soviet rule (53–56).

[41] The term *Unrechtsstaat* is problematic on several levels. First, it seems to imply a state of injustice (*Unrecht*), while historians, political scientists, and legal scholars use it to signify the absence of a constitutional state. Secondly, the term *Unrechtsstaat* was originally attached to National Socialist Germany (e.g., by Gustav Radbruch and Fritz Bauer), and only later applied to the GDR in order to buttress the totalitarianism theory as a means of justifying the supremacy of the FRG. Federal President Heinrich Lübke used the word *Unrechtsstaat* for the GDR in his proclamation of 1963, in which he declared June 17 the national holiday for the FRG to commemorate the uprising in the GDR in June 1953 (*Bundesgesetzblatt* (BGBl.) I 1963, 397). See Radbruch, "Gesetzliches Unrecht"; Reifner, *Das Recht des Unrechtsstaates*. Whether it is justified to apply the term to the GDR remains contested among historians and legal scholars. The Federal Constitutional Court has carefully refrained from designating the GDR a quintessential *Unrechtsstaat*, as legal scholar Alexander Blankenagel emphasizes in "Verfassungsgerichtliche Vergangenheitsbewältigung," 80.

[42] In "Politics of Remembering the GDR," Beattie, for example, stresses that "there is no doubt that underlying various state initiatives since 1990 has been a belief that the state should be involved in influencing public and collective

memories and that public funds should be spent promoting certain understandings of the GDR" (25).

⁴³ Hartewig in "'Proben des Abgrunds, über welchem unsere Zivilisation wie eine Brücke schwebt'" and Peitsch in *Nachkriegsliteratur 1945–1989* argue against claims that the GDR exclusively commemorated Communist victims of the NS regime and demonstrate that Nazi racism and concentration camps were topics in fiction and historical accounts early on. See, for example, Bredel, *Die Prüfung*; Heymann, *Marxismus und Rassenfrage*; Kahn, *Antisemitismus und Rassenhetze*; Langhoff, *Die Moorsoldaten*; Sachs, *In den Wohnungen des Todes*; Simonow, *Ich sah das Vernichtungslager*; Weisenborn, *Memorial*; Wiechert, *Der Totenwald*. Hartewig also emphasizes that the GDR functionalized the Holocaust for their founding narrative of antifascism (45). See Pinkert, "Pleasures of Fear," 26–27.

⁴⁴ Hell, *Post-Fascist Fantasies*, 17 (italics in original; hereafter cited as *PFF*).

⁴⁵ In "Unerledigte Widersprüche," Wolf emphasized the significance of surrogate parents. Anna Seghers played the role of a Jewish and Communist mother figure for Wolf, but other antifascists were crucial, too (29).

⁴⁶ Throughout *Dissonant Lives*, Fulbrook employs the term "1929ers" in her analysis of this generation's significance for the building of the GDR. She explains that her research on the 1929ers was initially provoked by a joke she heard repeatedly, "to the effect that 'Christa Wolf was born in 1929, like everyone else in the GDR'" (252). Fulbrook considers Wolf "the 'classic 1929er'" (*Dissonant Lives*, 293). See Wierling, "How Do the 1929ers and the 1949ers Differ?," 205–8; Ahbe and Gries, "Gesellschaftsgeschichte als Generationengeschichte," 481.

⁴⁷ Fulbrook, *People's State*, 37.

⁴⁸ Agde, *Kahlschlag*, 244; Magenau, *Christa Wolf*, 172–91; Soldovieri, "Censorship and the Law." Most notably, the plenum banned *Das Kaninchen bin ich* (1965; *The Rabbit Is Me*, 1990), a film by Kurt Maetzig based on a novel by Manfred Bieler only published after the fall of the Wall, and *Rummelplatz* (Amusement Park), a novel by Werner Bräunig. The latter was not published until 2007, but excerpts appeared in issue 10 (1965) of *neue deutsche literatur* (*ndl*), and a censored version of 170 pages appeared in the collection *Ein Kranich am Himmel* (1981).

⁴⁹ Wolf's "Diskussionsbeitrag" (contribution to the discussion) and her "Erinnerungsbericht" (report from memory) are reprinted in Agde, *Kahlschlag*, 255–66, and 344–54 respectively. The English version of the "Erinnerungsbericht," entitled "Rummelplatz," appeared in Christa Wolf, *Parting from Phantoms*, 42–53. In "Gerhard Wolf zur vierten Reise," his commentary on Christa Wolf's fourth journey to Moscow, Gerhard Wolf stresses that his wife had been the only person to object to Honecker's speech at the Eleventh Plenum (99).

⁵⁰ The so-called Brown Book was published in the GDR in 1965. It caused an international stir as it documented "the National Socialist past of some twelve hundred members of the elite who were now active in every professional sector in the FRG" (Ahbe, "Competing Master Narratives," 222). See Gibas, "'Bonner Ultras', 'Kriegstreiber' und 'Schlotbarone'."

⁵¹ Jürgen Kuczynski employs the term "loyal dissident" self-descriptively for his memoirs, *Ein linientreuer Dissident*. In *Im Dialog* (In Dialogue), Wolf describes

this position as "Identifikation ... im Widerspruch" (identification ... in contradiction; 75). See Bathrick, "Die Intellektuellen und die Macht," 240; Bogdal, "Klimawechsel: Eine kleine Meteorologie der Gegenwartsliteratur," 16–17; Emmerich, *Kleine Literaturgeschichte der DDR*, 457; Krauss and Vogt, "Staatsdichter, Volkserzieher, Dissidenten?," 73.

[52] Literary historiography alternately considers 1961, 1965, or 1967 as the decisive year for separating the East and West German literary spheres. In *Nachkriegsliteratur 1945–1989*, Peitsch considers 1961 the beginning of a process that was concluded by the 1970s (17–18, 30). In his *Kleine Literaturgeschichte der DDR*, Emmerich also stresses the significance of 1961 (177). In "Literaturgeschichtsschreibung der DDR," Schönert assigns significance to 1965 in a process that is concluded by 1970 (252). In *Nachrichten aus Deutschland*, Brenner emphasizes the difference between FRG and GDR literature, also pertaining to aesthetics, as early as 1967 (14).

[53] Jurek Becker, "Die Wiedervereinigung der deutschen Literatur," 360; Helbig, "Wandel statt Wende," 84; Frank Hörnigk, "Die Literatur ist zuständig," 26; Langermann and Takerta, "Von der versuchten Verfertigung einer Literaturgesellschaft," 2, 26; Ludwig and Meuser, *Literatur ohne Land?*, 15, 34, 45; Schmidt, "Über Redeweisen der Literaturwissenschaft," 51, 66–68. On censorship see Barck, Langermann, and Lokatis, *'Jedes Buch ein Abenteuer'*.

[54] Wolf, *Moskauer Tagebücher*, 153.

[55] Franke, *Kindlers Literaturgeschichte*, 9. Since the 1970s, scholarly publications on GDR literature emerged in the FRG. See, for example, Brettschneider, *Zwischen literarischer Autonomie und Staatsdienst* (1972); Sander, *Geschichte der schönen Literatur in der DDR* (1972); Raddatz, *Traditionen und Tendenzen: Materialien zur Literatur der DDR* (1972); Blumensath and Uebach, *Einführung in die Literaturgeschichte der DDR* (1975); Schmitt, *Einführung in Theorie, Geschichte und Funktion der DDR-Literatur* (1975). See Granzow, *Gehen oder bleiben?*, 41–54; Rosenberg, "Was war DDR-Literatur?" and Silberman, "Whose Story Is This?" 37–38.

[56] Article 1 of the GDR constitution of 1949 declared Germany inseparable. The revised GDR constitution of 1968 considered the two German states separate, but belonging to one German nation. The second revision of 1974 deleted the statement of intention to overcome the division and, identifying the GDR exclusively as a socialist country, any reference to one German nation. See Wolle, *Die heile Welt der Diktatur*, 63. Willy Brandt's *Ostpolitik*, the FRG's détente strategy towards the GDR since 1970, accepted the GDR as a sovereign state, but emphasized, for example in Brandt's government declaration of 1969, the importance to preserve the unity of the nation. http://www.hdg.de/lemo/html/dokumente/KontinuitaetUndWandel_erklaerungBrandtRegierungserklaerung1969/. See Emmerich, *Kleine Literaturgeschichte der DDR*, 178; Schönert, "Literaturgeschichtsschreibung der DDR," 253, 264.

[57] In "Konturen einer integrierten Nachkriegsgeschichte" (8) and in "Spaltung und Verflechtung" (30), Kleßmann demonstrates that the two German states interacted continuously and cannot be understood without the respective counterpart. Similarly, see also Bauerkämper, Sabrow, and Stöver, "Die doppelte

deutsche Zeitgeschichte," 15; Kleßmann, "Zeitgeschichte als wissenschaftliche Aufklärung," 6.

58 In "Competing Master Narratives," Ahbe argues that people identify with the class that represents the respectable pillar of society, even if their identification contradicts sociological criteria. "In the East this was the working class; in the West it was the middle class" (225; also see 229).

59 On 1989/90 marking the end of history, see Fukuyama, "The end of history?" and Heilbroner, "Triumph of Capitalism." Contradicting these claims, Christa Wolf, in "Abschied von Phantomen" (1994; "Parting from Phantoms," 1997), insists that socialist values and a GDR-specific attitude to money survived in the East (333 and 299 respectively). In "Competing Master Narratives," Ahbe compares East and West Germany in the twenty-first century and stresses differences in communication styles, social values, and association with a specific class (225, 227–31).

60 In "Remembering the German Democratic Republic," Clarke and Wölfel explain that after 1989, "East Germans become the Other whose difference, blamed on the failures of state socialism, helps to affirm the achievements of the Federal Republic" (12). In "Competing Master Narratives," Ahbe demonstrates that the hierarchy established in 1989 continues to have an impact in the twenty-first century (231, 238).

61 The notion of colonization was probably first voiced in the pamphlet "Aufruf für unser Land" (Appeal for our country, November 1989), which Christa Wolf published together with thirty other authors. In "Santa Monica," Wolf reflected on her version of Medea as a colonized foreigner and woman (244). On the link between gender and colonization in the German unification process, see Brüns, *Nach dem Mauerfall*, 189–203; Lewis, "A Difficult Marriage"; Morrison, "Feminization of the German Democratic Republic"; Scharpe, "Male Privilege and Female Virtue"; Gerstenberger, *Writing the New Berlin*, 16; Geier, "Enteignete Indianer und ausgebeutete Neger"; Cooke, *Representing East Germany Since Unification*. In fiction, the idea of the colonized East emerged, for example, in Becker, *Amanda herzlos*; Brussig, *Wie es leuchtet*; Delius, *Die Birnen von Ribbeck*; Grass, *Ein Schnäppchen namens DDR*; Hochhuth, *Wessis in Weimar*; Kroetz, *Haus Deutschland*; Maron, *Animal Triste*; Rosenlöcher, *Ostgezeter* and *Die Wiederentdeckung des Gehens beim Wandern*; and Schulze, *Simple Storys*.

62 Roth, "Der Westen als 'Normal Null'," 71. In "Politics of Remembering the GDR," Beattie designates East Germany "the post-unification underdog" (23). See Ahbe, "Ost-Diskurse als Strukturen der Nobilitierung," 110; Wedl, "Ein Ossi ist ein Ossi," 129.

63 In "Competing Master Narratives," Ahbe states that in 1994, 73% of West Germans, but only 33% of East Germans considered the GDR an *Unrechtsstaat*, and 50% of East Germans (compared to 15% of West Germans) denied this (223, 232, 240–41, 243).

64 See Clarke and Wölfel, "Remembering the German Democratic Republic," 11–12; Beattie, "Politics of Remembering the GDR," 33.

65 The so-called *deutsch-deutscher Literaturstreit* is documented in Anz, *Es geht nicht um Christa Wolf*, and in Deiritz and Krauss, *Der deutsch-deutsche*

Literaturstreit. See Deiritz, "Zur Klärung eines Sachverhalts," 15; Finlay, "Literary Debates."

[66] Greiner, "Die deutsche Gesinnungsästhetik," 208. See Brockmann, *Literature and German Reunification*, 1; Bullivant, *The Future of German Literature*, 70–71. In "Der Literaturstreit—ein Historikerstreit im gesamtdeutschen Kostüm?," Heidelberger-Leonard reads the literary debate of the early 1990s as a reissue of the West German *Historikerstreit* (Historians' Dispute) of the 1980s (74–75).

[67] In "Literatur als Medium des kollektiven Gedächtnisses," Erll stresses the dual function of cultural texts as media that store information and function as cultural reminder, and as objects of memory (255). In *Christa Wolf*, Magenau considers the *Literaturstreit* a discursive dispossession of GDR authors, and parallels it with the processes in the East German economy and civil society starting in 1990 (411). In *Stadt der Engel*, Wolf explicitly points to this strategy (16).

[68] On the gendered aspect of the campaign, see Kuhn, "'Eine Königin köpfen ist effektiver als einen König köpfen'"; Koch, *Ästhetik der Moral bei Christa Wolf und Monika Maron*. Evaluating Christa Wolf's role in the early 1990s, Clarke and Wölfel in "Remembering the German Democratic Republic" consider Wolf "a weapon with which primarily Western commentators sought to de-legitimize not just the GDR state, but socialist ideas in general" (5).

[69] Schlaffer's *Die kurze Geschichte der deutschen Literatur* subsumes all literature written in German after 1945 under German literature. In "Regionen deutscher Literatur 1870–1945," Hermsdorf, as well as Skare in "1989/90: Eine Wende in der deutschen Literaturgeschichte?" consider GDR literature a regional phenomenon (10; and 41 respectively). In his introduction to *Literatur in der Diktatur*, Rüther equates fascist and GDR socialist literature. In his introduction to *Die dritte Front*, Walther follows the same approach.

[70] The specific role literature played in the GDR also constitutes a major difference to Austrian and Swiss literature. While these two national literatures are sometimes also subsumed under the term "literatures of the German-speaking countries," both Austria and Switzerland are states that guarantee freedom of the press. Consequently, neither Austrian nor Swiss literature presents an exclusive space for debating relevant societal issues.

[71] Arnold, *DDR-Literatur der neunziger Jahre*; Radisch, "Es gibt zwei deutsche Gegenwartsliteraturen in Ost und West!" In *Nach dem Mauerfall*, Brüns stresses the importance of German Pop Literature since the 1990s as the first pan-German literature in which literary unification has taken place (243).

[72] For the practice of applying the terms East(ern) German, see for example Twark, *Humor, Satire, and Identity*; Fox, "Post-Communist Fantasies"; Iztueta, "Body and Grotesque as Self-Disruption." Only Twark self-consciously points to the limitations of this terminology (2).

[73] More precisely, this also includes writers who emerged in the Soviet Occupied Zone between 1945 and 1949, and who established themselves as communist writers in the Weimar Republic or while in exile during the Nazi years.

[74] While Kerstin Hensel was an established poet and playwright in the GDR, she emerged as a prose writer in 1989, when she published her first collection of

stories, *Hallimasch* (Armillaria) with Luchterhand in the FRG. Similarly, Kathrin Schmidt was a celebrated poet in the GDR and debuted as a prose writer in 1998 with *Die Gunnar-Lennefsen-Expedition*.

[75] Fulbrook in "Living through the GDR" (218) and Ahbe in "Competing Master Narratives" (223) contend that East German socialization continues to affect former GDR citizens. Barck in "Fragmentarisches zur Literatur" (321), Köhler in *Brückenschläge* (229), and Radisch in "Es gibt zwei deutsche Gegenwartsliteraturen in Ost und West!" (12), employ the term "Post DDR Literatur" (post-GDR literature). In "Post-Staatliche DDR-Literatur," Galli laments the lack of a definition of GDR literature written since 1990 (114).

[76] See Sedgwick *Epistomology of the Closet*, 11.

[77] See Laqueur, *Auf den Leib geschrieben*; Ecker, *Kein Land in Sicht*; Öhlschläger, "*Gender*/Körper, Gedächtnis und Literatur"; Wenk, *Versteinerte Weiblichkeit*; Öhlschläger and Wiens, *Körper-Gedächtnis-Schrift*, 9, 17.

[78] Yuval-Davis, *Gender & Nation*, 2.

[79] Heinrich von Kleist's poem "Germania an ihre Kinder" (Germania to her children), and his *Hermannsschlacht* (1821) can serve as examples. See Brüns, *Nach dem Mauerfall*, 156–57.

[80] Mayer, *Gender Ironies of Nationalism*, 6, 10, 16. Nations depend on biological purity in reproduction, which is therefore highly regulated. See Yuval-Davis, *Gender & Nation*.

[81] Butler, *Gender Trouble*, 173.

[82] Nusser and Strowick, *Krankheit und Geschlecht*, 8; Herrn, "Ver-körperung des anderen Geschlechts," 41–44.

1: Disease, Death, and Desires Pre-1989: Christa Wolf's Symptomatic GDR Bodies

Born in 1929 in Landsberg an der Warthe, now Gorzów (Poland), Christa Wolf grew up in fascist Germany and was strongly influenced by her family's Prussian values as well as by the Hitler Youth. When the teenager learned about the crimes of the Nazi regime in 1945, she welcomed the GDR's foundational antifascist project, to which she remained committed all her life. Starting with her novel *Der geteilte Himmel* (1963; *Divided Heaven*, 1965), Wolf became internationally known for her fictional and her essayistic texts, both of which interrogate the effect of historical and political events on individuals. After the Eleventh Plenum of the SED Central Committee in 1965, she adopted the role of a "loyal dissident" and became increasingly critical of the government. When the socialist state imploded, Wolf was without doubt the most significant GDR author. Her speech delivered on Alexanderplatz (Berlin) on November 4, 1989, and "Aufruf für unser Land" (Appeal for Our Country), which she published together with thirty other authors in November 1989, corroborate her political beliefs.[1] Wolf was one of the leading intellectuals who campaigned for what was called the "third way," a democratic socialist alternative to a capitalist society with a market-driven economy.

As was typical for her, Wolf, who had a history of reacting to political events in the form of physical maladies, responded physically to the GDR's demise. Numerous entries in *Ein Tag im Jahr 1960–2000* (2003; *One Day a Year 1960–2000*, 2007)—a compilation of her personal reflections on every year—recount the author's suffering from a variety of ailments over the years. The journal also points towards her increasingly skeptical attitude toward conventional medicine, which Wolf accuses of ignoring the "Geistkörperseele" (484: the unity of mind, body, and soul; 480). In her essay "Krebs und Gesellschaft" (1991; "Cancer and Society," 1997), a speech delivered at a German Cancer Society conference, Wolf developed a topic that is central to her oeuvre: physical illness as a manifestation of psychological injury and the way this reflects on individual and societal well-being. In this essay, she asks:

> Wie können wir wissen, ob nicht unser Körper der Austragungsort für die Widersprüche ist, in die jeder von uns angesichts unzumutbarer

Ansprüche der Gesellschaft . . . gerät, angesichts des drohenden Integritätsverlustes, wenn es der Person nicht gelingt, sich gemäß ihrem Wertesystem mit diesen Widersprüchen auseinanderzusetzen? Wie können wir hoffen, "Gesundheit" zu erfahren im körperlichen Bereich, wenn wir aufgehört haben, um die Integrität unserer Person zu kämpfen? (123)

[How can we know if our body isn't the place where we act out the contradictions we experience from the unreasonable demands of society . . . and from the threat of losing our integrity if we are unable to manage the contradictions in a way that is consistent with our system of values? How can we hope to experience "health" in the physical sphere if we have ceased to fight for our integrity as persons? (96)]

In this talk, Wolf investigates the link between illness and society, as well as the role of technology and hierarchical structures in medical institutions—the very topics at the center of previous essays such as "Krankheit und Liebesentzug" (1984; "Illness and Love Deprivation," 1993) and most of her novels, ranging from *Der geteilte Himmel* and *Nachdenken über Christa T.* to *Leibhaftig* and *Stadt der Engel.*

In fact, Wolf had grown increasingly critical of conventional medicine and medical technology over the years. We can observe this attitude in *Kindheitsmuster* (1976; *Patterns of Childhood*, 1980), where tenacious headaches prompt the narrator to go to the hospital to have her spinal column X-rayed, which leads to reflections on the mind/body split created by Western medicine. In *Störfall* (1987; *Accident*, 1989), the surgeons operating on the brain tumor of the narrator's brother rely entirely on the perfection of their technical instruments—which the narrator suspects to be too crude (20). Linking her brother's surgical procedure with the effects of the nuclear catastrophe in Chernobyl, the narrator spends the day of the operation criticizing science and medical research as male-dominated and lacking access to feelings and the psyche. This critique of Western medicine culminates in Wolf's 2002 novel *Leibhaftig*. Bridging the historical caesura of 1989/1990, her work consistently depicts symptomatic bodies exhibiting exigencies of contemporary society and the hubris of a healthcare system that unquestioningly believes in technological progress. Investigating the nexus between the development of disease and social conditions, Wolf positions herself within a modern tradition of emphasizing illness as a gateway to the unconscious and psychic alterity, as well as leading to a heightened sense of awareness.[2]

The symptomatic body of Wolf's novels epitomizes the agony that arises from social and political issues, and most especially from the legacy of Germany's fascist past. This concern is most central in *Kindheitsmuster*, but it can be observed in all those texts where both the GDR and the

FRG, before and after unification, are tied to Germany's fascist years through their respective founding narratives. In *Kein Ort. Nirgends* (1979; *No Place on Earth*, 1982) this connection surfaces in the form of psychological stress; in the case of *Störfall* or *Leibhaftig*, it manifests itself through serious, potentially deadly disease. Psychological and physical suffering, and even fatal illness, define *Nachdenken über Christa T.*, the novel that stages the first symptomatic body in Wolf's oeuvre. This body speaks and reacts to political and social events, and might be the reason literary critics in East and West have misinterpreted the novel.

In May 1969, in an article published in *Die Zeit* entitled "Christa Wolfs unruhige Elegie" (Christa Wolf's Uneasy Elegy), German literary critic Marcel Reich-Ranicki declared: "Christa T. stirbt an Leukämie, aber sie leidet an der DDR. Was bleibt, ist Kapitulation" (62; Christa T. dies of leukemia, but she suffers from the GDR. What remains, is capitulation). The famous yet controversial critic's misleading statement that turns Christa T. into an anti-socialist diagnosed with an illness induced by the GDR is likely the most influential assertion made about *Nachdenken über Christa T.* It garnered a great deal of attention, if not praise, in the FRG and sparked disagreement among officials in the GDR, where censorship delayed the publication, planned for 1968, by a year. Finally published in a small print run by Mitteldeutscher Verlag, *Nachdenken über Christa T.* was criticized, censored, and banned quickly. Reissued in 1972, it became a bestseller.[3]

So what exactly is the importance of this book? How could it possibly ignite so much interest—and so many misunderstandings and attacks on Wolf that affected her physically and psychologically?[4] How did the depiction of medical institutions, of Christa T.'s suffering from multiple ailments and a fatal disease, and of her untimely death cause so much political commotion? In order to tackle these questions, we must situate *Nachdenken über Christa T.* within Wolf's larger oeuvre, and then turn to the significance of Christa T.'s symptomatic body in the context of different aspects of the GDR health sector. In dialogue with medical-historical research, we shall investigate how *Nachdenken über Christa T.* contributes to a view of the past that challenges the hegemonic historiography of the GDR of the 1950s and 1960s.

The Symptomatic Body and the Fascist Past

Written in 1968, *Nachdenken über Christa T.* is often considered a landmark in Christa Wolf's literary production, her first book to break with the tradition of so-called *Ankunftsliteratur* (literature of arrival).[5] Without doubt, this novel epitomizes Wolf's pursuit of the new writing style she had explained in a conversation with Hans Kaufmann entitled "Subjektive Authentizität" (1973; "Subjective Authenticity," 1988). In her view, subjective authenticity aims to engage with objective reality in a productive manner meaningful to the subject while avoiding an unfettered subjectivism, which could obscure rather than illuminate reality (781–82). Still, the radical break implied in locating the shift from *Ankunftsliteratur* in *Der geteilte Himmel* to subjective authenticity in *Nachdenken über Christa T.* should be challenged, not least of all because Wolf already employs a body-centered and political discourse in *Der geteilte Himmel*. Both early novels focus on a young woman, estranged from her family, training to become a teacher, and struggling to reconcile her personal feelings and needs with the new socialist society's demands. However, the commonalities do not extend beyond these biographical elements. Whereas injury, hospitalization, and recovery in *Der geteilte Himmel* serve as the trigger for Rita's own recounting of her recent past in 1960/61, Christa T.'s struggles are played out on her body. Her long-lasting suffering manifests in a variety of illnesses, indicating a decisive shift in mood that underscores the altered political situation in the GDR: the tone of the narrative changes from the optimism of *Der geteilte Himmel*, which expressed the confidence associated with reform communism in the so-called "thaw years" following the building of the Wall in 1961, to distress (although not desolation) in *Nachdenken über Christa T.* This shift can be explained by the Eleventh Plenum in 1965 and by Wolf's removal from the list of candidates for the Central Committee following her critical intervention. Hope that the building of the Wall in 1961 would lead to democratic socialism waned after 1965. This explains why Wolf's fictional character Christa T., who suffers physically from the discrepancy between her personal desires and social expectations, seeks to resolve this struggle by developing a quasi-religious faith in the future of a humane socialism.[6]

Christa T.'s ongoing efforts to overcome the incongruity between her ideals and the realities of life in socialism lead to physical and psychological illness. Her body consequently becomes the focus of the nameless narrator who is reporting on the fate of her long-time friend. In the figure of Christa T., Wolf develops the prototype of the symptomatic body: it appears in most of her writing, but is most prominent in this novel and in *Leibhaftig*, written after unification. In *Nachdenken über Christa T.*, for the first time in Wolf's oeuvre, we observe a fictional character who repeatedly reacts somatically to socio-political events by developing maladies and serious diseases. In this novel, Wolf presents her life-long belief that the sick body functions as the site where contradictions between the individual striving for authenticity and the demands of society become manifest. With Christa T.'s symptomatic body, she launches her consistent exploration of the ways in which corporeality is able to confirm, indicate, criticize, and resist political and social norms. These qualities allow the symptomatic body to emerge as superior to the mind, and the body's physical reaction to political events can even serve to rescue both the body and the soul. Moreover, *Nachdenken über Christa T.* introduces Wolf's criticism of conventional Western medicine: by propagating a mind/body split, it negates the significance of the psyche for physical afflictions and healing, and it is entangled in a network of institutions that complicate the individual's claim to agency.[7]

Consistent with her aesthetic program since the late 1960s, in relating the individual's conflicts, Wolf employs a narrative voice that is clearly not omniscient throughout the novel. The narrator asks questions, invents episodes, and makes use of the subjunctive to convey possible paths Christa T. might have chosen. This narrative strategy corresponds with the author's belief that literature has a responsibility toward supporting social and political developments in the GDR, as she put it in "Lesen und Schreiben" (1968; "The Reader and the Writer," 1977). It fulfills this duty by developing prose that allows readers to imagine possibilities for life in a socialist country (47–48). After World War II, the narrator and Christa T., high-school friends from a village east of the river Oder, become separated as they flee from the Red Army. They meet again accidentally in Leipzig, where both are studying German literature to become teachers. The narrative technique explicitly aims not at re-constructing, but at constructing Christa T.'s life for the future (8). In this, it differs from *Der geteilte Himmel*, which aimed at re-constructing the events before Rita's accident in order to explain her hospitalization. Both narratives create empathy for their young and idealistic socialist protagonists, not least of all in depicting their pain, which is in both cases motivated by the struggle to deal with discrepancies they experience between their idealistic principles and the quotidian realities of socialism. But unlike Rita, who eventually finds her place in the new society, decides that the problems she perceives are temporary, and emerges a true socialist believer, Christa T. suffers physically whenever confronted with the realities of the GDR. When she finally meets and marries the veterinarian Justus, she quits her job and dedicates herself to her husband, her children, a brief affair, and to planning and building a house in the Northern districts. The particular historical events of the 1950s and 1960s, which challenge Christa T.'s belief in the demands of socialist society, leave their increasingly painful traces on her body. Repressed feelings of rebellion and disagreement surface repeatedly in a variety of psychosomatic maladies; they accumulate, resulting in a deadly disease during her pregnancy with her third daughter and the loss of her life.

It seems tempting to equate Christa T.'s retreat to the countryside and her eventual death with a rejection of the GDR. Her symptomatic body lends expression to Wolf's longtime belief that sickness is the result of modern society's demand that the individual adapt to false norms, as she insisted in "Krebs und Gesellschaft" (125). Yet if one considers the author's experiences in fascist Germany, which also emerge in the novel, both her own and Christa T.'s allegiance to the socialist project are thrown into sharper relief—albeit as criticism of the GDR. Confronted with the realities of war and its corollaries, Wolf came to regard socialism as the only feasible way to create a better future after the catastrophe of the Nazi past—a premise she reiterated consistently, even after the fall of the Wall and well into the twenty-first century.[8] In "Unerledigte Widersprüche" (Unsettled Contradictions, 1987/88), an interview with Therese Hörnigk, Wolf explained that for her personally and for her entire generation, socialism presented the only alternative to fascism. It allowed them to come to terms with the fact that even if one had been too young to actually participate in National Socialism, circumstances could have been different: in other words, one had narrowly escaped being directly culpable.

> Als wir fünfzehn, sechzehn waren, mußten wir uns ... von denen abstoßen, die in diesen zwölf Jahren [des Faschismus] ... schuldig geworden waren. Wir mussten diejenigen entdecken, die Opfer geworden waren, diejenigen, die Widerstand geleistet hatten.... Identifizieren konnten wir uns natürlich auch mit ihnen nicht, dazu hatten wir kein Recht. Das heißt, als wir sechzehn waren, konnten wir uns mit niemandem identifizieren. Dies ist eine wesentliche Aussage für meine Generation. (29)

> [When we were fifteen, sixteen, ... we had to reject those who in these twelve years [of fascism] had ... become guilty ... We had to discover those who had been victims, those who had resisted. ... Naturally we couldn't identify with them either, we had no right to. That means, when we were sixteen, we could not identify with anyone. This is a crucial statement for my generation.]

Wolf shifts the emphasis from individual experience—as it might surface in her writing as well—to her claim to speak for East Germans of her entire generation, the 1929ers, since they were all affected by the experience of fascism and later, of socialism. Culpability and separation from the guilty parent generation with whom Wolf and her peers cannot identify play a significant role in this context. In *Der geteilte Himmel*, for example, Manfred, a representative of the 1929ers, articulates his desire for distance from his parents' generation. He explicitly asks Rita why the parent generation, which has lost any credibility for moral guidance, does not want to admit that Manfred's generation grew up without parents (17). Similarly, in *Nachdenken über Christa T.*, biological parents are largely absent or do not play a significant role; and the foundational issue of potential guilt taken on for Germany's fascist years is at the center of the young protagonist's recollection of her flight from the Russian army.

Stuck in a village inn in the northeast of the collapsing Reich with many other Germans, Christa T. realizes in a moment of revelation that she is doomed when she hears Hitler's fanatic voice on the radio and sees her compatriots rise to intone the national anthem. While she is not yet able to comprehend the situation intellectually, the narrative informs us that she reacts physically:

> Ihr Körper hat, wie auch sonst, eher begriffen als ihr Kopf, dem nun allerdings die schwere Aufgabe des Nacharbeitens bleibt. . . . Die hier sitzen sind Verfluchte, und ich mit ihnen. Nur dass ich nicht mehr aufstehen kann, wenn das Lied nun kommt: Da ist es. Ich bleibe sitzen. . . . Ich hebe den Arm nicht mehr. . . . Ich singe nicht mehr mit. (23–24)

> [Her body, as usual, has understood before her brain has, and the brain now has the heavy task of catching up. . . . There is a curse on the people sitting here and on me as well. Except that she can't stand up any more when the song comes: there it is. I am staying here. . . . I'm not going to raise my arm any more. . . . I won't sing the song with them any more. (19)][9]

This passage relates how Christa T.'s body deals with her trauma. Placing the body before the brain, the syntax accentuates the primacy of the physical as characteristic for Christa T. Abiding by the physical sign as if it were a wake-up call, Christa T.'s mind follows her body. The shift in narrative voice—from a third-person perspective to a focalization through Christa T. and a first-person voice—accentuates the experience of physical paralysis and speechlessness: she cannot stand up, lift her arm, talk, or join the singing any more. The use of the present tense in the German original, supported by the modal verb "nicht können" (cannot) accentuates that there is no clear intention behind Christa T.'s lack of actions. When German fascism and World War II draw near, her body repudiates any participation in the fascist regime. This corporeal refusal to act distinguishes her from those around her. At the end of this scene, employing first-person narration in the German original, Christa T. relates, "I can't stand up any more." The "I" emphasizes her awareness of the body's power, which saps Christa T.'s energy in order to ensure her moral superiority in a disordered, immoral society. Her body initiates the intellectual process that aims at denying the collective body her voice, and poses a claim to subjectivity that might liberate Christa T. from what is left of the fascist ideological formation of her as a subject.

The primacy of the bodily signifier redefines moral legitimacy and accentuates Christa T.'s specific positionality as an absolved perpetrator:[10] as a teenager, she feels culpable for her lack of resistance and begins to understand the meaning of collective guilt and, to some extent, even survivor's guilt. Her age, however, assures that she cannot be blamed for the fascist genocide.[11] A close reading of the extent to which the novel focuses on Christa T.'s symptomatic body can reveal the complicated political implications—the imbrication of fascism and the beginning of a socialist state—conveyed by the incorporation of disease in this literary text. Physicians, enmeshed in the network of GDR state institutions influenced by Marxist-Leninist ideology, reinforce the demand for the individual's adjustment to society's needs, which in turn contributes to the protagonist's suffering. Illnesses therefore manifest the significance of both the public and the private spheres in the protagonist's ongoing struggle for a livable identity and point to the impossibility of escaping politics and history. The fundamental imbrication of the private and the public accentuates the political implications of Christa T.'s anguish and death, and suggests the necessary focus on history as the protagonist's secret, embodied memory. If we read Christa T.'s body attentively, we can glean a history that Wolf establishes to reveal what GDR historiography intended to deny—namely, the setbacks that even committed socialists faced in their fight for the socialist future.

Medical Institutions and Medical Training in the GDR

Nachdenken über Christa T. not only centers on the symptomatic body of a young woman, but also depicts various medical institutions and alludes to the redesigned university education for physicians in the GDR. This is hardly surprising, given that in the GDR, fiction was generally the venue for greater societal debates, and for medical discourses in particular. Doctors and nurses recall that controversial issues discussed in the circles of medical institutions were delegated to artists and intellectuals because doctors faced difficulties publishing critical opinions about the realities in their hospitals. Questions pertaining to ethics in the medical field and problems such as a scarcity of supplies and staff in hospitals were addressed in fiction, movies, and articles in popular magazines that had broad popular appeal and inspired discussion. While sometimes fictional accounts of glitches and strains in the healthcare system were censored, public readings of primarily fictional texts that were concerned with problematic developments in the medical realm took place and initiated debate.[12] They brought together experts from a range of fields, from doctors, nurses, and psychologists to lawyers, teachers, philosophers, and theologians. This practice supported the interdisciplinary flow of information, which contributed to the accuracy of literary depictions as well as the development of a productive synergy between intellectuals and practitioners.

It is remarkable that of all the diary entries, letters, and novels that Susanne Hahn—a practicing physician in the GDR—cites as evidence documenting the challenges individual patients faced in GDR medical institutions, none were published before the 1970s and 1980s.[13] This indicates that even beyond the significance of *Nachdenken über Christa T.* for Wolf's conceptualization of subjective authenticity, it was also one of the earliest novels to portray GDR medical institutions and an individual subjected to their therapies. This implies that the novel offers insight into the early effects of healthcare reforms, the norms underlying medical standards and practices in socialism, and the training of the medical staff along the lines of Marxist-Leninist thought.

In order to develop a mindset that would prevent aberrations comparable to the crimes committed in the medical field during the twelve years of National Socialist rule, future physicians in the GDR received a broader education with a focus on the humanities.[14] In 1951, required subjects such as Marxism-Leninism, political economy, dialectical and historical materialism, Russian, and physical education were added to the curriculum. In order to develop students' understanding of social factors and their role in the onset and spread of diseases, "Sozialhygiene" (social hygiene) was introduced in 1952. Since the 1960s, "Arztethik" (doctoral ethics), later renamed "Ethik in der Medizin" (ethics in medicine), complemented the medical education of future MDs, and in 1976, the obligatory political-ideological education of doctors in the first four years of their university training was expanded.[15]

There is a short yet significant scene in *Nachdenken über Christa T.*, in which a medical student in his final semester of medical school demonstrates both the effects and the shortcomings of these early reforms to the medical education of physicians. The self-assured fledgling doctor is Christa T.'s former high-school student. When he encounters her during a vacation in a restaurant in Bulgaria, he proclaims his new credo: "Der Kern der Gesundheit ist Anpassung" (110: the essence of health is adaptation or conformity; 111). The young man calls for adaptation at all costs because he considers it the core of health, and reveals himself in this as a future "sozialistische Arztpersönlichkeit" (socialist doctor personality) who follows the party line and readily takes on the role of his patients' ideological educator. Charged with implementing the norms for socially advantageous behavior and for health and sickness established by the government, physicians and nurses were educators of and healthcare providers for the socialist citizen and were thus involved in the state's power network.[16] They complied with the system and the discipline it imposed, and were vested with powers to exercise control, which ensured the implementation of ideological goals in conjunction with a healthcare system specifically designed for a socialist country.[17] Christa T.'s student embraces the belief that patients must subjugate their personal interests and bodies in the interest of socialist progress.

Though he is aware of Christa T.'s notorious lack of conformity, as his supercilious remarks regarding his teacher's impractical ethics expose, he implies in a dialectical turn that his teacher's lack of compliance with his own belief is both equal to and the cause of disease in GDR society (110). During the conversation, the nameless student accuses Christa T. of being a prime example of traditional German educators, who "haben schon immer an den Realitäten rütteln wollen . . . Anstatt daß Sie mal daran gingen, die Realität zum Maßstab zu nehmen und ihren Erfolg daran zu messen, ob es Ihnen gelungen ist, Ihren Schülern seelische Robustheit mit auf den Weg zu geben" (111: have always tried to undermine the realities . . . The right thing would have been to focus on the realities themselves as the true standard and to measure your success by the degree of psychological robustness you have given your students to sustain them through life; 112). The student reveals that he has fully adopted the standards that require him to accept the facts of socialism as practiced in the GDR as "truths," and to implement unquestioned ideological goals in his future professional work. His belief in the superiority of the realities of life—that is, socialism as it actually existed in the GDR, later known as *realexistierender Sozialismus* (real-existing socialism)—prevents him from recognizing higher, more idealistic standards. When he condemns Christa T. for allegedly attempting to condition her students in her teaching of literature (110–11), he shows that the growing number of mandatory classes in the humanities required as part of medical-school education was of limited efficacy. They did not necessarily lead to higher ethical standards, nor to a more holistic approach in how medicine was practiced since they were outweighed by the demand to conform to the realities of life.

Despite his advocacy for the socialist norms propagated in his university education, the future doctor's behavior betrays an appreciation of elite values. Not only can he afford to travel internationally as a student, he is also familiar with foreign local foods and markedly self-confident (110). He is accompanied by his beautiful fiancée, another aspiring doctor, whose conspicuous elegance indicates a privileged rather than a working-class background. Despite the partial success of the socialist education of doctors as revealed by Christa T.'s former student's declared belief in the necessity to cope with the realities of life, the young couple's behavior and their elegance puncture the illusion that doctors in the GDR identified with the working class.

This depiction questions the success of the SED's educational efforts. From the early days of the GDR, admission to medical degree programs was based on ideological allegiance, and the Stasi had joint decision-making and veto power. The SED and the Stasi favored the offspring of families who did not hold university degrees, and hoped that control over—and eventual elimination of—medical professional associations would contribute to an eradication of bourgeois norms in the healthcare sector (Süß, *Pm*, 243, 342). Yet even the political education of doctors, intended to mold them into exemplary socialist doctor personalities, did not prevent the emergence of a privileged, apolitical medical class. Among physicians educated in the GDR, such as Christa T.'s former pupil, elite conventions were, in fact, upheld—along with socialist demands for adaptation—until the country's dissolution.[18]

Yet changes occur over the years. In *Politisch mißbraucht?*, Süß quotes from a 1958 Stasi report that reflects the situation in the medical field around the time Christa T. encounters her former student in Bulgaria. This Stasi account condemns clinic doctors, in particular, for displaying an indifferent attitude toward the socialist state. Bourgeois ideology prevails, and as a consequence, head physicians—not the party—make decisions in hospitals and determine what accounts for appropriate conduct among doctors and nurses (*Pm*, 128). A report from 1967, however, emphasizes the generational succession within the medical intelligentsia over the previous decade. The graduates of medical-training facilities now appear closely aligned with the working class and with GDR society (*Pm*, 144).

"The fear that one might vanish without a trace": Depression, Psychiatry, and Self-Therapy

The discrepancy between her former student's belief in "the realities of life" and Christa T.'s ethics and ideals forms the core of the protagonist's interactions with her social environment. The idealism that anchors her unswerving belief in socialism is purely idealistic and draws on her profound identification with female authors of the romantic literary period, such as Bettina von Arnim and especially Karoline von Günderrode (64).[19] Like many of her romantic role models, she suffers from the incongruity between her ideals and the quotidian demands of society, and slips into depression. Wolf's notion of subjective authenticity reverberates in Christa T.'s effort to resolve her inner conflict and to overcome the resulting pathological sadness: the objective realities of life and subjectivity must be reconciled so that the individual can find a place in socialist society.[20]

The sadness and anxiety leading to Christa T.'s depression develop gradually and in tandem with political developments in the GDR. They first surface in the young woman's fear of vanishing without a trace. She wonders how to engage in the new society that she simultaneously dreads and desires (36). This hints both at the demand to give up subjective hopes and at an anxiety about citizens disappearing in Stalinist prisons and work camps that was fairly common in the early 1950s. Despite Christa T.'s admiration for the new society's ideals and the perfection of the state apparatus, she is terrified by the demand for self-sacrifice "achieved by self-extinction" for the sake of the new state (*The Quest for Christa T.*, 56). The German original offers a specific detail to characterize Christa T.'s distress that the translation omits: her fear is to end up as nothing but "a little screw" in the system, "sich auslöschen, Schräubchen sein" (*Nachdenken über Christa T.*, 58). This fear—combined with lovesickness—triggers her first deep depression, which is metaphorically significant on several levels.[21]

Christa T.'s horror of being reduced to a cog in the political machine evokes Lenin's call for literature in a socialist society to function as "a cog and a screw." In his essay "Party Organization and Party Literature" (1905), Lenin explicitly demanded that "Literature must become *part* of the common cause of the proletariat, 'a cog and a screw' of one single great Social-Democratic mechanism set in motion by the entire politically-conscious vanguard of the entire working class." Erich Honecker's demand that authors unquestioningly support the socialist state in their writings, as formulated at the so-called *Kahlschlag-Plenum* in 1965, clearly echoes Lenin's call for partisan writing. This suggests that Christa T.'s fear of becoming a little screw in the system and her resulting depression relate to the events of 1965. The young idealist's mood indicates more than a conflict between the dictate of partisanship and unquestioned belief in socialist progress on the one hand and her romantic yearnings on the other. Rather, this antagonism critiques the demand that GDR cultural politics placed on literature to subordinate itself to political affirmation. Christa T.'s illness thus embodies Wolf's call to rethink forms of writing in socialist society, to resist the demands of the government, and to insist on subjective authenticity.

In conjunction with the relationship between literature and depression, the historical timing within the fictional text points to its political significance. Conflating Christa T.'s two lost loves—her romantic feelings for Kostja and her commitment to the socialist idea—the narrative accentuates the proximity of the private and the political spheres. Her depression coincides with the people's uprising of June 17, 1953, which is silenced with the support of the very Soviet tanks the protagonist had heralded as liberators from fascism eight years earlier.[22] Violence and destruction, wrought both by the revolting citizens and the military, conflict with Christa T.'s unquestioning belief in the solidarity of a socialist society (73). As a result, her world—or, to stay within the framework of her own metaphor, her whole body—collapses: "[Es ist] als ob ganze Teile der Lungen seit Ewigkeit nicht mehr mittun. Kann man aber leben, wenn ganze Teile nicht mittun?" (72: As if whole areas of the lungs have been out of action for an eternity. When that is so, can one go on living?; 70). Christa T.'s body signals her reaction to the people's contempt for the new socialist state and the force the government felt justified in employing. Society's tensions and problems are channeled into and contained within Christa T.'s flesh, which, like the young state, struggles for survival. The young woman suffers physically and emotionally from her inner conflict: while she cannot relate to the discontented population's lack of enthusiasm for the socialist project, she also disapproves of the violence exercised by the Soviet army. Still, her allegiance to socialism requires that she accept the intervention of the tanks as necessary for progress, which exacerbates the constant pressure to adjust to and comply with the GDR.[23] This pressure to adapt to the state becomes so great that she endorses violence that endangers both the protagonist's physical well-being and the body politic. While Christa T.'s wish to die after June 17, 1953, does not, in fact, correspond to an actual rise in suicide rates, her mood surfaces as an explicit metaphor through which the narrative critiques the mandate that citizens adapt.[24]

When Christa T.'s depression culminates in a letter to her sister that is read as a suicide note, she is subjected to institutional psychiatry, where her affliction is interpreted according to official policies (71). The attending psychiatrist, in line with the principles espoused by Christa T.'s former student, views her severe depression as a refusal to participate in the socialist project and consequently as a subversive act: "Todeswunsch als Krankheit. Neurose als mangelnde Anpassungsfähigkeit an gegebene Umstände" (74: The death wish as sickness. Neurosis as deficient capacity to adapt oneself to existing circumstances; 72). His diagnosis renders Christa T. a sick outsider because she lacks the two main characteristics that distinguish the model socialist personality: optimism and health. In his extensive study on depression and suicide in the GDR, Grashoff emphasizes that, in the 1950s, socialism was considered the perfect prophylaxis against suicide because of its historic optimism:

> Neurotische Fehlentwicklungen, Pessimismus... rechneten die SED-Ideologen als dem Sozialismus "wesensfremd" den Erscheinungen zu, die... im Sozialismus ohne materielle Basis waren. Gleichzeitig beschworen sie das Idealbild einer "sozialistischen Persönlichkeit," die sich durch Aktivität, durch die "Fähigkeit, bewusst auf die Umwelt einzuwirken und diese sowie sich selbst nach eigenen Vorstellungen und Zielen zu verändern," auszeichnete. (Grashoff, *AD*, 281–82)

> [The SED ideologues considered neurotic aberrations, pessimism... part of those phenomena "alien" to socialism, which were... without any material basis in socialism. At the same time, they invoked the ideal of a "socialist personality" who was characterized by activity, by the "capability to consciously effect the environment and to alter both this environment and oneself according to one's own ideas and goals."]

In other words, socialism was the best prophylactic not only against physical, but also against psychological illness. In accordance with the prominent role medical institutions were assigned in advancing socialism by educating patients to embody the ideal of the positive citizen who ensures productivity and vitality for the triumph of socialism (Seifert, *GSV*, 12–13, 35), the physician establishes Christa T.'s malady as a medical and social anomaly.

By depicting Christa T. as deviant, *Nachdenken über Christa T.* becomes one of the first narratives to participate in the discourse on problems in GDR psychiatry, such as the condemnation of Freud's depth psychology and psychoanalysis, which achieved a more prominent position in GDR fiction of the late 1970s and the 1980s. Sibylle Muthesius (alias Boden-Gerstner) famously criticized GDR psychiatry as antiquated in *Flucht in die Wolken* (Flight into the Clouds, 1981). She wrote this book after her daughter Sonja had died due to inadequate therapy that essentially refused to treat her psychotic episodes. Despite Muthesius's prominent social position, the book was subject to censorship in the late 1970s before it finally became a bestseller in 1981. The significant time lag illustrates how difficult it was to add a public critical voice to this discourse.[25] Bearing in mind the publication history of *Flucht in die Wolken*, the significance of *Nachdenken über Christa T.* in initiating a discussion about depression already in the late 1960s becomes apparent.

In the GDR, suicide attempts, while not liable to prosecution, were condemned on moral grounds precisely because they allegedly pointed to an individual's disinclination to adjust and therefore expressed a pessimism incompatible with the fundamental political concerns of socialism.[26] A double discourse of morale and morality is at work here, since patients in the GDR were both legally and morally obligated to cooperate in preventing maladies. Insisting that it is "eine moralische Pflicht gegenüber der Gesellschaft, daß die Patienten auch über die Rechtspflichten hinaus an ihrer Gesundung mitarbeiten" (a moral obligation toward society that patients collaborate in their healing also beyond their legal obligations), GDR legal expert Konrad Franke utilizes arbitrary moral standards to justify demands for patient behavior that exceed legal obligations.[27] Ulrike Seifert considers Franke's statement proof of the "Einheit von Recht und Moral" (unity of law and morality) in the GDR, and deduces that jurisprudence effectively treated morality as "Ersatzrecht" (substitute law) and thus equivalent to law.[28] Within this legal and ideological framework, Christa T.'s death wish, resulting from the refusal to sacrifice her personal ideals and to instead accept social responsibility for the construction of socialism, signifies "false consciousness," a cowardly escape, or even dangerous rebellion. Diametrically opposed to the suffering of communists under fascist torture that receives praise and social approbation, the young woman's symptomatic body indirectly mocks the heroic fight to live out the communist idea through suffering. Accordingly, her therapy does not focus on supporting her subjectivity, but on eliminating the "false consciousness" that emerges in her psychic defects.

The narrative voice highlights this attitude by ironically inventing the direct speech the psychiatrist could have used: "Am besten, mein Fräulein, Sie kommen zu mir in die Therapie. . . . Sie werden sich anpassen lernen" (74: Best thing for you, Miss T., would be to come to me for therapy. . . . You'll learn to adapt; 72). The psychiatrist's educational goal and medical advice follows what Wolf has criticized in "Lesen und Schreiben" as psychiatry's desire to employ "de-sensitizing" methods to enforce adaptation to the norm (47). The doctor, invested with the political power to promote a supposedly universal subject position, privileges "rationalism" over personal care, consequently corroborating the link between the demand for adaptation, (psychological) illness, and a male-dominated "rational" medicine that underestimates psychosomatic suffering.[29]

The psychiatrist disregards Christa T.'s psyche and uses his expertise and rank to justify the mechanisms of treatment. As an individual who has difficulties adjusting to society, she poses a potential threat to socialism and must be treated. Portraying a character who has little recourse against this approach, Wolf's fictional narrative carefully reflects on GDR jurisprudence, which denied patients the sovereignty to refuse treatment plans proposed by doctors. Rather, patients were expected to actively support the putatively objective necessities of their mandated medical treatment, since only docile patients were considered able to reconcile their individual desires with the interests of society (Seifert, *GSV*, 351–52). By not considering potential triggers for Christa T.'s depression, but focusing instead on her future efficacy for society, this approach inserts into her therapy the very conflict that prompted her depression— namely, the discrepancy between her political ideals and the constraints implied by their implementation.

Many patients in the GDR experienced the clash between their individual interests and those of society in the medical realm, and solving this problem was typically at the core of therapy. More precisely, doctors were required to educate patients with regard not necessarily to their disease, but to correct social and socialist awareness: "Auch in der Arzt-Patienten-Beziehung ist die Rechtserziehung das Mittel zur Erziehung des Bürgers, 'in gesellschaftlichen Aspekten denken zu lernen, d. h. Verantwortung für das Ganze zu tragen,' ohne hierin einen Einschnitt in seine persönliche Sphäre zu sehen" (In the relationship between doctor and patient as well, legal instruction is the means to educate the citizen "to learn to think in social terms, i.e., taking on responsibility for society as a whole," without considering this an incursion in their personal sphere; Seifert, *GSV*, 354). This practice surfaces in *Nachdenken über Christa T.* when the young woman is informed that she is maladjusted and uncooperative.

Unsurprisingly, this diagnosis does not support her healing process, but instead increases her desperation when she maintains, "Ich erkenne alles, was falsch an mir ist, aber es bleibt doch mein Ich, ich reiß es doch nicht aus mir heraus!" (72: I know what's wrong with me, but it's still me, and I can't wrench it out of myself!; 70).

Christa T.'s inability or unwillingness to adjust places an obligation on her fellow students to work toward her social integration. In addition to the medical and the legal realm, a person's working collective or team in which they worked, or their worker's brigade (a slightly larger group established to increase productivity) was expected to contribute to the mandatory process of healing—read: adaptation.[30] Yet when other students from Christa T.'s cohort, taking on the role of the working collective, try to convince her that the required adaptation is justified in exchange for their free university education, the protagonist announces her refusal to pay "in fremder Währung" (87: in foreign currency; 87).

Obviously her "study group" is part of a network of institutions striving to protect the young woman's health—not because they are primarily interested in her well-being, but because her affliction affects their average exam results negatively and reflects badly on their mission to support Christa T.'s ideological education. Her refusal to adapt and contribute to her collective's success presents an affront to socialist society per se, since she undermines the basic principle that the fulfillment of individual desires is secured in the realization of societal interests, and especially within the "sozialistisches Leistungsprinzip" (socialist principle of efficiency; Seifert, *GSV*, 83). Since for Christa T.'s cohort the malfunctioning body is the equivalent of a political strike that undermines the workforce, on a par with the walkouts associated with the uprising of June 1953, the narrative establishes an additional layer of meaning. It points beyond the political significance of that uprising by revealing the extent to which the sick individual becomes subject to disciplinary tactics exercised not only in the medical realm and in the judicial system, but also in concomitant educational activities of the person's collective. In fact, this additional social means of exercising control and applying pressure to complement the corrective measures of the law should patients not willingly fulfill their duty to participate in their convalescence was considered particularly effective (Seifert, *GSV*, 354).

Christa T., however, is depicted as able to escape all these mechanisms. She retreats to the countryside where she aims at overcoming the tension between compliance with established norms and health on the one hand and resistance and illness on the other by embarking on a process of creative writing. She assumes agency with her decision to cure her depression by writing her exam thesis on Theodor Storm. This allows her to reconcile her two complementary sides: her romantic longing for socialist ideals and her intellectual desire to fit into socialist society, despite its conflict with her ideals. Balancing realism with the romantic ideal of identity construction in and through art, Christa T. finds her way to health (93–95). This therapeutic approach echoes Wolf's own demand for alternative medical treatment and, ultimately, subjective authenticity. Christa T.'s healing ascertains the power of literature to articulate resistance to established power structures and to gain a greater sense of self-awareness. The young woman emerges as a valuable member of socialist society precisely because she did not merely adapt, but rather searched for a way to balance her personal desires with the interests of society (93).[31]

Pregnancy, Childbirth, Abortion, and the Gynecology Ward

Despite her efforts to resolve the conflict between her personal aspirations and the needs and demands of society, Christa T. is not always successful. While compromise and concession prevail in her ongoing struggle to become a worthy constituent of the new socialist state, these behavioral patterns, which she developed as a university student, are inappropriate at times. This applies, for example, to her rational decision to marry the veterinarian Justus and to have children. Justus, whose name suggests that he is "just" or "right," appears as the sole male who is not associated with brutality, destruction, and death, and who can transcend the binary implied in the gendered allocation of values and ideas.[32] Like Christa T., he envisions a socialism that overcomes cruelty and the patriarchal structure inherited from earlier bourgeois gender systems. Marrying him allows Christa T. to negotiate her individual desires and society's demands for marriage and the bearing and rearing of children. She can overcome her single life, which had been considered "abnormal" because it extended beyond her time as a university student, as Sonja Hilzinger emphasizes in her afterword to the novel (215). Most importantly, she engages in a sexual relationship that does not tie sexuality to the fascist past, a constellation developed in early GDR literature that was influential for Christa Wolf, as Julia Hell has demonstrated in detail in *Post-Fascist Fantasies* and as outlined in the introduction to this study. Akin to her literary predecessors in *Aufbauliteratur*, Christa T. possesses a body that is constructed as the opposite of a sexual body that can be linked to fascism. Hers is a body whose sexuality is "disciplined," "contained" and can be considered "pure," since it serves the laudable economy of reproduction in the young GDR, which relied heavily on a young generation for its future.[33]

Reminiscent of various protagonists in Anna Seghers's oeuvre, Christa T. and Justus are desexualized even in their marriage. Justus's childless cousin in West Berlin, whose body—in contrast to Christa T.'s pregnant body—is artificially eroticized with long eyelashes Christa T. suspects to be false, repeatedly labels the couple "Kinder" (children; 125).[34] The two women emerge as each others' abject on the sexual level, a process that determines their subject formation on the political level. Like the two German states, they are linked by family relations, yet they are separate, alienated, and produce each other as a constitutive outside in Judith Butler's sense.[35] We can therefore add the markers "lack of sexual body/sexual body," "innocence/experience," and "authenticity/artificiality" to the dichotomies between socialism/capitalism, planned economy/market economy, and solidarity/individualism which I elaborated in the introduction as significant for the GDR's and the FRG's subject formation for their respective Other.[36] Christa T.'s pregnant socialist body, which links sexuality with reproduction for and in the socialist state, comes to stand for the GDR. Her innocence is produced by its distinct difference from the capitalist sexual body of the childless cousin who is associated with fascism and resides on the other, Western side of the German-German border. Devoid of sexual connotations that could link her and Justus's bodies to the fascist past, the narrative constellation in *Nachdenken über Christa T.* underlines the significance of the couple's pure communist bodies as signifiers for antifascism. Ultimately, it supports the official GDR rhetoric and its legitimating claim to power through the founding narrative of antifascism.

Despite the difficulties of all three of her pregnancies, Christa T. never complains, subordinating her wishes to the GDR's demand for children (131). This urgent need for children surfaces, for example, in the "Gesetz über den Mutter- und Kinderschutz und die Rechte der Frau" (Law for the Protection of Mothers and Children and the Rights of Women) from 1950. The legislation introduced financial support, enhanced hospital and medical care, increased the number of childcare facilities, doubled the mother's food rations from the sixth month of pregnancy on and extended maternity leave to twice what it was. By asserting the importance of children and the family for the socialist state, this law effectively suspended a woman's right to an abortion by eliminating the "social indicator" that had allowed women previously to have an abortion in the event of imminent social or economic crisis.[37] Throughout the 1950s, 1960s, and 1970s, there was a steady flow of pronatalist measures aimed at raising the birthrate. It included the extension of maternity leave, one paid day of housework each month for mothers, the introduction of child-benefit payments and—most significantly—special provisions for single mothers. These actions were aimed primarily at women, not necessarily at parents, revealing the government's interest in boosting birthrates and producing children for the future of socialism, as opposed to supporting bourgeois notions of family. Still, the ideal of a family modeled on the socialist collective in which women fulfill their "duty . . . to produce the socialist citizens of the future" persisted.[38] To counter the threat of a declining birthrate, particularly after the introduction of a new and less restrictive abortion law in 1972, which gave women the option to terminate a pregnancy within the first twelve weeks, the GDR introduced measures to encourage women to bear three or more children. In fact, the so-called "Dreikinderfamilie" (three-child-family) was considered necessary to maintain the size of the population in the GDR.[39]

When Christa T. decides already in the early 1960s to raise three children to benefit the socialist project, her sexuality is translated into maternal love, which allows her to contribute to the success of the socialist state in conformity with societal norms. Like her pledge to socialism, marriage and childbirth are the products of rational decisions and commitments to society's expectations. The narrator questions the motivation underlying Christa T.'s resolution to get married, as the use of the modal verb "müssen" (must) indicates: "So muss man sich binden?" (120: So must you accept certain ties?; 122). Unsurprisingly, the protagonist reacts physically to this rational decision that is made under a form of compulsion. Her body responds to the force of these social obligations when, due to the unborn baby, an old complaint flares up during her wedding night and forces her to visit the gynecology ward at the Berlin Charité the next day (126). We observe that Christa T.'s is body marked by a recurring, even habitual ailment. Over a long time, her flesh has become the unconscious repository of aspects of the past, such as the never-ending demand to adapt to her social and political environment.[40] The long-term incubation, so to speak, leads to the persistence of the condition and, furthermore, leaves the protagonist unable to consciously influence her condition or even successfully read her body.

Notably, not only the protagonist, but also the narrator possesses a body that speaks as soon as she approaches the medical institution. Reconstructing her visit to the hospital when Christa T. stayed there, the narrator remembers losing her way on the Charité grounds, experiencing "einen scharfen Schmerz" (128: a sharp pain; 131), and feeling injured by the "häßliche Rot der Klinikmauern ... und der nackte Hall meiner Schritte auf den ausgetretenen Stufen" (128: ugly red of the clinic walls ... and the naked echo of my footsteps on the worn stairs; 131). Via the narrator's symptomatic body, a body that responds to the state institutions by feeling damaged, the hospital is associated with injury, ache, shabbiness, emptiness, and desolation. Wolf's description of the ward that Christa T. shares with about twenty women, all lined up in a long row, and of the gloomy hospital corridor (129) augment the atmosphere of despondency and neglect; it also correlates with medical-historical accounts. Sabine Schleiermacher and Udo Schagen, for example, relate that about 80% of the Charité buildings were destroyed in 1945, and of the remaining 20%, many facilities could not be used because the

Nazis had neglected them even before 1945. Despite huge efforts by the administration in the Soviet Occupied Zone and later the GDR government, the famous Berlin hospital faced shortages in every respect, and its buildings displayed war damage until about 1960. When Christa T. is admitted to the gynecology ward of the Charité in 1956, the hospital was still suffering from a lack of space and shortage of clinic staff. The latter problem was only solved when the Berlin Wall was built, which from August 1961 on prevented physicians and medical personnel from leaving in vast numbers.[41]

The unavailability of medical staff might similarly account for the lack of care Christa T. receives when she goes into labor. The narrative does not mention doctors, nurses, or midwives supporting her during a delivery that is described as extremely difficult, only a doctor who later places the child on her breast (131). Yet the pain and suffering Christa T. must endure serve to "purify" her body—in Julia Hell's terminology—and once again underline the "purity" of her body that is staged as asexual even in childbirth. The feeling of desolation and abandonment Christa T. must have experienced in the clinic takes on political meaning when we consider the historical timing: her pregnancy and first delivery are framed narratively in the year 1956, and within the context of references to the violent end of the short-lived attempts to reform socialism in Hungary between October 23 and November 4, 1956 (130–31). In other words, when the protagonist experiences the discrepancy between her ideals of reforming socialism and their failed implementation as a rejection of her beliefs, her body reacts physically by developing complications during the delivery of the child for the socialist state.

Political and private events are clearly linked just before Christa T. gives birth, when the narrative depicts a number of friends listening to Western radio stations. In an unusually dark night, they "hörten aus allen westlichen Rundfunkstationen neben den Berichten über Kämpfe in Budapest das große, kaum unterdrückte Hohngelächter über das Scheitern dessen, was sie 'Utopie' nannten" (130: [heard] from all the Western radio stations, among the reports of fighting in Budapest, . . . the loud and almost blatant laughter at the demise of what they called Utopia; 133). The repeated use of "we" throughout this part of the text contrasts with the pointed "they" referring to those in the West laughing at the failed idealism of those in the East. This narrative constellation reveals that the friends identify with the political ideals of the socialist world even though they now have to get used to seeing "in das nüchterne Licht wirklicher Tage und Nächte" (131: by the sober light of real days and nights; 133). Particularly Christa T., who subscribed entirely and irrevocably to the new socialist world,[42] now must focus on living up to these ideals—by giving birth to her daughter Anna. The delivery of this child can be read as an allegory of the pain and exertions involved in turning the socialist ideals into reality. For both socialism and the baby, the initial position was critical in 1956:

> Das Kind lag schlecht. Sie brachte Stunden mit nutzlosen Anstrengungen zu. Natürlich erlahmte sie, aber sie flüchtete sich nicht in das Gefühl, ungerecht gequält zu werden.... Sie konnte nicht vergessen, dass sie das Kind wollte und dass der strenge Rhythmus von zerreißender Anstrengung und Entspannung nötig war, es hervorzubringen. (131)

> [The child was in a bad position. For hours she strained uselessly. Of course it weakened her, but she didn't retreat into the feeling that the pains were an injustice being done to her. She ... couldn't forget that she wanted to have the child and that the strict rhythm of rending strain and relaxation was necessary to produce it. (134)]

The same pattern produces the baby and socialism—alternately distressing, even painful strain and phases of easing; both need to be endured for a successful outcome. The narrative builds on the model of earlier *Aufbauliteratur*, which described social relations as family relations and featured antifascist heroes who suffered unspeakable pain under fascist torture—a pain that is inscribed in the body and leads to purification, as Julia Hell has detailed in *Post-Fascist Fantasies*. In childbirth, Christa T.'s suffering parallels the fascist torture communists were subjected to. Despite the agony she endures, Christa T. never complains. She accepts the pain as a component of both producing the child and the socialist state. The link between childbirth and politics in 1956 underlines that the process of painfully delivering her daughter for the antifascist GDR turns Christa T. into a revision of *Aufbauliteratur*'s antifascist heroes. It purges her of the "contamination" by National Socialist ideology and confirms her moral superiority.

Acute Fatigue and Self-Therapy: The Construction of the Perfect House

Once brought into the world, socialism and the baby resemble each other: they are vulnerable, in need of care, perfect in their own way—and they appear alien at first. Not unlike the new state, little Anna initially does not fulfill her mother's expectations, and Christa T. must learn to accept her daughter for what she is (132–33). And for the protagonist, both socialism and the child are worth subordinating her interests to her husband's needs and society's expectations. In the GDR of the 1950s, this still meant following the traditional model of marriage and child-rearing within the framework of conventional gender roles. Taking on the tasks that come with the role of mother and housewife, however, is shown to affect Christa T's life and well-being adversely.[43]

When asked, "what are you going to be?" the protagonist's answers highlight her loss of subjectivity—a condition diametrically opposed to Wolf's ideal of the "Subjektwerdung des Menschen" (48: human beings becoming "conscious subjects"; 212) as she explained in "Lesen und Schreiben." Far from articulating her aspirations, Christa T. lists the actions she envisions herself performing to serve other people's needs, such as preparing meals for the family, learning words like "cattle brucellosis" and "calving" and "tuberculin-tested," or caring about farmer Ulrich's pigs (135). The syntax of the list in the German original text underscores Christa T.'s transformation, which can only be described as a loss of agency: the first few sentences position the "I" before the described action, while subsequent sentences place other people's needs or deploy reversed word order, placing the verb before the subject in the sentence.[44] The constant reiteration of Christa T.'s subordination to others' desires and needs as expressed in the conspicuous rhetorical redundancy of the sentence structure emphasizes the re-constitution of Christa T.'s subservient identity through the acts she performs repeatedly. Her conscious attempt at inventing herself as wife and mother, however, weighs her down in that it requires her total adaptation to outside needs without allowing for individual subjectivity. Predictably, her body reacts accordingly. Christa T. understands the limitations of her new role when she describes her day as propelled by work: "Aber er [der Tag] hat ein Gewicht, gegen das meine beiden Hände auf die Dauer nicht ausreichen" (136: But the day is so heavy my two hands won't in the long run have the strength; 138). Exhausted by this work, which is alienated in Marx's sense,[45] the constant sacrifice for others leads to an extreme fatigue that is more than a premonition of the deadly disease awaiting her: "Niemals kann man durch das, was man tut, so müde werden wie durch das, was man nicht tut oder nicht tun kann. Das war ihr Fall" (136–37: This much is certain: what one does can never make one so tired as what one doesn't do or cannot do. That was the case with her; 140). The GDR of the late 1950s, still under the sway of the kind of conventional gender roles that Christa T. feels condemned to conform to, does not provide sufficient opportunities for the protagonist, a situation that causes her to fall ill. The double meaning of the German "Das war ihr Fall" is lost in the English translation. The German implies that the absence of prospects Christa T. experiences was not only the case with her, including her medical case, but also her downfall—the cause of her fatal disease.

Wolf repeatedly identified societal conventions as the cause of serious illness—"Krebs und Gesellschaft" is a case in point (123). In particular, she was concerned about a social attitude that considers women's sacrifice "normal behavior" to be rewarded, and female autonomy as "abnormal"—with the result that independent women ended up being burdened by feelings of guilt. As if to refute her former student's call for adaptation at all costs as the basis of health, Christa T.'s body demonstrates the failure of this medical approach when her conformity leads to pathological exhaustion and death. Even her alternative therapeutic approach—building her dream house—fails because it comes too late.

Initially, the effort is successful: Christa T. manages to temporarily defeat her fatigue and regain agency in her crucial project of building her house. Once again aimed at linking the public and the private, the dwelling symbolizes hope for an ideal socialist state: Christa T.'s plans reveal "daß es ja schon geboren war und daß niemand mehr das Recht hatte, es ins Nichtsein zurückzustoßen" (147: that it was already in existence and that nobody had any right to push it back into nonexistence; 150). Challenged by the inappropriate location that exposes the house to enormous winds, it must be defended against all obstacles and objections since it is, after all, "vollkommen in seiner Art" (148: perfect in its way; 150). Only getting to the house is said to be difficult; especially "das letzte Ende, den Hügel hinauf, war allerdings wirklich katastrophal" (147: The last stretch, up the hill, was really catastrophic; 151).[46] The starting date of the project, 1961, coincides with the building of the Wall—often considered the real founding year of the GDR since the Wall compelled GDR citizens to come to terms with quotidian life in socialism and required the regime to pursue legitimacy by increasing the standard of living.[47] Like the socialist state, which recovered briefly after August 1961 during the so-called "thaw years," Christa T. initially feels better. The fictional character mirrors the confidence of many East German intellectuals, such as Christa Wolf, who were convinced that the protected state would now progress as anticipated in Marxist-Leninist historical thought.[48] And in the same way that the GDR government and its supporters felt secure against outside intervention and Western capitalism after August 1961, the house can offer security and turn out to be a new *Heimat*, in which reality will finally measure up to its proclaimed ideal. Despite observable deficiencies, both Christa T.'s building and the state provide shelter; they appear to offer space for (individual) development and to sever all ties with the past. In the narrator's words, Christa T. "wollte ganz neu anfangen, nichts Altes sollte in das neue Haus mitgenommen werden" (156: wanted to start afresh; there weren't going to be any of the old things in the new house; 159). Like Christa T., who longs to disconnect from the past, the GDR dissociated itself from Germany's fascist history.[49] During the New Year's Eve celebration in 1961/1962, the friends who gather in the new building follow Christa T.'s optimism. The protagonist emerges as the vanguard in embracing GDR society based on the sense that a new era offering infinite possibilities has begun (163). At this point, Christa T.'s body is symptomatic of a feeling of victory: the protagonist seems to have triumphed in the fight against her potentially debilitating weariness. In constructing her house, she is breaking with the constraints imposed on the subject by hegemonic ideas of assimilation. Like her unfinished place on its way to perfection, the GDR will provide the socio-economic conditions for dedicated socialists to thrive; and it serves as the optimistic legacy Christa T. leaves behind when she dies.[50]

Leukemia, Death, and Intensive Care

When Christa T. falls seriously ill in 1963, GDR medical institutions promote scientific, "rational" medicine that excludes more holistic approaches to her body of the kind that she would have preferred. The GDR legal system emphasized physicians' obligations to elevate patients' hope and optimism by convincing them that their treatment was working, even in cases of terminal illness (Seifert, *GSV*, 168). Since the "socialist personality" believes in progress, is supposedly strong and generally optimistic, the very existence of incurable diseases was denied, even in scholarly publications.[51] Doctors were not obliged to disclose the truth about the condition of ailing patients, and it was common practice to discuss the status of the disease only with close family members, not with the patient. Particularly in cases of adverse prognosis, the prevailing practice of concealing the hopeless situation and the prospect of death was discussed among representatives of the medical and the legal systems. Until the very end of the GDR, however, physicians possessed the legal right—and were in most cases encouraged—not to disclose the bald truth. Instead, they were to employ what was officially termed the *schonende Lüge* (gentle lie), using appropriate wording and an incomplete description to deliberately keep patients in the dark in cases of unfavorable prognosis.[52]

From the first day of a series of stays in hospitals during Christa T.'s last year, the physicians in charge know that the patient is too sick to be cured (173). According to common practice, they notify the husband about her condition, and employ the *schonende Lüge* in conversations with Christa T. When she is transferred to another hospital, even her husband lies to her, elevating her hopes for better treatment while she is being rolled into the ward for the terminally ill (173). Later, Christa T. overhears the doctors discussing her illness and subsequently insists on being confronted with the truth: "So fällt im Eifer des Streites das Wort, das sie nicht hören dürfte: Leukämie. Ist es das, Frau Doktor, sagen Sie mir bitte die Wahrheit, ich will die Wahrheit wissen. Aber woher denn, wo denken Sie denn hin!" (174: so during their excited argument they utter the word she shouldn't hear: leukemia. Is it that, doctor? Tell me the truth, I want to know the truth. Certainly not, what can you be thinking of?; 178).[53] This passage signals a critical point in the narrative precisely because Christa T. insists on being told the truth, but is still confronted with lies. In this fictional text, Wolf explicitly raised a crucial issue and contributed to societal discussion already in the late 1960s. Not until the mid-1970s did some lawyers, theologians, and philosophers who were opposed to the practice of the *schonende Lüge* come forward with their views. However, the prevailing opinion in the medical and the legal realm supported the practice, as Müller's insistence on the *schonende Lüge* demonstrates: "Auch wenn der Kranke immer wieder . . . fragt und die volle Wahrheit, auch wenn sie den Tod bedeuten sollte, hören möchte, so will er sie im Grunde doch nicht wissen und erhofft von seinem Arzt eine optimistische und tröstliche Antwort" (even if the patient repeatedly . . . asks and wants to hear the whole truth, even if it should mean death, he really does not want to know it and hopes for an optimistic and comforting answer from his physician).[54] What emerges in this article by an ethics specialist is the firm belief not only in socialist optimism, but also in treating patients like small children because they are deemed incapable of dealing with the realities of life and death.[55] Christa T., however, sees through the lies the doctors tell her, and when the attending physician claims, "wir sind zur Macht gekommen, Sie, sie selbst" (175: We've got the better of it, and you too, you have; 178) she realizes that he needs her to play along to maintain the façade of his imperturbable belief in "rationalist" medicine. The overtly political phrasing in the German original, which claims that the doctors and the patient together "came to power," further underscores the notion that—in the triumphant "workers' and farmers' state"—medicine triumphs over disease.

The practice of the *schonende Lüge* and the belief in the success of socialist medicine are therefore linked. The medication the protagonist receives prolongs her life and supports her fight against death, as she informs the doctors: "Ich habe das Wichtigste noch vor mir" (176: For me the most important things are still to come; 179). The German original employs the singular in "das Wichtigste"—that which is most important—and points to an ideological universe, the one and only idea Christa T. believes in: the success of her ideal of socialism, which is symbolized by the house. This confidence corresponds to Wolf's basic conviction that good will prevail over evil, an implied certainty of quasi-religious salvation that is nothing less than the confidence that true Marxist socialism would be implemented during her lifetime.[56] This quasi-spiritual outlook on socialism and the success of socialist medicine arises in one of the nurses' pronouncements about the medical profession's ability to work wonders (174). Reflecting on the linguistic proximity of the words "Wunder" (wonder) and "Wunde" (wound), the protagonist understands that in this real-existing hospital, the patient herself must be responsible "für das reibungslose Funktionieren seines Wunders" (176: for the smooth functioning of the wonder; 180) that is supposedly performed in the medical system (176). In other words, unlike biblical miracles, wonders performed in a GDR hospital require the patient's optimism and participation.

What comes to the fore here is a crucial reflection on both Western medicine's claim to be universal and triumphant, and on the patient's position in the therapeutic process as determined by the framework of GDR law. The narrative criticizes both the factual substance of medical knowledge, which is acquired without informing the person affected about the cognitive processes by which it is validated or about the true outcome of this inquiry, and the patient's obligation to cooperate in the therapy administered. This duty, the so-called *Mitwirkungspflicht*, took the form of a legally binding obligation. It was supplemented by mandatory disclosure of any aspect of the concerned person's life that might impinge on the therapy, the so-called *Offenbarungs- und Informationspflicht*, and the legal compulsion to endure any medical measures and any doctor's directions, named *Duldungs- und Befolgungspflicht* (Seifert, GSV, 271–74). The legal system effectively relegated those affected by illness to the role of passive objects to be kept in the dark about their own condition. Depicting this situation in *Nachdenken über Christa T.*, Wolf's narrative highlights a dogmatic interpretation of Marxist-Leninist thought and the degree to which it permeated all realms of life, including the legal system and medical procedures. In fact, medical-historical evidence suggests that such Marxist-Leninist interpretations of disease even influenced therapeutic approaches, in particular concerning terminally ill patients. Prof. Kirchgäßner from the Department of Marxism-Leninism at the University of Greifswald, for example, maintained that the doctor-patient relationship should be based exclusively on Marxist-Leninist philosophy and the ideology of the working class. He considered this justified because some patients developed organic sickness stemming from an ideological instability, which could only be prevented by treatment based on Marxist-Leninist thought. Similarly, Rolf Löther, Professor at the Academy for Continuing Education of Physicians in Berlin emphasized that terminally ill patients, in particular, could only be treated within an ideological and ethical framework based on Marxist-Leninist philosophy.[57]

Subjected to intensive care in a hospital, Christa T. was obligated once again to adjust to the rules of an institution, this time those of the healthcare system, which did not offer alternatives to the prescribed treatment. The narrative criticizes the relations of power in the GDR generally and particularly discourses surrounding legal and medical institutions. Yet it should be noted—not least of all because this point presents a major difference to Wolf's post-unification works—that the protagonist believes in the future of socialist medicine, which will ensure an end of all suffering for coming generations:

Endlich! Schreibt sie an den Rand, und das heißt soviel wie: Jetzt stirbt man nicht. Es beginnt, was sie so schmerzhaft vermißt hatte: daß wir uns selber sehen; deutlich fühlt sie, wie die Zeit für sie arbeitet, und muß sich doch sagen: Ich bin zu früh geboren. Denn sie weiß: Nicht mehr lange wird an dieser Krankheit gestorben werden. (179)

[At last! she writes in the margin, and this is as much as to say: now there is no death. It's beginning, the thing she so painfully missed: we are beginning to see ourselves. Distinctly she feels that time is on her side, and yet she can't help saying: I was born too soon. For she knows that before long people won't still be dying of this disease. (182)]

The adverse conditions affecting Christa T.'s health are not attributed to socialism per se but to the missteps of the early years. Christa T.'s belief in the progress of socialist medicine can actually be supported by medical-historical research that shows the extent to which GDR medicine had improved since the 1950s. In the years 1978 to 1982, the centralized and free GDR healthcare system became more successful in combating cancer than most Western European countries, including the FRG, as a variety of international studies reveal.[58] The protagonist emerges as an optimistic and fearless socialist heroine who dies with her head held high, displaying a confidence that extends beyond death, and anticipates the (hopeful) beginning of a new time.[59]

The physicians responsible for Christa T.'s care may have lacked the ability to conquer the disease in the early 1960s, but the protagonist leaves her legacy to future generations, symbolized by the inheritance of her unfinished house, which is passed on to her three daughters.[60] Similarly, the ideal state—like the perfect house—will emerge as a space in which the sort of assimilation required in the GDR of the 1950s will disappear together with other bourgeois and capitalist traditions and the guilt of fascism. The tragedy of Christa T.'s suffering and her untimely death is thus attributed to unfortunate timing: precisely when she has found her calling, her place in life and in society, she falls sick and passes away. If we remember Elaine Scarry's argument that the "body in pain" depicted in literature signals societal crisis, Christa T.'s ailing body can easily be understood as symptomatic of the predicaments that made her suffer both in fascism and in socialism. Yet Scarry also emphasizes that portraying physicality can signal confirmation of the very ideology that is endangered, since the flesh points to the presumed "materiality" of the underlying idea(l)s (110–11). In this sense, Christa T.'s symptomatic body strengthens Marxist ideology when the protagonist dies voicing her unqualified support for socialism. She dies not because socialism failed her, but because "real-existing socialism" has not advanced fast enough to rescue her.

Like a female socialist Christ-figure, the eponymic Christa T. is purified by her suffering. She dies as a redeemer for future generations, and absolves those Germans who have participated in building an antifascist, socialist German state from their collective guilt. This explains the narrator's insistence that while the protagonist does not need us, we do need her (8). Her staging as a martyr follows the pattern Julia Hell identifies as originating in early socialist German literature: "within the specific German context of antifascism, the sublime body of the Communist is figured in a religious guise, as the body of the Christian martyr. In the struggle against fascism, the Communist body becomes a body-in-pain, refracted through a register mobilizing a dense network of religious connotations. This peculiar inflection points to an absolutely central element of the SED's official discourse of antifascism: its iconography of martyrdom and redemption" (Hell, *PFF*, 33–34). After long suffering from various maladies, Christa T. possesses the sublime body of the Communist. When she finally dies, her death emerges as the ultimate sacrifice for the socialist idea.

In death, her erstwhile depression and wish to die, which originated in her despair over the impossibility of merging her personal ideals with the realities in the GDR, is reevaluated along the lines of Soviet ethics that dominated GDR psychiatry, particularly since the 1950s. According to this view, the only excuse for giving up on life early would be a heroic, self-sacrificial death for the triumph of the communist idea, since such an end signified the dedication of one's life to the great goal of communist world revolution, even beyond one's lifetime.[61] In her self-sacrificial death, Christa T. atones for her earlier personal death wish, which was diametrically opposed to society's interests and needs. She finally prevails over her guilty body and is "purified" of its materiality. In other words, the Christian symbolism and discourse of sacrificial death as well as the demand to live a God-fearing life based on the individual's covenant with God are secularized and—barely disguised—transferred onto a society in which the socialist community assumes the role of God. Within this socialist deontology, the individual's covenant with God is superseded by a new covenant with the entire socialist community. Referring to the birth of Christa T.'s third child, the narrator expresses her belief that her friend took it as "Erneuerung eines alten Bündnisses, auf das sie sich von nun an wieder verlassen wollte. So hat sie es als Treuebruch empfunden, als sie wieder zusammenbrach" (178: a renewal of an old alliance, on which from now on she would again rely. So she regarded it as a breach of faith when she collapsed again; 182). While the English translation mentions an alliance, the German original states that Christa T. considered the birth of her third, healthy daughter just before she died a "Bündnis"—literally, a covenant. The German original emphasizes the subject of the "Treuebruch"—the "breach of faith." The context does, however, suggest that it was not socialism that failed Christa T. Instead, the protagonist believes that she betrayed the old and just-renewed covenant when she—or rather her symptomatic body—breaks down: her body, site of the social experiences of fascism and early socialism, emerges as not strong enough to keep the socialist covenant.

Yet within the structure of the narrative, Christa T. does not die in vain, but for a better future; accordingly, her significance reaches far beyond her lifetime. The narrator, emphasizing that she felt obliged to digress from her "real" friend's biography, deliberately does not reconstruct Christa T.'s life. Instead, she constructs it into the future in a dialectical process oscillating between memory and creative use of apparently "authentic" material, ranging from imaginary interviews with one of Christa T.'s professors to little notes Christa T. left behind.[62] Since the narrator claims that she cannot evade the protagonist's death—which she would have preferred—she makes sense of Christa T.'s end by turning her into a redeemer for coming generations and conveying an optimistic outlook for the future. While Christa Wolf repeatedly stated that her protagonist was modeled on her deceased friend Christa Tabbert, the narrator of the novel emphasizes that she was the one who came up with the name Christa T., "den Namen, den ich ihr gegeben habe" (77: the name I've given her; 75). The narrative accentuates Christa T.'s construction as a fictional figure. Particularly within the Christian imagery prevalent throughout the novel, the name Christa emerges as the female version of "Christ." Making ample use of biblical language and employing an eschatological time concept (54), the narrative further claims that the protagonist, evoking Christ, was "wiederauferstanden von den Toten" (29: resurrected from the dead; 25) when she walked the "Ruinenfelder" (29: ruins; 25) after the war. The ruins mentioned here allude both to the Bible and to Johannes R. Becher's verse for the GDR national anthem, thus associating this fictional female Christ-figure with the new German socialist state and underlining and reaffirming the new covenant of the believer with the socialist community in death. The deliberate construction of the character Christa T., the way her body becomes symptomatic of political events associated with early fascism, and the way she dies all confirm the belief in the ultimate success of the socialist experiment and reaffirm the GDR's founding narrative of antifascism.

Conclusion: The Symptomatic Body of the Impatient Redeemer

Christa T. dies of what is most likely leukemia, the only non-tumor-producing cancer and not associated with ugliness and degeneration.[63] Susan

Sontag, for example, points out in *Illness as Metaphor* that leukemia takes on what she calls the metaphorical meaning formerly ascribed to tuberculosis (17–18). Considered a romantic illness that ends a young life too early, tuberculosis can be viewed emblematically as a "pure" sickness of the soul causing a death that leads to great spiritual insights. Christa T.'s death, brought forth by leukemia, therefore emphasizes the degree to which the protagonist is represented as pure, innocent, and exceptional in her actions.[64] We learn that even as a child she was painfully aware of her uniqueness and distinctiveness (26, 59). Innocent of active participation in the fascist regime, she can die as a redeemer for the sins of fascism. She can be (re-)born for the socialist community and communist ideals because her desexualized body, which was never really contaminated by fascism, is further purified by years of suffering from psychological and physical maladies, which convey the limitations of real-existing socialism. Unlike the female protagonists in most of Wolf's later prose—particularly texts written after Wolfgang Biermann's expatriation in 1976 which amplify the inner conflict between the ideals of socialism and the realities of the socialist state—Christa T.'s death signals hope. In this, it contrasts markedly with the violence exercised in *Kassandra*, which is set up as a death-bed narrative with the proclamation on the first page, "Mit der Erzählung geh ich in den Tod" (5: Keeping step with the story, I make my way into death; 3).

Christa T.'s morally superior communist body, disciplined by years of disease painfully inscribed in the flesh as a reaction to the historical experiences of fascism and the early Stalinist years of socialism, emerges as the purest of the pure. The "pure death" of leukemia erases her physical, sexual corporeality—a "Veränderung, die sie 'altern' nannte" (175: change in her, which she called aging; 179). As a female, Christa T. additionally overcomes the destruction and violence associated with men throughout the novel. Decontaminated, she can declare the "truth." From this speaking position of the unreserved believer in socialism, Christa T.'s body can indicate problematic developments in the GDR healthcare system and in the advancement of socialism generally, ranging from the demand for social adaptation to the events of 1953 or 1956. Through this protagonist, Christa Wolf can reflect on GDR society and preserve the humanist values underlying socialist ideology that are sacrificed in quotidian life. Despite the criticism she articulates, Christa T.'s unswerving belief in socialist society never falters. Her faith in socialism extends to the supremacy of the healthcare system and its ability to cure cancer in the near future. The protagonist becomes a redeemer who can proclaim salvation for the future of GDR citizens: they will be delivered by the ideal socialism to come after her death. The narrative offers a secularized kind of eschatological redemption and with it the prospect of a lively, kind, and caring socialism that would not resemble Stalinism. In the late 1960s, the realization of that ideal seemed possible; the experiences of 1965 made it appear imperative. Following the so-called *Kahlschlag-Plenum*, even the most loyal socialists' beliefs were challenged by GDR reality, and the narrative cautiously indicates the exigency and the necessity for reforms in socialism in the last sentence, "Wann, wenn nicht jetzt?" (182: When, if not now?; 185).

For Wolf and other "loyal dissidents" and reform socialists, the urgency resumed in 1989, when the prospect for a revolutionary renewal of the socialist state briefly became conceivable after the fall of the Wall. And with it the female Christ-figure in Wolf's oeuvre returned.[65] In *Was bleibt*, the only piece of fiction Wolf published in this transition phase between the fall of the Wall and the end of the state, the author presents a young woman who gets up after a reading (supposedly in 1979) to ask the question central to this controversial novella: "auf welche Weise aus dieser Gegenwart für uns und unsere Kinder eine lebbare Zukunft herauswachsen solle" (90: how a livable future for ourselves and our children was going to grow out of this present situation; 286).[66] These words, spoken by a shy woman who overcomes her fears, trigger an open discussion among audience members who appear seized by a fever (90, 92). Ignoring the threat emanating from the Stasi, who were present, they speak up and no longer rely on the narrator as their mouthpiece. Instead, the protagonist listens to her audience and realizes that they have forgotten about her. For a fleeting moment in the narrative, the young woman, who represents the majority of the average population and not the intellectual elite, takes center stage and the fictional author is relieved of her role as defender of moral values.[67]

In wording that echoes the New Testament, this situation, which is reminiscent of a revelation, is described as "Wunder . . . Als stehe man vor einem Fest" (92: wonders . . . as on the eve of a celebration; 287–88). In other words, the young woman—a nurse and associated with healing—optimistically proclaims a future that has already begun and is about to finally signal the advent of a humane socialism fulfilling its utopian ideals.[68] In this new society, writers like the protagonist would find the new language they are longing for and, as indicated in the title, could deliberate about the central question: what should remain. The title of the German original, *Was bleibt*, refers to the last line of Friedrich Hölderlin's hymn "Andenken" (Remembrance), "Was bleibet aber, stiften die Dichter" (But what remains, the poets create). As the title lacks punctuation, the narrative neither affirms nor questions Hölderlin's credo. Rather, the portrayed writer appears content with leaving behind the distinct position of the author as a social force who functions in lieu of critical media. When average people claim agency and find their speaking position, the narrator is happy to listen to her audience, convinced that the position of poets will survive the political and social upheaval.

Yet faith in the ultimate success of the socialist experiment is stopped short. With the demise of the GDR in 1990, the utopian vision of a secularized paradise projected onto a dissolving community was lost. What remains is the question of the extent to which Wolf's humanist ideals, her struggle to negotiate between the individual's desire for authenticity and the demands of society, and her criticism of both Western medicine and GDR medical institutions, continue to find expression in the (ill) body that prevails over the mind. If Wolf's post-unification writings also employ symptomatic bodies, it will be revealing to see if the political messages inherent in these bodies contribute to writing (GDR) history through fictional texts.

Notes

[1] Wolf, "Sprache der Wende" (Language of the Turning Point). In "Aufruf für unser Land," this group of artists and intellectuals called for GDR autonomy, a socialist alternative to the FRG characterized by solidarity, peace, social justice, freedom, and environmental conservation.

[2] On authors associated with romanticism, realism, and modernism and the trope of illness, see Spackman, *Decadent Genealogies*, 211. In "Once Again: Illness as Metaphor," Crick elaborates intertextual references in *Christa T.* Analyzing texts from the 1980s, Dueck emphasizes in *Rifts in Time and in the Self* that Wolf "has drawn the connection of physical, psychic, and societal illness" and "has . . . situated the conflict of complicity and critique in her own body" (165).

[3] In a letter to Lew Kopelew, published posthumously in *Moskauer Tagebücher*, Christa Wolf reveals that West German criticism she characterizes as stupid made her a black sheep in the GDR (149). See Behn, *Wirkungsgeschichte von Christa Wolfs "Nachdenken über Christa T."*; Drescher, *Dokumentation zu Christa Wolf "Nachdenken über Christa T."*; Hartinger, *Wechselseitige Wahrnehmung*, 202–10; Therese Hörnigk, "Ein Buch des Erinnerns, das zum Nachdenken anregte"; Meyer-Gosau, "Ritt über den Bodensee"; Paver, "What we must invent"; Sevin, "Plea for Artistic Freedom." Christa Wolf's letter to Wladimir Steshenski, published posthumously in *Moskauer Tagebücher* (101) and "Gerhard Wolf zur vierten Reise," his commentary on Christa Wolf's fourth journey to Moscow, point out that *Nachdenken über Christa T.* could not be published in other socialist countries even after its success in the GDR after 1972. A Russian translation appeared in a volume entitled *Isbrannoje* (Selected Works) only in 1979 (97).

[4] In "Unerledigte Widersprüche" Wolf recalls the problems pertaining to the publication of *Christa T.* (56–57). In *Christa Wolf*, Magenau relates the effects on Wolf's health (218–30).

[5] Wolf's *Der geteilte Himmel* is often characterized as *Ankunftsliteratur*, named after Brigitte Reimann's *Ankunft im Alltag* (Arrival in the Everyday, 1961). Following the building of the Wall in August 1961, *Ankunftsliteratur*—after the emphasis on *Aufbauliteratur* during the 1950s—transmits a sense of the characters' arrival in GDR society. Typically, the heroes and heroines move beyond

their dreams about socialism, and instead realistically assess the possibilities in the GDR. See Emmerich, *Kleine Literaturgeschichte der DDR*, 176. Contrary to the majority opinion, Hell and Rechtien, like me, challenge the categorization of *Der geteilte Himmel* as *Ankunftsliteratur*. See Hell, *PFF*, 165; Rechtien, "Topography of the Self," 477–78; Klocke, "(Anti-)faschistische Familien und (post-)faschistische Körper."

[6] On the influence of the events of 1965 on *Nachdenken über Christa T.*, see Wolf's essay, "Jetzt mußt du sprechen," published posthumously in *Rede, daß ich dich sehe*, especially 116; Tate, *Shifting Perspectives*, 194; Therese Hörnigk, ". . . aber schreiben kann man dann nicht"; Drescher, *Dokumentation zu Christa Wolf "Nachdenken über Christa T."*; Hartinger, *Wechselseitige Wahrnehmung*, 192.

[7] Wolf, "Krebs und Gesellschaft," 123.

[8] In *Nachdenken über Christa T.*, one of the most explicit sentences reads, "unter den Tauschangeboten ist keines, nach dem auch nur den Kopf zu drehen sich lohnen würde" (53: Among the alternatives offered there isn't a single one that's worth a nod in its direction; 51). Also see 122–25, 130; and Wolf, "Unerledigte Widersprüche," 54–55.

[9] The belated shift in the narrative voice (from "she" to "I") in the translation suggests even greater distance between body and mind. In *Kindheitsmuster*, the protagonist Nelly similarly reacts physically in anticipation of the collapse of Nazi Germany.

[10] In *Making Bodies, Making History*, Adelson defines positionality as "a set of specific social and discursive relations in a given historical moment" (64).

[11] Memories haunting Christa T. disclose her feelings of culpability and underline that she is neither victim nor perpetrator. She remembers her friend Kalle, son of the gypsies whom she witnesses being deported (26), and the boy who dies during their flight (27). For the problematic categories of victims and perpetrators, see Martin, "Victims or Perpetrators?"; Schaumann, *Memory Matters*. Martin develops a "perpetrator continuum" (66), while Schaumann deals with the contested terms "victims," "perpetrators," "co-perpetrators," and "bystanders" (11–12).

[12] Hahn, "EF," 77; Luther, "Abriss zur Geschichte," 33.

[13] Hahn, "EF," mentions Geppert's *Die Last, die du nicht trägst* (1978), Görlich's *Eine Anzeige in der Zeitung* (1978), Muthesius' *Flucht in die Wolken* (1981), Thom and Thom's, *Rückkehr ins Leben* (1979), and Wander's *Leben wär' eine prima Alternative* (1979).

[14] The new curriculum for degree programs in medicine was published in the first postwar issue of the medical journal *Das deutsche Gesundheitswesen* (The German Healthcare System) in 1946. See Schleiermacher and Schagen, "Rekonstruktion und Innovation (1949–1961)," 231. The prevention of crimes like the ones committed by Nazi physicians was not acknowledged as an educational goal in the FRG. On differences between GDR and FRG physicians, see Festge, "Ethische Positionen," 94.

[15] Schleiermacher and Schagen, "Rekonstruktion und Innovation (1949–1961)," 232; Luther, "Abriss zur Geschichte," 24–33; Markgraf and Otto,

"Unfallchirurgie an den Hochschuleinrichtungen," 20–21. In "'Deontologija'," Bettin discusses the influence of Soviet deontology, the specific ethical culture of socialist medicine, on GDR ethics. Deontology emphasizes socialist values such as solidarity as opposed to the medical ethics in the West, presumed to be individualistic and doctor-centered.

[16] Seifert claims that the role of educator took priority over that of physician (*GSV*, 38–40, 355); Kirchgäßner, "Philosophische Aspekte des Arzt-Patienten-Verhältnisses," 25. In *Redefreiheit*, Ahbe, Hofmann and Stiehler quote Dieter Lohmann, Medical Director of the city hospital in Leipzig, who demanded that optimal patient care had to receive priority over the implementation of any ideology (526). This contribution, which met with strong approval by the audience, underscores how crucial an issue the predominance of ideology in medicine remained in the fall of 1989.

[17] Schleiermacher and Schagen, "Rekonstruktion und Innovation (1949–1961)," 216–17; Seifert, *GSV*, 42–43.

[18] Festge, "Ethische Positionen," 97; Hahn, "EF," 74; Reding, "Ärztliche und ethische Probleme," 93; Schleiermacher and Schagen, "Rekonstruktion und Innovation (1949–1961)," 230; Seifert, *GSV*, 60–61; Weil, *Zielgruppe Ärzteschaft*, 16.

[19] The reference to Bettina von Arnim accentuates Christa T.'s identification with female Romantics, and hints at the formal similarity between *Nachdenken über Christa T.* and von Arnim's *Die Günderode* (1839).

[20] Christa Wolf, "Subjektive Authentizität," 775; "Lesen und Schreiben," 31, 46–47; "Warum schreiben Sie?," 75.

[21] Christa T. appears wounded by love when Kostja leaves her (63–65), and her landlady considers her pains of the soul (71) her sickness.

[22] "Im Frühsommer dreiundfünfzig" (in the early summer of fifty-three; 72) more directly points to the June uprising than the English translation "in summer 1953" (70). Unlike earlier scholarship, which considered the unrest of 1953 a "workers' uprising," research conducted since 1990, after East German archives were opened, largely acknowledges "that citizens from all sectors of society took part in the unrest and that the events constituted a people's uprising" (Millington, *State, Society and Memories*, 19). On the events of June 1953, see Fulbrook, "Concept of 'Normalisation'," 19–20; Weber, *Die DDR 1945–1990*, 41–46.

[23] In "Unerledigte Widersprüche," Wolf similarly recalls being crushed by citizens' destructive behavior and the violence employed by GDR authorities (35–36).

[24] Udo Grashoff, *"In einem Anfall von Depression...": Selbsttötungen in der DDR*, 189 (hereafter cited as *AD*).

[25] Since Muthesius criticized GDR psychiatry, the Ministry of Health delayed the publication of the book in 1977. Though the famous fashion journalist and her husband, popular TV journalist Karl-Heinz Gerstner, were associated with the SED, *Flucht in die Wolken* could only be published in 1981. See Grashoff, *AD*, 464–65.

[26] This view is confirmed by various dissertations published in the GDR. See, for example, Hofmann, "Analyse von Suizidversuchen bei Frauen in Magdeburg,"

50; Kulawik, "Der Suizidversuch," 1; Seidel, "Der Suicid im höheren Lebensalter," 2; Schulz, *Die Untersuchung unnatürlicher Todesfälle*, 145.

[27] Franke, *Recht im Alltag*, 356.

[28] Seifert, *GSV*, 356. See Günther, "Das Arztrecht in der DDR," 89.

[29] See Wolf, "Krankheit und Liebesentzug," 738–39. In *People's State*, Fulbrook highlights that psychological care was underdeveloped in the GDR (98).

[30] On the significance of working collectives and brigades, see Fulbrook, *People's State*, 223–339. Fulbrook reports that they socialized and were "keeping a pastoral eye on those members who were suffering from physical ill-health or personal problems" (225–26).

[31] Christa T.'s self-therapy links healing and writing, an ongoing topic for Wolf. See "Lesen und Schreiben," 47; "Unerledigte Widersprüche," 27.

[32] On the significance of names, see Köhn, *Literatur—Geschichte*, 309. Wolf was convinced that patriarchy and class society deformed men more than women. Aware of the construction of gendered attributions, she called for the overthrow of systems and class structures that fossilize gender roles. See Wolf, "Projektionsraum Romantik"; "Berührung," 11, 14, 18; "Ich bin schon für eine gewisse Maßlosigkeit," 876.

[33] I am using Hell's terminology. See Hell, *PFF*, 109. However, in "Critical Orthodoxies," Hell interprets Christa T.'s reproductive sexuality as a relapse into the "re-sexualized" body, and concludes: "Reproduction turns the post-fascist body into a diseased body, links giving birth to death" (86).

[34] The words "Kind" or "Kinder" employed four times on one page in the original to describe Christa T. and Justus (125) are eliminated in the English translation (127).

[35] See Butler, *Bodies That Matter*, 3 and my protracted explanation in the introduction to this study.

[36] We can also observe such subject formation via abjection of the Other in *Der geteilte Himmel*. When Rita visits Manfred in West Berlin, they are already each other's Other because he left the personality traits associated with a socialist behind in the GDR (179). Rita's subject formation as a true socialist happens via abjecting Manfred during her brief visit to West Berlin, where Manfred emerges as lacking emotions, love, and strength.

[37] The law is reproduced in Thietz, *Ende der Selbstverständlichkeit?*, 70–75.

[38] Fulbook, *People's State*, 150–51; Sharp and Flinspach, "Women in Germany from Division to Unification," 183–84. For effects of these laws today, see Ahbe, "Competing Master Narratives," 230. On the expansion of the paid day of housework and its elimination after unification, see Sachse, *Der Hausarbeitstag*.

[39] Rücker, "Soziale Netze," 62.

[40] In *Erinnerungsräume*, Assmann similarly emphasizes that bodily inscriptions originate from long-term, unconscious adjustment, which makes them both stable and unavailable (224).

[41] Schleiermacher and Schagen, "Rekonstruktion und Innovation (1949–1961)," 207–8; David, "... *Es soll das Haus die Charité heißen*...," 491–514; Festge, "Ethische Positionen," 94, 97.

⁴² The narrative stresses: "Denn die neue Welt . . . gab es wirklich. . . . Aber was auch immer mit ihr geschah oder geschehen wird, es ist und bleibt unsere Sache. . . . Sie hat, jetzt spreche ich von Christa T., nichts inniger herbeigewünscht als unsere Welt" (53: For the new world that we were making . . . really did exist. . . . But whatever happened or will happen to that new world is and remains our affair. . . . What she wished for more intensely than anything, and I'm speaking now of Christa T., was the coming of our world; 51).

⁴³ In "Producing the 'Socialist Personality'?," Brock shows that in the mid-1950s, "half of all the women had a job; and this proportion increased by about ten percent in each following decade" (245). Similarly, Fulbrook emphasizes in *People's State* that "attitudes towards women and work began to change with the shift in generations in the 1970s and '80s" (158). In "Unerledigte Widersprüche" (48) and "Berührung" (14) Wolf lamented that the lack of daycare options in the 1950s forced women to sacrifice their autonomy and profession for the family.

⁴⁴ Sentences change from "*Ich* will, hätte sie zu sagen, jeden Tag früh aufstehen" (I want to, she would have to say, get up early every morning; 135) to "Dann will *ich* ihn losfahren sehen, will langsam nach oben gehen und den Tag über alles tun, was getan werden muss, eins nach dem anderen, so dass meine Arbeit den Tag voranschiebt" (Then I want to see him drive away, want to slowly go upstairs and do everything throughout the day that has to be done, one thing after another, so that my work pushes the day forward; 136).

⁴⁵ On the concept of "entfremdete Arbeit" (alienated work), see Marx, *Ökonomisch-philosophische Manuskripte aus dem Jahre 1844* (*Economic and Philosophic Manuscripts of 1844*).

⁴⁶ The new society, the new words, and the new human being are associated with a new house earlier as well (58). The image of the house as a symbol for the young GDR is not uncommon. Uwe Kolbe echoes the description of Christa T.'s house in his notion of socialism as the "Vorstellung, daß man gemeinsam an einem neuen historischen Gebäude arbeitet, und habe es auch seine Mängel und Schwierigkeiten, aber daß es doch das Bessere sei, speziell das bessere Deutschland" (vision that collectively, one works on a new historical building, and even if it has its deficiencies and intricacies, it is still the better, especially the better Germany; Kolbe cited in Dröscher, *Subjektive Authentizität*, 16). In post-GDR literature, Strubel employs the image of the house representing the GDR to be built in *Sturz der Tage in die Nacht* (92).

⁴⁷ Emmerich, *Kleine Literaturgeschichte der DDR*, 178; Barck, "Fragmentarisches zur Literatur," 313.

⁴⁸ On intellectuals welcoming the Wall see Dröscher, *Subjektive Authentizität*, 33–34; Emmerich, *Kleine Literaturgeschichte der DDR*, 178–80; Wolf, *Ein Tag im Jahr im neuen Jahrhundert*, 143.

⁴⁹ Unlike the FRG, which became home for many Nazis who could continue their professional careers as the so-called Brown Book revealed in 1965, the GDR dissociated itself from the Nazi past (Ahbe, "Competing Master Narratives," 222). In *Nachdenken über Christa T.*, the small house is declared worthy of support in its battle against the larger forces surrounding it, and alludes to the small GDR and the larger FRG (156). See Tate, *Shifting Perspectives*, 205.

[50] The image of the house returns in Wolf's oeuvre, albeit with contrary meaning. In *Sommerstück* (Summer Play), houses burn down; and towards the end of the novel, the dying Steffi refers to the GDR as an "Irrenhaus" (mad-house), which imposed a specific life onto her and forced her to struggle with it, causing liver cancer (208).

[51] In "An Stelle einer Einleitung," Bettin and Gadebusch Bondio emphasize that patients could not be termed incurable, but only "zur Zeit nicht heilbar" (currently not curable) or "auf der Grundlage der derzeit erreichten Erkenntnisse unheilbar" (on the basis of current knowledge incurable; 10–11). Reding, in "Ärztliche und ethische Probleme," insists on defining "unheilbar" (incurable) in relation to ideology (90). See Jahr, "Zur Diagnose und Therapie."

[52] Seifert, *GSV*, 173–78. In "An Stelle einer Einleitung," Bettin and Gadebusch Bondio similarly report that at least in 1976, the "schonende Lüge" (gentle lie) was still recommended practice (10–11). Hahn claims that the "schonende Lüge" was gradually abandoned during the 1970s ("EF," 78), but Günther in "Das Arztrecht in der DDR" insists that it persisted until the end of the GDR, particularly in cases of incurable cancer (89). See Berndt, "Gedanken zum Inhalt der Vorträge des Kolloquiums 'Ethik und Medizin im Sozialismus'," 4; Müller, "Das Problem der Wahrhaftigkeit."

[53] Maxie Wander relates her experiences in the Charité and in Berlin-Buch, of doctors lying to her about her diagnosis with malignant breast cancer. She accidently found out about her condition when friends and family had known about it for several months. Wander, *Leben wär' eine prima Alternative*, 25, 29–30, 60, 271.

[54] Müller, "Das Problem der Wahrhaftigkeit," 100.

[55] Since November 1989, the image of the GDR as an authoritarian, paternal state that kept its population in a prolonged state of childhood has dominated political and cultural discourses on the GDR. For early representations, see, for example, Henrich, *Der vormundschaftliche Staat*; and Maaz, *Der Gefühlsstau*. Debbie Pinfold has demonstrated that this image needs to be complemented by official representations of the GDR as a child who tries to negotiate its identity vis-à-vis its Soviet parental figures. See Pinfold, "'Das Mündel will Vormund sein'."

[56] See Wolf, "Lesen und Schreiben" (19) and "Unerledigte Widersprüche," where she describes why she and her peers believed that they "würden den Sozialismus, den Marx gemeint hatte, noch erleben. Auf der einen Seite Einübung in nüchternes, kritisches, analytisch-dialektisches Denken, auf der anderen eine Art Heilsgewissheit, wenige Jahre lang. In Christa T. habe ich etwas davon beschrieben" (would still live to see the socialism Marx had meant. On the one hand practicing sober, critical, analytical-dialectical thinking. On the other hand a kind of certainty of salvation, only for a few years. In Christa T., I described some of that; 41).

[57] Kirchgäßner, "Philosophische Aspekte des Arzt-Patienten-Verhältnisses," 25; Löther, "Ethische Aspekte der Beherrschung der Lebensprozesse," 14.

[58] Baust, "Ethische Problemsituationen," 117; Tanneberger, "Ethik in der medizinischen Forschung," 52–53.

[59] Hahn shows that the moralizing notion that in socialist society, one had to die fearlessly was only repudiated in the 1980s ("EF," 83). See Huyssen, "Auf den Spuren Ernst Blochs," 151, 153.

60 The notion of daughters born in the GDR and embodying hope for the future reappears in *Kindheitsmuster*. Precisely because this next generation, represented by Lenka in *Kindheitsmuster*, is not connected to so-called "values" of the fascist regime and questions authority in general, it can criticize the GDR.

61 Schischkin, *Grundlagen der marxistischen Ethik*, 401; Grashoff, *AD*, 276–83.

62 The narrator explains, "ich bekenne mich zur Freiheit und zur Pflicht des Erfindens" (47: I profess the freedom and responsibility of invention; 45), and the only aspect she cannot escape is Christa T.'s death, even though she would have preferred that (172). The narrative clearly projects Christa T. into and for the future (8, 122). On the constructedness of Christa T., also see Hörnigk, *Christa Wolf*, 117; Wilke, *Ausgraben und Erinnern*, 29.

63 The narrative does not explicitly name the disease, but mentions leukemia, cancer of the blood (174), and "Panmyelophthise" (177). Since Prednisone, a hydrocortisone administered to Christa T., is typically prescribed in both cases, the diagnosis presented in the novel remains ambiguous.

64 The narrator stresses the significance of purity for the socialist state when she recalls the friends contemplating the arrival of their socialist paradise, and the question they asked themselves: "Wer aber, wer würde würdig sein es zu bewohnen? Die Allerreinsten nur, das schien festzustehen" (54: Who, but who, would be worthy to inhabit it? Only the very purest, that seemed a certainty; 52). Nelly in *Kindheitsmuster* falls ill with tuberculosis in 1945—an illness believed to offer insights—at the moment the Nazi regime collapses.

65 An early scholarly article on *Was bleibt*, Janssen-Zimmermann's "Plädoyer für einen Text," pointed to the aspect of revelation in Wolf's novella, which has since been largely ignored (161).

66 Wolf dated *Was bleibt* June/July 1979 and November 1989, indicating that she revised the novella she originally wrote in 1979 after the fall of the Wall in November 1989.

67 This scene illustrates the positive function of oppositional literature, as Wolf explained it in "Zwischenrede" ("Momentary Interruption") in early 1990: "Durch Benennen von Widersprüchen . . . bei ihren Lesern kritisches Bewusstsein zu erzeugen oder zu stärken, sie zum Widerstand gegen Lüge, Heuchelei und Selbstaufgabe zu ermutigen . . . und nicht zuletzt, moralische Werte zu verteidigen, die der zynischen Demagogie der herrschenden Ideologie geopfert werden sollten" (18: to name the conflicts . . ., and thus to generate or strengthen a critical attitude in readers; to encourage them to resist lies, hypocrisy, and surrender of self; . . . and, last but not least, to defend moral values that in the dominant ideology were cynically earmarked for sacrifice; 10).

68 In *Was bleibt*, the hopes of 1989 that Wolf recalls in her 1990 speech "Zwischenrede" resonate; namely, that the fall of the old regime would lead to the revolutionary revival of the GDR (18).

2: Christa Wolf's Goodbye to Socialism?: Illness, Healing, and Faith since 1990

WHEN LEIBHAFTIG APPEARED IN GERMANY in 2002, literary critics and scholars often equated the protagonist with the author, and hastily interpreted the book as Wolf's final farewell to the GDR and to illusions about the socialist model underlying the state.[1] The novel relates the medical history of a nameless female writer in a GDR hospital, which is—according to the medical personnel—a mirror image of the depleted society (173). Without doubt, *Leibhaftig* presents a defining moment in Wolf's oeuvre, but can it be considered a good-bye? In order to answer this question, we must briefly consider Wolf's work from the 1990s.

In the first decade after unification, Wolf published primarily essays, speeches, letters, and short stories, in addition to her novel *Medea: Stimmen* (1996; *Medea: A Modern Telling*, 1998). Her first major prose text composed after 1990 rewrites an antique myth, much like *Kassandra* (1983). The two books are linked by the protagonists' feelings of alienation: they feel connected to their communities despite the lack of empathy they receive. Medea, particularly, feels hurt, betrayed, and exiled in her country. Not unlike Wolf following the so-called *Literaturstreit*, she is turned into a scapegoat. Medea appears as an indirect reproach to the West German media that had projected an exceedingly unfavorable image of Wolf. The GDR author emerged as the personified abject in the new political and social system based on her characteristics as East German, female, intellectual, political, critically engaged, and—after 1993—alleged Stasi collaborator. Aimed at silencing the author and her support for socialist ideals, the campaign ultimately failed since the abjected intellectual refused to be mute. After her brief cooperation with the Stasi from 1959 to 1962 was revealed, several of Wolf's accounts from 1992/93 demonstrate that the author experienced the media attacks corporally. In "Abschied von Phantomen," she describes her physicality as if it were one of the damaged bodies so abundant in her fictional oeuvre. She relates the physical sensation of being replaced "Stück für Stück, Glied für Glied . . . gegen eine andere Person, die in die Medien paßte" (330: piece by piece and limb by limb, by another person who was built to suit the media; 297). In *Stadt der Engel* (2010), Wolf's fictional alter ego expresses her feelings even more radically. She reports a dream she had in the early 1990s, in which her limbs were literally cut off in her sleep:

scheibchenweise abgesägt, abgetrennt, zuerst die Beine, dann die Arme, zum Schluß der Kopf, bis das Gehirn freilag und auch dieses zersägt wurde, und dazu rief eine männliche Stimme: So muß es sein. Dann ist da noch in Leuchtschrift mein Name, am Schluß verlischt auch der. . . . [Sie folgert:] Mein Körper entfernt sich von mir. (269)

[slice by slice, first my legs, then my arms, finally my head, until my brain sat there by itself and then that was sawed to pieces too, and then a male voice cried: So it must be! Then my name appeared in neon lights, and finally, at the end of the dream, that went out too. . . . [She concludes,] My body is leaving me. (203)]

Corresponding to Aleida Assmann's observation in *Erinnerungsräume* that corporeal inscriptions of trauma can also be traced back to experiences of psychological violence, Wolf felt the media attacks in her flesh (248). She perceived her body as being torn down for the purpose of rebuilding a "Wolf-façade" that lacked any relationship to her authentic self. As if she had been guillotined, the unofficial poet laureate of the GDR felt dismembered by the media of the victorious power.[2] Having declared her the favorite writer of the GDR regime, the media eagerly dethroned Wolf as the representative of the GDR body politic. They metaphorically tore apart the author's flesh and brain as they produced a caricature of her idealistic thought and her desire for a humane socialism.

The early 1990s had ushered in traumatic events for Wolf: the demise of the GDR and with it, the hope for a realization of her socialist ideals; the so-called *Literaturstreit*, which revealed her brief cooperation with the Stasi; and finally, the sense of betrayal she felt upon discovering that the Stasi had been observing her for decades. The first decade of the twenty-first century, then, could be considered a time of healing accomplished by shaping the traumatic events into narration. In this sense, the book at the center of this chapter—*Leibhaftig*—must be read together with *Stadt der Engel*. Both novels were written and published after Wolf had had the opportunity to deal with the traumatic experiences of the early 1990s, particularly during the year she spent in California (1992–93). Reading *Leibhaftig* together with *Stadt der Engel* and with a focus on the body allows us to understand Wolf's healing process as a prerequisite for her return to the literary body politic. Only after her recovery could she reclaim a social position in unified Germany that resembled the one she had held in the GDR.

Irene Kacandes suggests that "the production of this potentially healing narrative is hauntingly difficult . . . because the event that needs to be narrated may not have been experienced by the victim fully consciously in time."[3] The protagonists suffering from trauma therefore need to develop a "narrative memory," which Kacandes describes as "an ability to construct mental schemas that make sense out of experience" (*TF*, 91). This defines the project that drives Wolf's last two novels. Far from a goodbye to the GDR, *Leibhaftig* and *Stadt der Engel* reject the acceptance of the West as the winner of history and Wolf's own role of the personified abject, dismantled and silenced by the West German media. With these two novels, the author claims a voice and agency in post-unification Germany, and a place for the GDR in a unified German historiography that assigns the socialist state more than the abject, inferior position of an "abnormal" intermediate phase. Taken together, *Leibhaftig* and *Stadt der Engel* contribute to larger discourses on unified Germany by offering alternatives to the dominant images that have governed cultural memory and the media since 1990.[4]

Creating such "narrative memories" that challenge hegemonic cultural memory depends on communication. For Wolf, who had always been sensitive to words, the disturbances of the late 1980s and early 1990s primarily come out in the limitations of language. The protagonist in *Leibhaftig* verbalizes her mistrust in the ability of language to convey the truth when she declares that words are untrue, misleading, and potentially deceptive (83). These critical thoughts resonate with Kacandes's *Talk Fiction*: "numerous trauma victims, researchers, and clinicians warn that there is no 'authoritative telling' of the event" (94). Precisely because there are no intersubjective words for what the traumatized victim felt at the time, a telling of the event—a highly subjective experience—can only aim at approximating a representation of the trauma. Words cannot satisfactorily convey the corporeal pain emanating from physical and psychological wounds that never cease to hurt. Elaine Scarry echoes this observation in *The Body in Pain* when she explains that pain simply does not possess a referent in language (43–45). The realization that language is deficient and characterized by its ability to manipulate reality—just as terrible for the author Wolf as it is for her writer-protagonists at the center of *Leibhaftig* and *Stadt der Engel*—leads to Wolf's foregrounding of the symptomatic body for the process of remembering the past.

With *Leibhaftig*, Wolf returns to the severely ill, suffering body that we have discovered at the center of her pre-unification works, and particularly in *Nachdenken über Christa T.*[5] It reaffirms her early premise that the sick body serves as the site exhibiting the conflict between the individual struggling for authenticity and society's exigencies that she experiences as too complicated to address. Again, the body, indicating crisis and resisting social and political norms, is linked to metaphors of suffering and purification that are discursively associated with the victims of fascism and the GDR's founding narrative of antifascism. The pain-ridden patient, tortured by her dream-induced memories of traumatic historical experiences in GDR socialism and German fascism as well as by the surgeons cutting into her flesh, emerges as the ultimate symptomatic body.

Personal events linked to history and politics have left their traces on her mind and in her flesh—the location of individual and collective cultural memory.[6] Even more pronounced than in any of Wolf's earlier prose, the vestiges of trauma, now beyond the patient's control, surface in agony. As we will see, this pain links the patient with the victims of fascism, as it did in earlier works. Like the symptomatic bodies in Wolf's pre-unification oeuvre, the body at the center of *Leibhaftig* is stronger than the mind and able to support the search for memories that surface somatically on the patient's deathly ill body—a prerequisite for her recovery.

Stadt der Engel, even more complex and narrated in a subjective voice, continues the healing process. While the body does not loom nearly as large as in *Leibhaftig*, the ailing protagonist finally confronts those aspects of her past that she could not yet face openly in *Leibhaftig*. In addition to alternative healers, the protagonist in *Stadt der Engel* finds new friends among the intellectuals at the Getty Center in Los Angeles and the descendants of the predominantly Jewish émigrés who were forced to leave Nazi Germany. They support her identification with the antifascist resistance and with the GDR's founding narratives of antifascism, antiracism, and anticapitalism. As a result, Wolf's alter ego can finally come to terms with her personal history in a socialist state—from the temporal, spatial, and ideological distance of the United States in the early 1990s. Forced to reflect on her status in post-unification Germany because many Americans consider the protagonist an outcast in German society in the aftermath of the so-called *Literaturstreit*, the autobiographical narrator rejects emigration as an option and repatriates herself in her own cultural and political realm in unified Germany. In California and in the American Southwest, Wolf's alter ego can finally overcome her traumata, conclude the healing process, and confirm her entitlement to a position as voice of the public—not unlike the one Wolf occupied in the GDR. Given this remarkable development in Wolf's last two novels, this chapter parses *Leibhaftig* to reveal how the most afflicted symptomatic body in Wolf's oeuvre asserts the legitimacy of communist power through the discourse of antifascism. This reading is supported by an analysis of those aspects in *Stadt der Engel* which are relevant for understanding that the healing process at the end of *Leibhaftig* is only the beginning.

Leibhaftig: Fascism and Socialism Revisited from Post-Wall Germany

The narrative trajectory of *Leibhaftig* charts the progress of the main character's near-fatal illness in the final days of the GDR, from the delivery to the hospital at the beginning of the novel to recovery at the close. Initially ill with a case of appendicitis that was treated too late, the woman at the center of *Leibhaftig* develops sepsis, and the vicious strain of bacteria poisoning her body causes her immune system to collapse. The doctors fighting her death by means of conventional medicine fail to control her fever. The infection triggers high temperatures and necessitates several operations. The narrator oscillates between life and death, the realities of the hospital, stream-of-consciousness reflections on the past forty years, and the world of fever-induced dreams. The narrative perspective reflects the patient's existence in a state of limbo: at times conflated with the first-person narrator, she is also portrayed from a distance in third-person narration to convey the estrangement from the body's suffering. At times, first-, second-, and third-person narrative voices blur and highlight the impossibility of separating the multiple perspectives and approximating an undivided voice. The protagonist's imaginary dream-journeys depict her floating above Berlin and through the divided city's underground labyrinth, a metaphorical map of her brain. These tours lead her into a complicated past in which fascism and real-existing socialism serve as landmarks for a time in which personal and public history conflate. Reminiscent of Freud's analogy between archeology and dreams that need to be uncovered in order to allow insight into the psyche, each hallucination directs the patient into a layer of her previously suppressed memory to excavate layers of the past. The shreds of memories constantly change in perspective and historical time and confront the woman with uncongenial aspects of her involvement in public and private history.

In her feverish dreams, she is forced once again to face political events such as the Hungarian and Czech propaganda trials of the 1950s against Rajk and Slansky, the Soviet intervention in Czechoslovakia in 1968, or singer-poet Wolfgang Biermann's expatriation from the GDR in 1976. The most troubling sections concern her brief interaction with the Stasi. The narrative only hints at this contact during scenes that deal with the confrontation with Hannes Urban, an alter ego demonstrating what could have become of the protagonist had she also relinquished her socialist ideals for a career in the party. These passages reveal that the existential crisis the protagonist had to face during her stay at the hospital was related to her position vis-à-vis the GDR regime and its authorities. The burst appendix, the ensuing complications, and the hospital medical staff serve as screens on which questions of ethics and of "metaphorical devils" are played out. The core of this hospital narrative emerges just as the GDR is nearing its end and Urban decides to take his own life at the very moment that the patient begins to recover. By the end, we observe a protagonist who successfully fought for her life. She saves both mind and body, and can come to terms with the demise of the GDR because she endured the suffering associated with her illness. While she can emerge purified, she is only at the beginning of her healing process. She still needs to verbalize her trauma—the project of *Stadt der Engel*.

The GDR Hospital and Historiography

Unlike Christa T. who—despite her skepticism vis-à-vis Western medicine—believed in medical and socialist progress, the protagonist in the 2002 novel suffers in a late-GDR medical institution where she is subjected to what seems equivalent to forms of torture. Choosing this setting, *Leibhaftig* continues the GDR literary tradition of utilizing fiction as a venue for societal debates about topics including health and illness. This decision indicates a desire to employ literature as a medium of memory, using it to sustain cultural values and present memories of GDR life experiences that add to the cultural memory of present and future generations.[7] Beyond dealing with traumata through a body that becomes symptomatic, *Leibhaftig* showcases literature's contribution to historiography by informing readers in post-unification Germany about the practice of socialist medicine as a characteristic component of socialist society.

The protagonist's life is determined by two major factors: the desolate economic state of the hospital, which the doctors and nurses try to compensate for in collaborative acts of improvisation, and the patient's dependence on the predominantly male doctors and the trust they place in medical machinery. If the portrayed body is furthermore understood as an allegory for the body politic, the narrative's political references turn the protagonist's flesh into a seismograph of her country and its collapse. While the patient points to this reading when she emphasizes the metaphorical nature of her corporality (15), her body is actually more than a metaphor for the decaying GDR: it acts as a kind of interface on which the conflicts between the individual and the GDR regime are played out in disease and suffering. In this performance, the symptomatic body contributes its hidden historical knowledge to the historical narrative. It challenges totalitarian approaches to twentieth-century German history by referencing the founding narratives of both Germanys, by recalling the complications that determined life in the GDR, and by highlighting the protagonist's narrow survival.

Economic Deprivation and Social Equality

When a senior physician informs the patient that the hospital mirrors GDR society, which happens to be impoverished, he confirms the protagonist's impressions (173). The ambulance's bad shock absorbers, the latex gloves that keep tearing, the shortage of gowns, towels, bed linens, and life-saving medication represent the desolate economic conditions in the GDR and its hospitals. Only the improvisational skills of the medical personnel and their selfless attentiveness prevent the system from immediate collapse (5, 72, 173–75). This depiction is borne out by historical research. Mary Fulbrook's *The People's State*, for example, mentions that "only 30 percent of the equipment needed for heart surgery and transplantations were available in 1988; in the 1980s, the full range of drugs and medicines was never available" (93).[8] In his memoir, published in 1998, even former health secretary Ludwig Mecklinger reported on the chronic underfunding; and, according to Ilko-Sascha Kowalczuk, Erich Honecker admitted to the Central Committee of the SED that the situation in GDR hospitals in 1988 was scandalous.[9] Susanne Hahn reports in drastic detail the degree to which, as a physician, she experienced shortages in all realms of the public health sector. This included bed linen, influenza vaccines, disposable hypodermic syringes, and adequate dialysis equipment. The lack of disposable equipment caused infections and complications, while the long waiting periods for heart operations and the shortage of dialysis machines led to deaths. The medical staff had to compensate for these deficiencies by improvising and adding the so-called *menschlicher Faktor* (human factor)—additional attention to patients, which could be integrated at no expense.[10]

Notwithstanding her criticism, Hahn emphasizes the egalitarian nature of medical treatment despite the inadequate supplies ("EF," 82). Similarly, *Leibhaftig* stresses the absence of class differences as a determining factor: the senior surgeon assures the protagonist that everyone who needed medication from the West would receive it (175). Especially when read in conjunction with "Krebs und Gesellschaft," where Wolf laments that the post-unification medical system forced on the former GDR placed a higher value on cost-effectiveness than on patient care, *Leibhaftig* can be seen as highlighting the GDR healthcare system's positive aspects as well as its deficiencies (127). In fact, both "Krebs und Gesellschaft" and *Leibhaftig* echo the GDR's public credo regarding the mission of the socialist healthcare system. Medical professors Berndt and Hüller, for example, contrast the goals of doctors in capitalist and socialist systems. Unlike doctors in a socialist system, whose salaries are not based on the number of patients they treat, physicians in profit-oriented capitalist societies depend on generating revenue through the number of patients treated and procedures ordered. Berndt and Hüller conclude that these doctors have to turn their patients into profitable products if they want to survive financially. For the two physicians, this situation demonstrates that medicine is always influenced by ideology—socialist in the GDR, capitalist in the FRG—and that it supports the interests of a particular class—the working class in the GDR, and the more affluent classes in the FRG.[11] This correlates with Wolf's depiction of GDR medical staff. They appear invested in the patient's well-being and seek to compensate for deprivation. Distinguishing between the socialist values that governed medical institutions and their actual implementation in hospitals, *Leibhaftig* points to the discrepancy between ideal and implementation that characterized many institutions in the GDR.

While *Leibhaftig* does not specify the location of the depicted hospital, it appears to be a general hospital like the one to which Wolf was admitted in Schwerin in 1988 with a burst appendix. There is no indication that this is a special clinic like Berlin-Buch, the first hospital in Germany to open a ward dedicated to intensive care in 1958, which was reserved for the elite.[12] Rather, the physicians' collaborative fight for the patient's life in the novel highlights the interdisciplinary approach to intensive care for which the GDR was renowned. Though medical equipment was generally insufficient, *Leibhaftig* depicts it as routinely available. The novel not only integrates Wolf's preoccupation with the perceived threat of technology, it also hints at the unofficial flow of two- or three-year-old machines that FRG hospitals had discarded. They were brought to the GDR by colleagues from the West—who in turn received antiquated machines that were no longer operational for their planned museum on medical technology.[13] Thus, *Leibhaftig* downplays the granting of privilege—in the form of prioritizing politically committed and productive citizens—in favor of drawing attention to the egalitarian aspect of the GDR medical system.

War Machinery in the GDR Hospital

The medical machines the reader learns about range from an apparatus which displays the patient's heartbeat (118) and CAT scans (37) to an MRI apparatus (49) and a fluoroscope described as a cage filled with radiation (48). This terrifying technology, depicted as lurking in the clinic basement like the Minotaur in the labyrinth (50), serves to illuminate the patient's body from the inside (48) and permits a kind of surveillance—not unlike the observation by the Stasi the patient remembers in some of her nightmares (108). The machines' exercise of power in the medical realm, associated with images of cages in the underworld as well as tightly locked steel doors (50), evoke institutions of law enforcement such as the prison. The hospital appears linked to other state institutions that discipline individuals and their bodies in sometimes brutal ways.

The machines are associated with forms of violence that are strongly coded as male. They become part of the male/female binary so often represented in such troubling ways in earlier texts by Wolf. In *Nachdenken über Christa T.*, for example, Justus appears as the sole exception to other men in the novel because he is not associated with aggression and cruelty; and in *Kassandra*, men are largely portrayed as merciless and brutal while women are capable of solidarity. This male/female dichotomy reappears in *Leibhaftig*'s critique of a male-dominated medical realm that insists on its modes of obtaining, producing, classifying, and conveying knowledge based on its adherence to a presumably objective cognitive approach that relies on technology. Essentially, Western medicine in

Leibhaftig is metaphorically and structurally associated with male execution of power that ignores the psyche and alternative healing, and with industrial society and its unquestioned belief in progress and technology. Already in 1978, in "Berührung," Wolf had argued that men internalized this belief to a much higher degree than women. This allows patriarchal structures associated with bourgeois societies to linger in the GDR and leads to the inhumane and anti-socialist demand that women adapt (15, 18).[14] In *Leibhaftig*, this pressure to adjust to societal needs combined with the objectification by a medical system that turns the patient into a thing to be investigated contributes to the protagonist's suffering (101). As a result, she views herself not as being healed, but, on the contrary, as being physically injured by the surgery.

When the patient asks whether the surgeon is aware that he injures her by cutting into her flesh, "zu Heilungszwecken, gewiss" (132: for the purpose of curing her, of course; 90), she points to her physical and psychological distress. The unquestioned confidence in specific procedures ignores that the patient will incorporate the experienced pain permanently in her body memory, represented externally by the scars resulting from the wounds. These traces will prevent her from forgetting the traumatic experience, as her symptomatic body is turned into the site where the event is memorized.[15] The legal relationship between doctors and patients, unique to the GDR, reinforces this distress by denying the patient's agency. As elaborated in the introduction to this study, the GDR's *Betreuungsverhältnis* mandated that all prescribed medical interventions be carried out according to standard practice as treatment. Consequently, a patient's refusal of a recommended surgical procedure was impossible. The protagonist in *Leibhaftig* experiences the therapeutic measures that leave physical and psychological traces on her body as harmful, but her subjective response has no impact on her treatment.

The alleged "cure" is ironized when the patient contemplates asking the Professor what it is that he enjoys—and even experiences as causing pleasure—about cutting into her flesh. Suggesting that the surgeon derives pleasure from mutilating a patient, the narrative assigns the surgery sexual overtones and hints at (sexual) perversion and criminal offense. The repeated mention of cuts that will leave traces on the body as scars indicates an understanding of the female body as carrying the signs of male aggression and cruelty. The ravaging aspects of the treatment are stressed when the protagonist describes both her medication and the operations carried out on her body in terms of violent performances that symbolically re-enact war-time butchery: The male doctors are "dunkelgrün verkleidet" (63: clothed in the same dark green; 42), which hints at military camouflage. They follow "ein ausgeklügeltes Ritual" (137: a cleverly devised ritual; 93) when they perform a "Gemetzel" (138:

massacre; 94) on the patient's body. They get ready "zum Großangriff gegen diese verdammten Keime" (for a major offensive against those damned germs, 125), and plan to "beschießen" (fire at) the bacteria causing her fever "mit unserem schwersten Geschütz" (with our heaviest guns, 117).[16] Patients had no legal means of escaping such treatment due to the *Betreuungsverhältnis*, and the fierce language portrays the doctor-patient relationship as devoid of trust. In essays like "Krankheit und Liebesentzug," Wolf expressed her desire for a different doctor-patient relationship, one that would replace superiority on the physician's and subservience on the patient's side by a more reciprocal relationship (747).[17] This call to take the patient seriously and to grant her agency in the healing process exposes the GDR medical system as hierarchical and as premised on a docile patient.

The Passive Patient

While she loathes the doctor's aggressive approach, the patient in *Leibhaftig* is reduced to behaving like a good little girl and following orders (85). The novel consolidates the pattern already in evidence in *Nachdenken über Christa T.* Combining the physicians' military language with a self-ironic tone that mimics the infantilizing attitude of the legal system toward its sick citizens, *Leibhaftig* reproduces practices the GDR lawyer Christoph, quoted by Seifert, explained in 1980:

> Die Gesundheitseinrichtungen realisieren ihre Aufgabe grundsätzlich im Rahmen eines spezifischen Rechtsverhältnisses zu den von ihnen betreuten Bürgern. Eine entscheidende Besonderheit der Gesundheitseinrichtungen besteht darin, dass sie ihre Aufgaben nicht nur gegenüber dem Bürger erfüllen, sondern dass am Bürger selbst Maßnahmen der medizinischen und sozialen Betreuung durchgeführt werden. (Seifert, *GSV*, 359)

> [Fundamentally, the healthcare facilities fulfill their mission within the framework of a specific legal relationship with the citizens they care for. A significant specificity of the healthcare facilities consists in the fact that they not only fulfill their mission towards the citizen, but they perform measures of medical and social care on the citizen.]

Christoph highlights the enforced passivity of the patient in GDR law and in medical practice: something is done on and to a citizen's body that is to be understood as both medical and social remedy. Since socialist doctors had sworn to take responsibility professionally, politically, and as members of socialist society, patients were required to accept their physicians' proposed treatments as the best option for their individual health and, more importantly, for the health of the socialist community. Even the physician's formal obligation to inform patients about the proposed therapy (*Aufklärungspflicht*) and to seek consent could be bypassed without legal consequences for the doctor.[18] A patient's failure to cooperate could, by the 1970s, have serious legal consequences, for example, concerning labor law and rights to social security, and cause a patient's doctor to initiate educational reform measures (Seifert, *GSV*, 301). Patients' bodies become subject to the state and its legal and medical system in the doctors' performances on the citizens' bodies—even if the patient experiences the execution of the therapy as violent. Given the legal situation, citizens' bodies became—not only metaphorically speaking—subject to one body politic.

In *Leibhaftig*, we observe the patient cooperating in the therapy and enduring the prescribed remedies. When she agrees to follow the physician's orders, it causes her to reflect on previous mandatory medical exams. She recalls how, in the early years of the GDR, her body was repeatedly exposed to radiation (86). This flashback refers to routine screening measures the GDR undertook in 1961, when all citizens were legally compelled to undergo recurring X-ray screenings to combat tuberculosis on a regular basis.[19] Together with obligatory immunizations, they were part of the preemptive measures the GDR took in combating disease. *Leibhaftig* broaches the topic of the *Mitwirkungspflicht* for prophylactic healthcare as part and parcel of the GDR medical system's infantilizing attitude. When the patient reflects on her position in the hospital, which she associates with a regression to her childhood days when all that was demanded of her was cooperative behavior, she confirms that she is acutely aware of the mechanisms that exact her obedience (37–38). And when the head physician thanks her for her excellent cooperation, she even feels obliged to reassure the Professor of his accomplishments (117, 156). Corresponding to GDR law, *Leibhaftig* portrays a protagonist required to not only endure, but also to participate in the physicians' prescribed therapy, even though she experiences it as violent injury.

The demand for compliance in the doctor-patient relationship matches the general requirement to subordinate individual needs to the norms of socialist society—the same phenomenon that caused Christa T.'s illnesses. Linguistically, too, *Leibhaftig* suggests parallels to *Nachdenken über Christa T.* and *Mitwirkungspflicht*. In the novel from the 1960s, Christa T. reflected on the linguistic proximity of the words "Wunde" (wound) and "Wunder" (wonder) when a nurse reminded her that unlike in the Bible, miracles performed in a socialist hospital required the patient's cooperation (176). Similarly, *Leibhaftig* introduces puns to allude to *Mitwirkungspflicht* in the patient's reflections about her duty to read her forcefully inscribed body:

Heute habe ich mich zu fragen, was mein Körper mit mir vorhat. Ob er sich gegen mich auflehnt. Ich sehe meinen Körper, ich sehe die Schnitte, die ihn zeichnen. Was für eine Schrift wird meinem Körper da eingeschrieben, und werde ich sie je lesen können. Ist mir das aufgegeben? Aufgegeben, aufgeben, Wörter, deren Doppelsinn zu vermeiden ist. (132–33)

[Today I have to ask myself what my body has in mind for me. Whether it's rebelling against me. I see my body, I see the incisions marking it. What sort of inscription is being written upon my body? Will I ever be able to read it? Is that my charge? "Charge," "charged with": words whose double meaning is to be avoided. (90)]

The patient extends the duty to cooperate to reading her symptomatic body, which includes the incisions left by the surgeons as inscriptions on her flesh and her body's independent, rebellious behavior. In German, the reflections about this command to decipher her flesh take on disconcerting connotations: the German "aufgeben" also means "to give up," to "surrender," or even "to abandon." The choice of words conveys the patient's uncertainty: even if she follows the required *Mitwirkungspflicht*, the society represented by the medical team could just as easily abandon as rescue her. Depicting a patient who reflects on the double meanings of verbs when the medical staff requires her support in the therapy, the narrative emphasizes lack of choice: her cooperation is compulsory.

Both in the 1960s and in the twenty-first century, Wolf's protagonists reflect on society's use of language to highlight social demands that her protagonists experience as unreasonable. Notably, *Stadt der Engel* depicts a similar phenomenon and language use, albeit moved to another social institution after German unification. The necessity to position herself vis-à-vis the charges brought forward by the dominant media's incendiary reports about her brief Stasi collaboration takes on a new role. Hard-pressed by the events following the publication of *Was bleibt*, the protagonist in *Stadt der Engel* reflects on

> die endgültige Dunkelheit, erwünscht, . . . die befreien würde von dem Zwang, alles sagen zu müssen. In diesen Schacht nicht wieder, das kann niemand verlangen, aber wer sagt mir denn, daß ich mich nach dem richten müßte, was andere verlangten, richten, . . . ich liebe diese doppeldeutigen Wörter, sich richten, gerichtet werden, das ist richtig. Gerechtigkeit, du Donnerwort. (35)

[the final darkness, wished for, . . . to free me of the compulsion to have to say everything. Never to go down into that well again, no one can ask that of me, but then who says I have to go in the direction others ask me to go in—*richten*, . . . I love these words with equivocal meanings: *sich richten*, to go in the direction, or to conform; in the passive, to be condemned or judged; *das ist richtig*, that's right. *Gerechtigkeit*, Righteousness, thou word of thunder. (23)]

Wolf's last novel connects with both *Nachdenken über Christa T.* and *Leibhaftig*. The protagonist's desire for "the final darkness" insinuates Christa T.'s "death wish," which similarly originated in a yearning to escape a society that asked too much of the individual; and the extensive reflection on language alludes to comparable considerations in *Leibhaftig*. The words the protagonist in *Stadt der Engel* ponders hint at questions of fairness and of being judged. While they relate to the media treating her unfairly, they also resemble the patient's position in the GDR hospital: In both situations, the protagonist has no choice but to cooperate because she is at other people's mercy, whether it is the GDR medical system or the West German media in post-unification Germany. Since the protagonists in both novels feel subjected to similar power structures, which merely emanate from different realms, the exercise of power surfaces as independent of any specific political system. Indeed, the narratives highlight that while the historical situation is altered after 1990, the effects of those who have the means to control the individual—namely, the media—are at least as harsh as they were before. For now, however, let us return to the passive patient in *Leibhaftig* to learn more about the effects of authority in the medical realm.

The "Gentle Lie," Hierarchy, and Gender in the GDR Hospital

Leibhaftig, like *Nachdenken über Christa T.*, criticizes the *schonende Lüge* as an ongoing practice of turning patients into passive objects incapable of influencing their own therapy. In the GDR of the late 1980s, patients were still deemed unable to handle the truth about their medical condition, and physicians were encouraged to keep them uninformed. Already in 1974, Professor Berndt worried that patients' growing level of knowledge might lead to a situation in the future in which a doctor might be compelled to tell patients the whole truth.[20] For the time being and for years to come, however, patients in socialist society were declared incompetent when it came to managing the health of their own bodies.

Leibhaftig stages the GDR norm of physicians discussing a patient's life-threatening condition exclusively with their relatives. Initially, the patient is hardly surprised to learn that her partner or husband, the "you" she addresses throughout the narrative, speaks furtively with the doctors (16). When she discovers later that he knew about her imminent operation before she was herself informed—because he had discussed her therapy with the surgeon—she is alerted to the seriousness of her illness (50).

The patient, aware of the conversations but not of their content, accepts the daily clandestine meetings her spouse has with the *Chefarzt* (head physician; 77, 103, 119). Even when she has recovered at the end of the novel, the protagonist suspects continued private conferences based on the evidence that her husband happened to encounter the physician in the corridor (184). *Leibhaftig* therefore confirms those scholars and contemporary witnesses who assert that the *schonende Lüge* was practiced in the GDR until its healthcare system was dissolved. Moreover, the narrative reveals that the strategy meant to support healing by not alarming patients actually increased anxieties and contributed to doctor-patient relationships lacking trust and denying patients agency.[21]

In fact, the *schonende Lüge* preoccupied Christa Wolf repeatedly after her hospitalization in 1988. The entry for 1988 in the autobiographical *Ein Tag im Jahr* recounts that she heard a radio report in which a doctor insisted that one must not lie to cancer patients (424).[22] This indicates that in 1988, there was finally public discussion about the *schonende Lüge*—but it also confirms it as common practice. Similarly, *Stadt der Engel* conveys how the protagonist's friend Emma was forced to trick a nurse into revealing her diagnosis, thyroid cancer, so that she could arrange for her death as she saw fit (244). Absent the legal right to information about her body and her health, Emma's only recourse was to outsmart the medical staff. The *schonende Lüge* reveals a guardian state that wants to protect its allegedly incompetent citizens from unwelcome news. Medical machinery that requires patients to maintain uncomfortable positions for extended periods of time, complained about by the protagonist throughout *Leibhaftig*, adds to the hospital staff's desire for passive patients who comply with the requirements of the machines. While one might have come across practices like the *schonende Lüge* and the desire for cooperative patients in the FRG as well, patient docility and the *schonende Lüge* were not legally defined or prescribed by the state apparatus. On the contrary: since legal practice in the FRG has always demanded a patient's written consent for any medical intervention, they could hardly be left in the dark about their state of health. While the *schonende Lüge* as well as the demand for patient cooperation as enshrined in the *Duldungs- und Befolgungspflicht*, the *Mitwirkungspflicht*, and the *Offenbarungs- und Informationspflicht* are indeed characteristic of the GDR medical and legal systems, the enthusiasm for technology in the medical realm is a phenomenon the GDR shared with the FRG.

The gender differences and hierarchical structures among the physicians in *Leibhaftig* can hardly be attributed to socialism. In fact, a conversation between two physicians and the protagonist reveals significant differences between the GDR and the FRG pertaining to hierarchical structures within the hospital. The novel conveys that the head surgeon, alternatively addressed as the *Chefarzt*, or the Professor

will nicht mehr Chefarzt genannt werden, die Vorsilbe "Chef" liege ihm nicht . . . Kora sagt, die meisten Patienten, besonders die meisten Patientinnen, sagen sehr gerne "Chefarzt," ihr Wert steigt, wenn sie sagen können: Mich hat nämlich der Chefarzt operiert. Und mich nennen sie "Frau Doktor," obwohl sie wissen, ich habe den Titel nicht. (131–32)

[doesn't want to be called "Chefarzt" any longer, the prefix "Chief" doesn't sit right with him . . . Kora says that most of the patients, especially most of the female patients, like to say "Chefarzt," their self-esteem increases if they can say, "You know, the Chefarzt operated on me. And they call me "Frau Doktor," even though they know that I don't have that title. (89–90)]

With its more egalitarian relationship among doctors and nurses and a diminished gender binary, *Leibhaftig* highlights the effects of the reformed socialist medical education more clearly than *Nachdenken über Christa T.* Unlike Christa T.'s former high-school student who in the 1950s still upheld bourgeois patterns of behavior, the *Chefarzt* in *Leibhaftig* and his colleague Kora Bachmann have internalized the GDR's values. Demonstrating that hierarchical structures were largely eliminated, they propagate a classless society and deplore that some patients uphold elite structures because they derive self-esteem from their association with the *Chefarzt*. At the same time, the existence of the patients Kora Bachmann refers to indicates that hierarchical structures and traditional norms of status could never be abolished entirely in the GDR.

Even before all physicians and nurses were organized in the "Gesellschaft für Krankenpflege der DDR" (GDR Society for Medical Care), founded in 1985, reforms to the system like the elimination of privileges and hierarchical structures and the reduction of salary differentials had generated new forms of collaborative work, and gender became less significant. This "decline" in status had been painful for the older generation of physicians, but for those who received a GDR medical education flattened hierarchies were a matter of course. And while the changes might not have been as radical as the government had desired, eyewitness accounts suggest that physicians and nurses increasingly viewed each other as partners mutually committed to thinking and acting in socialist categories.[23]

The hospital staff in *Leibhaftig* is depicted as engaging in collaborative behavior without fail. When the patient asks for cold leg compresses instead of nausea-inducing shots to lower her body temperature, the *Chefarzt*, portrayed as solicitous and understanding, endorses her wish, but emphasizes that its fulfillment depends on nurse Thea (103).

Even though the *Chefarzt* is among those male physicians who staunchly believe in medical machinery, he can emphasize emotion when confronted with the patient's misery and highlights cooperation. Further, faced with insufficient scientific explanations for the collapse of the patient's immune system (125), some of the doctors even consider the soul as the troublemaker in the recovery process (161). In a conversation with the female anesthesiologist, the alarmed patient, however, insists, "die Seele finden Ihre Chirurgen niemals, so tief sie auch schneiden mögen" (160: your surgeons never find the soul, no matter how deeply they cut; 109). Underlying this discussion is a topic that has occupied Wolf all her life: undoing the split between body and mind. For the patient in *Leibhaftig*, who has just located her soul in her body, the discussion about the doctors' ability to find her soul at the core of her diseased flesh is cause for new anxieties.

A Faustian Bargain: Searching for the Soul in the Entrails

Unlike physicians, who merely see the soul as a potential troublemaker, the protagonist has discovered her soul within her body, and is now afraid of losing it. Her feverish dreams produce imagined journeys into her body, and she is shocked to realize that there is a realm in which the spiritual and the physical merge (97). Her body permits insights because of its affliction: listening to it, the protagonist understands that the mind/body split characterizing Western medicine is a constructed dichotomy. In her perception, the separation of body and mind dissolves into one specific area of her body, her appendix, which she recognizes as the locus of her soul. This fever-induced revelation provides insight into a dilemma already addressed in *Kindheitsmuster*; namely, our inability to understand the language of our organs due to our separation of the body's and the soul's memory (*Kindheitsmuster* 394). *Leibhaftig* suggests that memory and remembering reside in a unified body-soul realm, perceptible in the "Bloßlegung der Eingeweide" (137: exposed entrails; 93). This word choice evokes chapter 8 in *Kindheitsmuster*, which is subtitled "Entblößung der Eingeweide: Krieg" (Laying Bare of the Innards: War), and points to similarities between the protagonists of these two novels: in *Kindheitsmuster*, too, pain triggers dreams and insight (43), and Nelly knows and feels through her stomach (56)—not unlike the patient in *Leibhaftig* who, as a child, imagined her soul as resembling an appendix residing near her stomach (130–31). Echoing Aleida Assmann's *Erinnerungsräume*, which explains that the affective aspects of memory in particular cannot be controlled (256), *Leibhaftig* highlights how memory relies on the symptomatic body, not on the active pursuit to influence the process of remembering. However, if body and soul merge in the intestines, the excision of the infected appendix points to the loss of the soul and a contract with the devil (131).

The German title *Leibhaftig* alludes to this dilemma, since it means "in the flesh" and euphemistically denotes Satan. In the narrative, a nameless pathologist emerges as a life-saving devil who introduces himself as the ambassador from the underworld. His cold, lifeless handshake, slightly hoarse voice, scary smile, hollow cheeks, and not least of all the shock of jet-black hair carefully cut so that its tip falls low on his forehead, all contribute to the impression of a satanic figure (165–66). He holds a powerful position in the hospital because he knows both life and death. Not in love with life, familiar with mortality and deadly bacteria, and effectively fighting death, he emerges as the character closest to an omnipotent figure (170–71). A devilish figure, he points to the artificiality of the binary of life and death as well as the impossibility of separating good and evil. Indirectly, he addresses the questions that have traumatized Wolf with regard to her stance vis-à-vis the GDR regime and her involvement with the Stasi.[24]

The thoughts surrounding the "benevolent devil" develop further in a conversation between the patient and her husband, who explains his wife's elevated temperature as the work of the devil (119). Deliberately misquoting Johann Wolfgang von Goethe's *Faust*, the protagonist associates the predicament regarding the political involvement of art and culture with questions of ethics when she contemplates which devil could be responsible for her situation:

> Ob es auch einen Teufel gibt, der stets das Gute will und stets das Böse schafft? . . . Der Teufel . . . ist der allervernünftigsten Vernunft entstiegen . . ., der Traum der Vernunft gebiert Ungeheuer, habe ich das nicht auch mal Urban entgegengehalten . . . Ja, zugegeben, wenn die kleinen Geister sich des Traums bemächtigen . . . Dann hat die Zukunft nichts zu lachen, sagte er. . . . In unseren beiden Gesichtern war der gleiche Ausdruck von Zweifel und Schrecken. Wir hatten Berichte über den Rajk-Prozeß gelesen. Führte der Weg ins Paradies unvermeidlich in die Hölle? (119–20)

> [Is there a devil that always wills good and always does evil? . . . The devil . . . has risen from the most logical of all reasoning . . .—the dream of reason produces monsters, didn't I once hold that up to Urban . . . "Yes, admittedly, when petty demons appropriate the dreams . . . Then reason is in big trouble," he said. . . . The same expression of doubt and horror was on both our faces. We'd read reports about the Rajk trial. Did the way to paradise lead unavoidably through hell? (81)][25]

Echoing pre-unification writings by Wolf such as the essay "Glauben an Irdisches" (Belief in the Worldly, 1968) or the novel *Störfall*, the protagonist's reflections underscore that any good intention, including a socialism based on reason and with the promise of paradise, is likely to turn into its opposite as soon as one attempts to implement it.[26] In contrast to Goethe's *Faust*, Stalinism—imagined as Satan who demonstrates his power in perverse show trials like the one against László Rajk—is the devil whose actions, in contradistinction to the plans of Goethe's Mephistopheles, are initially motivated by the hope for a better society. Yet the horrific outcome of the original ideal causes the young socialists of the patient's memory to doubt their belief when they realize that the danger implicit in their values is tied to who will take action in history: if "petty demons" with bad intentions seize their ideals, their utopian vision is bound to end in hell. At the same time, these reflections hint at answers to the burning questions the author Wolf, too, faced in the 1990s: She had collaborated with the Stasi because she could not, at the time, even imagine that the wrong people had seized her ideals. The notion of hell creeping into her imagined paradise developed gradually over time; in *Nachdenken über Christa T.*, it was still an uncontaminated concept.

Stadt der Engel maintains that the quest for paradise in which all modern societies have engaged has led to the creation of hell on earth and that civilization, as a rule, brings forth monsters (118, 141). Where the pursuit of paradise on earth evokes socialism and alludes to *Nachdenken über Christa T.*, the monsters of civilization expand the concept of hell on earth to capitalist countries. While *Störfall*, which responded to the threat of nuclear power plants in reaction to the Chernobyl catastrophe of 1986, still asked whether modern civilizations necessarily had to produce monsters (37), Wolf's post-unification works *Leibhaftig* and *Stadt der Engel* confirm their existence for all modern societies alike. Whether these modern monsters emerge as nuclear power plants or intelligence agencies, they are everywhere. In *Stadt der Engel*, comparisons between the Stasi, the FBI and the CIA reveal that secret services, their language, and their structural modes of oppression are not specific to a particular political system: they rule the GDR and capitalist society alike. *Stadt der Engel* therefore calls attention to the murderous actions of the FBI and the CIA (184, 275).[27] Given that the novel revolves around the two questions that occupy the protagonist—why did she briefly collaborate with the Stasi and how could she have forgotten about this almost negligible collaboration—this comparison, though only touched upon in passing, could be read as relativizing the role of the GDR intelligence agency. This is not to say that the protagonist downplays the evil acts of the Stasi; on the contrary, she herself suffered under their surveillance and emphasizes the huge number of files on her that attest to decades of observation. However, the parallel portrayal of various intelligence agencies in *Stadt der Engel* emphasizes that moral duplicity and resulting failure is characteristic for contemporary civilizations per se, whether they are capitalist or allegedly socialist.[28] In *Leibhaftig*, hope remains with figures like the pathologist, a "benevolent devil" who is able to heal patients because he can overcome the artificial binary of good and evil. The personified opposite of the "petty demons" that horrify the patient, the powerful pathologist can appropriate rationalist thought for the idealistic vision of fighting death. Like the socialist idea, life depends on the right, idealistic actors for its successful implementation.[29]

Female Approaches to Healing

Dedicated to surmounting constructed dichotomies, *Leibhaftig* aims at overcoming the opposition of Western and alternative medicine. Wolf believed in alternative healing methods, as *Stadt der Engel* and essays such as "Krankheit und Liebesentzug" attest. In 1984, Wolf rejected the predominately scientific approach to medicine that focuses on advancing machines, drugs, and computers and pretends to be objective (729–30). She further pointed out historical developments that led to this form of dominant medicine being practiced by men, while women practiced as nature healers, midwives, and "herb-wives" (734). The author's skepticism vis-à-vis Western medicine is similarly present in *Stadt der Engel*. The protagonist fights her insomnia and joint pains with the support of Dr. Kim, a physician who believes in meditation, acupuncture, and dietary measures as remedies (67), and with the Feldenkrais therapist Rachel, who teaches her patient to accept that there is no need to be either perfect or innocent. This is what enables her to forgive herself for her brief Stasi collaboration (187).

In *Leibhaftig*, nurse Thea and the one female physician in the ward, Kora Bachmann, are referred to as descendants of the "herb-wives": their knowledge of natural medicine allows them to speed up their patient's recovery. *Leibhaftig* deplores the underrepresentation of women in leading positions in hospitals, which was largely due to the fact that despite the steadily rising proportion of female physicians in the GDR, most of them worked as general practitioners (Hahn, "EF," 80). Yet the historical dimension opened up in Wolf's 1984 essay reveals that the remains of gendered hierarchical structures in GDR hospitals cannot be attributed to socialist medicine, but are relics of the bourgeois order. A compassionate socialist society based on humanist ideals, in particular, depends on adopting values and medical practices linked with females. Associated with the night and the goddess Persephone, also known as Kore, the beautiful companion and guide through the netherworld, the anesthetist Kora Bachmann contributes to the patient's healing in unconventional ways. Responsible for leading the patient into the abeyance between the worlds, into Hades, before the operations, she maneuvers between the two worlds and negotiates existing borders (56, 96, 141–42).[30] In the patient's feverish dreams, Kora accompanies her on journeys into the labyrinth of the patient's brain, which corresponds with the underground network of passageways of Berlin, or on flights over the "untergehenden Stadt" (146: perishing city; 100). Here, the patient gains the insights about her past that are necessary for healing.

In *Stadt der Engel* the guardian angel Angelina—similar to Kora in *Leibhaftig*—watches over the protagonist when she is stricken with a high fever and guides her through imaginary spaces. A Ugandan cleaning lady at the Ms. Victoria boarding house where the protagonist stays during her time in California, Angelina is elevated to the status of an angelic guide, although she defies most biblical standards. Like her biblical prototype, she is visible only to the protagonist; yet unlike biblical angels— who are usually male, white, and come to the believer when it is time to die—Angelina is female, black, and comes to rescue the protagonist from death.[31] Far from being perfect, Angelina is content with doing the best she can, given that she is overworked and short of time (327, 384). Precisely because of her happy imperfection, she provides comfort and teaches that nobody can expect faultlessness from others. Like Kora in *Leibhaftig*, she serves as a "spiritual midwife," leading the protagonist towards the wisdom stored in her "Geistkörperseele" (unity of mind, body, and soul), which she is able to access during a trip to the American Southwest.[32] Experiencing the beauty of nature in the canyons and learning to appreciate the culture of Native peoples (385), the protagonist finds inner peace and finally flies with Angelina to Los Angeles. This imaginary flight stands for the protagonist's newly found freedom and actual healing in the "City of Angels." It emerges as the sequel to the fever-induced hallucinatory Berlin excursions with Kora in *Leibhaftig*, which serve as prerequisites for healing because they force the protagonist to face reality and initiate the painful recovery of mind, body, and soul.

Tachycardia and the Symptomatic Voice

From the beginning of *Leibhaftig*, the symptom through which the protagonist's body speaks most conspicuously is tachycardia, a form of cardiac arrhythmia characterized by a rapid beating of the heart. This ailment, which has repeatedly troubled the protagonist since the 1960s, becomes more severe in the late 1980s, when it develops into a life-threatening condition due to complications arising from the appendicitis. The tachycardia in the 1980s triggers flashbacks that point to the disconcerting history stored in the body: once unleashed, the cardiac arrhythmia can instigate recollections of the past that lead to insight. The chronic nature of the ailment indicates that the body has repeatedly tried to communicate what is disturbing for the mind and soul. Using as an example the first of many episodes of tachycardia the patient suffers in the hospital in the 1980s, we will discover how one onset of cardiac arrhythmia triggers a recollection of the patient's troubled relationship to the parent generation, and the memory of her first tachycardia in the 1960s.

The novel opens with an instance of tachycardia that provokes a flashback linking the deathbed scene of the protagonist's mother with the brutal overthrow of the attempts at democratization during the "Prague Spring" in August 1968: "Sie sind in Prag einmarschiert. Und höre meine Mutter flüstern: Es gibt Schlimmeres. Sie wendet den Kopf zur Wand. Es gibt Schlimmeres. Sie stirbt. Ich denke an Prag" (7: "They've marched into Prague." And hear my mother whisper, "There are worse things." She turns her head toward the wall. "There are worse things." She dies. I think of Prague; 4–5). The protagonist's medical history commences with a recollection of the GDR's participation in the military invasion of Czechoslovakia during the night of August 20 to 21, 1968. Since this attack was aimed at thwarting Alexander Dubcek's attempts to introduce what was termed "socialism with a humane face," the socialist state's participation in the offensive against Czechoslovakia is generally considered socialism's fall from grace, and points to the end of socialist ideals. Linking this moral and political disaster with the protagonist's dying mother, *Leibhaftig* marks 1968 as the end of hope for the implementation of socialist-humanist ideals.[33]

With the repeated "Schlimmeres," the diction replicates the words Wolf attributes to Anna Seghers in her response to the ravages associated with the Eleventh Plenum of 1965 in *Ein Tag im Jahr*, "Es gab schon Schlimmeres. Unter Stalin wurden die Leute an die Wand gestellt—jetzt nicht mehr" (73–74: There have been worse things. Under Stalin the people were put against the wall—not any longer; 81). Seghers, Wolf's antifascist Jewish figure of identification, is quoted qualifying the devastation of the Eleventh Plenum, the event that caused Wolf to doubt for the first time the possibility of realizing her socialist ideals, by relativizing it via a comparison with the executions under Stalin.[34] Decades later, Wolf blends her memories of her biological mother's death in 1968, which coincided with the "Prague Spring," with her fantasy of the pure Communist Jewish mother's reaction to 1965, creating a fictional mother figure for *Leibhaftig* in which the two mother figures merge. The tachycardia-induced hallucinations unchain the patient from ideological constraints. Unlike the author Wolf, the protagonist can openly grieve both mother figures and the events they symbolize.[35] Through the performance of the symptomatic body, the narrative points to what is the protagonist's primary conflict from the outset of the novel: the discrepancy between her socialist ideals and the quotidian reality in the GDR alongside the undeniable link between her own personal history and that of her country.[36]

The patient immediately floats into another flashback in which she recalls her very first tachycardia of 1963. This initial attack was triggered by her fear that a film she had co-produced would be censored after the official preview. The narrative links the distress evoked by the inevitable operation in the 1980s with the panic caused by the previous confrontation with state authorities in the 1960s through the physical experience of tachycardia (8–9). Yet the protagonist's feelings in 1963 were more complicated, or, more precisely, contradictory. She admits that on the one hand, she disliked that her collapse revealed what was going on inside her. On the other hand, this breakdown provided her with a valid excuse for her absence from the preview (9). In other words, the protagonist remembers the uncomfortable experience as simultaneously liberating, allowing her to escape public scrutiny. The narrative points to a pattern the patient will repeat in the hospital in the 1980s: the body not only allows her to gain insights about the past and personal feelings, as demonstrated by the instance of mourning the conflated mother figures, but it also opens up the possibility for temporary escape from uncomfortable circumstances, society's demands, and the very psychic conflicts that translate into bodily symptoms (81, 84).

Like Christa T., and like Nelly in *Kindheitsmuster*, this protagonist can rely on her body to protect her from unpleasant situations, and this points to the continuity in the way Wolf uses the symptomatic body after 1989. Yet there is more. Following the patient's recollection of the two contradictory feelings she experienced during her first tachycardia attack in 1963, she records a different physical response two decades later: "Tief in mir kicherte jemand mit mir über mich" (9: Deep within me, someone was giggling with me, at me; 6). Augmenting the characteristic relationship between mind and body that occupied Wolf so consistently, the narrative showcases three voices contained in one body; but only two of them belong to the persona embodied by the narrator. In addition, there is a third "someone" who can giggle about the "self" ("at me") with another part of the "I" ("with me"). The emerging, almost schizophrenic "I"-division, amplified by the attempt to locate another persona within one's own body, indicates a profound crisis of subjectivity. It is a crisis caused by remembering past historical events from the perspective of the narrative present in the late 1980s. As such, it signals what Julia Hell in *Post-Fascist Fantasies* called the "writing of memory as the interaction of the voices of the past with those of the present," which in Wolf's case emerges as "a relentless exploration of the inescapable historicity of voice, of its thorough imbrication in ideology" (*PFF*, 139). *Leibhaftig* thus builds on Wolf's early oeuvre, in which Hell attributed the absence of a "pure" voice untouched by ideology to "the *tension* between a desire for a 'pure' voice and the painful knowledge of the complex link between history and voice" (*PFF*, 139). The 2002 novel, with its voice split in three, brings together history, voice, and the body in even more sophisticated ways than in Wolf's previous works.

In fact, *Leibhaftig* explores voice even further when the combination of tachycardia and fevers leads to the protagonist's total loss of self-control, which culminates in the inability to control her voice. The resulting helplessness is experienced as traumatic, as the shift in narrative voice underscores:

> Es gibt keine Selbstbeherrschung mehr, die mir sonst so teuer ist, auch keine Beherrschung der Gliedmaßen. Nie hätte sie sich in normalem Zustand erlaubt, sich so aufzuführen, . . . nicht einmal mehr verständlich sprechen kann sie mehr, auch ihre Sprachorgane sind von dem Rütteln und Schütteln befallen. (80)

> [There's no more self-control—something dear to me—I can't even control my limbs. Under ordinary circumstances she would never have allowed herself to carry on that way, . . . she can't even speak intelligibly anymore, even her organs of speech are overcome by the shaking and chattering. (54–55)]

While the first-person narrator can communicate the lack of control over her frenzied body, the narrative shifts to the distanced third person to relate the malfunctioning of the voice. Reminiscent of Wolf's pre-unification character Kassandra, the narrative distance highlights the climax of the loss of control in the seizure (*Kassandra*, 47). Yet why is the inability to command her voice more distressing than the ungovernable limbs? In *Post-Fascist Fantasies*, Hell analyzes how in Wolf's earlier works, voice appears as "the symptom of the body's relationship to the past, often developing into a 'malfunctioning' of the vocal apparatus" (*PFF*, 250). In *Leibhaftig*, the total malfunctioning of the speech organs emerges as a "symptomatic voice," as historical experience is inscribed into the unregulated vocal apparatus, clearly indicating trauma. Citing Bessel van der Kolk and Onno van der Hart, Irene Kacandes insists that "traumatic memory 'has no social component; it is not addressed to anybody, the patient does not respond to anybody; it is a solitary activity'" (*TF*, 92). The socially and physically malfunctioning body in *Leibhaftig* underlines the solitary aspect of dealing with a traumatic event. At the same time, the body liberates the patient. Repeating the pattern of 1963 when the protagonist experienced both embarrassment and relief during the first tachycardic episode in her life, the body can free the patient from having to respond to society's demands—the very mechanism already at work in Wolf's pre-unification works, including *Nachdenken über Christa T.* and *Kindheitsmuster* (327).

In this twenty-first-century recollection of a hospital stay in the 1980s associated with the memories of the 1960s, the continued absence of an integrated voice hints at a larger problem. It signifies the main character's ongoing struggle to negotiate her commitment to socialist ideals with the diametrically opposed constraints imposed by a state apparatus that has always exerted pressure on her to collaborate. This political positioning as a "loyal dissident" in the GDR now surfaces as trauma. It emerges as cause for the symptoms her body develops, which then signal possible retreat from society and from the oppressive institutions that originally caused the disease. Since *Leibhaftig* links the protagonist's first tachycardia attack with the narrative present, it establishes her inner conflict, conveyed in the symptomatic voice, as chronic—a condition that requires the patient to go to the roots of her troubled past to be restored to health.

Fevers and Hallucinatory Excursions as Keys to the Past

To reveal the origins of the patient's symptoms, the protagonist of *Leibhaftig* must gain access to her suppressed past—a process for which she relies on her body.[37] This complicated process is reflected in the changing narrative perspective: a distanced third-person narrator relays that the infection caused the patient to focus exclusively on the body's signals. Accordingly, her brain ceased to work—with one exception: remembering (70–71). Yet the patient herself as first-person narrator qualifies this claim by assigning the body supremacy: "Nicht dass ich beliebig mein Gedächtnis anzapfen könnte. Doch an der festen Scholle in dem Meer von Unbewusstem, auf der ich mich halte, treiben Erinnerungsbrocken vorbei, ungerufen und unregulierbar" (71: Not that I can tap into my memory at will. But unsummoned and uncontrollable, clumps of memory drift by the sand bar I'm holding on to in this sea of unconsciousness; 48). Memories cannot be controlled, but pass by in random clumps. Consequently, agency remains limited to the body: because of the scars and wounds that serve as reminders of the past, it is more reliable than the mind and reveals itself to be incapable of manipulating the emerging "clumps of memory."

In "Konstruktionen in der Analyse" ("Constructions in Analysis"), Freud insisted that next to associations, memory chunks (such as Wolf's "Erinnerungsbrocken") are the most significant element for the psychoanalytic work of reconstructing a patient's suppressed past (45).[38] Even things that seem completely forgotten are merely buried and inaccessible to the subject (46). Aware of her body's supremacy over the brain and the significance of the past for her healing process, the patient in *Leibhaftig* guides her body into the fever-induced dreams that confront her with her role in Germany's fascist and socialist history. High temperatures and nightmares, often governed by images of rising floods washing the patient onto battlefields and causing her to suffer, serve as keys to the deepest regions of her memory, which would otherwise remain undisclosed (24, 106–7). Illness protects the patient from the social constraints that generated the disease, and simultaneously unlocks access to the hidden origins of her suffering.

Socialist and Capitalist Versions of Hell

Leibhaftig refers to the romantic notion of illness leading to insight that we observed in *Nachdenken über Christa T.*, and the novel turns to Freud's understanding of psychoanalysis as archeology that he mapped in "Konstruktionen in der Analyse" (45).[39] In *Leibhaftig*, the patient has to descend into the deepest regions of the mind, which are illustrated by various images of depth such as wells, mines, and labyrinths. The protagonist experiences her body as a mine into which she reaches to excavate its secrets (97).[40] In order to recover, she must work her way through these subterranean regions which correspond to the "Labyrinth in [ihrem] Gehirn" (139: labyrinth in [her] brain; 95). The stream-of-consciousness narrative captures the image of the mine and supports the dissolution of dichotomies, including historical time periods. To the protagonist's confusion, German fascism, capitalism, and socialism are confounded. One hallucination sends the patient wandering into a maze of Berlin catacombs that mirror her body's infected digestive tract. Particularly the inscription "LSR" for "Luftschutzraum" and the word "MAUERDURCHBRUCH" (112: AIR-RAID SHELTER and WALL BROKEN THROUGH; 76; capitalization in original) on one underground wall trigger feelings of despair. The patient associates these words marking the subterranean escape routes from World War II air-raid shelters with the Wall dividing Germany since 1961. The writing on the wall prompts memory, productive thought, and horror when she realizes that the corridors behind a crack in the wall seem to copy the underground labyrinths she paced before, albeit now with arrows on the walls pointing in the opposite direction (113). The blurring of time creates historical ambiguity: Are we dealing with East and West Berlin after 1961 and therefore with socialism and capitalism reflecting each other? Or does this dream conflate socialism and Nazi Germany, which inflicted World War II and air raids on Berlin and its population? Since Wolf explicitly rejected the equation of socialism and fascism, a reading that considers the ideological signposts of socialism and capitalism as being diametrically opposed yet leading to identical political power structures in real life seems most appropriate.[41]

This fever-induced insight and the concomitant blurring of historical time might have prompted some scholars to read *Leibhaftig* as the author's final farewell to socialism. Yet the leitmotif of the labyrinth points in another direction. Citing Bessel van der Kolk and Onno van der Hart, Irene Kacandes maintains that traumatic memory is "a return of the traumatic event as 'physical sensations, horrific images or nightmares, behavioral reenactments, or a combination of these'" (*TF*, 92). In *Leibhaftig*, the reenactments of traumatic events occur in nightmares featuring labyrinthine structures, which exemplify the repetition of traumatic incidents and reinforce the notion that history repeats itself. Various political systems seem to represent versions of modern hell, whether this hell emerges in the form of socialist or of capitalist alienation.[42] The patient's next anxiety to emerge, to be led perpetually through new halls of mirrors (113), underlines her fear that political systems, despite ideological differences, structurally mirror each other. Caught in a labyrinth that forces her to relive her traumata, her symptomatic body suggests that she is entangled in and betrayed by global history and various ideologies. *Leibhaftig* therefore not only comments on GDR history and the unification process, but also on the modern world that Wolf perceives as a hell ruled by global capitalism.

This topic also preoccupied the author in *Stadt der Engel oder The Overcoat of Dr. Freud*. The bilingual title of the German original and the English phrases interspersed throughout the novel highlight Wolf's perception of the world as dominated by Anglo-American capitalism, which catalyzes her criticism in all its manifestations, including post-unification East Germany.[43] The traumatic rupture associated with unification reverberates throughout *Stadt der Engel*. In particular, the subsequent imposition of capitalism onto the former GDR accompanied as it was by structural violence, exploitative mechanisms, inequalities, and racism, troubles Wolf's *Doppelgänger* narrator (36–38, 80, 130, 280). Since worse capitalist excesses are discernible in the United States, the problems are diagnosed as systemic and US-society as fatally sick (380).[44] Because of this social disease and the United States's murderous army and intelligence agencies, *Stadt der Engel* questions the legitimacy of capitalism and US supremacy as the universal norm (78).[45] In conjunction with the protagonist's identification with the victims of the Nazi regime, this criticism of capitalism supports her belief in the superiority of socialist ideals.

Identification with Victims of Fascism

While the patient in *Leibhaftig* positions herself within an age-old history of torture and pain (20), she strongly identifies with the victims of German fascism and its anti-humanist ideology as these find expression in racism, chauvinism, and totalitarianism. She claims to feel the agony of the afflicted and persecuted as a violent inscription literally burned into her body and mind (20). An unambiguous reference to the Jewish communist Rosa Luxemburg floating in Berlin's Landwehr Canal intrudes early in the novel and sets the tone (20). Supported by her body's symptoms, the patient places herself within the narrative of antifascism that legitimated power in the GDR, and specifically that of communist resistance under fascist torture. Yet the novel complicates this pattern by introducing the potential for guilt into the equation—albeit from a distanced third-person narrative perspective:

> Jetzt rächt es sich, dass sie von Kind an all die Schilderungen dieser Greuel immer nur hastig überflogen, dass sie im Kino die Augen geschlossen, beim Fernsehen das Zimmer verlassen hat, wenn es wieder losging. Dass sie nur ein einziges Mal in einem ehemaligen Konzentrationslager gewesen ist. (21)

> [Now revenge is being extracted for the fact that ever since she was a child, she'd just quickly skimmed over the portrayals of all those horrors, closed her eyes in the movies, left the room when such things started up again on television. For the fact that she'd only been in what used to be a concentration camp a single time. (14)]

The patient experiences her tormenting fevers as retaliation from a higher power for petty offenses that are hardly unforgivable. Her behavior—seemingly innate since the protagonist has acted this way since her childhood—establishes her as a sensitive person unable to face the Nazi horror. Even her self-reproach for an insufficient number of visits to Nazi concentration camps—the climax in her declaration of remorse—is hardly reasonable. Rather, the omniscient, distanced narrative voice insinuates that Nazi torture is replicated on the protagonist's infected, suffering flesh as a form of punishment for her deficiencies in acknowledging the suffering caused by Nazi crimes. In traumatic reenactments, the body makes historical knowledge available and acquires the right to relate to the victims of fascism because of their perceived shared agony. The first-person narrator's identification with victims such as Rosa Luxemburg or concentration camp prisoners dying during the death marches (23) aligns the protagonist with the GDR and its antifascist heroes.

When the patient locates her aunt Lisbeth's Jewish lover, Dr. Leitner, who had been persecuted by the Nazis, near the Berlin border-crossing known as the "Tränenbunker" (59: Bunker of Tears; 40), the fascist Third Reich and the GDR seem to converge briefly: they meet in a precarious space from which people desire to escape in vain. After a brief interruption, the feverish dream continues with the protagonist as a seven-year-old in the year 1936. She observes Lisbeth, Dr. Leitner, and their baby making their way through the labyrinth of Berlin basements—and contemplates whether she might have disclosed the illegal relationship (115). The fate of these family members occupied Wolf and her *Doppelgänger* narrators for many years: Dr. Leitner, Elisabeth, and cousin Manfred also appear in *Kindheitsmuster* and in "Krankheit und Liebesentzug" (745). The annotations in *Ein Tag im Jahr*, omitted from *One Day A Year*, disclose that Wolf modeled Dr. Leitner on the Jewish Dr. Alfred Lechner, who emigrated to the United States in 1938 (649). In *Leibhaftig*, the patient opens up to Kora Bachmann: she remembers that in 1936, her aunt insisted on Dr. Leitner's presence at Manfred's christening, a situation that the protagonist found hard not to divulge as a child (121–22). In the late 1980s, the feverish performance of the patient's body discloses historical information that connects her sense of being tortured by life-threatening fevers to the burden placed on her in 1936. Her pain triggers memories of her Jewish family members and fortifies her affinity with the victims of Nazi persecution and torture. Rather than distancing herself from socialism, the protagonist's deep identification with the heroes of the GDR and its founding antifascist narrative buttresses one of the essential constituents of the discourse legitimizing the socialist state.

In a clichéd scene following the christening anecdote, the protagonist is purified by water: the tears she cries further strengthen her association with the victims of Nazi terror:

> Da kommen mir die Tränen. Ich fange an zu weinen, das hätte ich längst tun sollen, ich weine und weine und kann nicht mehr aufhören, ich weine um Lisbeth, . . . ich weine um ihr Kind, Vetter Manfred, ich weine um Doktor Leitner und um unsere Familie, ich weine um mich. (122)

> [Then come the tears. I begin to cry, I should have done that long ago, I cry and cry and can't stop, I cry for Lisbeth, . . . I cry for the child, Cousin Manfred, I cry for Dr. Leitner and for our family, and I cry for myself. (83)]

The protagonist's insistence that her crying is overdue points to her sense of guilt for having withheld her grief for too long. The inability to mourn the Jewish victims of fascism who did not fight in the communist resistance, but lost their country and family ties, emerges as one of the suppressed feelings that caused the patient's ailment. Additionally, the association with the Jewish relative, accentuated by first-person narration and tears, cleanses the patient and her family of any guilt linked with the Nazi past, and establishes a new "covenant" with the Jewish victims. In this constellation, illness-induced physical suffering facilitates the engagement in "a politics of identification" with the victims of Nazi-Germany. This engagement pervades most of Christa Wolf's oeuvre, as Julia Hell argues in *Post-Fascist Fantasies* (*PFF*, 196): I contend that it is even more pervasive in her later works where it in fact predominates.

Stadt der Engel extends the protagonist's identification with the Jewish—and most often, communist—victims of the Nazi regime by focusing on the intellectual emigrants who established a so-called Weimar under the Palms in Los Angeles (207). Although she rejects emigration to the United States as a way to escape the German media flare-up that she experiences as a witches' cauldron (31), the protagonist identifies with emigrants like Brecht, Feuchtwanger, Heinrich and Thomas Mann, Schönberg, Weigel, Eisler, Bruno and Leonhard Frank, Werfel, Adorno, and Viertel. Her conspicuous admiration for the "parent generation"— those intellectuals who dedicated themselves to establishing an antifascist state—confirms the protagonist's rapport with the GDR's antifascist founding narrative as expressed in early GDR literature: the "dominant ideology's construction of social relations as family relations" (Hell, *PFF*, 61).[46] Portraying these emigrants and her elderly friend Emma, a committed communist who fought the Nazis and barely survived imprisonment,[47] the narrative counters hegemonic interpretations that disparage GDR antifascism by claiming that it was nothing but a founding "myth." Reflecting on the antifascist German writers listed as emigrants in a 1937 issue of *WORT*, the protagonist stresses that the GDR, based on its antifascist legacy, is morally superior to post-unification Germany, which will consign the antifascists to oblivion (347). This constellation tacitly establishes a near-equivalence between the new FRG and fascist Germany, and confirms the GDR founding narrative that considered fascism an outgrowth of the imperialist capitalist system.

This narrative strategy further elevates the protagonist's position to that of ambassador for the "Other Germany," who claims antifascist principles and rejects the FRG's politics of *Wiedergutmachung* (reparations, or literally "making good again") based on the conviction that the loss and damage presented by the Holocaust are irreparable (129).[48] While the GDR ceased to exist politically, the protagonist acts to ensure the persistence of the socialist-humanist values at the core of the GDR's founding narrative when she—in her words—accepts the role the Jewish emigrants and their descendants assign her: as a German, and thus as a representative of Germany, she mourns the victims of the Nazi regime with German Jewish Holocaust survivors and their children (103). From this cosmopolitan space of exile, Wolf's protagonist claims the voice of East Germans in post-unification German society— a critical, antifascist, intellectual voice that rejects the status of the abject assigned to her by the West German media.

Infections, Delayed Detoxification, and so-called *Wende* Suicides

A sense of culpability for German fascism and the desire to associate with its victims also come to the fore in those feverish dreams that suggest to the patient that she is poisoned. She concludes that she needs detoxification, purification, and purgation, and is surprised when she realizes this so late: "Die Infektion mochte früh erfolgt sein, die jahrzehntelange Inkubationszeit ist vorbei, jetzt bricht die Heilung aus, als schwere Krankheit" (93: The infection may have occurred at an early age, the decade-long incubation period is over, and now recovery is breaking out in the form of severe illness; 63). Neither the time nor the source of contagion is specified, yet the hint "at an early age" points to *Kindheitsmuster*. It suggests early contamination with authoritarianism inherent in the Prussian parenting style she was raised in, and Nazi ideology learned in the Hitler Youth and in a school system that propagated racism and chauvinism. Contaminated in her formative years, the patient in *Leibhaftig*, like Nelly in *Kindheitsmuster* and the protagonist in *Stadt der Engel* (88, 263, 286) developed an "authoritarian personality"—a deep-seated desire to please authorities instead of gaining freedom.[49] Now, decades later, this unquestioned belief in authorities must be painfully expunged by means of disease.

While *Kindheitsmuster* was a provocation to hegemonic GDR historiography because it pointed to the effects of the authoritarian character in the GDR,[50] *Leibhaftig* continues the fight against character traits acquired at an early age through the fevers that detoxify the body and purify the soul. The body develops symptoms that reveal its early contamination by fascism and engages in the purification process via illness. This ideological decontamination, the prerequisite for an arduous healing process, occurs in the final days of the GDR—not in post-unification Germany. After unification, the authoritarian character associated with fascism is overcome in a socialist society, not in a capitalist one—a significant observation particularly because *Stadt der Engel* continues to highlight the link between capitalism and fascism. Still, this recovery from fascist thought is long overdue—not unlike the patient's appendicitis, which she had left untreated for too long.

The patient is responsible for the complications because she ignored the physical symptoms indicating acute appendicitis. In the GDR, where health had ceased to be a private affair, delaying medical treatment demonstrated a failure to overcome bourgeois notions of individual liberty, to acknowledge freedom as the overlap of individual and communal interests, and to fulfill one's role in socialist society.[51] The *Arztvertrag* (contract between doctor and patient) of the *Bürgerliches Gesetzbuch* (BGB, German Civil Code), in effect in Germany until 1945 and in the FRG until 2013, stressed individual patient rights. In contrast, the GDR *Betreuungsverhältnis*, as detailed in the introduction to this study, placed emphasis on the subordination of individual rights to societal rights and, more generally, to public and legal norms (Seifert, *GSV*, 358). While the protagonist's initial resistance to medical treatment does not make her guilty de jure, she is accountable for neglecting her health. Because of the assumed conflation of individual and societal interests, she becomes guilty in a moral sense for not conforming to the general expectations of GDR society (Seifert, *GSV*, 268–69).

This aspect is underlined when the doctor she finally consults asks whether her negligence had been an attempt to commit suicide (130). This question constitutes more than concern for a patient who, perhaps partly due to political frustration, might contemplate taking her life. Until the final days of the GDR, suicide attempts were considered anti-socialist behavior indicating *falsches Bewusstsein* (false consciousness) and moreover unnecessary: after all, society provided for its citizens (Grashoff, *AD*, 278). Largely concealed by the government, official statistics on suicide were unavailable in the 1980s, although oppositional intellectuals such as Robert Havemann publicized what information they could obtain and contributed to a discourse opposing the regime's propaganda (Grashoff, *AD*, 297–98). Participating in this discussion in 2002, *Leibhaftig* draws attention to the discourse about the so-called *Wende* suicides and contributes to an aspect of late GDR history that is still largely obscured. Grashoff demonstrated that, notwithstanding claims to the contrary, neither the political repression of the GDR regime in the 1980s nor the fall of the Berlin Wall had any significant impact on suicide rates. Belying reports in West German newspapers from 1990 that declared that East Germany was facing a "suicide wave," the GDR in 1989 recorded the lowest rate of self-inflicted deaths since the founding of the state—albeit with a rise in suicides among SED party functionaries (Grahoff, *AD*, 235–36).

Leibhaftig exemplifies this topic in Hannes Urban, a character modeled on East German literary critic and *Kulturfunktionär* (cultural functionary) Hans Koch.[52] Just as he disappears from society, he emerges in the patient's agonizing dream-sequences, in which she tries to sort out the intricate ways their biographies are linked (123). In her last fever-induced dream, foreseeing his death causes the protagonist to choose life: she spots Urban's name next to those of dead relatives, written on a lattice door that serves as the gateway to Hades (162). A bluish light that tries to pull her through this door to the netherworld underscores both her proximity to death and her affinity to Urban, who in this dream constellation appears to be part of the family.[53] The two characters have been close since their university days, and as Urban makes clear, their ideological formation stems from the same "Brutkasten" (13: incubator; 9). Urban's choice of words points to early GDR prose texts that represented social relations as family relations, a pattern also employed by Wolf in *Der geteilte Himmel*. Yet while the traditional model structures fictional surrogate families around model communist parents whom the sons and daughters in the narrative could look up to, Wolf's 2002 novel gives the prototype a new twist: instead of ideal communists, an incubator "bred" Urban's and the protagonist's generation and this is responsible for what they have in common. Rescued by a machine before they could become guilty in the Nazi regime, this generation is linked with technology—whether they like it or not.

Accordingly, *Leibhaftig* replicates the romantic/realist dichotomy we had similarly observed between Christa T. and Kostja. Though they shared the same experiences when they were young and innocent (18, 49), Urban and the protagonist developed into each other's antagonist: While the protagonist takes on the role of a romantic believer in socialist ideals, Urban accepts the party line, becomes a career-oriented opportunist, and successfully advances in state institutions, sacrificing friends to promote his own career (18, 29, 99, 134–35). Their connection comes to the fore as another relationship of abjection: relying on abjecting the very aspects of socialism the other person embraces, the two former friends function as each other's "constitutive outside" for their "subject formation" in Butler's sense. *Leibhaftig* underlines that the GDR was, by no means, a homogenous community; and that citizens who self-identified as "socialists" were likewise not a homogenous group. Being presented as coming from the same metaphorical incubator, Urban and the protagonist appear as twins, as two sides of the same coin.[54] In a fever-induced dream, the protagonist's body forces her to realize that Urban represents what could have become of her, had she given up her ideals for a party career, or had the seductive force of socialism's executive powers, particularly the Stasi, been stronger (136).

Yet the two socialists' reasons for collaboration with the intelligence agency differ significantly. The protagonist's motivation is explained by her idealistic desire for a future "Hoffnungs- und Menschheitsstadt" (136: city of hope and humanity; 93), which references the biblical "city on a hill" from the parable of salt and light in Jesus's sermon on the mount.[55] Employing Christian imagery, *Leibhaftig* refers to the unquestioned belief in the perfect socialist society to come and the promise of the socialist covenant we are familiar with from *Nachdenken über Christa T.* Opposite her, we observe Urban's increasing identification with the Stasi, an organization he views as a "brotherhood" that provides him with comforting security and justification: (136–37) the ideal place for somebody who lacked an actual family that could have provided emotional warmth in his formative years.

Despite their differences, both characters are deeply implicated in the GDR and its foundational structures. In her feverish dreams the patient recognizes Urban as her twin and antagonist (67, 180). Her final reflection presents him as "der neue Mephisto . . . Verführung nicht mit Unsterblichkeit, sondern mit Stillstand" (183: the new Mephisto . . . Seduction not with immortality but with immobility; 125).[56] Unlike this representative of real-existing socialism, who surrendered because he lost faith and knew about its inevitable demise, the protagonist insists on the validity of her socialist ideals for the future and claims a role that corresponds to Wolf's favored self-image: the morally superior position of the loyal dissident.[57] Committed to the antifascist society of the GDR, she necessarily kept her distance from the GDR regime. Enlightened by subjecting her body to the mind's reflections about her past in her feverish dreams, the protagonist can be rescued while Urban—driven by cowardice—chose death as "das sicherste Versteck" (180: the best hiding place; 123).[58] Urban represents those SED functionaries who committed suicide when they foresaw the GDR's end, a phenomenon studied by Grasshoff (*AD*, 237–45).

In this figure, the novel, then, integrates the most prevalent rationales for choosing death offered in suicide notes of SED functionaries and Stasi officers from 1989/90. According to Grashoff, they maintained that they lost courage when faced with GDR citizens' increasing resentment, or that they developed a pessimistic outlook on the future because they no longer felt needed. Others remained unequivocally committed to their socialist belief and consequently wanted their suicide to be understood as an altruistic act and sacrifice for the socialist cause. Grashoff found one common denominator in all explanations: for the party functionaries of this generation—typically born between 1926 and 1939—who had derived their self-esteem from their political engagement, the internal distress was apparently stronger than the external. For many, the world collapsed with the end of the GDR, in which they had believed and to which they had committed their entire lives (*AD*, 238, 240, 243).

Like these functionaries, Urban in *Leibhaftig* had little faith left in socialism. Within socialist belief, however, committing suicide from a lack of hope, like cowardice, stands diametrically opposed to the exemplary suffering of communists under fascist torture. This might explain why some SED functionaries explicitly wanted their suicide to be understood as a heroic, self-sacrificial death for the triumph of the communist idea, for "the cause." Unlike the protagonist in *Leibhaftig*, who is "purified" by her near-fatal disease and thereby defends her ideals, Urban turns away from the fight for the socialist idea because it would have been too laborious (180). This commentary on the so-called *Wende* suicides intervenes in post-unification historiography in multiple ways: it highlights a phenomenon that has largely been ignored and it allows for sympathetic insight into choices made by GDR citizens who had remained loyal to their beliefs. Moreover, the narrative points to the difference between committed members of a GDR regime that was coming to an end and the so-called "loyal dissidents," who kept their critical distance to the government and anticipated—or even actively campaigned for—the end of the regime and a continuation of the GDR.[59]

Healing the Symptomatic Body

By the end of the novel, the protagonist has moved beyond any subliminal desire to take her life. When she leaves her bed to walk slowly to the window and face the sunshine and the lake, the woman who had barely escaped death appears resurrected.[60] The final lines of the novel cite Ingeborg Bachmann's poem "Enigma": "Du sollst ja nicht weinen, sagst du. Das, sage ich, steht auch in einem Gedicht" (185: "But you mustn't cry," you say. "That," I say, "is in a poem, too"; 126). Bachmann's words allude to the choir of angels absolving the sinner of her wrongdoing in the "Armer Kinder Bettlerlied" (Poor Children's Beggar Song) from *Des Knaben Wunderhorn* (The Boy's Magic Horn), an anthology of German folk poems collected by romantic writers Achim von Arnim and Clemens Brentano. This reference further sustains the reading that, once again, we encounter a resurrected female Christ-figure. Stronger than Christa T., who died as a redeemer for the sins of the fascist past to make possible a positive socialist future, this martyr figure has been purified and detoxified, has paid for the sins of various terror regimes, and now associates herself with the victims of German fascism from her position of resurrection.[61]

Purified, the protagonist proclaims the doctrine of the symptomatic body—namely, that salvation lies in granting the body superiority and in relying on illness to permit the unconscious to speak. Once again, the body is the site of historical experience, and suppressed knowledge of the past resides, quite literally, in the flesh, where it is only accessible if one renounces conscious interference. The process in which the body engages takes place in the disorganized, difficult to access, confusing labyrinths that the patient seeks out in her fever-induced dreams. In *Erinnerungsräume*, Aleida Assmann insists that these unordered and inaccessible spaces metaphorically stand for processes of remembering—in contrast to structured, orderly realms like the one we see at the end of the novel. These latter spaces indicate the storing of memories, and the end of the unstructured process of acquiring memories (162). After the body has immersed itself in disorderly, often seemingly unmotivated images of torture, suffering, and pain—a scenario that Wolf had previously employed more sparingly—the patient in the end appears comfortable in a well-organized environment. She approaches a heightened understanding regarding individual as well as political history that grants her a sense of consistency as her healing process continues.

With Elaine Scarry and her notion of the inherently political body, we can read this body's pain and healing as emerging from a national crisis—that is, the demise of the GDR. By staging the struggles—which are indeed resolved—as embodied in the protagonist, the narrative stresses the presumed "materiality" of the socialist ideas underlying the state.

As a result, the endangered socialist values that form the foundation of the GDR—particularly the legitimizing discourse of antifascism, which presents a dominant subtext in *Leibhaftig*—are confirmed by means of embodiment; or, in Scarry's words, by "the sheer material factualness of the human body [that is] borrowed to lend that cultural construct the aura of 'realness' and 'certainty'" (*The Body In Pain*, 14). By staging a recovering body, the narrative emphasizes the defeat of the calamities that both the protagonist and the socialist state had to face. In the recuperating, albeit weakened symptomatic body, the narrative recreates a GDR body politic based on the socialist state's original norms and values. Far from a goodbye to the socialist ideas on which the GDR was founded, this novel insists on these very ideals and the position of the loyal dissident—even after German unification. The GDR body politic might have been seriously wounded, but only the official parts related to the regime, as embodied in Urban, have been excised. The critical intellectual simultaneously devoted to the idea of an antifascist GDR and to dissidence towards the regime lives on. In the twenty-first century, Wolf replaces her criticism of the GDR government by reproaching global capitalism.[62] This approach requires the loyal dissident to take a stance vis-à-vis all political, ideological, economic, and social power structures underlying the capitalist order, which are perceived as hurting the weakest members of capitalist societies. Intervening in contemporary politics determined by global problems, the critical intellectual lives on to claim agency in writing. This allows her to archive her version of the past for future generations.[63] Unlike hegemonic historiography striving for a conclusive narrative, however, the patient's embodied experience allows for a plurality of manifold, even contradictory subjectivities—and for a protagonist who is both a subject of and subject to the historical construction of history. Inscribed by the historical knowledge in her flesh which surfaces in her suffering, the patient simultaneously resists societal norms and values, confirms the GDR's founding narrative of antifascism, and claims her position as a loyal dissident. Yet she only begins to recover from the traumata linked to life in the GDR.[64] The actual healing process is brought to completion in Wolf's 2010 novel, *Stadt der Engel*.

In her last novel, Wolf approaches the topic largely omitted from *Leibhaftig*: her long-time surveillance by the Stasi, her fleeting Stasi collaboration in the 1950s and early 1960s, and the so-called *Literaturstreit* that reached its most vicious stage when the media inflated the author's connection to the Stasi.[65] In the 2010 novel, the protagonist—like Wolf, a resident research fellow at the Getty Institute in Los Angeles for nine months in 1992/93, which coincided with the height of the media attacks on her—confronts the two burning questions she elided in the 2002 narrative: Why had she ever cooperated with the Stasi? And how could she possibly have forgotten about that collaboration? While the symptomatic body plays a vital role in the protagonist's managing of the crisis, we become privy to numerous conversations in which she articulates her most recent traumata.

In these conversations with various friends, she reflects on her potential guilt, on possible reasons for suppressing the relevant memories, and on the effects the media attacks have had on her (178–87, 257–59). Irene Kacandes suggests that "since the infliction of trauma involves some inability to act, the taking of action by turning the unassimilated experience into a story, seems to promote healing" (*TF*, 92). In *Stadt der Engel*, we encounter a protagonist who devises a narrative which, unlike *Leibhaftig*, explicitly addresses the traumatic discovery of her experiences with the Stasi, and emphasizes narration as a form of healing. Like *Leibhaftig*, *Stadt der Engel* is a memory project that not only discloses the past, but also highlights remembering as a selective, incomplete, and unreliable process that cannot be controlled by the individual. Consequently, the 2010 novel does not offer a conclusive answer to the questions that bothered Wolf so much, rather the protagonist realizes that she does not need to find such answers. This appears to free and heal her when, supported by her personal angel as well as new friends she made in California, she finally accepts her own imperfections.

Conclusion

With *Stadt der Engel*, Wolf not only freed herself but also her successive protagonists from their endless struggle for and with their humanist, socialist ideals. In this 2010 novel, the protagonist overcomes her traumata, ranging from her childhood years in Nazi Germany to the disclosure of her Stasi files and West German media attacks in the narrative present. While *Leibhaftig* exclusively relied on physical disease to work through and express these disturbances in a corporeality that one might call the ultimate symptomatic body, the protagonist in *Stadt der Engel* articulates her sorrows through physical pain and increasingly verbalizes them. She overcomes her distress in narration and learns to forgive and love herself. In both novels as well as in Wolf's pre-unification oeuvre, illness offers a retreat from unpleasant situations: it indicates and expresses suppressed feelings, memories, and traumata which surface on the body; and it heralds imminent danger, but also valuable insight. Similarly, the protagonists in Wolf's oeuvre pre- and post-unification are aware that they cannot control the processes of remembering so crucial for their respective healing process, which means they must rely on their symptomatic bodies. Unlike Christa T., who could successfully utilize writing as a cure, the protagonists in *Leibhaftig* and in *Stadt der Engel* are skeptical about the power of words and rely on the language of their bodies to show them the way to awareness. However, the protagonist in *Stadt der Engel* finally overcomes her reluctance to trust language: after contemplating the suspension of note-taking for her novel, she realizes that she depends on writing as a cure: "Den Selbstversuch abbrechen, den es bedeutet, zu schreiben: sich selbst kennenlernen wollen, bis auf den Grund, dachte ich, hätte ähnliche Folgen wie der Abbruch einer lebenserhaltenden Therapie bei einer schweren Krankheit" (233: Breaking off the writing, and what the writing meant—the experiment on yourself, the desire to get to know yourself down to the bottom—that would have been like stopping a life-sustaining treatment in the throes of a serious disease; 176). Life comes to the fore as a serious disease that can only be mastered by writing about it; the physical novel *Stadt der Engel* attests to both the protagonist's and to Wolf's final self-acceptance after physical and psychological suffering, and to ultimate healing.

Underlined by the protagonists' identification with the victims of the Nazi regime in Wolf's post-unification novels, this newly gained self-confidence includes adhering to, indeed affirming those socialist—and specifically anti-capitalist—values that have been at the core of Wolf's entire literary and political project. The author and her oeuvre assert their politics in insisting on the supremacy of the humanist—some might call them utopian—ideals central to socialism as opposed to capitalism. The latter emerges as flawed due to its systemic inequality, structural modes of violence, and moral bankruptcy, which brings capitalist countries into frightening proximity to fascism. Able to forgive themselves as well as the GDR for their lack of perfection, Wolf's late protagonists claim a specific space in post-unification Germany, a speaking position announced by the book jacket of *Stadt der Engel*: "Du bist dabei gewesen. Du hast es überlebt. Du kannst davon berichten." (You were there. You survived it. You can tell about it.) With this statement, the book and its writer claim the history of the bygone socialist state and its demise as part of a unified German historiography, and the role of contemporary witness and historiographer for the author. In other words, the author continues to interpret her social position as an obligation to critically reflect on this world and to preserve the socialist values absent in quotidian life, now in post-unification Germany and the world characterized by global capitalism.

A significant contribution to GDR historiography, Wolf's narratives provide information about GDR medical institutions as she experienced them and which largely emerge as a microcosm of the society, its achievements as well as deficiencies. Taking on the role of historiographer and reclaiming her critical voice within the FRG by setting the record straight and insisting that East Germans and their experiences in the GDR and on the road to unification must be heard, Wolf repatriates herself in her own cultural and political realm. In this attempt to influence both German and global society by means of literature, Wolf remains a socially engaged, political writer.

Notes

[1] On parallels between the protagonist and Wolf, who was hospitalized in Schwerin in 1988, see Caspari, "Im Kern die Krisis," 135; Cosentino, "Aus Teufels Küche," 123; Scribner, "Von 'Leibhaftig' aus zurückblicken," 214; Tate, *Shifting Perspectives*, 224. On Wolf's alleged farewell to socialism, see Costabile-Heming, "Illness as Metaphor," 203; Kaute, "Sprachreflexion in Christa Wolf," 55; Koskinas, "*Fremd bin ich eingezogen*," 172–73.

[2] Brüns, "Leibhaftig," 154.

[3] Irene Kacandes, *Talk Fiction*, 91 (herafter cited as *TF*).

[4] Rechtien made this point for *Leibhaftig* in "From *Vergangenheitsbewältigung* to Living with Ghosts," 125; Brüns, "Leibhaftig," 147.

[5] In *Shifting Perspectives*, Tate demonstrates that *Christa T.*, *Kindheitsmuster*, and *Leibhaftig* portray the same self (224).

[6] Öhlschläger, "*Gender*/Körper, Gedächtnis und Literatur," 230, 242.

[7] Erll, "Literatur als Medium des kollektiven Gedächtnisses," 255.

[8] See Wagner, "Polikliniken—ein gesundheitspolitisches Modell," 235; Müller and Kahle, "Organisation der Materialwirtschaft im Krankenhaus."

[9] Mecklinger, *Zur Umsetzung der Gesundheitspolitik*, 17; Kowalczuk, *Die 101 wichtigsten Fragen*, 70. Several physicians quoted by Ahbe, Hofmann and Stiehler in *Redefreiheit* support this assessment (521, 529, 559).

[10] Hahn, "EF," 76–77; Baust, "Ethische Problemsituationen," 119.

[11] Berndt and Hüller, "Zur Gesellschaftsabhängigkeit des ärztlichen Eides," 42–44.

[12] Baust, "Ethische Problemsituationen," 118. Berlin-Buch's intensive-care unit was the first in Germany (including the FRG), and better equipped than the Charité, which explains why writers Maxie Wander and Brigitte Reimann sought breast-cancer treatment in Buch. Wander, *Tagebücher und Briefe*, 33; Reimann and Wolf, *Sei gegrüßt und lebe*.

[13] Baust, "Ethische Problemsituationen," 118–19; Bause and Matauschek, "Zum Stand der Medizintechnik in der DDR," 198.

[14] In *Ausgraben und Erinnern*, Wilke points to the increasing essentialism in Wolf's oeuvre regarding violence and gender (84–85, 164–65).

[15] Assmann, *Erinnerungsräume*, 245–46.

[16] I am providing my own translation here because the published English translations—"attacking those damned germs" (*In the Flesh*, 85) and "We're going to turn our big guns on them" (*Flesh* 79)—do not catch the aggressiveness and the military undertones of the German original. Similarly, the English translation omits the aspect of pleasure (*Leibhaftig*, 132; *In the Flesh*, 90).

[17] Verwijs and Schäfer in "Der kranke Leib" note the negative doctor-patient relationship, but do not consider GDR-specific circumstances (42).

[18] Berndt and Hüller, "Zur Gesellschaftsabhängigkeit des ärztlichen Eides," 45; Seifert, *GSV*, 162; Günther, "Patientenschutz," 167.

[19] Seifert, *GSV*, 35, 275, 279. Prophylactic measures were a significant factor in the GDR medical system. Ahbe, Hofmann and Stiehler in *Redefreiheit* quote Dieter Lohmann, the medical director of the city hospital in Leipzig, who received strong applause from the citizens present when he demanded the abolition of routine screening measures in times of monetary scarcity in 1989 (527).

[20] Berndt, "Gedanken zum Inhalt," 4.

[21] Correspondingly, Wagner in "Polikliniken—ein gesundheitspolitisches Modell" relays that after the fall of the Wall, patients reported grievances in the GDR healthcare system, particularly the hierarchical, undemocratic relationship between doctors and patients (234). In "Krebs und Gesellschaft" Wolf criticizes the "gentle lie" referencing Maxie Wander's experiences (121).

[22] *Ein Tag im Jahr* and *Leibhaftig* contradict Hahn's claim that the "gentle lie" ended in the 1970s, and question Berndt's and Günther's justification for the practice of the "gentle lie," namely, concern that the truth could shorten lives. Hahn, "EF," 78; Günther, "Das Arztrecht in der DDR," 89; Berndt, "Gedanken zum Inhalt der Vorträge des Kolloquiums 'Ethik und Medizin im Sozialismus'."

[23] Hahn, "EF," 80–82, 84, 74; Festge, "Ethische Positionen," 97; Schleiermacher and Schagen, "Rekonstruktion und Innovation (1949–1961)," 230; Seifert, *GSV*, 60–61. Several physicians quoted in *Redefreiheit*, edited by Ahbe, Hofmann and Stiehler, demanded more respect, social prestige, a medical association exclusively dedicated to the interests of physicians, and higher salaries for MDs in the fall of 1989 (508–11, 522). Großbölting, "Entbürgerlichte die DDR?" and Jessen, "'Bildungsbürger', 'Experten', 'Intelligenz'" analyze the ambiguous situation with regards to bourgeois traditions among the general population as well as medical professionals. It corresponds with the nostalgia for cultural privilege and the simultaneous disintegration of bourgeois traditions in the GDR since the 1960s.

[24] The artificial dichotomies developed by early religions—God/devil, heaven/hell, and angel/devil—and which cause humans to separate their behavior and thoughts into the binary opposition good/bad, becomes the subject of several conversations in which Wolf's *Doppelgänger* narrator engages in *Stadt der Engel* (327).

[25] Wolf misquotes Goethe's *Faust: Erster Teil (Part I)*, 1335–36: "[Ich bin] ein Teil von jener Kraft, Die stets das Böse will und stets das Gute schafft" (47: [I am] part of that power which would / Do evil constantly and constantly does good; 42). The German "Führte der Weg ins Paradies unvermeidlich in die Hölle?" should be translated into "Did the way to paradise lead unavoidably to hell?"

[26] *Störfall*, 37. In "Glauben an Irdisches," Wolf reflects on Anna Seghers' oeuvre and asks, "Was könnte einen neuen Faust bestimmen, sich noch einmal—zum letzten Mal—dem Teufel zu verschreiben?" (What could lead a new Faust to once again—for the last time—commit to the devil?; 316).

[27] American intelligence agencies are associated with organized crime as well as fascist thought and language (176–77, 215–17, 241, 267, 275, 375).

[28] *Stadt der Engel* discusses the idea that capitalism will fail (108, 127), and the failure of socialism (289, 337).

[29] Schwarz and Wilde, "'Und doch, und doch . . .'" state that the traumatic experience of 1989/90 did not cause Wolf to break with her utopian ideals, but to separate them from the GDR (237–38, 243).

[30] Linking Kora Bachmann with Persephone and Ingeborg Bachmann, the narrative connects *Leibhaftig* with *Christa T.*, since the German phrase "beziehungsreicher Name" (a name rich in associations) is a direct quote from *Nachdenken über Christa T.*

[31] King James Bible, Daniel 10:5–7.

[32] In "Of Trauma, Angels and Healing," Kuhn describes how "Angelina serves as a spiritual midwife, allowing the narrator's latent wisdom to emerge" (180). In *Ein Tag im Jahr*, Wolf introduces the neologism "Geistkörperseele" (484: the unity of mind, body, and soul; 480).

[33] Brussig's protagonist Klaus in *Helden wie wir* (1995; *Heroes like us*, 1996) is born on the day the Warsaw Pact troops marched into Prague, thus associating his negative hero with the absence of the humanist ideals the GDR claimed.

[34] In "Unerledigte Widersprüche," Wolf explains her generation's desire to replace parents guilty of collaboration with the Nazis with representatives of the resistance: she found them in the GDR writers' association and particularly in Anna Seghers. Wolf characterizes these constructed father-son and mother-daughter relationships as unhealthy dependencies, since the authority of the parental figures and the GDR's political path could never be questioned (29–30).

[35] In "Unerledigte Widersprüche," Wolf explains that feelings such as sadness could not be expressed in the GDR in the 1950s and 1960s (27). The mother's deathbed situation is replicated in *Stadt der Engel* (113), while dreams that reference the mother (100–101) echo Wolf's pre-unification works, especially *Kindheitsmuster*. In *Stadt der Engel*, the protagonist can finally mourn her grandmother, too, who starved during the flight to the West in 1945 (405–6).

[36] Her mother's death set off Wolf's depression in 1968. See Magenau, *Christa Wolf*, 210; Wolf, *Ein Tag im Jahr*, 111. In "Fortgesetzter Versuch" (Continued Attempt), Wolf expresses her gratitude for Seghers, yet also estrangement (344).

[37] On the body in Wolf's oeuvre as passage between the unconscious and history see Weigel, *Bilder des kulturellen Gedächtnisses*, 6.

[38] Assmann, *Erinnerungsräume*, 246.

[39] Similarly, the narrator in *Kindheitsmuster* compares the work of remembering to that of a paleontologist; and in *Stadt der Engel*, Freud and the significance of uncovering layers of memory are already suggested by the subtitle.

[40] Alluding to E. T. A. Hoffmann's *Die Bergwerke zu Falun* (*The Mines of Falun*, 1819), the mines underline the romantic notion of illness also apparent in *Nachdenken über Christa T.* In *Leibhaftig*, the various images of depth take on different shades of meaning: in addition to the body as a mine, we observe the patient believing that she accesses Hades (56) and finding her way through the basement labyrinths of the hospital (50), of her apartment building (107–8), and of the subway station Friedrichstraße (25). In *Stadt der Engel*, the protagonist fears that the public represented by the newspapers might ask her to descend again into

"den Schacht" (35: that well; 23) again. Thus insinuating *Leibhaftig*, she rejects a repetition of the traumatic experiences.

[41] See for example *Ein Tag im Jahr*, 403; *Stadt der Engel*, 234. Given the reference to Ingeborg Bachmann, *Leibhaftig* can be read as the East German extension of Bachmann's 1965 essay *Ein Ort für Zufälle* (A Place for Coincidences), in which West Berlin is depicted as a traumatized city in decline. See Rechtien, "From *Vergangenheitsbewältigung* to Living with Ghosts," 140; Webber, *Berlin in the Twentieth Century*, 49.

[42] See Wolf, *Ein Tag im Jahr*, 618. Here, she also mentions the inspiration for the leitmotif of the labyrinth as hell, Jay Parini's novel *Benjamin's Crossing* (617–18). Labyrinths are also significant in *Kindheitsmuster*, *Medea*, and in *Stadt der Engel*. See Boa, "Labyrinths, Mazes, and Mosaics," 134–37; Gallagher, "Problem of Shame," 393–94.

[43] Boa, "Labyrinths, Mazes, and Mosaics," 147.

[44] For the protagonist, American society's state of disease manifests itself in class differences (49, 118, 302), racism and poverty that lead to illness (47, 68, 107–8, 153, 164–65, 169, 191, 241, 246–48, 276, 309, 336, 341–42), censorship (291), conformity (78, 312), war mongers in the White House (79, 142–43), the death penalty (26, 69, 170), and Americans taking pride in their nuclear bombs (377).

[45] The references to wars started by the USA link *Stadt der Engel* with *Kindheitsmuster*, which criticized capitalism, the Vietnam War, the Watergate scandal, and the Pinochet military coup in Chile.

[46] On the protagonist's association with the emigrants, see 41, 206–9, 303–4, 337–40, 343–50. On her admiration as well as the physical pain she experiences due to the impossibility to engage in controversies with that generation, see 111, 140, 160–61, 188, 316. If we remember Wolf's declaration that her generation had no right to identify with the victims of and those resisting to National Socialist rule in "Unerledigte Widersprüche," quoted in the previous chapter, this growing identification in her latest novels is all the more notable.

[47] Bircken, "Lesen und Schreiben als körperliche Erfahrung," considers Emma a fictionalized Anna Seghers (207, 212). Haase, "Christa Wolfs letzter 'Selbstversuch,'" sees communists like Berta Waterstradt and Anna Schlotterbeck merged in this character (223).

[48] This statement echoes Wolf's early criticism of West German attempts to come to terms with the past, which she voiced in "Subjektive Authentizität" (785).

[49] On the authoritarian personality, see Fromm, "Sozialpsychologischer Teil," 77–135; Schaumann, *Memory Matters*, 78–80; Tate, *Shifting Perspectives*, 213. My reading corresponds with Rechtien, "From *Vergangenheitsbewältigung* to Living with Ghosts," 133. Paul, "'Aber erzählen läßt sich nichts ohne Zeit'," relates the intoxication to the GDR (119).

[50] Bridge, *Women's Writing and Historiography*, 59.

[51] Seifert, *GSV*, 61, 261; Kirchgäßner, "Philosophische Aspekte des Arzt-Patienten-Verhältnisses," 21.

⁵² Hans Koch (1927–1986) personified the perfect GDR career: from officer of the Freie Deutsche Jugend (Free German Youth) and an academic position in the SED's Institute for Social Sciences at the Central Committee of the Socialist Unity Party, the country's most important think tank, to member of the GDR Parliament and posts in the Writer's Union, the Ministry of Culture, the Central Committee, and finally in the politburo. Müller-Engbergs, *Wer war wer in der DDR?*, 445–46.

⁵³ Throughout the narrative, the protagonist contemplates their relationship (42–43, 71, 123–24).

⁵⁴ Caspari also notes the similarities between the protagonist and Urban ("Im Kern die Krisis," 136). Meyer-Gosau considers the two to be hostile socialist siblings ("Den Staat im Leibe," 85).

⁵⁵ In Matthew 5:14, Jesus tells his listeners, "You are the light of the world. A city that is set on a hill cannot be hidden."

⁵⁶ In "Aus Teufel's Küche," Cosentino reads this constellation as the divide between stagnating real-existing socialism and the belief to own utopia (123).

⁵⁷ In "Pleasures of Fear," Pinkert proved this point with the example of Wolf's *Kindheitsmuster* (25–26, 34). See Wolf, *Im Dialog*, 75.

⁵⁸ See Costabile-Heming, "Illness as Metaphor," 214.

⁵⁹ Tate critically notes that the "problem inherent in this [Wolf's] allegorical way of presenting the conflict between GDR intellectuals and 'authority' is not just that it effectively absolves the narrator of responsibility for what went wrong, but also that it leaves a mystery surrounding the identity of the forces actually determining the course of events, by presenting Urban as a pawn in an even more sinister game" (*Shifting Perspective*, 234).

⁶⁰ Both Kurz and Meyer-Gosau read this scene as a resurrection (Kurz, "Besprechung," 357; Meyer-Gosau, "Den Staat im Leibe," 85).

⁶¹ *Leibhaftig* stresses the detoxification, purification, and purgation achieved by the fevers and the pain (93). Wolf's story "Nagelprobe" (1994; "Trial by Nail," 1997) supports this reading. Written in 1991, it stages the first-person narrator as a female Christ figure, who seems resurrected at the end of *Leibhaftig*: "Prinzip Hoffnung. Genagelt ans Kreuz Vergangenheit. Jede Bewegung treibt die Nägel ins Fleisch" (169: The Principle of Hope. Nailed to the cross the Past. Every movement drives the nails into the flesh; 135).

⁶² See Costabile-Heming, "Illness as Metaphor," 216.

⁶³ Rechtien argues that *Leibhaftig*, by portraying the GDR "as a concrete place that was home to its citizens," ensures that "its loss is declared the subject of mourning" ("From *Vergangenheitsbewältigung* to Living with Ghosts," 125).

⁶⁴ Costabile-Heming also insists that at the conclusion of the novel, "the protagonist remains a patient" ("Illness as Metaphor," 215).

⁶⁵ On Wolf's collaboration with the Stasi between 1959 and 1962, see Vinke, *Akteneinsicht Christa Wolf*.

3: Retrospective Imagination in Post-GDR Literature: Gender, Violence, and Politics in Medical Discourses

As THE PRECEDING CHAPTERS HAVE SHOWN, medical discourses and symptomatic bodies dominate Christa Wolf's oeuvre. Often mimicking the GDR author's style, East German literature published since unification conspicuously employs these strategies to deal with the GDR and its collapse from a historical distance. This tendency toward historicization is prevalent in the novels examined in this chapter: Kathrin Schmidt's *Die Gunnar-Lennefsen-Expedition*, Thomas Brussig's *Wie es leuchtet*, and Kerstin Hensel's *Lärchenau*. All three highlight the everyday life of fictional characters from different paths of GDR life by presenting symptomatic bodies and portraying medical institutions. Yet these novels do more than portray the GDR: they interlace various historical phases in twentieth-century German history through medical discourses. Specifically, they establish trajectories from Germany's fascist past, extending at times even as far back as the nineteenth century, to the GDR and post-unification Germany. Placing the GDR and its demise within larger historical discourses and creating a diverse image of the country by means of the novels' characters, these narratives effectively complement collective memory. To this end, they reconstruct GDR history, and, if necessary, rectify the collective memory archive.

Collecting, storing, and communicating alternative images of the GDR and its decline, they continue two important characteristics of critical GDR prose fiction: they introduce socially relevant discourses and they defy expectations that literature should provide a specific, supposedly "true" interpretation of history which contributes to hegemonic discourses of the past. The predominantly auctorial style of narration in all three novels foregrounds the desire to participate in society and to represent a variety of age groups and their specific GDR life experiences. Here they differ from Christa Wolf's characteristic use of the first person in the service of subjective authenticity, while radicalizing her claim to speak for an entire generation, as she expressed it in "Unerledigte Widersprüche" (29). Brussig, Hensel, and Schmidt populate their imaginative novels with a broad spectrum of characters who belong to various social backgrounds, ages, and, in some cases, ethnic and sexual minorities. The majority are from the East, and they are always juxtaposed with

West Germans. In this narrative contrast, they play with the notions of the abject, for example, by aligning the dichotomy East/West German with female/male, only to undermine it; or by claiming the validity of East German subject formation by insisting on the appeal of values such as solidarity over individualism.

This narrative constellation signals a focus on the East German experience that is typically underrepresented in hegemonic historiography. Brussig's novel asserts this emphasis when a photographer explains the significance of the unfolding narrative about the events of August 1989 to August 1990. Much like Erich Maria Remarque's *Im Westen nichts Neues* (1929; *All Quiet on the Western Front*, 1929) which assembled the experiences of soldiers at the front during World War I, *Wie es leuchtet* claims to provide an archive of the experiences of the last months of the GDR, equally valid for everyone (13). While similarly including a great variety of subject positions, Schmidt's novel *Die Gunnar-Lennefsen-Expedition*, unlike Brussig's *Wie es leuchtet*, does not include easily recognizable public figures. Instead, Schmidt's narrative explains the purpose of its imaginary journey and the resulting expedition diary as "Grabpflege ... für die, die im Fischzug der Geschichte wegen vermeintlichen Mangels an Größe durch die Maschen des Netzes gerutscht waren" (grave care ... for those, who during history's fishing expedition had slipped through the net due to alleged lack of greatness; 68). In other words, this expedition sets out to include those who are often marginalized—specifically based on gender, sexuality, or class. While Hensel's *Lärchenau* does not state an intention to contribute to historiography, the myriad of characters in the novel present a panoramic representation of society. Therefore, they all—albeit not as explicitly as Brussig—continue Wolf's agenda: fictional stories as alternative histories written into the often damaged flesh of a novel's characters.

In post-GDR fiction, we find a conspicuous number of symptomatic bodies. These bodies—of protagonists as well as of minor characters who sometimes serve as "counter figures" in larger narrative constellations—take on a wide variety of shapes and serve manifold purposes. They include pregnant women as well as individuals declared "mad" for political reasons. Representatives of these two groups are required to submit to the mandates imposed by medical institutions, where some of them can muster their bodies for opposition, while others become victims of the medical profession and the Stasi. Still others unknowingly become subjects in experiments conducted on human beings—both inside and outside of hospitals, but always performed by physicians. We observe characters who resist the gender binary, some of whom exercise resistance through their bodies, while others' failures signal a country in distress during the transformation processes of 1989/90. Several symptomatic bodies are directly linked to radical changes associated with the fall of the

Wall, and to the impossibility of facing—both physically and metaphorically—everyday life after November 9, 1989, with GDR eyes.

"We Germans are now the happiest people in the world!"[1]

In the character of Sabine Busse, Brussig's *Wie es leuchtet* draws on the topos of blindness. Perfectly capable of living independently in the GDR, the woman realizes that since November 10, 1989—the day after the fall of the Wall—loss of sight is deemed an illness (527). Eager to partake in this new, visual, and complex world, Sabine consents to eye surgery performed by the West German Dr. Sternhagen (337). The doctor's brother, journalist Leo Lattke, is desperately looking for a good story and for this reason the doctor agrees to grant him exclusive access to the story.[2] Daydreaming about the success of his feature and his future, Leo Lattke reveals his anticipation:

> Wenn er beschreiben kann, wie jemandem zum ersten Mal im Leben die Binde von den Augen genommen wird, dann wird er die Gefühle beschreiben, die die Nation mit sich erlebte—das märchenhafte Ende eines unnatürlichen Zustandes . . . Der Blinde sollte aus dem Osten sein, und er sollte schon immer . . . blind sein. In dieser Story ist alles drin . . .: Ost-West, Mangelwirtschaft, geraubtes Leben, Neubeginn . . . Blindheit als Metapher für ein Leben hinter der Mauer. (347)

> [When he can describe how the blindfolds are removed from somebody's eyes for the first time, then he will describe the very feelings that the nation experienced with itself—the fairy-tale end of an unnatural condition . . . The blind man had to be from the East, and he should have been blind always . . . This story has everything . . .: East-West, economy of scarcity, robbed life, new beginnings . . . Blindness as metaphor for a life behind the Wall.]

In his unsophisticated reverie, Lattke imagines himself and his brother as saviors, redeeming East Germans from their actual and metaphorical blindness, a blindness caused by the prison and darkness of the Wall that held half a nation in bondage: an "unnatural condition" resolved by the "natural" course of history that leads to unification thanks to West German saviors. The anticipated, newly gained eyesight will allow the East German man to finally see the "right," superior political system; it will manifest the West German notion of the so-called *Wende* as the historical moment marking the anticipated failure of socialism. Overcoming the blindness he was born with—in other words, GDR-socialized from the beginning—the man would end his miserable existence, his metaphorical "castration" by socialism.³ He would be turned into a seeing, potent man who would adjust to capitalist society and be "the happiest man in the world"—the title of the feature Lattke has composed in advance. The person who can fit Lattke's profile needs to be fabricated—both physically by surgery and as a founding myth for the new German republic in West German news reports such as Lattke's. An artificial creation, this man serves as living proof of Berlin mayor Walter Momper's proclamation of November 10, 1989, that "we Germans are now the happiest people in the world."

The fictitiousness of this supposedly "natural" historical development indicates the problematic outcome of the scheme. When Lattke learns that his protagonist is actually a woman, his plans are initially frustrated, but Sabine is quickly utilized to highlight the feminization of East Germans and East Germany (381). The timing highlights her allegorical function, since Sabine physically gains her eyesight in March 1990, the month of the first free elections in the GDR. These elections resulted in the success of conservative parties, which paved the way for German unification, and the defeat of the civil-rights activists who had campaigned for free elections: the *Neues Forum* (New Forum) and various other groups who jointly formed the *Bündnis 90* (Alliance 90) in hopes for a humane socialism.⁴ Drunk with happiness like the German nation in November 1989, Sabine—in Lattke's report—echoes the words she recalls from that fall: "*Wahnsinn! ... So ein Tag, so wunderschön wie heute*" (*Madness! ... Such a day, so wonderful as today!*; 530; italics in original). Yet quickly, her eyes turn out to be incapable of taking in the flood of new information: they see everything, but they do not recognize anything (532). Three weeks after the surgery, Sabine's world is still turned upside down (533), and she is more blind than she had ever been (537).

Sabine's story implicitly alludes to a speech delivered by author Monika Maron at a 2002 historians' conference, reprinted in the *Süddeutsche Zeitung*. Maron referenced neuroscientist Wolf Singer's 2000 report about patients who had successfully undergone surgery but whose eyesight was impaired by neurological issues. Unable to process information, they became depressed and, donning dark glasses, retreated into a blind person's life as a way of coming to terms with the irreversible condition. Maron interpreted Singer's depiction as an allegory of disorders she perceives in East Germans: not accustomed to employing certain senses and abilities, they could not activate them now, so they blamed their enablers—that is, the West—for their deficit, and retreated into GDR nostalgia.⁵ In addition to this neuroscientific interpretation of blindness, *Wie es leuchtet* allows for the conclusion that Sabine's blindness could derive from her lack of a quasi-religious belief in the capitalist system (338). Reversing Jesus's success stories in which healing blindness depends on the blind person's belief, Sabine fails to gain her vision because she lacks faith in liberal democracy and capitalism.[6] Socialized in the GDR, her eyes resist the temptations of the West. They further raise a crucial question that has been discussed since the Enlightenment: is seeing an inborn physical-optical ability or an acquired cognitive-mental process based on experience?[7] Sabine's symptomatic body provides the insight that her perception of the world is culturally determined, yet that culture has disappeared with her country, and she cannot return to her former state of innocence. Her greatest wish ten weeks after the surgery is to be able to retreat from this new state which leaves her feeling confused and physically violated (537).

Sabine represents an uncanny reminder of one of Christa Wolf's protagonists. Referring to the tension between terror-inducing control and comfortable security provided by the GDR government, Wolf's Kassandra confesses that she has always granted herself periods of partial blindness. In fact, she emphasizes that, had she acquired sight all of a sudden, it would have destroyed her (48). Unlike Kassandra, Sabine gave in to the West's temptations and gained her eyesight precipitately—which ruined her. Building on the symbolic meaning Wolf assigned to her seer Kassandra, Sabine appears as a cautioning prophetess who—albeit in different ways than imagined by Lattke—represents the damaged GDR. Her symptomatic body, capable in socialism but not in capitalism and violated within the historical process, serves as a bearer of cultural memory and emerges as both medium and effect of the historical operations that produced it. Her body's performance reflects one more character's realization that she will never belong (543). Such characters demonstrate how the radical changes associated with 1989/90 left East Germans on the verge of collapse—and in a country where they would always be the abject. The feeling of not belonging and the abjection of the East are underlined when Leo Lattke's magazine rejects his report because Sabine's story, which is at the center of it, does not correspond to the normative discourse of joy and euphoria established by West German media for celebrating the incorporation of the East. Sabine's actual experience of unification and her body remain abjected in post-unification Germany.

Medicine as Social Agency against Women: Comparing the GDR and the FRG

In Schmidt's *Die Gunnar-Lennefsen-Expedition*, the protagonist's pregnancy is central to the narrative, not least of all because it prompts the eponymous journey. The complex novel, which stylistically evokes magical realism, ironically visualizes the GDR of the 1970s from a perspective informed by post-1989 politics. The plot revolves around Josepha

Schlupfburg, a 21-year old print worker in a small town in Thuringia. She possesses supernatural powers and is pregnant with Shugderdemydin, the so-called "black-and-white child" whose Angolan father is absent, as are most other fathers in the novel. This boy challenges the racist German primacy of blood as the defining factor for nationality and citizenship with his very body, since his ethnic German, Jewish, and African heritages do not blend, but become visible in black and white "blotches" on his skin and defy any racial classification.[8] Her pregnancy impels Josepha, orphaned herself and raised by her great-grandmother Therese, to explore her family history. Aiming to rewrite history for her son from the kind of subject position typically excluded from hegemonic historiography, Josepha decides to join Therese in embarking on an expedition to an unknown destination in both space and time (19).[9] They can remain in their living room since they use a fantastic means of transportation, the so-called imaginary screen, to travel back in time (27). Both the screen—a kind of historical cinema designed to display history—and the expedition diary in which they record the new history mock conventional historiography and challenge hegemonic notions of gender, race, and class.

Josepha's symptomatic body is positively affected by her pregnancy. She becomes more energetic, develops a "tattoo" on her thigh that visualizes the historical knowledge she gains, and a fissure on her skin that signals her increasing awareness of instances of political and social injustice. This includes problems she anticipates for her son as a child born out of wedlock who challenges traditional notions of both race and family. Yet the state's definition of pregnancy as a condition that requires monitoring by medical institutions subjects both the woman's body and her child to state interference and regulation. In contrast to Luce Irigaray, though, who asserts that "maternity supplants the deficiencies of repressed female sexuality," the *Gunnar-Lennefsen-Expedition* assigns the female reproductive organs preeminent strength.[10] Inspired by the physical changes brought about by her pregnancy, Josepha feels motivated to challenge conventional, so-called universal approaches to gaining knowledge. Since scientific support for her expedition in the form of Freud's works is unavailable in the GDR, she spontaneously replaces psychoanalysis with a bottle of cognac (18).[11] Josepha's unique method of acquiring a new kind of historical knowledge humorously reveals that the approaches for attaining, storing, and conveying information are socially constructed as a conventional norm (36).

Both the expedition diary Josepha keeps and her pregnant body are visual representations of the historical learning process. Josepha's physique is turned into a mnemonic site when her so-called "mütterliche Linie" (maternal line; 94), painfully tattooed into her skin and reminiscent of a Freudian *Dauerspur* (permanent trace) that stands for the unconscious acquisition of cultural memory, increasingly shines out from beneath the subcutaneous layer of her skin (107, 114).[12] Even more painfully than in Wolf's *Leibhaftig*, history—configured here as genealogy—is inscribed into the flesh. Reminiscent of Michel Foucault, who insists in "Nietzsche, Genealogy, History" that "descent attaches itself to the body . . . [which] manifests the stigmata of past experience," the body is displayed as produced by a variety of regimes beyond the individual's control (356). While Josepha acquires new knowledge, her body changes continually; its inscription remains in a dynamics of constant re-signification. The body records Josepha's increased awareness of the interaction of power and knowledge, which produces, regulates, and disciplines both her flesh and the body politic. At the same time, her ongoing physical transformation highlights that the new history, too, can only approximate historical truth by offering a variety of subject positions. Literally turned into a site of historiography, the embodied "motherly line" epitomizes the intricate ways in which the biological and the historical are tied to one another.[13]

Another physical inscription depends on the fetus and points to the baby's future. Induced by blending the "Eiblick" (fetus's gaze) with the mother's "Einblick" (insight; 302), Josepha develops an increasingly large and painful "haarfeinen Spalt [in ihrer] bis dahin erstaunlichen Panzerung gegen physische und psychische Übergriffe" (fine split [in her] previously astonishing armored protection against physical and psychic assault; 98). The split in Josepha's body comes to the fore as a fissure in both skin and conscience (98). Concerning her intellect and her emotion alike, it elevates her social and intellectual awareness and sustains the superiority of the pregnant body, which can expose the oppressiveness of the petit-bourgeois town and the state authorities' exercise of power in the GDR (115). The split parodies the logocentrism of Western intellectual thought and ascribes to the female sex supremacy because of its ability to reproduce. While this narrative strategy remains in the traditional male/female binary, the signs indicating inherent preeminence are reversed, and pregnancy now appears as an ironic citation of hegemonic phallogocentric domination. When the pregnant woman's belly replaces the phallus, the narrative establishes a new economy that is devoid of male hegemony and presents femininity outside of the sexual difference traditionally identified as the lack of the phallus.

The split is complemented by the fetus's encouraging kicks (311), which inspire Josepha to make recalcitrant speeches in which she criticizes Stasi spying methods and incites her co-workers to rebellion, resulting in repercussions from the intelligence service.[14] The narrative insinuates that the gynecologist breached doctor-patient confidentiality when she informed Josepha's brigade about the pregnancy (98) and notified the Stasi about her refusal to subject herself to regular examinations and to disclose the father's identity (37–39, 121). The latter offense challenges both the GDR's definition as a nation through bloodlines and the institution of the family—sufficient reason to involve the secret service.[15] Collaboration between the Stasi and physicians, usually as IMs (*Inoffizielle Mitarbeiter*; Unofficial Informers), was not uncommon in the GDR. According to Sonja Süß, about three to five percent of GDR physicians acted as IMs, and the vast majority was recruited after 1970 (*Pm*, 273). Francesa Weil, whose study *Zielgruppe Ärzteschaft* (Target Audience Physicians) is based on nearly five hundred Stasi files and interviews, points out that these numbers indicate that the average number of IMs among physicians exceeded that among the general population at about one percent in 1989 (20). These high numbers point to both the significance the Stasi assigned the medical profession and the physicians' willingness to collaborate, which they largely did out of political conviction.[16]

The number of female IMs among medical professionals (fifteen percent of all IMs in the medical field) correlates with that of the general population and is therefore rather low (Weil, *Zielgruppe Ärzteschaft*, 39). In "Ärzte als inoffizielle Mitarbeiter" (Doctors as Unofficial Informers), Weil explained that IMs primarily spied on their colleagues (77%), particularly those they suspected of planning to leave the GDR; 27% passed on information about FRG citizens; and 24–25% imparted knowledge about their patients (A1594). This seems to signal a breach of doctor-patient confidentiality, even according to GDR law. Both the GDR and the FRG reformed the old §300 *Strafgesetzbuch* in 1968, which led to §136 StGB-DDR in the GDR and §203 StGB-BRD in the FRG. GDR and FRG law differed with regards to the intended penalty in cases of a breach of trust by lawyers, doctors, dentists, psychologists, midwives, and pharmacists: FRG law stipulated up to a year of imprisonment, while GDR law considered the threat of punishment with a conviction on probation, a fine, or a denunciation sufficient. However, GDR physicians' obligation to report a crime extended to political offenses such as treasonous demagoguery (§106,2 StGB-DDR), treasonous human trafficking (§105 StGB-DDR), or the preparation of unlawful border crossings (§213,3 StGB-DDR). Failing to report the plan, preparation, or implementation of these "crimes" could, according to §225 StGB-DDR, lead to imprisonment for up to ten years.[17] The legal situation could therefore cause conflicts if patients informed their physicians about plans to illegally protest the government or leave the country. However, the law did not warrant IMs' breaching of doctor-patient confidentiality, and no order issued by the Ministry for State Security has been found to suggest that physicians were asked to spy on their patients. Sonja Süß, for example, emphasizes this indicates that the Stasi was aware of the illegality of their unofficial inquiries about patients (*Pm*, 263). Yet at least 25% of IMs in medical institutions conspiratorially disregarded GDR law and conveyed information pertaining to diagnosis, therapy, or their patients' personalities or social problems. Internists, surgeons, general practitioners, psychiatrists, dentists, sport medicine specialists, and *Chefärzte* (head physicians) outnumbered clinicians in the lower ranks. Next to the dominance of male over female informants, the high number of medical students among the IMs is striking.[18]

Indeed, the situation was even more complex, and *Die Gunnar-Lennefsen-Expedition* engages with its full scope. In the GDR, physicians were not simply "doctors in socialism" but "socialist doctors" (Seifert, *GSV*, 40, 363–456). Required to think and act in socialist categories, they had to accept the close proximity of the state's medical system and its intelligence agency. Due to this cooperation, the right to doctor-patient confidentiality was suspended by statutory obligations to notify the authorities in cases of cancer, epidemic diseases, and suspicion of crimes—a constraint on confidentiality that was apparently not understood by the majority of the population.[19] In *Die Gunnar-Lennefsen-Expedition*, Josepha first learns about the limits of doctor-patient confidentiality when she refuses to disclose what she considers private information: the Stasi begins interfering in her life when she insists on keeping the identity of her son's father a secret. When Josepha contests hegemonic concepts of race and kinship, the literary text alludes to controversial discussions about notions of family that extend beyond the GDR. In contrast to the FRG, where children born out of wedlock were legally disadvantaged even in the 1990s, the GDR supported single mothers.[20] Despite a preference for socialist families, which were considered one of "the building blocks of the socialist future," the GDR *Familiengesetzbuch* (Family Law) of 1965 relaxed the divorce law.[21] In concert with women's increasing employment rates, this led to their greater independence and altered notions of marriage and family. New laws passed in 1972, in particular the support for single mothers and the legalization of abortion which lowered maternal mortality rates, reflect the GDR's progressive attitude.[22] These effects emerge in *Die Gunnar-Lennefsen-Expedition*; for example, when the doctor informs Josepha that she still has sufficient time to decide whether she wants to live by herself (38). After unification, women from the former GDR lost support for single motherhood as well as access to abortion, unless it was deemed necessary for specific medical, ethical, social, or eugenic reasons. At the same time they were disproportionately affected by high unemployment rates in East Germany.[23] *Die Gunnar-Lennefsen-Expedition* therefore portrays life in the GDR in 1976 while at the same time critically commenting on post-unification Germany.

Given the legal status of single women in the GDR, Josepha's problems are more likely to arise from her reluctance to participate in preventive measures and to disclose information she deems private than from her rejection of the socialist family. Since the notion of privacy receded in the socialist healthcare system, which considered individual health within the societal context, pregnant mothers were socially obligated to care for their unborn baby's health.[24] Moreover, due to the reciprocal relationship of rights and obligations in a socialist legal framework, basic rights do not extend to individual protective rights vis-à-vis the state. In the world of *Die Gunnar-Lennefsen-Expedition*, Josepha's insistence on individual choice presents a case of treasonous demagoguery and renders her an object of surveillance by several state institutions, including healthcare providers, the legal system, and the Stasi. The latter threatens to place her in the "care" of psychiatrists, justified by her alleged inability to raise a child (352). Based on the state's interest in the health of the following generation, the Stasi recruits Carmen Salzwedel, Josepha's best friend, as an IM to spy on her (363, 365).[25] Justifying their interference with concern for the well-being of the child, the Stasi emphasizes that the medical institution's and the state's interests coincide. In the GDR, the health of children and teenagers was systematically monitored from birth to their eighteenth birthday. The first three years of health examinations took place at the *Mütterberatungsstelle* (institution for the counseling of mothers), and this is the institution Josepha visits to receive her official documents. Social welfare workers checked on families of newborns and small children regularly to guarantee the general well-being of the young GDR citizens.[26]

While there was no statutory obligation to participate in these programs, expectant mothers were de facto forced to partake because the *Mütterberatungsstelle* distributed the state subsidy for the expected child (Seifert, *GSV*, 276). Located at the intersection of the medical and the legal realm, welfare for pregnant women depended on the individual's submitting to various state institutions—a situation reflected in the *Gunnar-Lennefsen-Expedition*. In accordance with GDR law, Josepha receives the first installment of money for her child only after she agrees to the first of several examinations—in the last trimester of her pregnancy, which the doctor interprets as the successful adaptation of the patient she considers recalcitrant (257–58).[27] For Josepha, her subjection to the regulating measures built into the GDR healthcare system means defeat, as her fantasies about the Stasi closing her file reveals. She imagines a memo saying, "'Objekt hat feindlich-negative Handlungen schlußendlich aufgegeben' oder 'Objekt distanziert sich in verabredeter Weise'" ("object ultimately gave up adversely-negative acts" or "object dissociates herself as agreed on"; 280).[28] Josepha becomes part of a process of regulation and normalization that serves to define the parameters of her personhood. As Judith Butler elaborates in *Undoing Gender*:

> A regulation is that which *makes regular*, but it is also, following Foucault, a mode of *discipline and surveillance* within late modern

forms of power ... As an operation of power, regulation can take a legal form, but its legal dimension does not exhaust the sphere of its efficaciousness. As that which relies on categories that render individuals socially interchangeable with one another, regulation is thus bound up with the process of *normalization*. Statutes that govern who the beneficiaries of welfare entitlements will be are actively engaged in producing the norm of the welfare recipient. (55; italics in original)

Despite her efforts to resist state powers, Josepha has to realize that the state uses her pregnancy to regulate, discipline, and police her within an entire network of institutions.

It is not Josepha's conscious decision but her pregnant body—in other words, the reason for the state's increased interest in Josepha—that resists the GDR power structures and her own inclination to surrender. For example, the papers verifying the pregnancy repeatedly slip out of Josepha's hands: clearly, her body refuses to accept the official documents, which consequently elude control—not only the institutions', but also Josepha's (37). Yet even the insistently pregnant body is forced to comply with the regulations that determine Josepha's subjection to GDR law as a condition for receiving state support. Forced to comply, Josepha becomes "socially interchangeable," to invoke Butler: she is turned into one of many expectant mothers in the GDR. Yet the laws that govern the social behavior required for welfare not only regulate a normed and normalized socialist personality, but effectively define and even stigmatize the person's identity: Josepha learns that her file at the gynecologist's office carries a red "A" for "*Assotzjaalenkortei*" (register for social misfits; 171; italics in original), which is only removed after she consents to regular examinations. The references both to Hawthorne's *Scarlet Letter* and to discourses of National Socialism render Josepha a social outcast and hint at a proximity of the socialist and fascist states as far as matters of state control camouflaged as pronatalist "welfare" are concerned. The GDR state institutions are portrayed as encouraging behavior that constructs normalized identities, which are defined by their ability to fit social norms—exactly the process we observe in *Nachdenken über Christa T.* Despite the superiority of the GDR healthcare system over that of the FRG until the mid-1970s, particularly pertaining to infant and maternal mortality and to life expectancy—a success that can be attributed to the measures depicted in *Die Gunnar-Lennefsen-Expedition*—the novel decidedly criticizes these restrictive policies because they deprive women of agency.[29]

The fictional text evaluates GDR maternal health further by contrasting it with the care Ottilie receives in the FRG. Ottilie, Josepha's grandmother in Bavaria—the daughter of her great-grandmother Therese, who participates in the expedition from the couch—is hospitalized in the FRG when she becomes pregnant at age 60. The mother-to-be and her unborn son have to endure constant fumbling, pressing, auscultating, and ultrasounding, all of it inflicted by male doctors (96). The physicians want to gain knowledge about the mysterious female body that exhibits a "späte Schwangerschaft, [die] nicht mit sich rechnen [lässt], [und] sich jenseits der Regeln menschlicher Ontogenese im Zeitraffertempo [vollzieht]" (late pregnancy one cannot count on [and] which progresses in fast-forward motion beyond the rules of human ontogenesis; 61). Alluding to medical and mathematical language, the narrative ridicules the epistemic processes by which the head physician Dr. Zehetmayr, in particular, unsuccessfully attempts to gain medical insights. He is primarily focused on Ottilie's body as an object of research and of his "Geschäftsinteressen" (financial interests; 96). He is unable to collaborate with the lower-ranking ward physician, his colleagues in other fields, and the nurses. As a result, the gynecologist is out of his depth, since Ottilie is considered a "Mischpatientin" (mixed patient) for whom psychiatry and gynecology alike feel responsible (62). In other words, to understand Ottilie's body and the late pregnancy, the medical professionals would need to collaborate and listen to the patient. However, they disregard her wisdom about her body, which has become so astonishingly symptomatic, since it does not meet scientific criteria. Due to the lack of cooperation, and since neither of the doctors can explain Ottilie's pregnancy with scientific knowledge, they declare both her body and mind ill by diagnosing psychic instability and pregnancy psychosis (63).

Depicting hierarchical structures, the dominance of male doctors, and the priority of financial interests over the health of the patient, *Die Gunnar-Lennefsen-Expedition* criticizes precisely those negative aspects of the capitalist German medical system that the GDR was dedicated to eliminating from the start. As Christa Wolf's depiction of the GDR hospital in *Leibhaftig*, corresponding to the vast majority of medical-historical research, demonstrates, hierarchical structures and particularly the position of the *Chefarzt* were structurally eliminated. Despite the fact that some patients had internalized the old hierarchical structures and still preferred to be treated by the *Chefarzt*, the relationship among doctors and nurses in the GDR was largely egalitarian. Neither this equality nor the interdisciplinary approach to patient care, which was characteristic for GDR clinics, finds an equivalent in Schmidt's depiction of the FRG hospital. Since unification meant adoption of the FRG medical system for the former GDR, *Die Gunnar-Lennefsen-Expedition* also doubles as a commentary on medical institutions in post-unification Germany—a system that had served as part of the GDR's abject before 1989, as various medical documents reveal.[30]

Christa Wolf had warned against a westernization of GDR healthcare early on. In her 1991 essay "Krebs und Gesellschaft" Wolf, quoting the Berlin Physicians Association, pointed out that in the FRG medical system, which was superimposed on the former GDR, profitability and optimal techniques of coded accounting are more important than patient care (127). Similarly critical, *Die Gunnar-Lennefsen-Expedition*'s comparative approach reveals differences as well as similarities between the two countries' approaches to healthcare, such as for example their overall lack of comprehension of the female body. And while in the FRG there is no socialist system charged with influencing a patient for the benefit of her newborn and society at large, class-oriented and institutionalized male-dominated power structures and doctors interested in making a profit deny the mother-to-be agency. Most importantly, however, both systems are characterized by misogynist practices: at least in the area of gynecology and maternal care, the FRG hardly presents an acceptable alternative to the GDR.[31]

Pregnancy and Childbirth in *Lärchenau*

The title of Kerstin Hensel's *Lärchenau* refers to an imaginary village in the East German countryside, located about an hour northeast of Berlin. This novel—announced by the book jacket as a medical romance with a grotesque twist—also features expectant mothers. One of them is Dr. Gunter Konarske's wife Adele. The couple is at the center of *Lärchenau*, which begins with their shared day of birth in 1944 and ends with Adele's premature death some time after German unification. The brief part of the novel that portrays pregnancy and childbirth is assigned its significance via two clearly established oppositions. First, the novel sets up a contrast between two women—Adele Konarske and a so-called "gypsy" named Baba Prohaska—who can produce healthy children on the one hand, and a nurse Angela—wife of the local physician Dr. Krause—and her unsuccessful attempts to bear children on the other. When Dr. Konarske, who is aware of the Krauses' futile efforts to have offspring, interferes by secretly administering a fertility-enhancing serum he had previously used on pigs, Angela becomes pregnant—but her pregnancies end in miscarriages. A second major distinction is set up between Adele's delivery in a GDR hospital in the 1970s and Baba Prohaska, who gives birth on Lärchenau's village green in 1990. Baba is the daughter of a family of so-called "gypsies" who arrive shortly after the fall of the Wall and are forced to live on the outskirts of Lärchenau (277). Her social position and her physical body serve to highlight mechanisms of exclusion and inclusion of members of specific social groups, mechanisms that determine—in all political systems portrayed here—the historical, social, and cultural positionality of the various characters.

In contrast, Adele emerges as privileged because of her husband's position as a medical doctor in a leading hospital. In her own imaginary world, she receives favorable treatment because she deems herself as "von unerhört hoher Geburt" (of unheard-of high ancestry; 339) as daughter of the "Führer," a false memory perpetuated by her late mother (26–27). Growing up in the GDR, Adele, who imagines the "Führer" as a king and confuses Wilhelm Pieck, the first president of the GDR, with her mother's reference to Hitler, believes Pieck to be her biological father (96–97). Adele's naïve and confused belief ironizes what was the decisive model for early GDR literature and Christa Wolf: the portrayal of social relations as family relations centered around the figure of the communist father as antifascist hero and role model. Yet in *Lärchenau*, GDR education is unsuccessful in establishing a classless society: the cap with the emblem of the torch, the symbol of the GDR youth organization, replaces Adele's tin foil crown, the signifier for her imagined noble lineage (93). The family model mobilized in early GDR literature is revealed as ironically cementing conservative norms: it actually contributes to the favorable treatment Adele receives in the hospital when she gives birth.

While *Lärchenau* does not portray mandatory prenatal medical exams, it does impart knowledge about privilege granted in GDR hospitals. Her husband's position in the clinic ensures Adele's exceptional position. In a GDR hospital, which typically would suffer a shortage of space and medical staff, Adele resides in a single room, is readily approved for a Caesarian section so that she may determine the day of her son's birth, and regularly summons the higher-ranking physicians to examine her scar (199). Adele's behavior in the hospital as well as her son Timm's luxurious layette, which astonishes the social welfare worker who visits the young mother at home, reveal the GDR's failure to establish a classless society—despite its efforts to eliminate the remnants of social privilege (200).[32] Unlike Schmidt's *Die Gunnar-Lennefsen-Expedition*, which portrays the medical system as it would have been encountered by the majority of GDR women, Hensel's *Lärchenau* highlights the experience of the privileged minority in a satire of bourgeois relics in GDR society.

In contrast to Adele, Baba goes into labor on the village green, to which her family has carried her. Holding on to a tree branch, she quickly gives birth to three children, supported only by her mother-in-law Mitschka, who offers magic spells and prayers (355). Mitschka is endowed with positive traits reminiscent of a witch and a midwife. In her knowledge about foraging food from the woods, in her appearance, and through the scent of wild garlic and bark mulch that accompanies her at all times, she is identified by her proximity to nature. Her prophecies, which come true, reveal her superior secret wisdom; and when she takes charge during the delivery of her three grandchildren, Mitschka's self-confidence and poise emphasize that her wisdom extends particularly to women (348–55, 371–72, 420). Her symptomatic body—marked by a tattooed number burned into her flesh in a Nazi concentration camp

(353)—and psychic trauma (376) reveals that her knowledge exceeds the realm of natural remedies. Unlike Mitschka, whose body stores and reveals individual as well as collective German Nazi history, the inane and fatuous farmers of Lärchenau live in a state of oblivion: when they read Mitschka's bodily inscription as a hieroglyph (in the German text the misspelling as "Hyrumglüfe" adds to the irony), as a telephone number, or as an unambiguous sign for the woman's insanity (353), they demonstrate a lack of historical awareness that corresponds with the racism they verbalize while Baba gives birth. Afraid that the traditional practice facilitated by Mitschka would return Lärchenau to the Stone Age and cause death (354), the local farmers exhibit the result of official policies: since both German states largely ignored the Sinti and Roma as victims of Nazi persecution, prejudice and closed-mindedness dominate contemporary public discourse. The population of Lärchenau can neither recognize Mischka's body as an object of cultural memory, nor celebrate the arrival of three new Prohaska family members. This might indicate the contingency and repeated exclusion of ethnic minorities in post-unification Germany. However, it is significant that Baba's three babies are healthy and outlive the ethnic German population, which is either unable to reproduce, like Angela, or loses their offspring prematurely, like the Konarskes their son Timm. *Lärchenau* thus establishes a silver lining on the gloomy horizon of increasingly right-wing thought in post-unification Germany, an aspect to which we will return in chapter 4 in the discussion of the last part of Hensel's prose text.

Focusing on the interaction of the ethnic German population with former victims of Nazi terror, Hensel pursues the same goal as Wolf, though her path may differ: In Wolf's writings pre- and post-1990, inmates of concentration camps as well as so-called "gypsy," Jewish, and communist sufferers from German fascism made repeated appearances, which allows the protagonists to identify with the victims. Hensel, however, refrains from offering any means of identification with those who suffered or were murdered. The narrative perspective she chooses—that of an omniscient narrator—renders this impossible. Similar to Wolf, though, Hensel employs symptomatic bodies, their archived knowledge, and alternative medical traditions to indicate and to criticize how ideas of ethnic homogeneity determine who is excluded from the national community of post-unification Germany.

Gender Games

Playful attempts to overcome the gender binary in literature are neither new nor specific to GDR literature, as Wolfgang Emmerich emphasizes in his afterword to *Geschlechtertausch* (Gender Exchange, 1980; 102–6). The thin volume assembles three short stories by Sarah Kirsch, Christa

Wolf, and Irmtraud Morgner, all of which describe their respective female protagonist undergoing a sex change: they need to be transformed into men in order to function effectively in careers that have been determined by the male norm.[33] Wolf's "Selbstversuch. Traktat zu einem Protokoll" ("Self-experiment") is particularly complex. The female protagonist's imagined sex change or so-called self-experiment leads to his temporary inability to love. It calls into question hegemonic notions of sex and gender while fundamentally critiquing male rationalism—that is, a belief in facts and numbers—and scientific methodology and discourse in general. When the protagonist, named Anders (Other) by her male boss, assumes agency and chooses to end the self-experiment on her own, s/he resolves to start her own experiment; namely, the attempt to love (100). Yet as Friederike Eigler has pointed out, there is more to it, as "the treatise [mentioned in the German subtitle] ultimately calls for a different approach to the sciences, one that considers the ethical and social implications of bio-technological research not as separate from but as part and parcel of its epistemological foundation."[34]

Wolf's story was one of the first to address women's participation in as well as criticism of and resistance to dominant scientific discourses and approaches linked with the topic of hegemonic notions of gender and sex. As we observe in *Die Gunnar-Lennefsen-Expedition*'s approach to rewriting history, these themes are still prevalent in post-GDR literature. Particularly the topics Wolf addresses explicitly, such as ethical and social implications of bio-technological research and of gender and/or sex changes, continue to occupy a central place in the novels analyzed here. They differ from their predecessors from the 1970s, however, in one central respect: while the three stories published in *Geschlechtertausch* all portray a transition from female to male, post-GDR literature portrays the reversal—that is, male-to-female sex changes, or decisions in favor of the female sex in the case of intersexuality.

The "Vatermutter": Intersexuality in the GDR

In Kathrin Schmidt's *Die Gunnar-Lennefsen-Expedition*, the intersexual Lutz/Lucia challenges hegemonic notions of sex, "natural" gender roles, and kinship models along with established power structures. Lutz/Lucia's body is characterized as an oversized vagina, which serves as the repository for an equally immense penis. Lucia works as a saleswoman in a local department store, after Lutz decided to live as a woman in order to escape the ten years of military service to which he had voluntarily committed upon his graduation from high school (153). In Lutz/Lucia's ability to utilize this extraordinary sexual constitution as a strategy for conscientious objection, a new symptomatic body opens up fresh possibilities for acting one's conscience and escaping obligations that run counter to it. At the same time, this body facilitates a lifestyle that heralds newly imagined kinship models. Engaged in a love relationship with a married couple, Lutz/Lucia is part of a family comprised of three adults and five children, one of whom he fathered and two of whom he bore (153). The portrayed family challenges both heteronormativity and heteromonogamy. In the fictionalized GDR, it lays out Judith Butler's vision of a universe she described in *Undoing Gender* as a world in which "individuals with mixed genital attributes might be accepted and loved without having to transform them into a more socially coherent or normative version of gender . . . [and in which it is understood that] a continuum exists between male and female that suggests the arbitrariness and falsity of the gender dimorphism as a prerequisite of human development" (64–65). In such a world, masculinity and femininity become fluid and finally allow for a dialogue defeating the sexual binary. Lutz/Lucia's body enables the unique positionality of a "Vatermutter" (fathermother; 175): it serves as a physical incarnation for a human being who exists and loves in the interstices of a binary distinction imposed on a continuum and demonstrates that this binary is not exhaustive. Lutz/Lucia's body and life choices underscore how common notions of sex receive meaning from an individual's identification with the underlying norms; and that consolidation of the dominant gender categories depends—to invoke Judith Butler's *Gender Trouble*—on a stylized repetition of acts along the lines of these norms (140). Since Lutz/Lucia's bodily acts evade clearly gendered signification, they emphasize the potential for resistance to social hegemony by modifying established categories for unambiguously gendered forms of interaction. Because the signifiers emerge as flexible, diverse, and socially constructed, they can be challenged and re-negotiated, and serve to contest sex-based supremacy.

Although state representatives are at first unhappy at the sight of this body refusing categorization within the gender binary, institutions in Schmidt's fictional GDR tolerate this kinship model, which presents deviance from the recognized norm, as long as it does not interfere with the upbringing of the next generation (154). The narrative portrays socialist society as exercising less brutality on intersexed children than is common in capitalist countries, where the intersex movement is still fighting unwanted surgeries today.[35] As Ulrike Klöppel emphasizes in her 2010 analysis *XXOXY ungelöst* (XXOXY unresolved), the binary gender distribution from birth appears as an ever-existing factual constraint. Even in current discussions about policies pertaining to intersexual newborns, it goes unquestioned.[36] Particularly when compared to current perceptions, the GDR appears to have been rather progressive. Of the very few monographs that have appeared to date on the topic of the legal situation of intersex persons, the first one, Hans-Jörg Lammers's *Über die Intersexualität beim Menschen* (On Intersexuality in Humans), was published in the GDR in 1956. Lammers describes the discrepancy between scientific medicine and the legal system, and considers the gap in legislation the root of the problem. While medicine acknowledges that only a three-tier gender classification could do intersexual individuals justice, the legal system only recognizes two sexes. As a result, Lammers argued, intersexual individuals had to be allowed to choose their preferred gender identity independent of medical findings (111–15). In the same year, Heinz Pockrandt and Heinz Brunkow, two physicians at the Berlin Charité, published "Zwitter und Scheinzwittertum beim Menschen" (Hermaphroditism and Pseudohermaphroditism in Humans). They emphasized that decisions about sex should be based primarily on the prospect of integrating intersex individuals into society (929–30). They further demanded that if the gender identity of intersex persons could not be changed legally, they should receive a certificate granting them the right to live in the desired gender and to carry an appropriate name (930).

By 1975, the decade in which Lutz/Lucia in Schmidt's fictional GDR could live as a so-called "Vatermutter," gender identity was usually assigned based on objective psychological criteria (*XXOXY*, 559). Otto Prokop, director of forensic medicine at the East Berlin Humboldt Universität, declared genital surgery a therapy legally recognized as safe in his standard textbook on forensic medicine in the GDR.[37] Lutz/Lucia's body—at first sight part of the fantastic elements in Schmidt's fictional text—represents the legal situation of intersexed individuals in the GDR in the 1970s surprisingly accurate. S/he also contradicts the prevalent notion that a sexually ambiguous body hampers healthy psychological and social development (*XXOXY*, 16). Because her/his life in the interstices of the gender binary is socially accepted in the GDR Schmidt imagines in *Die Gunnar-Lennefsen-Expedition*, the socialist country appears devoid of practices that construct the intersex individual's body as a medical and psychological problem in need of an expert solution.

Ambiguous Gender and Violence in the GDR

In contrast to Lutz/Lucia, who can live peacefully, Kerstin Hensel's *Lärchenau* presents Helge Hemlock, a delicate youth, who is victimized because of his gender ambiguity. While he seems to possess a biologically male body, both appearance and name highlight the uncertainty of his gender.[38] He is wheat-blond, tender as a girl, has a snub nose and lips that move like a snail, and wears small gold-rimmed glasses. Most importantly, he is said to move from feminine into masculine within seconds, and often does not know himself where he belongs (215–16). His ambiguous gender makes Helge a victim of Stasi collaborator Hans-Werner Giersch. Motivated by self-hatred induced by problems with his own sexual identity and his long-lasting attraction to the conspicuously effeminate boy, Giersch uses his power to send Helge to prison in 1988 (268). When Helge is released in August 1990, he is traumatized:

> Als . . . Helge Hemlock mit einer großen Schädelnarbe nach Lärchenau zurückkehrte, fand er seinen Platz nicht mehr und mochte mit niemandem reden. . . . Nur Pfarrer Niklas gelang es, den verstörten Mann zu sich zu nehmen. Er kleidete Helge neu ein, schenkte ihm eine Pudelmütze . . ., unter der die Narbe schmerzte. . . . Sprunghaft, unartikuliert, doch für den Pfarrer verständlich erzählte Hemlock von dem, was ihm im Zuchthaus widerfahren war. (279)

> [When . . . Helge Hemlock returned to Lärchenau with a large scar on his head, he did not find his place any more and did not want to talk with anyone. . . . Only Reverend Niklas managed to take in the distraught man. He provided Helge with new clothes, gave him a pom-pom hat . . . under which his scar hurt. . . . Erratically, inarticulately, but in a way that was comprehensible to the clergyman, Helge talked about what had happened to him in jail.]

The experiences of his detainment are inscribed in Helge's body and psyche alike. Physically, the painful scar on his skull ensures that the traces of the horrific experiences in the Stasi prison become permanently manifest and stored as historic knowledge in his body—but they cannot be accessed due to the trauma.

Lärchenau does not disclose details pertaining to the Stasi prison, which affirms that Helge suffers from post-traumatic stress disorder. Since trauma and traumatic effects cannot be verbalized adequately,[39] the fact that the narrative does not offer Helge's words points to the fundamental dilemma: healing depends on the victim's ability to recollect the traumatic experience—which is, however, mostly inaccessible to conscious recall—and on repeatedly narrating the events to a variety of people. Furthermore, the process of accessing trauma requires a "sympathetic, committed listener" because "'remembering and telling' about trauma is a social act, not an individual one" (Kacandes, *TF*, 94–95). Since only the clergyman can support Helge in verbalizing the traumatic experience and a single sympathetic listener is insufficient for successful healing, Helge's recovery is endangered. The transformation of trauma into narrative memory further depends on integrating those "large realms of experience or aspects of one's identity [that] are disowned" due to the traumatic event.[40] Since Helge's body and rattling voice are unintelligible for the villagers, he cannot successfully overcome his trauma and his historical knowledge cannot be imparted (279).

Helge's symptomatic voice is not unlike the one we could perceive in Wolf's *Leibhaftig*. His malfunctioning vocal apparatus points to his body's disrupted relationship to the past, which also destroys his present and future. Unlike Wolf's protagonists, who were to some extent liberated by their symptomatic voices, Helge's fettered vocal apparatus does nothing but signal traumatic historical experience. When Reverend Niklas accuses his congregation of indifference and insidiousness in the GDR as well as in post-unification Germany and describes Lärchenau as a place where the devil has made its headquarters, he loses his position. Helge, as a consequence, freezes to death on his mother's grave. His end, as Hensel seems to suggest, marks the notion that post-unification Germany, even more than the GDR, provides a space for the devil and his collaborators (278–79, 434–37). Those who do not fit in, who inhabit the interstices of sexual or social existence and who could tell about the past and the crimes committed, are eradicated, and their memories are eliminated with them.

Yet there is more to Helge Hemlock. In Hensel's novel, we find another revealing game played with early GDR *Aufbauliteratur*. In the uneven relationship between Helge and his tormentor Hans-Werner Giersch, a variation of the post-fascist body as described by Julia Hell emerges. In *Lärchenau*, however, it is not the sexual body associated with the fascist past that surfaces as the source of Helge's trauma, but rather somebody like Hans-Werner Giersch who has suppressed his sexual desires in a homophobic GDR and hence turns to violence.[41] Moreover, here the victim suffering indescribable pain is no longer the communist, but the innocent and apolitical Helge, whose only "offense" consists in possessing a gender-ambiguous body. When he reappears after his release from prison in 1990, his body is not marked by fascist torture, but inscribed by the realities of real-existing socialism. And yet, post-unification Germany is no better than the former GDR for Helge. The text suggests that not only there are similarities between the structural violence under fascist and socialist rule, but also, specifically, that aggression against sexual minorities endures post-1990.

Transsexuality in the GDR

Thomas Brussig's *Wie es leuchtet* also makes a contribution to "gender games." In this novel, we encounter a group of seven so-called "unvollendeten Transsexuellen" (unfinished transsexuals; 177) who experience the demise of the socialist system on their bodies. After psychological and psychiatric counseling and tests, they were finally approved for sex changes in the GDR. Yet when the only team of doctors qualified to carry out the procedure leaves for the West in the summer of 1989, the transsexuals' male-to-female sex changes are first suspended mid-process and then reversed when, due to the lack of hormones, they gradually regain their male bodies. Abandoned in what reporter Leo Lattke considers a sexual no-man's land (314), these victims of a country in transition represent the calamities associated with the political changes in their bodies. Linking their individual fate to the historical processes, their physicality points to a stability in the GDR system that evaporated into chaos on the path to unification. In her militaristic choice of words, Heidi, formerly Rainer, reveals the hostility inherent in the transition process: "Es ist wie Krieg, den der Körper gegen die Seele führt, und die Bomben sind Hormone. . . . Als der Nachschub für die femininen Bataillone ausblieb, begann ihr Körper die Konterrevolution: Die Brüste verkleinerten sich, und ihre Ausdünstungen waren ihr männlich" (It is like a war, which the body wages against the soul, with hormones as bombs. . . . When the supplies for the feminine battalions failed to materialize, her body began the counterrevolution: Her breasts shrank, and her effluvia appeared male to her; 320). Heidi opposes to the bygone order of the socialist GDR—associated with revolution, progress, and femininity—the transition period of 1989/1990, a time linked to chaos, setback, counterrevolution, and masculinity. The East German Heidi, desiring a female body, feels forced into a male existence when the GDR dissolves and the sellout to the West begins with the exodus of GDR physicians.

The fundamental East-West dichotomy is replicated in the way the two societies interact with transsexuals. While GDR society lacks a transsexual scene but largely accepts Heidi/Rainer's sexuality, the West does not present an alternative even though it would offer the possibility of immediately continuing hormone therapy. Surprisingly, the reason for this is precisely its liberal transsexual scene. The reader learns that Heidi feels supported in the East, where she does not experience any resentment. She realizes that in the West, she would be considered a strange bird, restricted to "einer Szene . . ., die sich für nichts interessiert als für sexuelles Raffinement" (a scene . . . that is interested only in sexual sophistication; 321). Socialist society is depicted as accepting sexuality—including forms of it that fall outside the heteronormative framework—as a "natural" part of individuals' lives, whereas capitalist society is associated with blatant sexual behavior. *Wie es leuchtet* therefore echoes the early GDR literary convention we encountered in Christa Wolf's oeuvre: like Christa T., whose East German pregnant body appears pure particularly in contrast to her West Berlin cousin's artificially sexualized body, Heidi appears almost naïve because she is only interested in acquiring the body that will harmonize with her felt gender identity. Her innocence rests not least of all in her body's explicit separation from the desire for sexual sophistication associated with the other side of the newly opened German-German border.

Heidi's desire to fit both into her social environment and into the opposite gender identity points to the political and legal aspects of transsexual life in the GDR and during the so-called *Wende*. Beginning in the 1950s and 1960s, physicians in the GDR acquired special permits aimed at facilitating life in their preferred gender identity for transsexuals. Since the mid-1960s, forensic pathologists supported requests to the Office of Vital Records to include a second—or alternative—first name that matched the desired sex on the person's identification card. And since the mid-1970s, the GDR facilitated surgical and hormonal sex reassignments both for intersex individuals and for transsexuals (*XXOXY*, 560–61). In February 1976, the GDR Minister of Public Health issued the "Ordinance on the Gender Conversion of Transsexualists," which officially regulated gender change in the GDR—more than four years before the FRG ratified a similar law. The GDR ordinance was aimed at offering qualifying transsexuals easier access to medical interventions and the opportunity to change their gender identity. It gave them the legal right to change their name and civil status if a psychiatric assessment approved their belonging to a sex other than the one registered on their birth certificate after the surgical and hormonal gender reassignment had been completed.[42]

These rights, however, came with certain obligations: persons wanting to implement a gender conversion were required to dissociate themselves from homosexuality and promise to undergo sex reassignment surgery. Moreover, they had to commit to socialist values and present themselves as loyal GDR citizens. In return, socialist institutions committed to fulfilling the individual's wish to fit in—which included the necessity to conform to the GDR's heteronormativity and conservative gender stereotypes that were present at the institutional level and deeply ingrained in everyday life in the GDR.[43] In other words, the notion that, in a socialist state, the interests of the individual and of society must be aligned at all times is replicated in the GDR's policies concerning transsexuality. Again, we observe the two sides of healthcare in socialism: the ideological emphasis on the collective implies that the individual is physically incorporated in the socialist state and must adjust to its hegemonic notions of gender and sex; in turn, the individual can rely on the solidarity of the collective. The way *Wie es leuchtet* describes Rainer's path to becoming Heidi corresponds to GDR procedures and practices. This includes the psychiatric therapy following a suicide attempt, the time s/he had to wait for the surgery for reasons of age, the hormonal therapy, the first surgery, and the interruption of the process when her physician left for the West (316–20). The transsexuals portrayed in *Wie es leuchtet* were raised in a social, legal, and medical environment that was largely aimed at supporting them. In 1989, that environment fell apart.

After Heidi eventually completes the sex change with the help of foreign physicians who volunteer to finish the process after they read

Lattke's report, she ends up in prostitution. This is more than an ironic commentary on the 1950s and 1960s GDR practice of predicating gender reassignment on the reassurance that it was not aimed at engaging in promiscuous behavior (*XXOXY*, 560). And it is more than an intertextual reference to Thomas Brussig's hero Klaus Uhltzscht in the novel *Helden wie wir*, who is a corrupt Stasi officer in the GDR and after the fall of the Wall offers sex for sale as a pornographic actor. Rather, Heidi's prostituted flesh represents the novel's critique of the peaceful revolution of 1989 that quickly fell prey to the DM (Deutsche Mark), the hard currency of the West. Her East German innocence is contrasted with the corruption of the West, personified in the journalist Leo Lattke, who immediately scents a story when he sees the pictures of the seven transsexuals whose surgeries were abandoned (197–98). By agreeing to the publication of her story in the West German media in order to increase her chances of receiving the desired surgery, Heidi demonstrates that after the fall of the Wall, the success of her therapy hinges on promoting herself—in contrast to the GDR, where it was contingent on the support she received from society and physicians in return for her loyalty to the state and her acceptance of heteronormativity. In other words, there is a price to be paid for the transition in both societies—only the "currency" differs. *Wie es leuchtet* shows how after the fall of the Wall, Heidi's story and her body are turned into a marketable commodity—much like the pictures of November 1989 that dominated the global mass media. Unlike Lattke's report on Sabine Busse, which was unpopular because it lacked enthusiasm, Heidi's story sells as well as the images of November 1989, which turned the peaceful revolution aimed at reforming socialism into an inauthentic image of the events.[44] Prostituting the new body she acquired in the capitalist system emerges as the most honest and authentic decision Heidi can make. In this act, she claims her body's physical existence in the new sex and at the same time symbolically performs the historic experience of a community being absorbed into the capitalist system, where the individual's value depends on her or his market price.

Heidi's decision to play along with the new rules of the capitalist system moreover aims at subverting the heteronormativity and hegemonic gender norms that govern the GDR and the FRG alike. She enjoys playing with both her identity as an East German and her sexual identity, and with the confusion she can cause in men by troubling their assumptions about what determines femininity:

> *In Heidis Nähe ahnten manche Männer, wie trügerisch ihr ... Bild von Mann und Frau ist.... Zwar reichten die Phantasien der Männer nicht aus, um Heidis unweibliche Herkunft zu erkennen— manchmal aber für eine Erschütterung dessen, was unter weiblich zu verstehen sei.... Die meisten Männer waren aus dem Osten. Mit dem*

Westgeld . . . wollten sie sich echten westlichen Sex kaufen. Sie bekamen einen Mann aus dem Osten, frisch transformiert. . . . Für diejenigen aber, die ostdeutsches Material suchten, . . . war sie aus dem Osten. Die Männer aus dem Osten waren ihr die liebsten. (500–501; italics in original.)

[Close to Heidi, some men developed an idea about how deceptive their view of man and woman . . . is. . . . Much as the fantasies of the men were not sufficient to detect Heidi's unfeminine origin, they sometimes sufficed for unsettling [their views of] what should be understood as *female*. . . . Most men were from the East. With West money . . ., they wanted to buy real Western sex. They got a man from the East, newly transformed. . . . But for those who were looking for East German material, . . . she was from the East. She liked the men from the East best.]

While she does not entirely overcome the male/female binary, Heidi poses a challenge to hegemonic notions of normative sexual bodies and emphasizes the falsity of gender dimorphism. Yet *Wie es leuchtet* also identifies the distinction between East and West Germans as equally problematic. Since Heidi prefers East German men because they lack experience with prostitutes, she does not deny the difference. Rather, she points to the performative aspects underlying her self-representation both as a woman and as an East German. In Brussig's depiction of Heidi, particularly after the introduction of the West German Mark in the East on July 1, 1990, a world emerges in which nothing can be taken at face value and everything is determined by money. While the fluidity between East and West as well as between female and male undermines the hegemonic categories defining the abject on which West German subject formation depends, capitalism emerges as the most dominant factor in the equation—and has taken over in the East. Brussig's is a world in chaotic flux, in which everyone and everything is in camouflage. Here, East Germans emerge as belonging to those abject beings who are ready to become West German subjects in unified Germany by accepting the West German—and particularly capitalism's—"Normal-Null-Status" (normal-zero-status). Until they have fully committed and adapted to the West German norms, however, they remain the abject and useful for West German subject formation.

"Charité Berlin. The Horror Clinic"[45]

In the early 1990s, the West German media published articles portraying a demonic power conglomerate consisting of the Stasi and their supporters in the GDR medical system. In addition to scientists who were accused of having performed medical experiments on human beings, psychiatrists were blamed for collaborating with the Stasi to dispose of political opponents. The *Bild* article that furnished the section title, for example, claimed in August 1991 that healthy opponents of the GDR regime, allegedly pathological troublemakers, disappeared in institutions, where they were operated on and their organs cannibalized. Similar claims had been made by the news magazine *Stern* in the spring of the same year. Journalist Uta König mentions political abuse of psychiatry comparable to the Soviet Union and claims that the Stasi deported GDR citizens they wanted to muzzle to the psychiatric clinic "Waldheim."[46] In the following years, several media outlets similarly reproached former GDR psychiatric institutions, with the case of then-secretary of the interior in Saxony, Reverend Heinz Eggert, receiving particular attention. On January 1, 1992, Eggert accused GDR psychiatrists of collaborating with the Stasi in an *ARD Brennpunkt* report, a public television program with high popularity ratings. Eggert claimed that physicians had been involved in *Zersetzung*, the Stasi-specific measures aimed at a person's public degradation with the goal of causing the individual's breakdown—an accusation which he later had to retract after the District Attorney's office concluded its preliminary investigations in December 1992. This is not to say that the Stasi were not involved in Eggert's case, that his attending physicians were not Stasi-IMs, or that doctor-patient confidentiality was not breached: all of these accusations voiced by Eggert were, in fact, correct. Up to fifty IMs were observing Eggert, including physicians, because the Stasi considered him a dangerous enemy. However, the psychiatric institutions where Eggert was treated in 1983/1984 were not involved in the measures aimed at *Zersetzung*, and Eggert was not forcibly admitted to a psychiatric institution (Süß, *Pm*, 58–69).

With such reports in the back of our minds, reading Kathrin Schmidt's *Die Gunnar-Lennefsen-Expedition*, which hints at the problematic situation of GDR psychiatry, causes some unease, particularly since the author is herself a trained psychologist who practiced in several medical institutions in the GDR. The novel depicts a case of social exclusion based on politics that are indicative of the Stasi-psychiatry network. Josepha's *Meisterin*, the supervisor originally loyal to the GDR, first becomes unusually benevolent and then goes AWOL. Her compassion for her co-workers indicates the beginnings of the supervisor's critical distance to the government, which culminates in the desecration of a portrait of the head of state (113, 116). On her last day at work, a portion of Josepha's cherry dessert hits the aforementioned painting and, as a consequence, the president develops cherry-red lips with a heart-shaped pout (99). The ensuing wild sexual encounters with the painting depicting the head of state in which the supervisor engages both dishonor and sexualize the president and his image. They reverse and mimic the narrative pattern developed in early GDR prose texts which was so influential for Wolf; namely, the model of the desexualized body of the communist, antifascist hero at the center of novels that allow for identification (Hell, *PFF*, 19). Since in this model popular in *Aufbauliteratur* sexuality links the subject to its fascist past and the new subject depends on the obliteration of the sexual body, the ironic depiction of the portrait of the head of state whose sexuality is unleashed by Josepha's cherry dessert and the supervisor's uncontrolled sexuality mock the early GDR narratives. Schmidt's ridiculed and sexualized version of the GDR father figure at the center of the communists' symbolic politics of power can claim neither power nor the position of the pure antifascist hero.

The ideal of the Communist father is further satirized as the portrait of the president is said to utter a constant stream of profanities, which ridicules the fantasy of a pure communist voice (116). As we saw in the two preceding chapters, the links between the symptomatic body, its constantly endangered pure voice, and history have been defining factors for Wolf. They continue to be thematized in *Die Gunnar-Lennefsen-Expedition*, and are ironized not least of all because the head of state's attempt to reclaim his repressed subjectivity is linked to nothing but the painted portrait of his head. The voice uttering profanities is separated from his material body, which consequently can remain pure. The literary nexus of ideological inscription in the flesh, voice, and history that was so important for Wolf returns here in ironic form. Since the actual head of state and the numerous portraits of him that are found throughout the GDR cannot assume one speaking position heralding the "truth," voice emerges as consisting of multiply-layered and conflicting voices. The supervisor undermines parts of the founding GDR narratives and exposes the ideal of the Communist father as a fantasy; she is found guilty of collaboration with the class enemy (117, 120). When the *Meisterin* regains her material sexual body in the erotic folly with the portrait of the president, she loses her immunity to non-socialist ideologies and becomes susceptible to ideological inscription other than the dominant communist discourse. Her lack of identification with the antifascist founding fathers and her seduction of the head of state's portrait are most likely interpreted as treasonous demagoguery, a punishable offense according to §106,2 StGB-DDR. Consequently, the Stasi declares that she has committed the despicable act of defecting to the class enemy after she was infected with an illness called the West (120–21).

Apparently inspired by the above-mentioned media coverage of the confinement of opponents to the GDR government in psychiatric institutions, which was illegal even by GDR standards, *Die Gunnar-Lennefsen-Expedition* stages the disappearance of the *Meisterin* as a kidnapping to a psychiatric clinic (124). Josepha witnesses the Stasi and the attending physician collaboratively combing through the drawers in the supervisor's home, which was subject to ongoing surveillance (117–18). In search of her boss, Josepha first looks in "Pfafferode," the closest psychiatric clinic, and then investigates the nursing homes of the district and even of the county (121), locations suggesting that the novel builds on the media reports of the early 1990s. While the Stasi's declaration that the supervisor was infected with an illness called the West indicates that she might have defected to the West or been bought off by the FRG, Josepha believes that her former boss may have disappeared into a clinic linked with the Stasi.

By the mid-1990s the majority of cases investigated in four of the five new states had been rebutted by commissions of inquiry. The final report of the Berlin commission of inquiry states that in all cases in which the commission looked into medical histories or Stasi files, no indication of a political abuse of psychiatry was discovered. By 1996, all commissions had finished their reports and published their results. In summary doctor-patient confidentiality was breached by IM doctors, but there are no known cases of hospitalization for political reasons. While the Stasi attempted to commit political opponents to psychiatric institutions, they never succeeded because physicians refused to hospitalize them. Also, no evidence for brain surgery or castration performed on political opponents, nor other political abuses of psychiatry, could be found (Süß, *Pm*, 107). In Brandenburg, however, the commission found several cases of forced institutionalization of psychologically conspicuous, potential troublemakers (Süß, *Pm*, 110). In the fictional world of *Die Gunnar-Lennefsen-Expedition*, the supervisor's changed ideological belief as it emerges in her newly materializing sexuality—a sexuality that moreover dishonors and ridicules the head of state—could easily be interpreted as a source of irritation for the Stasi, especially if she previously collaborated with them. Interpreting her renunciation of her faith in socialism as mental illness or madness (115–18, 121–23), the Stasi in Schmidt's world could conceivably have subjected the *Meisterin* to a psychiatric state institution. A highly imaginative text in the tradition of magical realism, *Die Gunnar-Lennefsen-Expedition* creatively engages with a topic that not only pertains to the GDR, but also to the ways post-unification Germany deals with the memory of the bygone state.

"GDR Sold Patients for Experiments on Human Beings"[47]

In February 1991, the influential German weekly magazine *Der Spiegel* was first to claim that West German pharmaceutical companies tested their products in the GDR. The article, entitled "Das ist Russisches Roulette" (This is Russian Roulette), maintained that in turn, GDR labs pocketed millions in hard currency for these so-called experiments on human beings

(80, 85). Shortly afterwards, the famous Berlin Charité came under attack by *Der Spiegel* for the experiments on human beings already mentioned in "Das ist Russisches Roulette," for collaboration with the Stasi, and for criminal practices in procuring human organs. The condemnation of what *Der Spiegel* called the former flagship clinic of the SED regime aimed at discrediting the core of GDR healthcare.[48] If the practices and ethical standards of the flagship of GDR medicine evoked the specter of Nazi experiments, what was to be expected from other institutions?

According to the *Spiegel* report "Das ist russisches Roulette," the deal, which aimed at generating a profit for the GDR, was first concocted in 1983 by—among others—the minister for health, Ludwig Mecklinger, and functionary Schalk-Golodkowski (85). The latter was known for doing business with the West to procure hard currency for the GDR. *Der Spiegel* reported how since 1984, GDR citizens in several hospitals had been abused as cheap guinea pigs for pharmaceutical companies from numerous Western countries—without legal rights in case of adverse health effects, without their knowledge, and mostly without their consent, but with disastrous consequences for their health, including death (80). Clinic physicians were portrayed as willing collaborators, since they received the technology necessary to conduct the tests from the pharmaceutical companies. The acquisition of this equipment meant that the hospital's economic deprivation could be mitigated, to the benefit of the majority of patients (87). *Der Spiegel* singled out Prof. Stephan Tanneberger, head of the GDR ethics commission, and depicted him as an inhumane SED comrade who was supposedly known as the greatest advocate of clinical experiments across the GDR, and interested solely in scientific fame and financial gain (82, 90). The allegedly slack GDR laws enabled physicians like Tanneberger and clinics like the famous Berlin Charité or the district hospital Karl-Marx-Stadt (today Chemnitz) to engage in the experiments, which they did eagerly (90).[49]

The Senate of Berlin, shocked when confronted with the reports in *Der Spiegel*, immediately appointed an independent commission to look into the allegation, which ruled that the accusations made in the news magazine were entirely unfounded. The commission consisted of five members, equally critical of the GDR regime and the pharmaceutical industry, and headed by Professor of Medicine Ruth Mattheis, then Chairwoman of the ethics commission of the Medical Board of Berlin.[50] In September 1991, their report concluded that based on the information conveyed to the commission, there was no reason to believe that in the testing of medical products in the GDR, fundamentally different guidelines or procedures were employed than in the FRG.[51] In fact, the allegedly slack GDR laws were in part stricter than their FRG equivalents, particularly pertaining to ethical standards.[52] Since Schalk-Golodkowski brokered the deals between the Western pharmaceutical companies and the hospitals, the alleged bonuses doctors received were never paid. Instead, the profits went into the GDR budget. Moreover, the number of tests of medical products *Der Spiegel* reported turned out to be exaggerated, and the risk was misrepresented: *Der Spiegel* had described primarily phase I and II experiments, which are the most dangerous, when in reality, most of the medical product tests had been phase III trials—clinical tests focused, for example, on expanding the indications for prescribing a drug.[53] The commission's report showed that two out of one hundred and twenty studies did not meet international standards—not because they were dangerous, but because there was hardly any expected benefit for the patients. The one problem the commission discovered was the insufficient consent sought from the individual patients.[54] Given the GDR *Betreuungsverhältnis*, the lack of zeal with which consent was pursued is hardly a surprise. Since even the physician's obligation to inform patients about their therapy, and to seek consent could be bypassed without any legal consequences for the physician, the problematic situation of patients receiving unapproved medications could be expected.[55]

This is by no means to deny that the legal situation in the GDR created and propagated problematic patient passivity. On the other hand, as far back as 1974 physicians engaged in the testing of medical products developed in the GDR distinguished between *Erprobung* (trial) and *Versuch* or *Experiment* (experiment). In a co-authored article, Hans-Georg Hüller, H.-G. Berndt, and I. Amon, for example, state the conditions for testing new medications in 1974. They highlight the scientific necessity of a test or experiment; its social, moral-ethical and scientific prerequisites; the certainty, or at least likelihood of reaching a positive outcome, that is, one that is beneficial for the patient/test person; and the reasonableness of the test or experiment.[56] They further stress that the obligation to inform patients about the therapy and to seek consent need to be "adjusted" to the specific situation when patients receive new medical products or medication not yet approved for a specific indication. This does suggest a problematic willingness to influence patients towards acknowledging that their interest, having their health restored, coincides with secondary scientific interests—which in the GDR was always also interpreted as the interest of furthering socialist society, as Hüller, Berndt and Amon concede.[57]

Still, the supremacy of the *bonum communae* over the *bonum privatum* is not a GDR-specific phenomenon, but could be observed in most European countries and was widely discussed in the FRG in the 1970s, explicitly with regard to testing new pharmaceutical products. The existence of public debate is probably the aspect in which the FRG differed most decisively from the GDR. Richard Toellner, referencing Alexander Mette, Gerhard Misgeld, and Kurt Winter, authors of *Der Arzt in der sozialistischen Gesellschaft* (The Physician in Socialist Society) maintains that the GDR had definitely decided that everything which advances the interests of the "progressive class," the working class, and its party, ethically takes precedence.[58] Discussions in the FRG obviously had to consider other aspects than the progress of the "progressive class."

Apparently based on the reports in *Der Spiegel*, Brussig's *Wie es leuchtet* alludes to the medical experiments on human beings through the character of Professor Hense, who works at the district hospital in Karl-Marx-Stadt mentioned in *Der Spiegel* in 1991 (152–58). In a meeting with the hospital staff, which is portrayed as very hierarchically structured, Professor Hense is questioned about the experiments. Sitting with the other head physicians and the medical director, Professor Hense admits to having used pharmaceutical preparations from West German companies, but repeatedly denies having participated in experiments on human beings. His argument echoes those brought forward by Professor Tanneberger in the *Spiegel* reports (153, 156). The owner of a vacation home furnished with West German consumer goods (154), Professor Hense is depicted as an arrogant Stasi collaborator (156). The narrative's internal focalization finally configures him as a character to be denounced: "Die Zeit arbeitete für ihn, das spürte Prof. Hense. Noch zwei, drei Minuten, höchstens noch eine Frage zu dem Thema, die er in gewohnter Selbstsicherheit beantworten mußte, dann war es geschafft. Dann würde die Wende andere Opfer fressen" (Time was on his side, Prof. Hense could sense that. Another two, three minutes, at the most another question on the topic, which he had to answer with his habitual self-confidence, then he would have made it. Then, the *Wende* would devour other prey; 157). Both the narrative perspective and the word choice stage Professor Hense as aloof and as somebody who experimented with medications on his patients—not for their sake, but for his own profit. He appears as a predator who benefitted from his proximity to the GDR regime and the hard currency he received to purchase his West German consumer goods. The wording he repeatedly rejects—namely, that he conducted "Menschenversuche" (experiments on human beings)—not only echoes the allegations brought forward in *Der Spiegel*, but also places his actions in close, uncanny, and ahistorical proximity to medical experiments performed in Nazi concentration camps. Particularly since Hense accentuates the link between medical institutions and state power when he states that "naturally" the experiments were supported by the Stasi (156), the narrative insinuates comparable proximity between state interests and medical research in the GDR and fascist Germany. Given the great awareness of GDR physicians regarding the abuse of medical science in experiments on human beings in the fascist concentration camps or in euthanasia projects, topics that repeatedly emerge in discussions among doctors in the GDR, such correlation is puzzling.[59]

Because Brussig's novel also suggests a similarity between the GDR and Nazi Germany elsewhere—that is, the GDR police are compared to the SA—*Wie es leuchtet* may be read as supporting both the FRG founding narrative and the post-unification hegemonic historiography that construct the GDR as totalitarian and in uncanny proximity to the National Socialist regime.[60] Given that Brussig's fictional text is written in a highly satirical mode, however, this depiction of Professor Hense at the district hospital in Karl-Marx-Stadt also serves to play with Western fears and prejudices about the GDR as they emerged in the *Spiegel* reports. In the context of the critical stance *Wie es leuchtet* assumes toward the media personified in Leo Lattke, the allusion to the *Spiegel* reports aims to tease Western anxieties and biases. After all, the exclusion of Sabine Busse's story and the inclusion of the transsexuals' experiences in Lattke's news magazine demonstrate that the West German media is interested in publishing items that support normative discourses which celebrate the successful incorporation of the GDR in the FRG. Portraying discussions surrounding the GDR medical system, Brussig positions himself in the GDR tradition of utilizing fiction as a vehicle for conveying politically, socially, and historically relevant information. In choosing to depict Professor Hense as a physician who conducted medical experiments for his profit in the fictional world of *Wie es leuchtet*, the novel remains ambiguous: it conveys an image of the GDR healthcare system that might serve to question physicians' efforts to restore the health of their patients in often challenging conditions—and it ironizes West German expectations to find the GDR portrayed as an immoral dictatorship, willing to sell its citizens for a profit.

"A rather trusting attitude toward medical measures prevailed in the GDR"[61]

Kerstin Hensel's *Lärchenau* employs a different approach to present the most dramatic example of the effects of so-called progress in biomedicine. Hensel's narrative also references the massive media reports about the Charité with its male protagonist, Dr. Gunter Konarske, a physician and professor at the famous Berlin clinic who engages in tests that also involve human beings. For his biomedical experiments, he relies on the results of the clandestine reproductive experiments he conducted on hogs in Lärchenau (204, 207–9). Humans and pigs are closely associated throughout the novel. The hogs stage a revolution reminiscent of George Orwell's *Animal Farm* (249–52); Konarske breeds a rose hybrid that smells like pigs and calls it Princess Adele after his wife (225); and he provides a pig-costume for his son to wear for carnival (212–13). These events foreshadow the experiments on human beings and particularly on Adele.

In the late 1960s and early 1970s, Dr. Konarske is internationally celebrated for his world-class research in human engineering in the GDR (192, 260). He receives the "Vaterländischen Verdienstorden in Bronze . . . für hervorragende Forschungsleistungen auf dem Gebiet der Humanmedizin, und man ernannte ihn zum *Geheimnisträger*" (patriotic order of merit in bronze for outstanding achievements in research in the field of human medicine, and he was appointed a *person with security clearance*; 202; italics in original). By italicizing the *Geheimnisträger*, the narrative highlights the GDR medical realm as part of a network of state institutions executing power and invokes the reports in *Der Spiegel*. Given that Dr. Konarske, though not a member of the SED, had been part of the travel cadre who could take trips to the West since the early 1970s (206, 260), a privilege granted only to highly reliable members of the profession, his collaboration with the Stasi as an IM is very likely.[62] His bourgeois lifestyle with his wife Adele as a "*FrauzuHause*" (stay-at-home wife; 185) who plans extravagant parties, reads West German magazines, watches West German TV, and enjoys her private swimming pool, supports the suspicion that Dr. Konarske is employed by the Stasi—precisely because it counters the ideal of the socialist doctor personality. Gunter Konarske perfectly represents the ideal doctor-IM in the 1970s, as characterized by Francesca Weil in *Zielgruppe Ärzteschaft*:

Der innerhalb der Ärzteschaft zum Einsatz kommende IM sollte über einen Hochschulabschluss verfügen, ein interessantes Hobby haben, in seiner Ausdrucksweise gewandt sein, bürgerliche Umgangsformen pflegen und möglichst als politisch indifferent . . . und nicht als "aktiver Genosse" bekannt sein. Zudem waren ein gesichertes Einkommen, ein PKW sowie eine gut eingerichtete Wohnung wesentlich für die Auswahl. (38)

[The IM to be deployed within the medical profession should have a university degree and an interesting hobby, be articulate, cultivate bourgeois manners, and ideally be known as politically indifferent . . . not as an "active comrade." Moreover, a regular income, a private car, and a well-furnished apartment were essential for the selection.]

Dr. Konarske, who regularly upgrades his car and builds additions to his house, fits the Stasi requirements to become part of the ever-expanding network of IMs in the medical field. Particularly interested in medical doctors who assume leadership positions, such as Hensel's fictional professor, the Stasi controlled every larger medical institution in the GDR by the 1980s, a fact that apparently went unnoticed by the majority of the medical staff.[63]

At the same time, collaboration also implied privileges. For example, even though the lack of private medical insurance companies in the GDR resulted in the absence of private patients, high-ranking doctors could also treat patients privately in exceptional cases[64]—and Dr. Konarske's private consultations are said to be legendary in *Lärchenau* (238). Patients who were beneficial for the hospital or a doctor's private residence, such as craftsmen, or in Dr. Konarske's case, a car mechanic (234), as well as patients who supplied doctors with Western products or hard currency, apparently often enjoyed favorable treatment.[65] In *Lärchenau*, this topic is broached when even as a student Gunter Konarske receives West German coffee, chewing-gum, or magazines for his wife (177) and as a physician he advances to more expensive products and hard currency (183). While the Stasi monitored doctors such as Dr. Konarske, who is under observation by the fictional IM Felge (204–6), they tolerated such behavior because interference would have further increased the number of discontented doctors leaving the GDR illegally or applying for permission to leave the socialist state.

As part of the privileges Dr. Konarske enjoys, he was able to afford a private laboratory in the basement of his villa starting in the 1980s, which allows him to carry out in the private realm those parts of his research that are incompatible with GDR law. This plot device serves two purposes: first, it comments on the actual situation of doctors in GDR hospitals, who had to conduct significant amounts of their research in their leisure time because the day-to-day operations in the clinic did not leave time for scientific investigation.[66] Second, it shifts violence to the private realm. As a result, the narrative can evade the debate about the factual existence of questionable experiments in the GDR, but still introduce the brutality of the portrayed medical research with the psychological and sexual violence Gunter revels in vis-à-vis Adele.[67] The borders between the public and private realms in medical research are therefore blurred in *Lärchenau*.

Hannelore and Uwe Körner, both doctors in executive positions at the Berlin Charité, report that notions of ethics pertaining to experiments with animal and human cells first came into play during the 1970s, when transplantation experiments on animals among and between species were successful.[68] Medical-historical studies indicate that, despite difficult conditions, professors at the Charité produced impressive results in biomedical research that did not lag behind capitalist countries. Like Hensel's Professor Konarske, they conducted genetic experiments, including some tests with human cells, long before the fall of the Wall. However, this research was strictly regulated. Körner and Körner emphasize that experiments with human embryos in the GDR required the permission of an independent commission consisting of philosophers, lawyers, biologists, and gynecologists.[69] Still, the possibility in principle of experimenting on human embryos underscores the significance that medical research assigned to medical and social progress, and the belief that improvements in scientific research would advance socialist society and its ethical standards. This confidence explains Körner and Körner's certainty that GDR citizens generally trusted medical procedures.[70]

Yet this is exactly the point Hensel challenges with her fictional portrayal of medical research in the GDR. *Lärchenau*'s story relates how even the GDR's reformed university education for medical professionals, with its emphasis on humanist education, could not overcome the break in humanist traditions that is marked by Nazi crimes, particularly those committed in medical experiments carried out in concentration camps. Before 1989, nurse Angela, the wife of Dr. Krause, remains unaware that she is the victim of Dr. Konarske's repeated attempts to use the fertility-enhancing serum he had already used on hogs on a human being. Twice he secretly drugs his colleague, who successfully impregnates his wife, who then carries several embryos (222, 236). Yet both times, Angela miscarries in the seventh and fifth month respectively (236, 238). While the couple give up their hopes for healthy progeny, Dr. Konarske promptly overcomes his failure. In his private research lab, he swiftly places the fruits of nurse Angela's miscarriages in alcohol and sets out to disprove the failure of his study (238–39). In the privacy of Konarske's basement, Angela's fetuses contribute to a parade of glass vessels that contain floating limbs, intestines, twisted tissue, noses, ears, and mouths of alien animalistic creatures (443). This image, and particularly the fetuses in alcohol stored away as material for research, immediately evokes the famous fetus collection housed at the Berlin Medical-Historical Museum of the Charité. The majority of the original collection of malformed fetuses started by Rudolf Virchow was destroyed during World War II. However, the corpus grew by about seven thousand items during GDR times, when it was unnecessary to obtain the family's permission for an autopsy[71]—a practice that was, according to Heinz David, former director of the Institute for Pathology at the Charité, beneficial for scientific medicine.[72] When the museum reopened in 1998 after renovations, many newspaper reports included photographs of the fetuses in alcohol that seem to have inspired Hensel. Via nurse Angela's fetuses, *Lärchenau* creates a historical context of monstrous experiments that stages the GDR as both the result and the source of dangerous experiments on human beings. The historical framework reaches back even further than the Nazi concentration camps to the founder of the famous Charité, Virchow, and his nineteenth-century collection of monstrous fetuses; it also foreshadows experiments after German unification.

The preliminary results of Dr. Konarske's experiments to create human-animal hybrids emerge in the shape of a laboratory mouse he surreptitiously bred from Adele's genes in his private laboratory, which features a human eye situated on its back (293). While this mouse is reminiscent of a picture from *Der Spiegel* of a mouse featuring a human ear on its back, which was bred in Boston in 1995,[73] the existence of the "Adele-mouse" might have been derived from GDR genetic research on mice, a field in which the GDR occupied a pioneering position: Konarske might have overstepped the official regulations for experiments with human cells, which required permission by a committee.[74] Adele meets the mouse during the days of the so-called *Wende*, and is terrified by this new body that bodes ill for the future. Yet the mouse only foreshadows Adele's role as a guinea pig for Dr. Konarske's later experiments on his naïve wife, which continue his GDR-inspired research on the "new human being" in post-unification Germany—a topic we shall revisit in chapter 4.

Conclusion

The novels by Brussig, Hensel, and Schmidt discussed in this chapter generate images of the GDR, including its important final months, that serve to supplement, balance, and modify the existing collective memory. They also respond to mass media representations of the GDR that circulated after unification—often to satirize these representations. Instead of merely reconstructing the socialist state, their historical distance introduces critical deliberation about the past—which includes the years since the fall of the Wall, and the hegemonic discourses that developed since 1989/90. This two-pronged approach of both recreating and historicizing the GDR makes history accessible. Since the novels' reflections about the past also involve the role of the West German media and their often inaccurate depictions of the GDR and so-called scandals, such as alleged human experiments and exaggerated Stasi involvement, these novels demonstrate the power of literature: it can not only refer to such discourses, but also critically engage with them and thus contribute to historiography in unique ways. This is also true for satirical and parodic strategies, which are important in all three novels analyzed in this chapter.

As we can see, even the fantastic discourses in Schmidt's *Die Gunnar-Lennefsen-Expedition* demonstrate how fiction can create authentic images and transport knowledge. All novels discussed here make conspicuous use of what I have termed symptomatic bodies; bodies such as those of the pregnant Josepha or Brussig's transsexuals reveal everyday life experiences in the GDR, and carry on writing conventions typical for the GDR and for Christa Wolf's oeuvre. This includes playful variations of gender games; ironized versions of the GDR's traditional portrayal of social relations as family relations arranged around a dominant father figure; and ironized as well as horrifying variations on the significance of sexuality. The novels clearly confirm the GDR tradition of reflecting on society and its relevant discourses, often by means of employing a symptomatic body at the center of the narrative, which participates in a process of generating a representative memory culture that includes the East German experience. At the same time, these fictional texts encourage their readers to critically engage with media portrayals of the GDR and its demise that feed into dominant collective memory discourses. This implies that these novels depend on images of the GDR that already exist in the collective memory, which they either affirm or defy and ironize.

While all three novels connect to the GDR past, their discourses surrounding bodies also link the narrative present to Germany's fascist past. In Schmidt's novel, the tie appears in the racist exclusion of the multiracial child, whose body includes his ethnic German, Jewish, and African heritage and who, unlike Lutz/Lucia, cannot claim a space in the GDR, the FRG, or post-unification Germany.[75] Racial exclusion seems to trump sexual exclusion in Schmidt's version of the GDR, which is supported by Brussig's depiction of transsexuals who appear well integrated into GDR social life. While Brussig highlights the GDR past, the media depictions of medical experiments to which *Wie es leuchtet* refers link this fictional GDR to Germany's fascist past as well as to discourses that are relevant in the Berlin Republic. Most explicitly, Hensel evokes Germany's history of murderous exclusion in a variety of symptomatic bodies and medical discourses surrounding experiments on human beings. In all three novels, the symptomatic bodies and the medical practices to which they are subjected suggest a trajectory reaching from Nazi Germany—indeed even the nineteenth century as alluded to in *Lärchenau*—to the GDR, and to post-unification Germany. Particularly in *Lärchenau* and *Wie es leuchtet*, the fall of the Wall activates the previously dormant monsters of the fascist past, which negate the possibility for healing and wholeness of many protagonists.

Notes

[1] "Wir Deutschen sind jetzt das glücklichste Volk auf der Welt!" Berlin mayor Walter Momper on November 10, 1989, and quoted in Brussig, *Wie es leuchtet*, 347.

[2] Krauss in "Zonenkindheiten" (97) and Durzak in "Der Roman der deutschen Wende?" (40) point out that Leo Lattke is modeled on *Der Spiegel* journalist Matthias Matussek.

[3] Since *Wie es leuchtet* alludes to the idea of unification as a marriage between a male West and a female East, the notion of a "castrated," feminized East emerges and points to Freud's analogy between castration anxiety and the fear of blindness as he expressed it in "Das Unheimliche" ("The Uncanny").

[4] Child, *Fall of the GDR*, 128–29; Jarausch, *Uniting Germany*, 128.

[5] Maron, "Lebensentwürfe, Zeitenbrüche."

[6] For Jesus healing a believer, see Mark 10: 51–52.

[7] Diderot, "Lettre sur les aveugles à l'usage de ceux qui voient."

[8] The so-called "schwarzweißes Kind" (black-and-white child) alludes to Feirefiz, Parzival's half-brother in Wolfram von Eschenbach's medieval verse-novel *Parzival*. For the black-and-white child challenging hegemonic notions of race and kinship, see Klocke, "Die frohe Botschaft der Kathrin Schmidt?," 154–56.

[9] For the significance of this feminist expedition, see Breger, "Postmoderne Inszenierungen," 108–9; Eigler, "(Familien-)Geschichte als subversive Genealogie," 262–63.

[10] Irigaray, "The Sex Which Is Not One," 325. In *Gedächtnis und Geschichte in Generationenromanen seit der Wende*, Eigler emphasizes that pregnancy and motherhood in *Die Gunnar-Lennefsen-Expedition* are socially and historically contextualized (115).

[11] In *Kleine Literaturgeschichte der DDR*, Emmerich emphasizes that GDR librarians were ordered to destroy so-called "decadent literature," for example by Freud or Kafka (119).

[12] On the significance of the Freudian *Dauerspur*, see Weigel, *Bilder des kulturellen Gedächtnisses*, 49–50.

[13] In *The History of Sexuality*, Foucault proposes to make the body "visible through an analysis in which the biological and the historical ... are bound together" (152).

[14] Josepha's speech "Filter und Folter" (Filter and Torture; 299) and her incendiary chant "Hic Rhodos, hic salta" (374) are rebellious. The latter alludes to Marx's "The Eighteenth Brumaire of Louis Napoleon" (1852) in which he calls for the continuation of the proletarian revolution.

[15] Unlike the involvement of the Stasi in the medical system, the link between state control, medicine, and racism was not GDR-specific, as Foucault demonstrates in *The History of Sexuality* (149).

[16] Weil, "Ärzte als inoffizielle Mitarbeiter der Staatssicherheit," A 1598; Weil, "Im Dienste der DDR-Staatssicherheit," A3250–51; Richter-Kuhlmann, "Ärzte als inoffizielle Mitarbeiter," 22.

[17] Süß, *Pm*, 259–60; Weil, "Ärzte als inoffizielle Mitarbeiter der Staatssicherheit," A1594.

[18] Weil, *Zielgruppe Ärzteschaft*, 40; Weil, "Ärzte als inoffizielle Mitarbeiter der Staatssicherheit," A1594–95, 1598; Weil, "Im Dienste der DDR-Staatssicherheit," A3248; Süß, *Pm*, 271, 275. Süß found significant differences among the various categories of IMs and their likelihood to breach the doctor-patient confidentiality.

[19] Günther, "Das Arztrecht in der DDR," 90.

[20] On the legal situation in the FRG, see Ostner and Schumann, "Steuerung der Familie durch Recht?," 292.

[21] Fulbrook, *People's State*, 153.

[22] Knopf and Fritsche, "Müttersterblichkeit in der DDR," 220; Rücker, "Soziale Netze," 66; Fulbook, *People's State*, 152–53, 160.

[23] Gerhard, "German Women and the Social Costs of Unification"; Nickel, "Women in the German Democratic Republic and in the New Federal States."

24 Seifert, *GSV*, 61; Löther, "Ethische Aspekte der Beherrschung der Lebensprozesse," 18; Kirchgäßner, "Philosophische Aspekte des Arzt-Patienten-Verhältnisses," 21.

25 Instead of judging IMs for Stasi collaboration, the novel offers reasons that make the individuals' collaboration palpable. It therefore indirectly comments on the public circulation of Stasi documents by the West German media that did not differentiate among IM categories and used questionable Stasi documents to abject East Germans. See Lewis, "Reading and Writing the Stasi File," 377; Pinkert "Toward a Critical Reparative Practice," 183.

26 Ringel and Schneider, "Öffentliches Gesundheits- und Sozialwesen der DDR," 73.

27 For the twenty-six weeks of her maternity leave (which began six weeks before the estimated date of delivery and ended twenty weeks after childbirth), a mother received her salary plus 1,000 Marks. This money was paid in installments and depended on participation in preventive exams. After childbirth, she received an additional 750 Marks plus another 400 Marks paid in four installments after each visit to the *Mütterberatungsstelle* where the baby was examined every time. Since only 90% of women participated, women were obligated to register pregnancies with the *Mütterberatungsstelle* beginning in 1988. Since 1976, mothers could prolong their fully paid maternity leave for up to a year starting with the second child. This benefit was extended to first-time mothers in 1986. See Rücker, "Soziale Netze," 62–64; Friedemann, "Prävention in der DDR," 247–48.

28 In "Rekonstruktion und Innovation (1949–1961)," Schleiermacher and Schagen emphasize the link between healthcare and social welfare, and the focus on women, babies, children, teenagers, and families with many children (213). On educational measures, see Seifert, *GSV*, 360.

29 Knopf and Fritsche, "Müttersterblichkeit in der DDR"; Wagner, "Polikliniken— ein gesundheitspolitisches Modell," 231; Wiesner, "Zur Gesundheitslage der beiden Bevölkerungsteile DDR und BRD," 22; Wolf and Fritsche, "Zur Entwicklung der perinatalen und Säuglingssterblichkeit in der DDR." In *Redefreiheit*, Ahbe, Hofmann and Stiehler quote Dr. Wolff, the head physician of the obstetrics department of the Leipzig gynecological hospital who emphasizes the excellent results they achieved in her department with regards to infant mortality, even by international standards (552).

30 Berndt and Hüller, "Zur Gesellschaftsabhängigkeit des ärztlichen Eides," 42; Harych, "Zur Zukunft der Polikliniken und der ambulanten Versorgung in der DDR," 104; Thiele, "Das Gesundheitswesen in einem deutschen Staat," 12.

31 In "Krankheit und Liebesentzug," Christa Wolf pointed to gynecology's long and deep-seated tradition of contempt for women and its desire to regulate and restrict women by establishing strict rules for behavior during pregnancy and childbirth, and for infant care (733, 738). While her lecture, delivered at a conference of the Work Group on Psychosomatic Gynecology, held in Magdeburg on November 2, 1984, had a different function in the restricted public sphere in the GDR than Schmidt's novel of 1998, it is remarkable that Schmidt points to the same issues.

32 On the GDR's attempts to eliminate bourgeois customs, see Hockerts, "Grundlinien und soziale Folgen," 526.

[33] Christa Wolf's and Sarah Kirsch's stories were originally published in the GDR in a volume entitled *Blitz aus heiterem Himmel* (A Flash Out Of The Blue, 1975), edited by Edith Anderson.

[34] Eigler, "Rereading Christa Wolf's 'Selbstversuch'," 401–2.

[35] In "Medikalisierung 'uneindeutigen' Geschlechts," Klöppel details the ongoing practice of genital surgery on children despite protests of the intersexual movement (33). See Klöppel, "Geschlechtergrenzen geöffnet?," 35–37; Wunder, "Intersexualität: Leben zwischen den Geschlechtern," 36.

[36] Klöppel, Ulrike. *XXOXY ungelöst*, 583 (hereafter cited as *XXOXY*).

[37] Prokop, "Das zweifelhafte Geschlecht," 503.

[38] Helge is a male and a female given name in Germany, while it is exclusively a male given name in Scandinavia.

[39] Kacandes, *TF*, 94; Assmann, *Erinnerungsräume*, 259.

[40] Caruth, *Trauma: Explorations in Memory*, 152.

[41] The GDR decriminalized homosexuality in 1968, yet homosexuals were discriminated against in everyday life. See Grau, "Sozialistische Moral und Homosexualität"; Klöppel, "Die Verfügung zur Geschlechtsumwandlung," 169; Sweet, "Bodies for Germany."

[42] The GDR ordinance called "Verfügung zur Geschlechtsumwandlung von Transsexualisten" was issued on February 27, 1976, while the FRG passed a similar law, the "Transsexuellengesetz" (transsexual act; TSG) on September 10, 1980. The FRG law went into effect on January 1, 1981 (BGBL, 1654). See *XXOXY*, 554, 561; Klöppel, "Die Verfügung zur Geschlechtsumwandlung," 168. Klöppel emphasizes that medical and legal developments in both German states impacted each other, and were influenced by John Money's Baltimore experiments since the mid-1960s (*XXOXY*, 589, 591–94).

[43] Klöppel, "Die Verfügung zur Geschlechtsumwandlung," 171.

[44] On visual images, see Bohn, Hickethier, and Müller, *Mauer-Show: Das Ende der DDR*; Geier, "Mediating Immediacy," 104; Wehdeking, *Generationenwechsel*, 41–53.

[45] "Charité Berlin. Die Horrorklinik." Headline *Bild Zeitung*, August 29, 1991. Quoted in Süß, *Pm*, 16.

[46] Süß, *Pm*, 11. Süß quotes from a series of articles published in *Stern* on April 26, 1990; May 3, 1990; and May 10, 1990.

[47] "DDR verkaufte Menschen für Menschenversuche." Headline *Berliner Kurier*, December 4, 2012.

[48] "'Es geht um unsere Ehre,'" 60. See also "Als gesund entlassen."

[49] In "Ethik in der medizinischen Forschung," Tanneberger offers information on the testing of medical products in the GDR (58–62). In "Medizinische Ethik in der DDR," Toellner questions Tanneberger's position due to a lack of figures on the level of information about risk factors, and insufficient information on biomedical tests in the GDR (72).

⁵⁰ In addition to Mattheis, the commission consisted of Peters, as a representative for health in the Berlin Senate; Helmut Coper, pharmacologist at the West-Berlin Free University; Ulrich Moebius, co-founder of "arznei-telegramm" and an outspoken critic of the pharmaceutical industry; and Otto Prokop, an Austrian-born forensic pathologist who practices at the Charité. See Stein, "West-Medikamente in Ost-Berlin," 28.

⁵¹ Stein, "West-Medikamente in Ost-Berlin," 27. The debate was revived in May 2013, when *Der Spiegel* published two reports characterized as "scandalizing" by the Medical Board of Berlin. Various newspapers reprinted the *Spiegel*'s claims, while *Die Zeit* offered a balanced discussion of the topic in "Die Halbwahrheiten über DDR-Menschenversuche."

⁵² This applies to the GDR "Arzneimittelgesetz vom 27. November 1986" (Pharmaceutical Act of November 27, 1986).

⁵³ In "Wortmeldung zum Thema," Stephan Tanneberger and Hartmut Bettin reproach media outlets like *Der Spiegel* for crediting sensational journalism instead of scientific reappraisal, and for ignoring medical-historical research.

⁵⁴ Stein, "West-Medikamente in Ost-Berlin," 27–28.

⁵⁵ On the legal situation, see Berndt and Hüller, "Zur Gesellschaftsabhängigkeit des ärztlichen Eides," 45; Seifert, *GSV*, 162; Günther, "Patientenschutz," 167.

⁵⁶ Hüller, Berndt, and Amon, "Versuch und/oder Erprobung am Menschen," 48.

⁵⁷ Ibid., 47, 49.

⁵⁸ Toellner in "Medizinische Ethik in der DDR," implies that the major difference was not between the GDR and the FRG, but between continental European countries and Anglo-American culture and its emphasis on the individual (71). Also see Toellner, "Medizinische Ethik im Alltag," 25.

⁵⁹ Festge, "Ethische Positionen," 94; Fischer, "Euthanasie in der Diskussion," 70–71; Hüller, Berndt, and Amon, "Versuch und/oder Erprobung am Menschen," 47; Thom and Caregorodcev, *Medizin unterm Hakenkreuz*.

⁶⁰ See, for example, the police control of a demonstration in Karl-Marx-Stadt: "Wie die Nazis standen sie da, in ihren Schaftstiefeln . . . Jawohl, wie Nazis, wie die SA" (They stood there like the Nazis, in their high boots . . . Yes, like Nazis, like the SA; 60). One character reflects in internal focalization after his arrest on October 7, 1989: "Die Stimmen der Aufseher hallten, und Daniel wußte, daß alle Demonstranten jetzt dasselbe denken [*sic*]: an dreiunddreißig, an die Verhaftungen durch die SA" (The voices of the wardens clanged, and Daniel knew that all demonstrators were thinking [of] the same thing now: of thirty-three, of the arrests by the SA; 79).

⁶¹ "Es überwog in der DDR ein eher vertrauensvolles Verhältnis zu medizinischen Maßnahmen." Körner and Körner, "In-vitro-Fertilisation," 137.

⁶² Körner and Körner, in "In-vitro-Fertilisation," emphasize that visits to Western countries were rarely possible before 1985, while the restrictions were relaxed later (129, 135).

[63] Weil, "Im Dienste der DDR-Staatssicherheit," A3249–50; Markgraf and Otto, "Unfallchirurgie an den Hochschuleinrichtungen," 23; Süß, *Pm*, 107.

[64] Hockerts, "Grundlinien und soziale Folgen," 523. On the absence of private patients, see Markgraf and Otto, "Unfallchirurgie an den Hochschuleinrichtungen," 21.

[65] Hockerts, "Grundlinien und soziale Folgen," 540.

[66] Markgraf and Otto, "Unfallchirurgie an den Hochschuleinrichtungen," 22.

[67] Dr. Konarske enjoys the bizarre wedding ceremony in the basement of the Charité, which turns into hell for Adele (181). Throughout the novel, sexuality is invariably linked with violence, and Dr. Konarske is said to be most aroused when he realizes that he successfully created pain and terror for Adele. At the same time, Adele experiences sexual excitement each time her husband humiliates her. See, for example, 192–93; 226.

[68] Körner and Körner, "In-vitro-Fertilisation," 133. In "Medizinische Ethik in der DDR," Toellner states that discussions on ethics in research on human cells and embryos started later in both German states compared to the United States, Great Britain, and Sweden (64–65, 70).

[69] Körner and Körner, "Ethische Positionen zum vorgeburtlichen Leben," 151–53.

[70] Körner and Körner, "In-vitro-Fertilisation," 137.

[71] Gerstenberger, *Writing the New Berlin*, 59. See Atzl, Hess, and Schnalke, *Zeitzeugen Charité* for interviews with former and current employees who emphasize that the majority of the fetuses were created after 1945, and predominantly after 1950. See especially the interviews with David (52), Schildhaus (83), Reinecke (117–18), and Krenn, who considers the legal uncertainties after unification responsible for the decline in acquired fetuses (139).

[72] See the interview with David in Atzl, Hess, and Schnalke, *Zeitzeugen Charité*, 53. David's view is confirmed by Martin, who in *Zeitzeugen Charité* considers the lack of autopsies after 1990 one of the regrettable setbacks after unification (64).

[73] Evers, Franke, and Grolle, "Zucht und deutsche Ordnung," 312.

[74] The first to successfully experiment with stem cells derived from mice in Germany was Anna M. Wobus, who conducted her research at the "Institut für Genetik und Kulturpflanzenforschung der Akademie der Wissenschaften der DDR in Gatersleben" (Institute for Genetics and Research on Cultivars of the Academy of Sciences of the GDR). Körner and Körner, "Ethische Positionen zum vorgeburtlichen Leben," 151; Münz and Wobius, *Das Institut Gatersleben und seine Geschichte*.

[75] On Lutz/Lucia's social position in contrast with the black-and-white child, see Klocke, "Die frohe Botschaft der Kathrin Schmidt?"

4: Haunted in Post-Wall Germany: Sickness, Symptomatic Bodies, and the Specters of the GDR

RECENT POST-GDR NOVELS often do not portray the GDR per se, but feature symptomatic bodies to reveal vestiges of the GDR lingering in contemporary German society. Precisely because the socialist state has long since ceased to exist, the protagonists at the center of these fictional prose texts are taken by surprise when the specters return to haunt them— even outside the territory of the bygone country. As Antje Rávic Strubel explains, "ich siedle gern meine Texte, die sich immer wieder . . . mit dem Thema beschäftigen, wie weit wirkt eine Gesellschaft noch in die andere hinein, außerhalb von Deutschland an" (I like to choose settings outside of Germany for my texts, which time and again deal with . . . the topic, to what extent does one society still affect the other).[1] Strubel's decision to deal with the remains of the GDR in her prose texts by choosing locations outside Germany may be unusual; depicting the ongoing effects of the socialist state on post-unification Germany is not. In particular, the socialist state's idiosyncrasies and specific means of exercising power remain a topic in East German writing.

The ongoing portrayal of the late GDR, and especially its effects on post-unification Germany, confirm that the bygone state still plays a crucial role in post-GDR writers' cultural and historical memory. Specific practices in hospitals and in medical research, as well as the power of former Stasi officers, all point to the ongoing influence of GDR structures. At the same time, the fictional texts analyzed here highlight both similarities and differences between the GDR and post-unification Germany in exerting control over individuals. They demonstrate ways in which FRG laws and customs in institutions lend themselves to being utilized for maintaining configurations of power that originate in the GDR. Portraying the GDR roots of these control mechanisms and their influence on the health and the bodies of East German individuals in the twenty-first century, post-GDR writers like Antje Rávic Strubel, Kathrin Schmidt, and Kerstin Hensel show a desire to contribute to collective memory beyond the immediate GDR experience. This is not to say that they claim the right to speak the one and only "truth" about the history of the socialist state and the GDR's influence on the present. As Antje Rávic Strubel put it in an interview with Beret Norman and Katie Sutton, "I'm not talking about how things really were or how they really are, but how they are perceived through the lens of a specific character in a specific situation."[2] In other words, these post-GDR writers offer individual East German experiences that can, like pieces of a mosaic, contribute in their entirety to a post-unification German history that does not exclude the East German experience. In the same interview, Strubel also insists that her fiction does not stand unconnected to the reality of East Germans' experiences. About readings from her novel *Sturz der Tage in die Nacht*, she reports: "people react more strongly to the topic of the secret service [than to the incest]. In the former West I had responses of disbelief. People can't imagine that some of the old structures still exist. . . . In the East I hear the opposite. People . . . tell me they had to put the book aside . . . because they couldn't bear it" (105). East Germans' testifying to an inability to cope with texts referring to an unsettling continuation of Stasi influence indicate both the power the secret service exercised in the GDR and the fear it still precipitates in former GDR citizens. At the same time, Strubel's statement reveals the extent to which the realities of GDR life remain incomprehensible to West Germans, even twenty-five years after the fall of the Wall. This status quo points to the ongoing division of German experiences in the supposedly unified country and to the possibilities inherent in literature: fictional texts by East German writers can have the important—and as yet, underappreciated—effect of allowing West German readers access to East German experience. While literature does, of course, stage imaginary, mediated and vicarious experiences, post-GDR fiction still presents an in-depth and intense form of making East German knowledge available for West Germans so that it can find its way into a pan-German history.

In these most recent texts, symptomatic bodies that are haunted by, or somehow reminded of, their GDR past serve exactly this purpose. They invite readers to experience the lives of GDR citizens in ways that can add to—and challenge—hegemonic historiography. The sometimes traumatic, never "ostalgic" resurrections of the socialist state that influence the fictional characters' health take a variety of forms and serve different purposes. In the last part of Kerstin Hensel's *Lärchenau*, the increase in medical experiments on human beings after 1990 engages with post-unification discourses regarding bioethical questions and suggests that the lack of state control exacerbates the plight of the individual due to privatization. Kathrin Schmidt's 2009 novel *Du stirbst nicht* reverts to illness-induced dreams that—reminiscent of Christa Wolf's *Leibhaftig*—force the patient to revisit her memories of the GDR and face her trauma. Unlike Wolf's novel, however, Schmidt's prose text highlights the continuation of GDR-specific practices in the medical realm—even after unification—that limit a patient's agency, and compares ways of exercising power pre- and post-1990. Antje Rávic Strubel's *Sturz der Tage in die Nacht*, similar to the works of Wolf and Schmidt, features a symptomatic body suffering from fevers that allow her to gain insight about her entanglement in political affairs of which she is unaware. This body reveals the impossibility of escaping one's GDR past and particularly the Stasi—even if one withdraws to a small Swedish island. *Sturz der Tage in die Nacht* discloses how a generation of East Germans who have no recollection of life in the GDR is nonetheless affected by its power structures in twenty-first century Germany. By passing on knowledge of the GDR, its norms, beliefs, and authoritative systems of control that remain influential in the Berlin Republic, all three novels participate in socially pertinent discourses relating to the GDR past.

The literature examined in chapter 4 features predominantly East German characters, who are rarely juxtaposed with West Germans. This indicates a lessening of the desire—more prominent in the earlier texts discussed in chapter 3—to assert an East German identity by insisting on supposedly superior GDR values such as, for example, solidarity over individuality in order to challenge the West German abjection of the East. Rather, certain power structures that deny individuals agency and the freedom to organize their lives are revealed as not necessarily unique to the GDR. Specific modes of destruction and control were, however, able to thrive extremely well in GDR institutions such as the Stasi and the healthcare system. Individuals who benefitted from such practices seek loopholes in the FRG legal system that allow them to continue to exert power in post-unification Germany—which particularly affects East Germans. To illustrate these points, we return to the discussion of Hensel's *Lärchenau*: the last third of the novel focuses on the effects of the GDR university education of physicians and of bio-medical genetics experiments conducted in post-unification Germany. My analysis sets the fictional text in dialogue with Peter Sloterdijk's essay *Regeln für den Menschenpark: Ein Antwortschreiben zu Heideggers Brief über den Humanismus* (1999; "Rules for the Human Zoo: A Response to the *Letter on Humanism*," 2009). This approach reveals the extent to which the topic of the former GDR and heated societal debates on genetic research can intersect with one another in post-unification Germany and, in the process, unleash monsters similar to the ones portrayed in Christa Wolf's oeuvre.

Rules for the Human Zoo in *Lärchenau*

German philosopher Peter Sloterdijk's *Regeln für den Menschenpark* is based on a speech he delivered at a philosophers' conference in Elmau (Bavaria) in July 1999. Even before its publication later that year, the text sparked the so-called Sloterdijk debate in the culture sections of all major German newspapers and newsmagazines, first and foremost among them *Die Zeit* and *Der Spiegel*.[3] What had happened? While this is not the place to analyze specific aspects of Sloterdijk's essay, a brief summary of pertinent arguments will be helpful at this point. Building on Plato, Nietzsche, and Heidegger, Sloterdijk's *Regeln für den Menschenpark* declares the end of humanism, interpreted by Sloterdijk as a project taming humans by means of education and literary traditions. This mission has failed both because of the advent of the new media and because it led to inhumanity, an argument he supported with references to Heidegger and Nietzsche. Sloterdijk moreover suggests that thanks to genetic research, we can now realize Plato's idea of breeding humans just as humans breed animals—which clearly hints at Nietzsche's notion of the *Übermensch*. Employing vocabulary that, particularly in Germany, is associated with Nazi medicine and Auschwitz—terms such as "Selektion" (selection), "Menschenzucht" (human breeding), and "Anthropotechniken" (anthropotechnologies)—Sloterdijk suggests that manipulation of the DNA not only of plants and animals, but also of human beings can lead to forms of cultural change that he considers desirable. Arguing for the existence of specific genes that carry "morals," he suggests that genetic breeding should take on the tasks that humanism has failed to fulfill. Unsurprisingly, the final point, in particular, caused a public uproar in Germany.

Bioethical questions had received attention in the German media for some time, but the Sloterdijk Debate moved them to the forefront, as the September 27, 1999, edition of *Der Spiegel* demonstrates. Announcing a dossier on the topic "Gen-Projekt Übermensch" (Genetic Project *Übermensch*) on the front cover, *Der Spiegel* assembled a whole array of articles and interviews on the topic. This also contained the image of a mouse implanted with a human ear, discussed in the previous chapter. The last third of Kerstin Hensel's *Lärchenau*, which deals with Dr. Konarske's problematic official and unofficial research in post-unification Germany, ostensibly builds on 1999 newspaper reports on bioethics. In fact, the novel engages with Sloterdijk's text, particularly with its claims that humanism has come to an end and needs to be replaced by genetic research.

In *Lärchenau*, questions pertaining to the—allegedly finite—validity of humanist ideals are represented via three generations of the Konarske family, starting with Dr. Gunter Konarske's father, Dr. Rochus Lingott, and ending with his son, Timm. In Hensel's text, the end of humanism is clearly linked with German fascism and with Dr. Lingott's death in a Nazi concentration camp. Dr. Lingott is portrayed as the last compassionate doctor who was in touch with nature and treated people in Lärchenau with natural remedies and true sympathy. Significantly, he dies at the very site of horror that laid the foundation for his son's research. Despite his biological relationship with his father, Gunter, from birth, appears balefully and lastingly contaminated by fascist thought, which proves to be stronger than the genetic profile he shares with his natural father. Born to Hitler's fanatic voice and the Wagnerian sounds of the *Götterdämmerung* (Twilight of the Gods; 9) on the radio, Gunter emerges as Hitler's symbolic son, a relationship underscored by the midwife's comment that his mother, Rosie, had given the Führer a lovely child (20). Adele also imagines Hitler to be her father, and thus she and Gunter appear similarly linked to fascism from birth. Devoid of humanist values, they emerge as the perfect team: Gunter, in possession of knowledge and power, can utilize Adele as a research object for the realization of his anthropogenetic ideals.

Historical, social, cultural, and moral destruction and violence, foreshadowed in the *Götterdämmerung*, are manifest in Gunter and those surrounding him—including his son Timm. Reminiscent of Christa Wolf's *Kindheitsmuster*, which centers on the idea that the paradigms and behavioral patterns learned by children in the Nazi years not only remain with them into adulthood but are also passed on to the next generation, Timm inherits his father's love for cutting into flesh. Like Gunter, who even as a small child enjoys playing with sharp medical instruments (64) and visiting the local butcher shop because of the large knives used there (71), Timm loves the meat market and his career choice, to become a butcher, appears natural, as if inevitable (266). Healing, which was Dr. Lingott's life's work, is entirely replaced by his grandson's forceful and passionate cutting up of meat. This foregrounding of violence points to the irrevocable loss of humanist ideals in the Nazi years; reminiscent of Christa Wolf's *Kindheitsmuster*, in this as well, it stands in contrast to the official GDR narrative of antifascism. Fittingly, Timm is born on the same day as his mother and father, which highlights the continuation of a dormant Nazi tradition in the ethnic German family. The tradition resumes after unification, when Timm becomes a neo-Nazi and dies (430). Before 1990, Timm, like his father, keeps the fascist monster inside. Dr. Konarske's research produces horrors like the mouse with the additional human eye he bred from Adele's genes which is released only after the fall of the Wall (293). The new creature foreshadows Adele's future as her husband's guinea pig after unification. Thus Dr. Konarske's life-long fascination with monstrosities is linked with Germany's monstrous history, and the doctor emerges as the personification of the end of humanism declared by Sloterdijk.

Corroborating Sloterdijk's idea that opportunities for realizing humanist thought and ideals by means of education have run their course, Dr. Konarske functions as an example of how the GDR's educational efforts, implemented to reform the university education of GDR doctors and overcome the influence of Nazi contamination, were in vain. Although he is a product of these reforms—he takes up his studies at the *Humboldt Universität* in Berlin in 1965, after the introduction of medical ethics as part of the education of future physicians—he fails to develop into a socialist doctor personality. Dr. Konarske thwarts all attempts to implement humanist ideals underlying the socialist idea, the very ideals Christa Wolf held onto in her oeuvre until the end. He points to the failure of socialist efforts to "tame" or "domesticate" citizens, to invoke the terms Sloterdijk used in describing the end of the humanist project. Instead, Dr. Konarske interprets his role in serving the "Gesellschaft des neuen Menschen" (society of the new human being) not as treating illness, but as designing new, enhanced humans, whom he imagines as hybrid combinations of humans and animals (167). The optimized breeding techniques he develops on hogs and unsuccessfully attempts to transfer to humans, as nurse Angela's repeated miscarriages underscore (236, 238), reveal his belief in "selection" with the aim of engaging in "human breeding"; and the third-eye laboratory mouse featuring Adele's genes exemplifies his engagement in anthropotechnology. Dr. Konarske's experiments, driven by his own ambitions and hubris, refer to precisely those components of Sloterdijk's text that remind Germans of their fascist past. They also belie socialist ethics which—in response to crimes committed by medical professionals under National Socialism—expected socialist doctors to be politically engaged for the "gerechte und humane Sache" (just and humane cause) and extended the Hippocratic oath to emphasize a physician's obligation not only to the patient, but also to socialist society at large.[4]

In *Lärchenau*, only local Dr. Krause emerges as a socialist doctor willing to serve the villagers. Yet lacking charisma and the ability to impregnate his wife, he appears weak and not very attractive from the start. When his severe visual impairment degenerates into blindness after German unification, Dr. Krause's inability to read the signs of the future highlights that the world does not belong to humanist-socialist ideals, but to Dr. Konarske and his colleagues, who similarly engage in genetic research. The macabre wedding celebrations for the Konarskes in the basement of the Charité at the end of the 1960s foreshadow this course of events. The inscription above the entrance to the cellar room, which reads "ÜBERALL HIMMEL ÜBERALL HÖLLE" (everywhere heaven everywhere hell; 180; capitals in original), predicts humanity's prospects in general, and Adele's future with Gunter, her future God (179), in particular. In contrast to Dr. Lingott, whom Gunter Konarske imagines not as his forefather but as his fore-God (392), Hensel's God-to-be Dr. Konarske dreams of creating and propagating the new human being. He uncannily resembles the God responsible for breeding imagined in Sloterdijk's *Regeln für den Menschenpark*: a researcher in possession of the "Wissen, das Macht gibt" (49: knowledge that power gives; 25), "der wahre Züchter . . ., [der], weil er aus Einsicht handelt, den Göttern näher steht als den konfusen Lebewesen, die er betreut" (the true breeder . . ., [who] because he acts from insight, stands closer to the gods than the confused populace he looks after, 49).⁵ Yet this breeder, so close to the gods, is not merely interested in caring for his creatures. Rather, as Sloterdijk's *Regeln für den Menschenpark* explains, it is not about "die zähmende Lenkung der von sich aus schon zahmen Herden, sondern [es geht] um eine systematische Neu-Züchtung von urbildnäheren Menschenexemplaren" (leading herds that have already tamed themselves with the aim of taming them, but [it is about] systematically breeding new exemplary human beings that are closer to the archetype, 50).⁶

Such systematic breeding of new, optimized, prototypical creatures is exactly the foundation of Dr. Konarske's ideal: he is not interested in taming Adele, the intentionally domesticized FrauzuHause (stay-at-home wife; 185) merely for the sake of keeping her at home in the traditional sense of a housewife. Instead, he increasingly controls her for his anthropogenetic objectives, which he developed in the GDR, beginning with his university education. After unification, the devil lurking in Dr. Konarske's clandestine reproductive experiments with the hogs in the GDR is unleashed: under the new conditions, the doctor can utilize Adele's genes for his vision of the perfected hybrid individual, the most perverted symptomatic body, "das Hausweib in der Hausmaus" (the housewife in the house mouse; 346). The narrative reveals that even in the GDR, where the vast majority of women were integrated into the workforce in the 1970s, those who occupied power positions like Dr. Konarske could rely on bourgeois class structures granting privilege and on traditional gender systems that protected domestic violence in all its forms. Dr. Konarske's domestication efforts intensify, however, after 1990, when—long after the GDR has come to an end—he locks up his wife in their house (442). Serving as a kind of "zookeeper" for his research object, he takes on the role in conventional family structures that Christa Wolf assigned men in "Krankheit und Liebesentzug": namely, that of the "Gefangenenwärter" ("jailer-husband") of his "schwache, ahnungslose, unmündige, bürgerliche Frau" (738: bourgeois woman: weak, uninformed, dependent; 77). In other words, after unification old-fashioned conditions gradually prevail over progressive social tendencies that had developed in the GDR and allow Dr. Konarske to extend his role as a prison guard to all aspects of his wife's life. The private realm of the Konarske residence, resembling Sleeping Beauty's castle and increasingly shielded from external interference, emerges as a heterogeneous site of violence: it acts as a social shelter against external hazards and concurrently functions as the locus of absolute social control and internal violence vis-à-vis the "housewife in the house mouse." Hensel's narrative integrates a view of how life in the GDR, both in the domestic sphere and in research, laid the foundation for the devastating outcome of gender-specific violence that had apparently been lurking for decades and emerged post-unification. Since Gunter uses Adele for his research purposes in the private realm, the narrative structurally parallels male aggression vis-à-vis women in general, and violence in the relationship between doctor and patient in particular—especially when the patient has become a research object.[7]

While Sloterdijk ignores the specificity of women's experience as objects of male fantasies of creation, he does reflect on the necessity of regulating technology's interference in human genes when he states that in the face of modern biogenetics

> wird es in Zukunft wohl darauf ankommen, das Spiel aktiv aufzugreifen und einen Codex der Anthropotechniken zu formulieren. Ein solcher Codex würde rückwirkend auch die Bedeutung des klassischen Humanismus verändern—denn mit ihm würde offengelegt und aufgeschrieben, daß Humanitas nicht nur die Freundschaft des Menschen mit dem Menschen beinhaltet; sie impliziert auch immer—und mit wachsender Explizitheit—, daß der Mensch für den Menschen die höhere Gewalt darstellt. (45)

> [it will become necessary in the future to formulate a codex of the anthropotechnology and to confront this fact actively. Such a codex will retroactively alter the meaning of old humanism, for it will be made explicit, and codified, that humanity is not just the friendship of man with man, but that man has become the higher power for man. (24)]

Given that Sloterdijk declared humanism dead, his imagined codex cannot be founded on ethics. Rather, it has to manifest and reveal the power relations between the "breeder" and the "bred," domesticated animals—imagined in *Lärchenau* as Gunter's version of the "new human being," a hybrid of human and animal, or more generally for Sloterdijk, the optimized human being. All such a codex can do, then, is to establish rules for the human zoo, rules that regulate and conclusively stabilize power relations between the god-like creator and his timid and subservient creatures. In other words, the rules of breeding will supersede an ethics founded on humanist norms.

Where does this lead in the unified Germany of *Lärchenau*, where the GDR's efforts to teach their doctors ethics were to no avail and where former GDR physicians meet their even more ruthless West German counterparts? In Hensel's world, the "breeders" from the East and the West find the perfect conditions for collaboration when the Munich-based private "Institut für Rekonstruktive Neurobiologie" (Institute for Reconstructive Neurobiology; 274) takes over the research institute of the Berlin Charité in August 1990.[8] When private—in other words, commercial—interests take over the previously state-controlled institution, Dr. Konarske can cooperate with Professor Dickescheidt, who, like Gunter, is famous for his success in cell biology (314). Professor Dickescheidt encourages the human experiments Dr. Konarske planned to perfect using his wife as his guinea pig. After unification, when the public realm has officially dissolved into the private, Gunter's "chimärisches Zukunftsmodell" (chimerical model for the future; 346) of the mouse, prepared in the GDR, can become reality: "Das Tier mit der Extraportion Mensch" (The animal with the extra portion of the human; 346). Eager to win the Nobel Prize for which his work developing the Stem Cell Act has already been nominated, Gunter trains Adele to regularly inject herself with a serum in case he is not around to administer it. This serum, he declares, contains "vitamins" aimed at creating a new biotype (315). Since this results in gradually reversing the natural aging process to the extent that Adele resembles a six-year-old child, we can also read it as a comment on the obsession with youth increasingly prevalent in capitalist countries since the turn of the century.

Adele receives the first shot while she is comatose. As her husband administers the injection, Professor Dickescheidt encourages him and observes the procedure (332). When they penetrate the body of the unconscious Adele with the needle, this presents her in a position of being symbolically raped by both men. At this point, the physician from the East and the West appear united in their shared scientific goals, motivated by nothing except the lure of worldwide fame and fantasies of male self-procreation. Playing with the post-unification motif of the female East's symbolic rape and abjection by a West imagined as male, *Lärchenau* highlights the damaging effects of German unification, particularly for women. Dr. Konarske, however, also emerges as an abjected loser of the unification process: in 2007, just before he is ready to retire, he realizes that his former collaborator Dickescheidt, who in the meantime has moved on to conduct his research at a US university, has tricked him. When Konarske receives an email informing him that Dickescheidt has received the Nobel Prize in Medicine for his epigenetic phenomenon-activation (441), all the East German doctor can do is weep in frustration.

Still, Adele emerges as the true victim because she does not possess the knowledge that comes with power—which in Sloterdijk's world renders her the "bred animal" at the mercy of the "breeder." Her symptomatic body is perverted because her malady manifests on the surface level as an artificially induced well-being, which in reality and over time makes her ill and leads to her death. Moreover, her suffering from the dominance and violence she experiences particularly in the twenty-first century materializes as a progressive undoing of physical inscriptions on her body, which she cannot comprehend. The results of the serum injections are inscribed in Adele's flesh as a bizarre elimination of historic bodily traces, since the regression back to a six-year-old child deprives her of her archived body knowledge. When she is finally slain by a drunken Russian soldier who has the same name, Oleg, as the man who saved her life in Russian-occupied Berlin after the war (84, 444), Adele's and the GDR's decline come to a sudden and violent close. The socialist experiment, as embodied in Adele, has ended. Adele's death, which includes her symptomatic body's consignment to oblivion, stands for the forceful expulsion of lived GDR experience from the historical process.[9] Moreover, the protagonist's regressing, severely injured, and finally forgotten body as well as the decaying socialist state that eventually dissolves without a trace present the failure of attempts to reinstate the humanist ideals that were lost with fascism. The success of the capitalist system in the unification process and at the beginning of the twenty-first century marks the point in history when the new age of genetic research, eagerly anticipated by Dr. Konarske and Dr. Dickescheidt fifteen years earlier, expedites the destruction of capacities for remembering history.

Adele's gradual loss of the body as a site of cultural inscription corresponds to the growing power of scientists engaged in genetic research. Her body points to a scientific success that presupposes the loss of humanist values and historical memory and further problematizes Sloterdijk's visions of the future. Posing a variety of future-oriented questions, Sloterdijk had stated:

> Ob aber die langfristige Entwicklung auch zu einer genetischen Reform der Gattungseigenschaften führen wird—ob eine künftige Anthropotechnologie bis zu einer expliziten Merkmalsplanung vordringt; ob die Menschheit gattungsweit eine Umstellung vom Geburtenfatalismus zur optionalen Geburt und zur pränatalen Selektion wird vollziehen können—dies sind Fragen, in denen sich . . . der evolutionäre Horizont vor uns zu lichten beginnt. (46–47)

> [But whether this long-term process will also eventuate in a genetic reform of the characteristics of the species—whether a future anthropotechnology portends an explicit determination of traits; whether humanity as a species can transform birth fatalism into optional birth and into prenatal selection—these are questions in which . . . the evolutionary horizon before us begins to dawn.][10]

The world imagined in *Lärchenau* denies the possibilities Sloterdijk presents. Adele's regression and her violent death as well as nurse Angela's miscarriages stand for the impossibility of optimizing future human beings by means of prenatal selection and influence or by later genetic manipulation. The narrative thus rejects the notion of a "master race" of *Übermenschen* imagined by the Nazis and bizarrely evoked in Sloterdijk's dreams of a genetically optimized human species. In fact, the contrast with Baba Prohaska's healthy children, delivered by natural birth without the slightest support of modern medicine, not only refutes the "brave new world" imagined by Sloterdijk and Dr. Konarske alike, but also opens up a new horizon: hope lies outside the ethnic German population because ethics are based on a set of cultural norms and cannot be replaced by a bred genome. Since the humanist values the ethnic German population lost in fascism are only preserved in the few descendants of survivors of the Holocaust, prospects of a future determined by humanist values are vested in the so-called gypsy family forced to live on the fringes of society. By demanding a space in the center of the village to initiate the life of the newest generation when Baba gives birth, the family asserts their cultural norms. They demonstrate that rescue for the ethnic German population is only to be found in the margins of society, which have never been contaminated by fascist thought.

Like Christa Wolf towards the end of her life, Hensel projects modern civilization, particularly when associated with capitalism and—even worse—fascism, as producing monsters. Yet while Wolf's protagonists see the danger of humanist ideals ending up in the wrong hands—namely, those of petty demons—Hensel's narrative depicts the end of humanist ideals within the ethnic German population. In her world, the GDR emerges as having failed to re-educate its population along the lines of socialist-humanist values. The pre-conditions for the creation of genetic monsters could develop in socialism as well as in capitalism, and her monsters surface in uncanny ways as actual monstrosities that negate any remaining humanist values. In the ethnic German population, in socialism and capitalism alike, genetic engineering attempts to replace social criticism, and test tubes and research labs assume the place of utopia after the death of humanism.

Written in the Flesh, Revisited: *Du stirbst nicht*

In Kathrin Schmidt's award-winning 2009 novel *Du stirbst nicht*,[11] monsters do not materialize as explicitly as in Hensel's novel; rather they surface in ways reminiscent of Christa Wolf. As in Wolf's *Leibhaftig*, this tale of illness and recovery features medical institutions, albeit in post-unification Germany. *Du stirbst nicht* portrays a woman's quest for agency and positionality after she wakes up from a coma caused by an aneurysm. The symptomatic body at the center of the novel receives and continually changes its identity as the protagonist, a writer and psychologist like Schmidt, acquires knowledge about her past and her illness. Despite Schmidt's sober and often self-ironic tone, which could not differ more from Christa Wolf's presentations of suffering, the proximity to Wolf's *Leibhaftig*—published seven years prior—is impossible to miss, and *Du stirbst nicht* expressly invites the comparison (228).

Both books narrate tales of survival: similar to Wolf's protagonist, Schmidt's patient Helene Wesendahl depends on reconstructing her past so that she can heal. Her recovery is a slow and painful process. She needs to come to terms with the paralysis that afflicts the entire right side of her body, her inability to control bodily functions, her constant drooling, her lack of language and memory, and her immobility—all of which are a source of humiliation and shame. For her recuperation, she depends on learning to read her body's symptoms: she must recognize and interpret the warning signs it sends in reaction to disturbing news in the narrative present, and she has to understand that it supports her in overcoming the suppressed trauma caused by the demise of the GDR and resulting unification. The novel provides only a single indication of this trauma, and Helene's recollections of the GDR only constitute a small portion of the remembered experiences. Still, memories of the GDR and the so-called *Wende* surface not only as part of her positionality in post-unification Germany, but also as significant for understanding her illness and for her ability to heal. In order to analyze the memory work undertaken by her body, it is first necessary to examine aspects of the novel that appear to be related to Wolf's *Leibhaftig*: experiences of aggression in the medical and in the legal systems, and power structures that are reminiscent of those depicted in Wolf's GDR hospital.

Aggression and Deceit in Post-Unification Medical Institutions

Helene Wesendahl encounters the power structures of two clinics and a rehab center over a period of several months. With few exceptions, these institutions and their staff are portrayed as violent and acting against the patient's interests. Since Helene's body forces her to behave in ways unthinkable under "normal"—that is, "healthy"—conditions, she challenges the hospital's power structures from the beginning and is repeatedly punished. Unaware of her body's condition after she wakes up from the coma, she first pulls out the metal clips in her head, and later the stomach tube through which she is fed. Her actions lead to increased measures that are literally presented as "punishment" by the nurse: "*Ach Mensch, muss das denn sein? . . . Zur Strafe werde ich Sie fixieren und Ihnen die Decke wegnehmen*" (Really, did you have to do this? . . . As a punishment I'm going to immobilize you and take your blanket away; 18; italics in original). Helene, who has difficulties recognizing her family members, understands neither her illness nor her whereabouts. She suffers from major linguistic deficiencies and is not able to resist the nurse and her practices of subjugation. Unable to recall appropriate words and protect her vital interests, Helene becomes the victim of the nurse's rude language and the target of her corporal punishment. Similarly, the patient's body is disciplined when the nurses leave her in a painful state of semi-consciousness for hours while she suffers from a biliary colic. This time, they consider the chastisement "justified" as a reaction to Helene's refusal to take medication that, as it turns out, would have had adverse effects. In contrast to the considerate and polite tone of the GDR nurses portrayed in Wolf's *Leibhaftig*, the post-unification hospital depicted in Schmidt's narrative shows nurses yelling and as empowered to punish patients, to endanger their well-being, and to add to their misery.

There is a single instance of a nurse attempting to protect Helene—in this case, from a ward physician who wants to force the patient to subject herself to a form of psychological treatment that Helene, a trained psychologist herself, dismisses as unsuitable. The nurse is promptly reprimanded by the doctor. The patient's subsequent reflection reveals a major difference compared with GDR hospitals: "Ärzte haben es eben nicht gern, wenn in der Hierarchie weit unter ihnen rangierende Chargen etwas tun, was einem Belehren gleichkommen könnte, denkt Helene" (Physicians just don't like it if those ranked much lower in the hierarchy do something that might amount to teaching them a lesson, Helene thinks; 220). Contrary to Wolf's depiction of a GDR clinic that stressed collaboration and the egalitarian relationship among doctors and nurses in a society that propagated the elimination of class distinctions, Schmidt's depiction of a hospital highlights the re-introduction of traditional notions of status and hierarchical structures in medical institutions after unification. Rank figures as more important than the patient's well-being, and doctors and nurses only collaborate when they team up against the patient.

While Wolf's protagonist in *Leibhaftig* also complained about being turned into an object of violence, the perceived aggression—contrary to the depiction in *Du stirbst nicht*—was always related to therapy. In Wolf's clinic, physical force was never exerted by the female nurses, but exclusively by some male physicians and medical machines. In *Du stirbst nicht*, the patient feels similarly threatened by technology. Not unlike Wolf's patient, who suspects that she is being kept under surveillance by a monitor, Helene misinterprets the intravenous drip as a means to connect her to a network that controls her remotely. Her belief that she is at the mercy of a gang of murderers who are intent on killing her along with everyone else in the clinic shows us that she experiences the hospital as truly violent (11). The language evokes *Leibhaftig* as well in the extent to which medicine is dominated by male discourse; it points to the aggression that results in associating the hospital's doctors—who are exclusively male—with the military. The physicians appear as a troop of men (16, 25) who are responsible for having inserted the metal clips the protagonist identifies as "metallene Panzersperren" (metal tank barriers; 17, 30). Later, Helene needs the approval of an entire squad of doctors (136, 229) in order to be transferred to a rehab center. Here, similarly, the men sharing her table in the dining room appear as its occupying force (241). In short, the patient feels subjected to the war machinery of an army rather than to medical staff focused on healing her illness. Her weakened body is unable to resist either the hospitals' existing power structures or the unquestioned belief in medical machinery and the potent yet dangerous medication that is administered in maximum doses. As a result, Helene becomes increasingly dependent on her husband Matthes as a corrective force in the face of the medical institutions.

When the protagonist develops an allergic reaction to the pills she is prescribed following a misdiagnosed epileptic seizure, Matthes furtively brings in an alternative practitioner. He diagnoses imminent kidney failure caused by the medication and proposes homoeopathic drainage to rescue the patient. When Helene and Matthes decide to secretly discontinue the dangerous pharmaceutical drugs in favor of homeopathic pills, the narrative intensifies the conflict between Western medicine, which reduces the protagonist to being little more than an object of medical interest, and alternative medicine focused on healing—a contrast similarly evoked in *Leibhaftig*. Particularly since both the physician's diagnosis and the proposed therapy were contraindicated as dangerous, *Du stirbst nicht* criticizes Western medicine doubly for its presumably objective approach as well as for the therapeutic measures it prescribes. When Helene, happy with the success of the alternative treatment, finally discloses her independent decision, the violent response from authorities infringes on the protagonist's most basic rights.

Over the course of her weeks in various medical institutions, Helene repeatedly claims agency. Early on, for example, she refuses to take an antidepressant: "Sie macht kein Geheimnis daraus, dass sie es [das Antidepressivum] nicht nimmt, aber niemand registriert das" (She is not cagey about not taking the antidepressant, but nobody notices it; 36). The hospital staff care so little about the patient that they do not even seem to register her resistance. Thus, Helene is able to influence her therapy only due to the medical staff's initial disinterest. This changes suddenly when she declines psychotherapy in the hospital. After her rejection of the contraindicated epilepsy medication, she is subjected to the full force of the medical staff. Three doctors and two nurses assemble to inform her, "Sie dürfe das nicht. . . . Sie müsse. Zurückstecken. Die Verantwortung trügen sie. Nicht Helene. *Was, ich trage keine Verantwortung?*" (She was not allowed to do that. . . . She had to. Back down. They bore the responsibility. Not Helene. *What, I am not bearing responsibility?*; 308; italics in original). Denying her the right to take responsibility for her own body, the members of the medical profession team up against the patient and claim authority over her disease—behavior that appears bizarre, given the legal situation in the FRG. Instead of finding a solution in dialogue, they expect the patient to "back down," which clearly means that she is supposed to disregard her own interests in favor of those expressed by the medical professionals.

These doctors and nurses appear stuck in an attitude towards the patient that is reminiscent of GDR law, where both patients' ill bodies and their behavior were to be treated, where individuals were supposed to be persuaded to "back down" for the greater good, and where passive patients had to accept the proposed therapy. In other words, certain aspects of GDR medicine seem to live on, which is hardly a surprise. Hartmut Bettin and Mariacarla Gadebusch Bondio agree:

> Beim Pflegepersonal ... kann ... von weitgehenden personellen Kontinuitäten ausgegangen werden.... Das heißt, dass viele, die in ... medizinischen Einrichtungen arbeiten und forschen, in der DDR geboren, sozialisiert und teilweise akademisch ausgebildet worden sind. Als Medizinstudierende, Ärztinnen und Ärzte ... sowie Krankenschwestern und Pfleger haben sie in medizinischen Einrichtungen der DDR gewirkt, Erfahrungen gesammelt, gewisse Prägungen erfahren.[12]

> [pertaining to the nursing staff ... we can assume extensive continuities with regards to staff.... That means that many who work and research in ... medical institutions were born, socialized, and in many cases received their academic education in the GDR. As students of medicine, physicians ... and nurses they worked in medical institutions of the GDR, gained experiences there, and were shaped in certain ways.]

Medical-historical research maintains that due to obvious continuities among medical staff, behavior and ethical attitudes that were specific to the GDR and socialist medicine persist. In other words, while the political state ceased to exist, its citizens inevitably perpetuate its practices and norms. *Du stirbst nicht* addresses this topic repeatedly by referencing the GDR's *Duldungs- und Befolgungspflicht*—an "obligation" the medical personnel in Schmidt's novel expect to be fulfilled by Helene and against which the patient rebels. Lingering GDR practices also surface in the patient's alleged obligation to cooperate in the therapy. In the novel, this extends to the reports the hospital sends to the rehab center. They are not limited to information pertaining to the patient's medical situation, but assess her personality and her willingness to cooperate in the therapy whose successful outcome is contingent upon her cooperation, and for which she is held liable. The speech therapist, for example, claims that the patient "erwies sich als *nicht kooperative Patientin ... Sehr kooperativ* steht hingegen im Bericht der Physiotherapeutin" (proved to be a *noncooperative patient...* The physiotherapist's report, however, says *very cooperative*"; 136; italics in original). Employing language that is characteristic of the GDR medical system, both reports explicitly evaluate the patient's inclination to cooperate. By italicizing the relevant words in the text, *Du stirbst nicht* draws attention to what Christa Wolf similarly conveyed about her stay in the GDR hospital in *Leibhaftig*: the requirement to actively participate in therapeutic measures, even if the patient experiences them as brutal, contraindicated, or simply futile.

The patient in *Du stirbst nicht* is clearly not prepared for anything resembling such GDR practices in the post-unification hospital, and is therefore surprised to hear the clinic staff ask her whether she had considered a *"Betreuungsverfahren"* (guardianship procedure; 309; italics in original). In post-unification Germany, taking on the medical staff can apparently lead to similar legal repercussions as in the GDR. In this hospital, the socialist notion that individual health and interests must be subordinated to those of the community lives on. As a result, Helene's body is in danger of being subjected to the state's legal system because of the influence the medical system can exert. The threat implied in the medical staff's suggestion of undergoing a guardianship procedure combined with their sudden display of insincere friendliness causes Helene's body to respond: "Hab acht, sagt ihr Bauch, . . . da rollt was an, was du nicht übersiehst, was dir aber gewaltige Bauchschmerzen verursachen kann . . . Helene spürt den Schmerz . . . Die Galle" (Watch out, says her belly, . . . something is rolling in, something you don't comprehend, but which can cause an enormous bellyache . . . Helene feels the pain . . . The gall bladder; 309). Echoing the physicality of Wolf's protagonist, Helene's body sends warning signals, here in the shape of a biliary colic that jolts her brain into activity. Prompted by the painful attack, Helene considers the exercise of state power over the individual's body along the lines of the multiple meanings of the word "reichen"—very much in the style of Wolf's contemplations on language. The meanings of the German "reichen" upon which the protagonist ruminates range from "to be enough" in the sense of "I've had enough" to "to be adequate," or "to be sufficient." When she ponders the significance of the subjunctive creeping up in her thoughts, she suddenly remembers an elderly, demented neighbor who had initiated such legal action:

> [Sie [hatte] zu Helene davon gesprochen, sich *entmündigen* lassen zu wollen . . . Seit Anfang der Neunziger gab es aber Entmündigungsverfahren in der Bundesrepublik nicht mehr, sie wurden durch die Betreuungsanordnung ersetzt, die in einem gerichtlichen Verfahren getroffen wurde. . . . Helenes Starre löst sich ein wenig, sie glaubt zu wissen, dass sie nach einem gutachterlichen Prozess nicht mit einer Betreuungspflegschaft, die für sie . . . eigentlich doch nichts anderes ist als eine *Entmündigung*, zu rechnen hätte. (310–11; italics in original)

> [She had spoken to Helene about wanting to be declared legally *incapacitated* . . . But since the early 1990s, there were no legal

incapacitation processes any more in the FRG, they had been replaced by a guardianship order that was instituted in judicial proceedings. . . . Helene's numbness loosens a bit, she feels she knows that in her case, an expert's report would be unlikely to result in a guardianship arrangement, which for her . . . really did not amount to anything else but an *incapacitation.*]

Through Helene's memory of her elderly neighbor, the narrative delivers an accurate portrayal of the legal situation in the FRG. With the new *Betreuungsanordnung* (guardianship order) from January 1, 1992, regulated in the *Bürgerliches Gesetzbuch* in BGB §§1896–1908, incapacitation was replaced by the guardianship procedure. This procedure does indeed grant potential candidates for a *Betreuungsanordnung* more rights than the previous law regulating incapacitation, not least of all with regards to granting the basic rights warranted in the German Basic Law. However, it is still possible to appoint a legal guardian against an individual's will in cases of diagnosed psychiatric illness—with unwillingness to participate in psychological treatment as one of the indicators. Since Helene repeatedly refused to accept psychological treatment in the clinic, she has already endangered herself. Specifically, BGB §1906 (3) clearly states that the guardian can consent to an *ärztliche Zwangsmaßnahme* (a mandatory medical measure) if the person placed under guardianship is unable to understand the necessity of a medical measure or to act upon such understanding because of psychological illness or a mental or psychological disorder. The threat represented by the medical staff's intention to order guardianship for Helene initially aims at unsettling the patient, to the extent that the staff is hoping she will concede to the treatment they prescribed. A second step would, however, imply a greater risk: Once Helene was assigned a guardian, she would lose the freedom to intervene in her therapy—also according to FRG law. She would lose any agency, and be turned into a passive patient without an opportunity to resist the doctors. In other words, while the legal situation may be very different from the GDR, the medical staff seem to have found loopholes in FRG law that allow them to continue practices in the hospital that serve their desire for passive, "cooperative" patients.

At the end of the day, Helene depends on her husband's interference, and on his rejection of the idea to submit his wife to a guardianship procedure. She is relieved that "Matthes . . . gesagt [hatte], dass *seine Frau* geschäftsfähig, im Vollbesitz ihrer geistigen Kräfte und keinesfalls ein Fall für ein Betreuungsverfahren wäre" (Matthes . . . had said that *his wife* was contractually capable, of sound mind, and on no account a case for a procedure to incapacitate her; 313–14; italics in original). Italicizing the words "his wife," the narrative highlights that without the legal protection of the heteronormative relationship in the institution of marriage, Helene would have been subject to the doctors' will—including the threat of imminent death due to the unnoticed allergic reaction to the epilepsy medication and resulting kidney failure—and unwarranted incapacitation. In other words, the medical institution in the FRG respects the husband's judgment only because Helene's and Matthes's relationship is legalized by a state institution. This realization receives an ironic twist, since Helene previously remembered the reason for their wedding in the GDR: they had been informed that they could receive an apartment for their family of five—Helene was expecting her third child at the time—provided that they got married. *Du stirbst nicht* thus relativizes historical research on single mothers, childcare, and divorce in the GDR by including Helene's private reflections on the past. The protagonist felt punished by the unsatisfactory living conditions that forced two adults and two children to cohabitate in two small dorm rooms (64). The location of the childcare facilities additionally made it difficult for Helene to follow her career. This points to the discrepancy between progressive laws that clearly supported single mothers just like married couples, particularly after the reforms of 1972, and the quotidian experiences in the GDR.[13]

In everyday, real-life socialism, old-fashioned notions of morality continued, including the preference for children to be raised in conventional families. They forced Helene and Matthes into a lifestyle they had never imagined for themselves, and which had significant implications for their life in post-unification Germany. Helene's contemplation of how the institutional regulation of social norms had influenced her private life, seen within the context of the threat of incapacitation in the FRG, presents a comment on the similarities of power structures in Germany pre- and post-unification. Despite the political differences, the network of various state institutions continues to impact the individual's private life; and because marriage as the legalized form of a heteronormative relationship continues to have the exact same influence in the post-unification FRG that it had had in the GDR, it is Helene's only rescue.

Legal Inequality Post-Unification

Du stirbst nicht further emphasizes the state preference for heterosexual marriage and the violence exercised in concert between the medical and the legal realm in its portrayal of another character, Viktor/Viola. When Viktor decides to live as Viola and wants to take advantage of medical treatment to achieve bodily transformations, s/he has to submit to a medical system that categorizes her/his body as "'transsexual', bound up with a classification as 'mentally disturbed,'" as Jannik Franzen points out in "Disordering Heteronormativity." He concludes, "Transition opens a field of tension between the self-determination of gender and dependency on treatment professionals, who deny trans* patients personal autonomy over their bodies" (192). In other words, in order to achieve the desired bodily transformations, Viktor in *Du stirbst nicht* has to submit to a procedure that as much as certifies him as mentally ill and denies him responsibility for his body and his will—which effectively parallels the threat of incapacitation Helene endures. Even in the twenty-first century and after the latest reforms of the TSG (*Transsexuellengesetz*; transsexual act) in the FRG in 2009, trans individuals are considered abnormal and psychologically unstable, which results in the unquestioned assumption that they require the supervision of healthcare professionals.[14] Hinting at the power network behind the law, Franzen emphasizes that within a short time medical and psychological disciplines managed to establish "a powerful assessment and treatment apparatus" (192). In other words, outside the gender binary, transsexuals are entirely at the mercy of doctors and lawyers in power positions.[15]

In contrast to Schmidt's Lutz/Lucia, the intersexual individual we observed living exempt from major state interference in the GDR of *Die Gunnar-Lennefsen-Expedition*, as well as Heidi, the transsexual whose sex change was supported in the GDR of *Wie es leuchtet*, Viola experiences intense state interference and finally death. Helene first met Viola in the context of an article she was writing on divorced couples (133), and learned in this context about the cruelty of the TSG, which forces transsexuals like Viktor/Viola into undergoing "sex-adapting" surgery and into divorce. De Silva's "From Moral Downfall to Trans*_Homo Marriage" confirms the legal situation presented in *Du stirbst nicht*, which was written when the TSG from 1981 was still in effect. At that time, the TSG determined as prerequisites for a revision of personal civil status that "the applicant must be 'permanently unable to reproduce', and 'must have undergone a surgical intervention to alter external sex characteristics'" (157). Moreover "any previously entered marriage bond must be dissolved through divorce, as a prerequisite to apply for a change in personal civil status" (159).[16] In an attempt to "protect" the heteronormative majority population from being irritated by men who give birth and women who father children, the TSG from 1981 forces trans individuals to undergo dangerous surgeries which can threaten their lives simply to achieve a change in civil status.

While present-day hormone therapy and a sex operation can allow individuals like Viktor/Viola to alter their sex, which, to some extent, can have a liberating effect, these possibilities also imply a forced compliance with the gender and sex binary, which is promoted by the TSG. Klöppel, too, emphasizes that within the binary classification system for gender and sex, the legal-medical framework opens up a space for alterations. However, these modifications merely present the same firmly established gender and sex binary in new clothes (*XXOXY*, 584). In the demands formulated by the TSG, the FRG emerges as forceful as the GDR in its requirements for individuals to align their behavior with the expectations of society: while the individual does not have to express a desire to commit to socialist—or in the FRG, capitalist—society, the requirement to submit to the sex and gender binary and to fulfill heteronormative gender stereotypes similarly infringes on the individual's rights.

Motivated by his desire to conform to the socially sanctioned sex binary, Viktor decided to change his sex without being fully aware of the legal ramifications. After the surgery, Viola is forced into divorce since she cannot be married to a woman, which also leads her to lose custody of her sons. Since Viola has exclusively loved women all her life, both before and after the surgery, the law also denies her any future legal marriage. Insisting on her trans identity as a woman and simultaneously desiring women, Viola emerges as dangerously "queer": she defies the gender/sex binary, as well as heteronormative sexual practices.[17] When Helene finally comprehends the goal of the legal requirement that forces people like Viola to undergo a "sex-adapting" operation, that is, cementing the binary concept of sex, she is indignant about the brutality of a law that demands such a profound intervention (187).

As if they heard Helene's outcry, the Federal Constitutional Court has since abolished the requirement both for genital surgery (2011) and for a divorce (2009) as prerequisites for a change in civil status.[18] With these latest court decisions, judges appear to concede the injustice imposed on people like Viola, who was prevented from living her desired self-image as a "Vatermutter" (fathermother; 321). Because Viola's self-designation evokes the "Vatermutter" Lutz/Lucia in *Die Gunnar-Lennefsen-Expedition* and thereby suggests a comparison between the situation in the GDR and the FRG, *Du stirbst nicht* has the potential to send a strong statement about gender conventions in post-unification Germany. At the time *Du stirbst nicht* was written, the FRG offered fewer possibilities for a life outside the heteronormative sex and gender binary than the GDR imagined by Schmidt. For post-unification Germany, Schmidt exposes a legal situation that negates certain individuals their right to agency: Viktor/Viola's agency is denied by the TSG, and Helene's agency is threatened by the *Betreuungsverfahren*. Helene, however, remains protected by a heterosexual marriage, while her transsexual friend is left without a safety net and finally dies, most likely from suicide.[19]

Remembering the GDR

Next to the comparison between the GDR and the FRG implied by the discourse surrounding transsexuals and Schmidt's ideal of the "Vatermutter," *Du stirbst nicht* offers GDR memories that are important for the protagonist's healing process. While both her capacity for language and her memory are severely impaired, Helene actively attempts to remember her past. Aware that the weeks before the aneurysm have practically been erased, while memories of the extended past are more readily available, she follows an imaginary memory thread, her *Erinnerungsfaden*, to regain her memory (39). Unlike Wolf's *Erinnerungsbrocken* (*Leibhaftig*, 71)—the memory chunks that float by uncontrollably and depend on the body's dominance over the brain in *Leibhaftig*—Schmidt's *Erinnerungsfaden* requires active participation in the memory process, which is excruciating—and pushes the body aside. Reminiscent of Aleida Assmann's *Gedächtnisspur* (memory trace), Schmidt's *Erinnerungsfaden* presupposes knowledge of the past. With reference to Freud, Assmann explains that we need a memory trace in order to remember events. This *Gedächtnisspur* depends on information that has been previously noticed and stored because one cannot remember blind spots.[20] Schmidt's *Erinnerungsfaden* thus explicitly points to both the content of the knowledge to be uncovered and to the cognitive processes to be regained. Contrary to Wolf's protagonists, who are attempting to unearth knowledge hidden in metaphorical "mines" and pinpointing their various "blind spots," Schmidt's protagonist aims at uncovering parts of a past she knew, not traumatic experiences that were suppressed. The approaches therefore have to differ and this also clarifies the diverging functions of the respective symptomatic bodies: while Wolf's protagonists rely on their bodies to speak to them and make knowledge available that was previously not accessible, Schmidt's protagonist depends on the body to allow her to follow the *Erinnerungsfaden*.

At the same time, Helene Wesendahl reveals significant information about her illness and its link to her work with the *Erinnerungsfaden*. She claims that she had never before spent that much time "erinnern zu üben" (practicing to remember; 111). Generally pleased with the results, she is nevertheless frustrated that the last weeks before her aneurysm—which, in her words, "schließlich das Innerste nach außen beförderte" (finally brought out that which had been innermost; 111)—are only fragmentarily accessible. Helene's words reveal an awareness of her symptomatic body that makes previously secret aspects of her personality available for public view, and also to herself. Among these former mysteries is an occurrence whose significance Helene could not acknowledge at the time it happened. Only with the support of her body can she understand the loss of the GDR and subsequent German unification as traumatic events in her life. Apparently, the loss of her East German *Heimat* (homeland) deeply troubled her—until she experienced her life-threatening disease.

> Überhaupt hatte die Erfahrung des Verschwindens [der DDR], ohne von der Karte getilgt zu werden, nicht vor dem Platzen des Aneurysmas, vor der Dunkelpause, über allem gehockt wie ein

Bussard, bereit, jederzeit nach Beute zu schnappen? Das unterschwellige, blitzschnelle Abwägen . . ., ob jemand von *hier* oder von *drüben* kam. . . . Nur die Dunkelpause konnte das ausgelöscht haben, oder? (100; italics in original)

[Before the aneurysm burst, before the dark pause, did the experience [of the GDR] disappearing without being erased from the map not squat above everything, like a buzzard always ready to grab prey? That subliminal, lightning-quick deliberation . . . whether somebody was from *here* or from *there*. . . . Only the dark pause could have erased that, right?]

The life-threatening disease experienced as a befogged interruption of daily life emerges as a life-changing experience: it entirely transforms the way the protagonist views the world and it allows for insight into the effects of a historic event on the individual. Previously, the disappearance of her country and its social, political, and economic system had resulted in aggression, as it emerges in the image of the inner raptor waiting for prey. Only the coma and the symptomatic body it generated possessed the power to both acknowledge and overcome the trauma that had determined the protagonist's life since the demise of the GDR and unification—and that previously had been a blind spot.

The terms *Betreuungsverfahren* (310) and *Entmündigung* (incapacitation; 311) function not so much as signs for East Germans who experienced the GDR and its aftermath in terms of "linguistic powerlessness," as Deidre Byrnes suggests in "Writing on the Threshold" (180). Rather, the increasingly confident and less fearful voice Byrnes rightly acknowledges points to the patient's final overcoming of the East/West division and to her rise above the position of the abject. In her entirely happy memories of summers with her family in a little village near Anklam in the 1980s, she recovers and claims her own, authentic East German voice and memories. And in her recollection of the summer of 1989, she summons up the East German experience of a lost revolution and the destruction of their lives. Helene remembers how Matthes and she, who had apparently started to socialize with members of oppositional circles in the mid-1980s (105–8), became increasingly excited, expecting to play a significant role in reforming the GDR once the regime collapsed. However, their initial excitement, which resonates with the dream of creating a humane socialism, was quickly disappointed, and the couple was left disillusioned with the aftermath of the peaceful revolution of 1989 (246). What emerges in Helene is the very trauma of the destruction of hopes for the future that we can also observe in Christa Wolf's fiction and essays, even if Schmidt denied having felt deep resignation in an interview.[21] In Helene's increasingly self-confident voice, Schmidt's protagonist can formulate her disillusionment and expose the East German experience of the years following German unification: the subsequent summers are entirely determined by the closure of the neighborhood *Konsum*, the GDR supermarket, and the local *Landwirtschaftliche Produktionsgenossenschaft* (LPG), the GDR collective farm. Unemployment, exploitation of the few people who have found new jobs, alcoholism due to increasing frustration among the village population, a plummeting birthrate and—along with it—scarcity of children and hope for the future, lack of communication and interaction among the villagers, and most importantly, death: these are the developments that define people's lives after 1989 (246–49):

> Erschrocken hatten sie [in der zweiten Hälfte der 90er] die vielen Gräber Gleichaltriger gesehen . . ., in den Fünfzigerjahren Geborener, . . . als hätte hier eine ganze Generation sich verabschieden wollen. . . . Ähnlich wie die Dörfler selbst, die unter dem Eindruck des von allen geahnten Endes erstarrt schienen, hatten sie nicht mehr hinsehen wollen, wie es sich dort totlief. Wie sich ein Dorf . . . aus dem Leben trank inmitten herrlich blühender Landschaften, . . . die keine Leute mehr brauchten, um in voller Blüte zu stehen. (247)

> [Frightened, they saw [in the second half of the 1990s] the many graves of their peers . . ., those born in the 1950s, . . . as if an entire generation had wanted to bow out. . . . Similar to the villagers themselves, who—under the impression of the end that had been anticipated by everyone—seemed frozen, they did not want to observe any more how it fizzled out. How a village . . . drank itself to death in the midst of gloriously blooming landscapes, . . . that did not need people anymore in order to be in full bloom.]

After she survives her illness, Helene articulates what are explicitly East German memories, determined by apocalyptic sentiments that stand in stark contrast to the images presented in the West German media. The actual physical death of an entire generation, of those too young to retire and too old to adapt easily to the new political system, is at the center of her experience. Yet it is the conspicuous reference to Helmut Kohl's famous proclamation that gives rise to East Germans' deep resentment of German unification: on July 1, 1990, on the occasion of the Monetary, Economic, and Social Union taking effect, Kohl declared that by Germans' joint efforts, the five so-called new states would soon be turned into *blühende Landschaften*, blooming landscapes in which it would be worth living and working.[22]

As Helene's reflection highlights, these *blühende Landschaften* existed before unification—and they were actually inhabited by people who enjoyed the blooming scenery as well as working in the rural area. Reversing Kohl's declaration, the protagonist demonstrates the East German claim to a right to interpret political developments and challenge the West German depiction of the events. Strengthened by the experiences of her symptomatic body, Helene finds a voice that demands that East German voices be included in a pan-German history. To be clear, Schmidt's novel explicitly opposes any *Ostalgie*, or nostalgia for the GDR, not least of all in the protagonist's rebuff of her friend Raphael's retrospective glorification of certain aspects of GDR life.[23] At the same time, the narrative insists on making knowledge about the GDR as well as the unification process public, not least of all so that structural similarities of repression in both the GDR and in post-unification Germany become visible.

Specters of the Stasi

Not unlike Schmidt's novel, Antje Rávic Strubel's *Sturz der Tage in die Nacht* (2012) reveals distressing manifestations of the GDR past that affect the protagonists' present and reveal that GDR power structures, particularly the destructive effects of the Stasi forces, are still alive in the twenty-first century. In Strubel's novel, too, the female protagonist relies on her symptomatic body: it signals the uncanny emergence of GDR history in her personal life, a history she thought she had left behind, and it allows her to gain knowledge about the extent to which her GDR past determines her present in the twenty-first century. *Sturz der Tage in die Nacht* tells the story of forty-one-year-old Inez, an ornithologist conducting research for her dissertation on Stora Karlö, a small Swedish island and bird sanctuary, and twenty-four-year-old Erik, who accidentally ends up on the island in the summer of 2009. The two East Germans, who as the story unfolds are revealed to be mother and son, fall in love with each other without being aware of their biological bond. Yet their relationship is affected by Inez's GDR past or, more accurately, by Rainer Feldberg, a former Stasi officer, who arrives on the same ferry as Erik. The two main story lines of *Sturz der Tage in die Nacht*, the incestuous relationship between Inez and Erik, of which they only gradually become aware, and the continuing influence of the Stasi and its practices on East Germans even twenty years after the fall of the Wall, intersect—and they play out most violently on Inez's body.

Even though Inez has not been in touch with Feldberg for over twenty years, her body immediately recognizes him. When he steps off the boat, her body weakens and she needs support. "Sie habe etwas gebraucht, um sich festzuhalten, und nach meinem Arm gegriffen" (She needed something to hold on to, and reached for my arm; 53), Erik remembers Inez telling him later. In twenty-first-century Sweden, Feldberg's appearance represents a deep disruption as the GDR past that Inez thought she had left behind, both temporally and spatially, intrudes on the island. Inez's conscious decision to leave post-unification Germany to escape the potential return of the specters of the GDR is undermined when they show up in Sweden—in the figure of Feldberg. The safe space offered by the secluded bird sanctuary is revealed as deceptive. Its security is lost the instant Feldberg arrives, because his appearance renders Inez's reason for being on Stora Karlsö invalid, as the narrative informs us (53). Inez's body understands the reemergence of the Stasi as a villainous force in the woman's life. It emerges as an eerie reminder of the GDR and continuing Stasi control of her private life; and it heralds evil for everything that is alive.

After 1990, Feldberg utilized his professional abilities of spying and *Zersetzung* for his private business, an agency he calls MEGA OPERATION & RISK PROTECTION (333). He therefore had never lost track of Inez (335), whom he knows as his former colleague Felix Ton's sixteen-year-old girlfriend. In 1984, she became pregnant. Coerced by her boyfriend, Inez agreed to put her newborn son up for adoption because Ton, pressured by Feldberg, considered family life counter-productive for his career. In the GDR, Feldberg organized and supervised the adoption process and also kept an eye on Erik in the subsequent years—without the young man's knowledge. Through former Stasi informants who hold positions in state agencies after unification, Feldberg remains well connected even after 1990. This enables him to foil Inez's plans to learn about her son's whereabouts after the fall of the Wall and to gain access to the island in an official position that allows him to control Inez.

As the story unfolds, the significance of Inez's body and its warning signs that do not betray her become more evident: Feldberg acts under orders from Felix Ton, now a successful Brandenburg politician for the conservative CDU (*Christlich Demokratische Union*, Christian Democratic Union). Ton runs for a seat in the Federal Parliament and wants to find his son so that he can utilize him as part of an *operative Legende*, a legend he and his campaign manager, Feldberg, concoct in typical Stasi manner (97–98).[24] At the end of Feldberg's diabolical operation, Ton is to appear as Inez's victim, with her having allegedly denied him his rights as a father. For his press-supported campaign, which ironically emphasizes family values and the need to prosecute former Stasi officers, the politician stages himself as a father longing to be reunited with his long-lost son. This constellation, which in Ton's ostensible desire to reprimand Stasi collaborators puts the fox in charge of the henhouse, demonstrates the persistent influence of Stasi methods in politics. In fact, the power of the former secret service extends to manipulating political content in post-unification Germany: they can—as respected members of democratic parties such as the conservative CDU—take care of former Stasi officers by allegedly shedding light on the GDR past. The former

Stasi slogan, which designates the GDR Ministry for State Security the *Schild und Schwert der Partei* (shield and sword of the party), attains a new twist in the context of post-unification Germany, when Feldberg emerges as Ton's shield and sword, hired exclusively to destroy Inez's life and her reputation on the island.

The woman's physical reaction warns her of the threatening *Zersetzung* and indicates her latent knowledge—based on past experience—of Stasi methods. Aware of ongoing Stasi influence, she anticipates Feldberg's old Stasi connections in post-unification Germany. Therefore, Inez, warned by her body, foresees that Feldberg's activities will thwart her research and destroy her island life. While her body signals peril, the purpose of Feldberg's appearance and menacing actions remain obscure until he seemingly by accident leaves behind a newspaper article that informs Inez about Ton's career. With that information in hand, it dawns on her that Feldberg will infiltrate her surroundings with false information to destroy her reputation, thus preventing her from effectively tarnishing Ton's name by revealing the nature of their relationship and his Stasi affiliation.

Feldberg's second line of attack, letting Inez unknowingly engage in an incestuous relationship with her son—a relationship the former Stasi officer could then use against her—remains undisclosed to Inez for a long time. Only shortly before leaving the island does Feldberg strategically place several mysterious hints aimed at unsettling Inez. Her body reacts violently:

'Neunzehnhundertvierundachtzig. *Es war ein klarer kalter Tag im April, und die Uhren schlugen* dreizehn. . . . Er wird fünfundzwanzig, Inez. . . . Das sind genau sechzehn Jahre. Ist dir das noch nicht aufgefallen? . . . Ihr zwei seid ein schönes Paar. Nicht wahr, Inez. Das findest du auch. Ist es nicht ein bisschen so wie nach Hause kommen?' (135; italics in original)

[Nineteen eighty-four. *It was a bright cold day in April, and the clocks were striking thirteen.* . . . He'll be twenty-five, Inez. . . . That's exactly sixteen years. Haven't you noticed that? . . . The two of you are a handsome couple. Right, Inez? You think so, too. Isn't it a bit like coming home?]

Feldberg's dual approach targets Inez's private life and lays the groundwork for the revelation that Erik is her son. Referencing the beginning of George Orwell's *1984*, it indicates that the ongoing Stasi threat is ubiquitous and will continue in any given societal or political structure. This approach corresponds with Strubel's opinion of the Stasi, which for her represents destruction and manipulation as well as the meanest characteristics people can develop, usually out of greed and narcissism. At the same time, she is convinced that such an organization is not exclusive to the GDR, but a phenomenon that generally exists in every society.[25] In his self-portrayal as Big Brother, Feldberg accordingly not only reveals that he is observing Inez and Erik, but also conveys to Inez that her desire to leave "home" and her GDR past are in vain. Precisely because Stasi-like methods of surveillance and destruction can and will survive in any given society, Inez is forced to realize that with Feldberg, the dreaded "home" has caught up with her in Sweden in 2009—even if she still does not recognize her son in her lover. When Feldberg additionally leaves behind a poisoned razorbill named Friederike, Inez's subsequent realization "Das hört nie auf" (That will never stop; 140) applies both to the Stasi menace and to men desiring to destroy nature. Feldberg's lesson cannot be misunderstood: by killing Inez's favorite bird, he tells her that he can and will take everything she loves. She gets the message: when she contemplates that one day she might find another bird she would visit every morning and who would recognize her, she understands that she would lose that one, too—and comes down with a fever the same night (157).

Given that Inez never suffers from fevers or headaches, the flu and the accompanying delirium into which her body retreats to gain information about her past are telling.[26] The fever episodes, which come in waves that each time allow Inez to retrieve another memory, let her dive into her GDR past in an attempt to figure out who she was and what her feelings and thoughts were at the age of sixteen. Supported by the fever attacks, Inez remembers individual events involving Feldberg and Ton in 1983 and 1984. She can recall certain smells, specific conversations, even words and old, forgotten vocabulary, "das das Fieber aufspürte" (which the fever tracked down; 158–59). However, she has to admit that her body's abilities are limited: she cannot figure out how she felt when she was fifteen or sixteen (180). Closer to the end of the fever episodes, Inez admits (as the text presents in internal focalization), "Die Person, die sie mit fünfzehn oder sechzehn gewesen war, ließ sich nicht mehr aufspüren. Da half auch kein Fieber" (The person she had been when she was fifteen or sixteen could not be tracked down. Even a fever could not help; 184). While the fever actively supports the body in "retrieving" certain facts relating to her past, a process of which she seems to be highly aware, the repeated emphasis on the unavailability of access to her feelings obtrudes. This constellation, in which Inez realizes that her ability to solve the riddle depends on access to her past emotions, implies that she expects Feldberg to know the very sentiments that remain barred to her, and points to the overarching significance she assigns to the Stasi officer. In fact, her first fever-induced dream reveals his magnitude: like a giant, Feldberg approaches her and casts a growing cloud over the site until he overshadows everything. The scene climaxes when he presents her with the dead razorbill, which reveals that because he has access to everything, including her most private emotions, he knows how to hurt her most effectively—and will not hesitate to do so.

Felix Ton is another constant presence that Inez experiences physically during her feverish hallucinations. The reemergence of a dream she had as a teenager, but did not manage to decipher then, is hardly surprising:

> Felix war der schillernde bunte Vogel, der Arara . . . Der Arara saß zutraulich auf einer Wiese . . . Sie lief auf ihn zu, aber als sie ihn fast erreicht hatte, flog er auf. . . . Ein paar Meter weiter wartete er auf sie, bis sie ihm so nah kam, dass sie ihn beinahe berühren konnte, und hob wieder ab. Auf diese Weise querten sie die Wiese. . . . bis . . . sie sich von oben sah; wie sie einem schillernden Vogel hinterherlief, der von Drähten geführt wurde, die an einem Brückenkran befestigt waren. Der Kran überspannte die Wiese. Es war nicht der Wind gewesen, der ihm die Flügel aufgeklappt hatte, sondern eine Fernsteuerung. (175)

> [Felix was the enigmatically colorful bird, the macaw . . . The macaw sat trustingly in a meadow . . . She ran towards him, but when she had nearly reached him, he flew off. . . . A couple of meters further, he waited for her, until she came so close that she could nearly touch him, and then he took off again. In this manner, they traversed the meadow. . . . until she saw herself from above; how she ran behind an enigmatic bird that was guided by wires, which were attached to an overhead crane. The crane spanned the meadow. It had not been the wind that had opened his wings, but a remote control.]

As her dream reveals, her teenage attraction to Ton rested on the enigmatic and exotic touch he brought into her gray life, underscored by the fact that she could never actually get hold of him. However, the now-obvious revelation that Ton never acted freely but was remotely controlled had remained inaccessible to her in the 1980s. The reemergence of her teenage dream does, in fact, also grant access to knowledge about the situation in 2009: since the shimmering bird is piloted by a crane straddling the entire pasture—that is, everything—it is reasonable to assume that Ton still does not act entirely of his own accord, but remains strongly linked with Feldberg.

Ton and Feldberg, then, emerge as the perfect team: Ton's eloquence and casual manner, his ability to establish, sustain, and utilize ties are supported by Feldberg's aloofness and his will to destroy (194). This fever-induced realization triggers Inez's desire to stop Ton by threatening to inform the press about his Stasi past. It reveals that Inez, unaware of her incestuous relationship with Erik, also remains oblivious to Feldberg's agenda (194–95). When he informs her that he is leaving the island to provide Ton with the instruments he needs to disable the forces operating against him in the election campaign (134), Feldberg reveals that once again, he is one step ahead of Inez: in control of her professional and personal reputation on the island and in possession of proof regarding her sexual relationship with her son, Feldberg has effectively acquired information for Ton that is most harmful for Inez if made public.

As Strubel explained in an interview with Beret Norman and Katie Sutton, "while the individual evil is controlled and limited by laws, the incest taboo as a moral issue is sometimes connected to one of the most anarchic powers: love. To ignore this taboo can have a much stronger threatening impact on an established order."[27] In fact, the incest taboo is more than a moral issue: Feldberg and Ton also have German jurisdiction on their side, which perceives a violation of the incest taboo a much greater threat to society than the Stasi collaboration of former GDR citizens. Neither part-time nor full-time Stasi employees can be prosecuted because their activities were not actionable under GDR law. This interpretation applies exclusively to former GDR citizens: as former Federal Public Prosecutor General Kay Nehm explains, they had no sense of wrongdoing because they believed they were serving their country, while West German Stasi informants knew that they rendered themselves liable to prosecution under the law of their country.[28] By contrasting the offense associated with ignoring the incest taboo with the guilt of Stasi officers, who are not liable to prosecution in post-unification Germany, *Sturz der Tage in die Nacht* displays the same "palpable uneasiness and . . . residual mistrust in the capacities of both the new German state and its citizens to tackle the past head-on" that Faye Stewart has detected in Strubel's *Fremd gehen*.[29] FRG law does not appear capable of dealing with Feldberg and Ton: according to legal practice, neither would have to face consequences for their actions. Inez and Erik, however, would most likely be sentenced to up to three years of prison according to §173 *Strafgesetzbuch*, because incest between a parent and a natural child is considered the gravest offense. Attacking society at its core—the traditional family—the anarchic love relationship between Inez and Erik presents a greater threat to post-unification Germany than Ton's behavior, even though it is entirely unethical: he lies to his potential voters, uses Feldberg's Stasi strategies and connections, and employs the former Stasi officer to destroy Inez's life.

The East German desire to leave post-unification Germany does not stand as a singular phenomenon, and at first glance, Inez's flight to Sweden seems to parallel the escape of Christa Wolf's protagonist to California in *Stadt der Engel*. However, the reasons for seeking temporary refuge in a foreign country could not be more different: while Wolf's protagonist seeks to leave behind the slander of the West German media, Inez flees Germany to escape the specters of the GDR. Wolf and Strubel both mobilize images of haunting, trauma, and repression as well as bodies suffering from fevers and hallucination, yet the plot components differ. While Wolf's main character appears to have achieved closure to her trauma at the end of the novel, Strubel's protagonist recognizes that the unresolved GDR past has not been overcome. In "Gender, Identity, and Memory," Helen Finch claims that Strubel's earlier novels "challenge binary clichés of gendered nationhood" and disrupt dichotomies, among others "temporal binaries that pit the divided German past against the re-unified present" (82). In *Sturz der Tage in die Nacht*, Strubel forces us to acknowledge that Stasi control and its traumatic effects continue to reach into the lives of Germans twenty years after unification, because power structures that were not unique to the GDR but apparently developed particularly well in the socialist state also thrive in post-unification Germany.

Conclusion

Violence increasingly defines the historical and cultural memory of the unified Berlin Republic. The novels analyzed here all point to continuities of aggression. In Hensel's case, they originate in Germany's fascist past and stand for the loss of innocence and humanist values, while Schmidt's and Strubel's narratives highlight trajectories that reach from the GDR into post-unification Germany. The paradigm of the exercise of power in various realms of society suggests the continuity of violent and exploitative structures that establish existing relations of domination as an effect of established authority: bio-medical research and the medical realm in Hensel's *Lärchenau*; both the healthcare system and the legal realm in Schmidt's *Du stirbst nicht*; and the legal system as well as an uncanny, privatized version of the Stasi in Strubel's *Sturz der Tage in die Nacht*. Since the texts—individually and taken together—reveal that the ways in which dominant power structures affect individuals are largely independent of specific political systems, it seems irrelevant which institutions represent authority or whether they are privately run or state-organized. In fact, the threat emanating from the privatized research institution in Hensel's post-1990 *Lärchenau* exceeds that of the previously state-owned medical institution, while the Stasi menace looms just as large twenty years after unification as it did in the GDR, as Strubel's *Sturz der Tage in die Nacht* indicates. Similarly, Schmidt highlights how certain practices that dominated the GDR medical system and were portrayed in Wolf's *Leibhaftig* continue to deny patient agency, while additional violence caused by a return to class traditions, such as increased hierarchical structures in the hospital, add to the patient's misery.

The novels discussed here further show that personal history is always informed by a historic dimension, which surfaces in symptomatic bodies that are often inscribed by the violence inflicted upon them—similar to what we have observed in Christa Wolf's texts. The bodies in these texts are all haunted by—or reminded of—their GDR past. They elaborate the network of medicine, science, law, and Stasi surveillance that continues to characterize the nexus of power and legitimacy in post-unification Germany. All three novels, very much attuned to the GDR literary convention of placing social commentary in the realm of fiction, feature symptomatic bodies reacting to societal discourses. At the same time, they all point to the ongoing relevance of the GDR past and GDR institutions in post-unification Germany. They confirm the capacity of literature to witness historical trajectories and changing life situations and respond by offering alternative models for narrating history. These novels not only add to a retrospective evaluation of the GDR; they also contribute to larger debates on unified Germany and to pan-German historiography in ways that challenge the dominant media discourse since 1990.

Notes

[1] Opitz, "Verhängnisvolle Vergangenheit."

[2] Norman and Sutton, "Memory is Always a Story," 104.

[3] The debate developed following the publication of Assheuer's "Das Zarathustra-Projekt" and Mohr's "Züchter des Übermenschen" in September 1999. Sloterdijk answered in two open letters in *Die Zeit*, in which he also attacked Habermas, who was then prompted to enter the discussion. The debate inspired a special issue of *Environment and Planning D* on "The Worlds of Peter Sloterdijk" in 2009. Following an introductory essay by Stuart Elden and Eduardo Mendieta, *EPD* published Mary Varney Rorty's translation of *Regeln für den Menschenpark*, "Rules for the Human Zoo."

[4] Bettin, "'Deontologija'," 44. The GDR used an oath based on the Hippocratic oath that emphasized the physician's obligation vis-à-vis socialist society, its citizens, and the GDR (Seifert, *GSV*, 40–41). In some cases students created their own oath, which stressed the significance of socialist society, the socialist constitution of the GDR, solidarity, societal progress, and social equality. See, for example, the oath the graduates of the department of medicine at the University of Greifswald wrote, which is reproduced in Berndt and Hüller, "Zur Gesellschaftsabhängigkeit des ärztlichen Eides," 44–45.

[5] Mary Varney Rorty's translation, "Rules for the Human Zoo," does not always reflect the meaning of the original German text. In these cases, I provide my own translation in the main text and supplement it with Rorty's translation in the notes. Here, Rorty's translation reads: "the true shepherd . . ., [who] because he leads through insight, stands closer to the gods than the confused populace he governs" (25).

⁶ Rorty's translation reads: "pacifically directing the herd which has already tamed itself; it is a question of systematically generating new, idealized, exemplary individuals" (25).

⁷ On gender and violence, see Dackweiler and Schäfer, "Gewalt, Macht, Geschlecht," 9.

⁸ The only present-day "Institut für Rekonstruktive Neurobiologie" belongs to Bonn University, a public institution.

⁹ Iztueta in "Body and Grotesque as Self-Disruption" reads Adele's reversed aging process as a metaphorical representation of unification and its consequences (146). She understands Adele as an "experimental object" (156), but her interpretation of Adele's rejuvenated body as symbolizing the "'rebirth' of the weak, dying GDR into a new, renovated and polished Federal Republic" (157) remains unconvincing.

¹⁰ Rorty's translation reads: "But whether this process will also eventuate in a genetic reform of the characteristics of the species; whether the present anthropotechnology portends an explicit future determination of traits; whether human beings as a species can transform birth fatalities into optimal birth and prenatal selection—these are questions in which the evolutionary horizon ... begins to glimmer" (24).

¹¹ In the fall of 2009, Schmidt won the prestigious German Book Prize. For more information on the prize and a general introduction to the novel, see Byrnes, "Writing on the Threshold"; and Klocke, "A Woman's Quest for Agency."

¹² Bettin and Gadebusch Bondio, "An Stelle einer Einleitung," 7.

¹³ Knopf and Fritsche, "Müttersterblichkeit in der DDR," 220; Rücker, "Soziale Netze," 66; Fulbrook, *People's State*, 152–53, 160.

¹⁴ As Mittag and Sauer stress in "Geschlechtsidentität und Menschenrechte im internationalen Kontext," this notion is not exclusive to the FRG. Rather, the internationally acknowledged systems for classifying illnesses list transsexuality, diagnosed as so-called disturbed gender identity, either as psychological health disorder (in the Diagnostic and Statistical Manual of Mental Disorders) or as a mental and behavioral disorder (in the International Statistical Classification of Diseases and Related Health Problems) (58).

¹⁵ Klöppel emphasizes the collaboration of law and medicine as part of a power network that determines the lives of both inter- and transsexual individuals (*XXOXY*, 583–84).

¹⁶ In "Geschlechtsidentität und Menschenrechte im internationalen Kontext," Mittag and Sauer stress that in seventeen out of the forty-seven states of the Council of Europe, sterilization is a mandatory prerequisite for a change in civil status (58).

¹⁷ On the definition of queer, see Warner, *Fear of a Queer Planet* and *The Trouble with Normal*.

¹⁸ De Silva, "Vom Sittenverfall zur Trans*_Homo-Ehe," 152–54. See the court decision: www.bundesverfassungsgericht.de/entscheidungen/rs20110111_1bvr329507.html.

[19] On Viktor/Viola and the circumstances of her death, see Klocke, "A Woman's Quest for Agency," 235–37.

[20] Assmann, *Generationsidentitäten und Vorurteilsstrukturen*, 47.

[21] Fietz, Pezzei, and Schilke, "Ich wusste schnell wieder, wer ich bin." On parallels between Schmidt and Helene, see Cosentino, "Einige Gedanken zu Christa Wolfs *Stadt der Engel*."

[22] Kohl, "Fernsehansprache."

[23] Raphael praises Sweden, where much reminds him of the bygone GDR, but the protagonist contradicts his nostalgic claims (333–34).

[24] *Operative Legende* (functional legend) is Stasi-speak for a plausible pretense, often also a false identity, which is constructed to deceive people about the true intentions of the Stasi. In order to appear credible, these legends were largely based on verifiable facts. Typically, Stasi officers constructed a fictitious backstory for IMs, who had to remember the story that became their new "truth." For details, see Suckut, *Wörterbuch der Staatssicherheit*, 240–41.

[25] Opitz, "Verhängnisvolle Vergangenheit."

[26] Jeremiah, "Shameful Stories," 75–76.

[27] Norman and Sutton, "Memory is Always a Story," 104.

[28] Bönisch and Lamprecht, "Züge von Menschlichkeit," 87. See BGH 3 StR 324/94. http://www.hrr-strafrecht.de/hrr/3/94/3-324-94.php.

[29] Stewart, "Queer Elements," 65.

Conclusion

In Antje Rávic Strubel's *Sturz der Tage in die Nacht*, Erik is called the heir to the East (39)—the heir to a country he cannot even remember. Even in 2009, the young man who was five years old when the Berlin Wall came down identifies as an *Ossi*, the colloquial term employed particularly by East Germans who proudly self-identify as having been raised in the former GDR (37). It is important to him to know whether Inez is also from the East—quite a surprise for the forty-one-year-old woman, who has tried for years to escape her GDR past (36). She explains her dislike of the categorization "East German," which she feels turns her into the abject who does not conform to the West German standard—even for Erik, a young *Ossi*:

> Du willst hören, wie das Leben und die Liebe und die Hoffnung zerstört werden, . . . so dass du . . . denkst, in so einem Arbeiter- und Bauernland möchtest du aber nicht gelebt haben, wie gut, dass das vorbei ist, dass das bloß eine Geschichte ist. Nur der Mensch, der täglich auf seinen zwei Beinen durch diese Geschichte gelaufen ist, hat nicht auf einmal zwei neue Beine . . . Und das kränkt ihn, Erik. Und es kränkt ihn auch, dass er gezwungen ist, sich auf diese Weise an sein Leben zu erinnern. . . . Es kränkt ihn, dass das sein Leben gewesen sein soll. (111)
>
> [You want to hear how life, love, and hope are destroyed . . . so that you . . . think, you would not have liked to live in such a workers' and farmers' country, fortunately, this is all past and just a story. But the person who every day walked on their two legs through this story doesn't suddenly have two new legs . . . And that hurts, Erik. And it also hurts that they are forced to remember their life in such a way. . . . It hurts that this is supposed to have been their life.]

In her defensive response to Erik's inquiry, Inez exposes the emotional suffering of East Germans who are continuously confronted with interpretations of the GDR as a dictatorship and an *Unrechtsstaat*. Pointing to the exclusive focus on the destruction of people's lives, loves, and hopes, which denies GDR citizens the right to having lived a "normal life" on their own two feet, Inez invokes what Martin Sabrow called a *Diktaturgedächtnis*. Wounded by Stasi operations before and after 1989, she still distances herself from a narrative that exclusively focuses on the antagonism between the repressive SED regime and its victims (108). Like most of Strubel's novels—first and foremost *Fremd gehen* and *Tupolew 134—Sturz der Tage in die Nacht* demonstrates that there is no single historic truth, and consequently there cannot be one valid way of remembering the past. Inez reveals how the construction of the GDR as an *Unrechtsstaat* upsets average East Germans who are forced to justify and qualify their life experiences so that they fit West German expectations. Her reaction to Erik's question further shows the extent to which the young man's understanding of the socialist state has been influenced by the official discourses that dominate public commemorations in the Berlin Republic as well as in the West German media. East Germans obviously can neither escape the image of the GDR created by the West nor their—frequently traumatic—East German heritage, whose specters still haunt the present, as chapter 4 has revealed.

This observation rekindles a question this study posed at the outset: Why is the GDR such a persistent topic, even in post-GDR literature of the twenty-first century? As media research repeatedly confirms, the German identities that originate from the forty years of separation have not evened out since 1989, but are constantly reproduced; and the image of East Germans as the abject, launched on TV and in newspapers, continues to buttress West German subject formation.[1] This phenomenon explains the ongoing presence of the socialist state in the mass media dominated by West Germany; and it accounts for GDR and post-GDR writers' desire to remember the country in which they lived in ways that challenge these distorted and monolithic images.

Analysis of Christa Wolf's twenty-first-century texts has revealed how her writing activates what Sabrow identifies as *Fortschrittsgedächtnis*. Her last novel, *Stadt der Engel*, with its criticism of global capitalism, could not be more explicit on this point. To this end, Wolf continued to employ stylistic features that were characteristic for her pre-1990 writing, particularly symptomatic bodies and Christian imagery. In fact, symptomatic bodies proliferate in Wolf's late fiction. They are shown to foster access to historical knowledge and to corroborate the GDR's founding narrative of antifascism by highlighting the protagonists' identification with Jewish and communist victims of the Nazi regime. Through the trope of suffering female flesh, both *Leibhaftig* and *Stadt der Engel* substantiate the moral preeminence of socialist-humanist ideals. From this speaking position, Wolf's protagonists criticize specific facets of GDR life, such as the economic deprivation of hospitals and the belittling of citizens that produces passive patients devoid of agency. *Leibhaftig* most emphatically communicates how challenges in the GDR medical system—a system shaped by Marxist-Leninist thought and a corresponding legal system—are symptomatic of problems in the advancement of socialism generally.

At the same time, the ideological influences on the healthcare system have positive effects such as promoting a spirit of collaboration among doctors and nurses. Such signs of solidarity are missing in the capitalist societies portrayed in *Stadt der Engel*. Moreover, the suffering of the protagonist in *Leibhaftig*—which can be read as emerging from a national crisis, that is, the end of the GDR—finally comes to an end. Since both pain and final healing are embodied in the protagonist, the narrative emphasizes the presumed "materiality" as well as the continued validity of socialist ideas. And Wolf and her protagonists are not alone: with novels like *In seiner frühen Kindheit ein Garten* (2005) and *Weiskerns Nachlass* (2011), Christoph Hein similarly challenges the hegemonic narrative that stages the FRG as morally superior to the GDR and the neoliberal economic system as fair. In *Die hellen Haufen* (2011), Volker Braun picks up the discourse of East German colonization by the West to support his ongoing belief in the superiority of socialist ideals: while a 1992 East German worker's uprising against the West never materialized, Braun's story—by imagining such a revolt—expresses the desire for socialist ideals such as solidarity and opposition to the capitalist system. Explicitly advocating the ideals underlying a humanist socialist state that intellectuals in the GDR envisioned in 1989 but which remained unrealized, these GDR authors adhere to their preferred political stance.

As the analysis of post-GDR fiction in chapters 3 and 4 has shown, these texts do not succumb to *Ostalgie*. While this prose is in—sometimes explicit—dialogue with Christa Wolf's oeuvre and particularly with her portrayal of symptomatic bodies that enable access to historical knowledge, it does not follow Sabrow's *Fortschrittsgedächtnis* or corroborate the supremacy of socialist thought—or, in fact, of any ideology. Rather, these post-GDR novels engage with memories of the GDR along the lines of what Sabrow identified as *Arrangementgedächtnis*, or they refuse the idea that there is a "true" way to remember the bygone state altogether. For the purpose of detailed textual analysis, chapters 3 and 4 concentrate on select prose by four post-GDR writers. The findings can, however, be transferred to a larger body of post-GDR texts. The fictional world of Eugen Ruge's 2011 novel *In Zeiten des abnehmenden Lichts*, for example, is populated with characters that feature symptomatic bodies. Like the prose texts analyzed in the second part of this study, *In Zeiten des abnehmenden Lichts* refrains from presenting a monolithic image of the GDR. Instead, representatives of various generations and paths of life make their voices heard: they range from admirers of Stalin and the generation invested in building the socialist state after 1945 to GDR citizens who found their place in society and cannot tolerate their children who dismiss socialist ideals and leave the country before the fall of the Wall.

Like Ruge's novel, the texts examined in chapter 3 reveal the authors' desire to present everyday life in the GDR from a critical distance, yet conveying knowledge that presupposes real-life experiences in the socialist state. Bodies that become symptomatic through the brutal inscription of historical and political events, Stasi interference, and actions of physicians contribute to a re-writing of history from subject positions that have been marginalized in hegemonic discourses. Some bodies allegorically represent the state of the nation and express their resistance to the rushed unification process, like Brussig's Sabine Busse or the transsexual Heidi. Others possess the power to permit access to previously hidden historical knowledge and can simultaneously behave rebelliously vis-à-vis the state, as does Josepha in Schmidt's *Die Gunnar-Lennefsen-Expedition*. In the end, however, Josepha must surrender to the state authorities. Similarly, Nelly, the main character in Julia Franck's 2003 novel *Lagerfeuer*, as well as her grandmother cannot withstand the combined force of the legal system, the police, and the Stasi: while Nelly's body is turned into a Trojan horse when a gynecologist brutally implants an unknown object into her abdomen before she is allowed to leave the GDR for West Berlin, her Jewish grandmother is stopped at the border and forcefully has the crowns and bridges removed from her mouth (30–31). *Lagerfeuer* thus establishes a trajectory between violence exercised in Nazi concentration camps and GDR institutions—not unlike Thomas Brussig's *Wie es leuchtet* and Kerstin Hensel's *Lärchenau*. Bodies such as those of Hensel's Helge or Mitschka, into which the crimes of the GDR or Nazi Germany are violently inscribed, are predominantly disillusioning: they cannot be deciphered by the depicted German majority population and point to a lack of historical knowledge in contemporary Germany.

The fictional texts analyzed in chapter 4 explore what it means to be East German in the twenty-first century: being exposed to the specters of the GDR, or even to present-day repercussions of Germany's fascist past. In all the novels, bodies suffering from increasing violence loom large. In Hensel's *Lärchenau*, Adele's body points to the effects of fascism on both the GDR and post-unification Germany. By juxtaposing Adele's awful end with the celebration of life in the so-called gypsy family, the novel suggests that hope for Germany may lie in the margins. In Schmidt's *Du stirbst nicht* and in Strubel's *Sturz der Tage in die Nacht*, symptomatic bodies, in the tradition of Wolf, can retrieve significant memories of the GDR—although Strubel's Inez has to realize the limitations of both her agency vis-à-vis the Stasi and of her feverish body, as it does not allow for access to her feelings. In contrast, Schmidt's patient Helene increasingly gains knowledge about her past. However, she has to endure procedures in the post-unification hospital that imply the continuation of undesirable GDR-specific practices in the twenty-first century. *Du stirbst nicht* therefore also highlights structural similarities of repression in the GDR as well as in post-unification Germany—both in the medical and in the legal realms.

Julia Franck's *Lagerfeuer* extends this comparison—not unlike Christa Wolf—to the parallels the main character perceives between the GDR Stasi and the American CIA: her body reacts by developing symptoms such as burst blood vessels in her eyes when she realizes that CIA interrogation techniques correspond to Stasi methods (91). Inge Lohmark, the protagonist in Judith Schalansky's novel *Der Hals der Giraffe* (2011; *The Giraffe's Neck*, 2014), highlights the significance of the educational realm for reining in individuals—independent of a political system: "Es war doch alles die gleiche Chose. Man nehme demokratisch und frei und ersetze es durch sozialistisch.... Es ging... darum, die Kinder an... die jeweils vorherrschende Ideologie zu gewöhnen" (150: So it was the same thing all over again. Take democratic and free and substitute it for socialist.... It was about getting the children used to... the dominant ideology of the moment; 140). Inge not only employs metaphors of illness and health to describe the social and political systems pre- and post-1989 which, in her view, are equally sick, but quotes verbatim the credo Christa T.'s former student proclaims in Wolf's *Nachdenken über Christa T.*: "Der Kern der Gesundheit ist Anpassung" (110: the essence of health is adaptation or conformity; 111).[2] In Inge Lohmark's reflections on the contemporary Berlin Republic, the GDR in retrospect emerges as no better or worse than the FRG: both systems are sick, and both systems call for conformity.

Post-GDR literature offers a multitude of imaginative fictional scenarios that complement GDR history with the authentic voices of those who lived in the bygone state; those who, as Inez in Strubel's *Sturz der Tage in die Nacht* puts it, daily walked through this story (and history) on their own two legs. In fact—directly, like Brussig, or indirectly, like Strubel, Hensel, and Schmidt—they point to the influence of the West German media in constructing the GDR and its demise in ways that serve West German subject formation via abjection of the East. As a result, none of the portrayed East Germans ever feel that they are on an equal footing with West Germans. Nurse Lena in Brussig's *Wie es leuchtet*, for example, experiences a distinct lack of happiness by the fall of 1990. She explains it with the desire of West Germans to hear East Germans tell them a simplified version of history; that is, how terrible the GDR was and how fantastic the present is. Based on this experience, Lena concludes that she will never belong (543)—a feeling that is echoed in other post-GDR novels such as Jenny Erpenbeck's *Aller Tage Abend* (2012; *The End of Days*, 2014). One of Erpenbeck's protagonists realizes that years after German unification, "heißt die neue Zeit bei ihm immer noch *die Zeit der Gewinner*" (265: he can't stop calling the current era *Age of the Winners*; 222; italics in original). Even though now "sitzt auch er in dieser richtigen Welt" (265: he too is sitting in this right world; 223), he feels left out. Reflecting on the signs with the images of dogs not allowed in butcher shops, restaurants, and swimming pools, he feels like the proverbial underdog: banned from Western society which tells him: "*Ich muss draußen bleiben*" (I have to remain outside; 265; italics in original).[3]

East Germans depicted in post-GDR fiction often seem to remain excluded. Yet post-GDR writers utilize their fiction to make their voices heard and engage with post-unification debates. As we have seen, several of them specifically zero in on media depictions of Stasi influence on the medical realm and medical experiments on human beings.[4] For the most part, these writers juxtapose the dominant notion of the GDR as a dictatorship with images of the socialist state that complicate these discourses without downplaying problems. Specifically, they also point to violence exercised in the FRG medical and legal realms; for example, when it comes to dealing with transsexual individuals—a topic that comes to the fore in Brussig's *Wie es leuchtet* and Schmidt's *Du stirbst nicht* as well as Sibylle Berg's 2012 novel *Vielen Dank für das Leben*. As a result, these post-GDR authors participate in writing GDR history by claiming a space for their memories and interpretations of past events. They invite readers who did not live in the GDR to close their gaps regarding knowledge of the bygone state; and they qualify West German notions of FRG supremacy and claim a place for the GDR in pan-German history.

In the conspicuous degree to which numerous younger post-GDR writers author playful, inventive, and imaginative texts that—among others—draw on GDR literary traditions yet always include a characteristic twist, they add authentic voices to the collective memory archive. Iris Radisch's characterization of post-GDR literature of the 1990s as a political literature in the best sense of the word—a literature that exposes, deconstructs, and destabilizes German society—retains its validity well into the twenty-first century.[5] Stylistically, the post-GDR fiction examined in this study is multifaceted: the magical realism typical for all of Schmidt's early prose and particularly *Die Gunnar-Lennefsen-Expedition*, the satirical overtones characteristic of Brussig's writing including *Wie es leuchtet*, and the often grotesque characters that inhabit Hensel's *Lärchenau* like most of her prose differ from the sincere manner of Schmidt's *Du stirbst nicht* and the fascinating complexity of Strubel's *Sturz der Tage in die Nacht*. Yet all these texts share at least two qualities: like many of Christa Wolf's protagonists, characters in these post-GDR novels develop physical symptoms in answer to political events, or when they feel threatened by institutions that often collaborate to infringe on an individual's rights; and unlike Wolf's texts, post-GDR fiction refrains from taking an open, specific political stance—yet it is highly critical of society and political in Radisch's sense.

Post-GDR literature presents a space where different versions of the past are probed—versions of the past that also provoke dialogues about the present and the future. The ongoing depiction of medical institutions and of bodies that display historical and political experience in East German fiction is perhaps the most conspicuous feature of this literature's social and political dimension. Unlike the few examples of West German literature that employ a GDR or post-GDR environment and a medical institution as setting for their poetic depiction of an apolitical plot development, the post-GDR texts analyzed here utilize tropes for voicing political criticism that are at the center of GDR literature.[6] In their socially engaged writings, these post-GDR writers extend GDR literary conventions—conventions that often originate in GDR *Aufbauliteratur* and are typically aimed at supporting official narratives such as the founding narrative of antifascism—in the twenty-first century and creatively play with them. It is impossible to ignore, for example, Schmidt's joy in telling frivolous stories that mock the suffering of Communists prevalent in early GDR *Aufbauliteratur* in *Die Gunnar-Lennefsen-Expedition*. In *Lärchenau*, Kerstin Hensel mobilizes the same pattern to expose mechanisms of power and injustice that remain the same in all political systems, Nazi Germany, the GDR, and unified Germany alike. The rich fabric of Hensel's text invites us to disentangle the complex narrative threads—and thus gain insight into unfamiliar stories of the past and their influence on the present.

Inspired by lively fictional texts, this study turned to medical-historical research, GDR publications on medical ethics, legal work, and feminist theory to reveal the continuities and variations in literary inventions and portrayals of what I have termed symptomatic bodies and the depiction of medical institutions in East German prose fiction from 1968 to 2011. These interdisciplinary excursions, particularly into the realms of medicine and law, reveal the idiosyncrasies of the GDR and the socialization of its citizens. Recognizing the specificities of medical institutions within a Marxist-Leninist power network allows us to appreciate the state of rebellious alarm that materializes in symptomatic bodies—in the GDR, during the days of the so-called *Wende*, and in post-unification Germany when the specters of the GDR come to haunt these individuals. The reasons for the suffering of the mind and flesh differ among these texts: the traumata may reach back to the GDR or to Nazi Germany, often only provisionally masked by seeming stability. In all cases, however, the symptomatic bodies claim a voice and, with it, agency to participate in writing GDR and pan-German history.

Notes

[1] Ahbe, "Ost-Diskurse als Strukturen der Nobilitierung," 110; Wedl, "Ein Ossi ist ein Ossi," 129.

[2] "Und der Kern aller Gesundheit war die Anpassung" (Schalansky, *Der Hals der Giraffe*, 151).

[3] The published translation reads: "No dogs allowed" (223).

[4] Stasi methods of gaining access to the medical field are, for example, also a topic in Tellkamp's *Der Turm*.

[5] Radisch, "Es gibt zwei deutsche Gegenwartsliteraturen," 13.

[6] Marion Poschmann's *Die Sonnenposition* (2013), which won the Wilhelm Raabe literary award in 2013, is an example of a poetical, yet apolitical text set in an East German psychiatric institution.

Glossary

Ankunftsliteratur. Following the building of the Wall in August 1961, *Ankunftsliteratur* (literature of arrival) transmits a sense of the characters' arrival in GDR society. The heroes and heroines realistically assess the possibilities in the GDR.

Arrangementgedächtnis. Martin Sabrow defines *Arrangementgedächtnis* (memory of accommodation) as the memory of the GDR that focuses on quotidian life and emphasizes the complexity of lived experiences of GDR citizens.

Aufbauliteratur. This literature of socialist construction was propagated in the GDR in the 1950s to support the building of a socialist society.

Aufklärungspflicht. In GDR law, *Aufklärungspflicht* (obligation to enlighten) describes a physician's formal obligation to inform patients about a proposed therapy and to seek consent. It could, however, be bypassed without legal consequences for the doctor.

Berlin Republic. This term is often used to describe the new unified FRG, which declared Berlin its capital in Article 2 of the unification treaty of 1990, even though the West German city Bonn remained the seat of government until 1999.

Betreuungsanordnung/Betreuungsverfahren. This guardianship order or guardianship procedure from January 1, 1992, is regulated in the *Bürgerliches Gesetzbuch* (German Civil Code) in BGB §§1896–1908. It replaces incapacitation in the FRG.

Betreuungsverhältnis. The GDR *Betreuungsverhältnis* (medical care relationship) emphasized the subordination of individual rights to societal rights, and considered prescribed medical interventions carried out according to standard practice to be therapy. Patients had no legal right to refuse a recommended therapy or surgery.

Bürgerliches Gesetzbuch. German Civil Code, commonly abbreviated BGB.

Diktaturgedächtnis. According to Martin Sabrow, the *Diktaturgedächtnis* (memory [of the GDR] as a dictatorship), which defines the GDR as a dictatorship or an *Unrechtsstaat*, is the dominant memory of the GDR in post-unification Germany.

Duldungs- und Befolgungspflicht. In GDR law, the *Duldungs- und Befolgungspflicht* (obligation to endure and follow) describes a patient's legally binding obligation to endure any medical measures and to follow doctor's directions.

Fortschrittsgedächtnis. Martin Sabrow defines the *Fortschrittsgedächtnis* (memory of progress) as the memory of the GDR that highlights the progressive aspects of the state and insists on socialism's legitimacy as an alternative to capitalism.

IM (Plural: IMs). IM is short for *Inoffizieller Mitarbeiter* (Unofficial Informer) to the *Staatssicherheit*.

Kahlschlag-Plenum. The term *Kahlschlag-Plenum* (clean-sweep plenum) refers to the Eleventh Plenum of the Central Committee of the ruling SED in 1965, which banned numerous films and books.

Literaturstreit (also *deutsch-deutscher Literaturstreit*). This term refers to the so-called (German-German) debate on literature that was carried out in major German newspapers in the early 1990s. It was triggered by the publication of Christa Wolf's novel *Was bleibt* ("What remains"), but soon developed into a campaign aimed at critical and political literature generally.

Mitwirkungspflicht. In GDR law, the *Mitwirkungspflicht* (obligation to cooperate) describes a patient's legally binding obligation to cooperate in the therapy administered.

Mütterberatungsstelle. In the GDR, the *Mütterberatungsstelle* (institution for the counseling of mothers) was responsible for prenatal as well as postnatal care for children up to the age of three. The *Mütterberatungsstelle* also distributed the state subsidy for the expected child.

Offenbarungs- und Informationspflicht. In GDR law, the *Offenbarungs- und Informationspflicht* (obligation to disclose and inform) describes a patient's legally binding obligation to disclose all aspects of life that might impinge on the therapy.

SED. SED is short for *Sozialistische Einheitspartei Deutschlands* (Socialist Unity Party of Germany), the ruling party in the GDR.

Stasi. Stasi is colloquial for *DDR Staatssicherheit* (GDR State Security), which is short for *Ministerium für Staatssicherheit* (Ministry for State Security), also abbreviated as *MfS*.

Strafgesetzbuch. German Criminal Code, commonly abbreviated StGB.

Unrechtsstaat. This term seems to imply a state of injustice (*Unrecht*), but historians, political scientists, and legal scholars use it to signify an "unconstitutional state" or, literally, a state in which the rule of law does not exist. It was originally attached to National Socialist Germany and only later applied to the GDR, a practice that remains contested among historians and legal scholars.

Wende. Literally "turn" or "turning point," this term is used to describe the changes in GDR society in 1989 and 1990. Many intellectuals and East Germans reject the term *Wende* because—unlike "peaceful revolution"—it elides the involvement of activists who fought for their freedom and intended to reform the GDR.

Zersetzung. *Zersetzung* (demoralization measures) refers to Stasi-specific measures aimed at a person's public degradation with the goal of causing the individual's public and private destruction.

Bibliography

Adamietz, Laura. "Geschlechtsidentität im deutschen Recht." *Aus Politik und Zeitgeschichte* 62, no. 20/21 (2012): 15–21.
Adelson, Leslie A. *Making Bodies, Making History: Feminism and German Identity*. Lincoln: University of Nebraska Press, 1993.
Agde, Günter, ed. *Kahlschlag: Das 11. Plenum des ZK der SED 1965*. Berlin: Aufbau, 1991.
Ahbe, Thomas. "Competing Master Narratives: Geschichtspolitik and Identity Discourse in Three German Societies." In *The GDR Remembered: Representations of the East German State since 1989*, edited by Nick Hodgin and Caroline Pearce, 221–49. Rochester, NY: Camden House, 2011.
———. "Ost-Diskurse als Strukturen der Nobilitierung und Marginalisierung von Wissen: Eine Diskursanalyse zur Konstruktion der Ostdeutschen in den westdeutschen Medien-Diskursen 1989/90 und 1995." In *Die Ostdeutschen in den Medien: Das Bild von den Anderen nach 1990*, edited by Thomas Ahbe, Rainer Gries, and Wolfgang Schmale, 59–112. Bonn: Bundeszentrale für politische Bildung, 2010.
Ahbe, Thomas, and Rainer Gries. "Gesellschaftsgeschichte als Generationengeschichte: Theoretische und methodologische Überlegungen zm Beispiel DDR." In *Die DDR aus generationengeschichtlicher Perspektive: Eine Inventur*, edited by Annegret Schüle, Thomas Ahbe and Rainer Gries, 475–571. Leipzig: Leipziger Universitätsverlag, 2006.
Ahbe, Thomas, Rainer Gries, and Wolfgang Schmale, eds. *Die Ostdeutschen in den Medien: Das Bild von den Anderen nach 1990*. 2009. Reprint, Bonn: Bundeszentrale für politische Bildung, 2010.
Ahbe, Thomas, Michael Hofmann, and Volker Stiehler, eds. *Redefreiheit: Öffentliche Debatten in Leipzig im Herbst 1989*. 2014. Reprint, Bonn: Bundeszentrale für politische Bildung, 2014.
Allan, Sean, and John Sandford, eds. *DEFA: East German Cinema, 1946–1992*. New York: Berghahn Books, 1999.
"Als gesund entlassen." *Der Spiegel*, September 2, 1991.
Anderson, Edith, ed. *Blitz aus heiterem Himmel*. Rostock: VEB Hinstorff, 1975.
Anz, Thomas, ed. *Es geht nicht um Christa Wolf: Der Literaturstreit im vereinten Deutschland*. Frankfurt am Main: Fischer, 1991.
Arnim, Bettina von. *Die Günderode*. 1839. Reprint, Frankfurt am Main: Insel, 1983.
Arnold, Heinz Ludwig, ed. *DDR-Literatur der neunziger Jahre: Sonderband Text + Kritik*. Munich: edition text + kritik, 2000.

Assheuer, Thomas. "Das Zarathustra-Projekt." *Die Zeit*, September 2, 1999.
Assmann, Aleida. *Erinnerungsräume: Formen und Wandlungen des kulturellen Gedächtnisses*. Munich: C. H. Beck, 1999.
———. *Generationsidentitäten und Vorurteilsstrukturen in der neuen deutschen Erinnerungsliteratur*. Vienna: Picus, 2006.
Assmann, Jan. *Das kulturelle Gedächtnis: Schrift, Erinnerung und politische Identität in frühen Hochkulturen*. Munich: C. H. Beck, 1992. Translated as *Cultural Memory and Early Civilization: Writing, Remembrance, and Political Imagination* (Cambridge: Cambridge UP, 2011).
Atzl, Isabel, Volker Hess, and Thomas Schnalke, eds. *Zeitzeugen Charité: Arbeitswelten des Instituts für Pathologie 1952–2005*. Münster: LIT, 2006.
"Aufruf für unser Land," November 29, 1989. http://www.hdg.de/lemo/html/dokumente/DieDeutscheEinheit_aufrufFuerUnserLand/index.html.
Bachmann, Ingeborg. *Ein Ort für Zufälle: Mit dreizehn Zeichnungen von Günter Grass*. Berlin: Wagenbach, 1965.
———. *Liebe: Dunkler Erdteil. Gedichte aus den Jahren 1942–1967*. Munich: Piper, 1984.
Backman, Donald, and Aida Sakalauskaite, eds. *Ossi Wessi*. Newcastle upon Tyne: Cambridge Scholars, 2008.
Barck, Simone. "Fragmentarisches zur Literatur." In *Die DDR im Rückblick: Politik, Wirtschaft, Gesellschaft, Kultur*, edited by Helga Schultz and Hans-Jürgen Wagener, 303–22. Berlin: Christoph Links, 2007.
Barck, Simone, Martina Langermann, and Siegfried Lokatis, eds. *"Jedes Buch ein Abenteuer": Zensur-System und literarische Öffentlichkeit in der DDR bis Ende der sechziger Jahre*. Berlin: Akademie Verlag, 1997.
Bathrick, David. "Die Intellektuellen und die Macht: Die Repräsentanz des Schriftstellers in der DDR." In *Schriftsteller als Intellektuelle: Politik und Literatur im Kalten Krieg*, edited by Sven Hanuschek, Therese Hörnigk, and Christine Malende, 235–48. Tübingen: Max Niemeyer, 2000.
Bauerkämper, Arnd, Martin Sabrow, and Bernd Stöver. "Die doppelte deutsche Zeitgeschichte." In *Doppelte Zeitgeschichte: Deutsch-deutsche Beziehungen 1945–1990*, edited by Arnd Bauerkämper, Martin Sabrow, and Bernd Stöver, 9–16. Bonn: Dietz, 1998.
Bause, Ulrich, and Jochen Matauschek. "Zum Stand der Medizintechnik in der DDR." In *Das Gesundheitswesen der DDR: Aufbruch oder Einbruch. Denkanstöße für eine Neuordnung des Gesundheitswesens in einem deutschen Staat*, edited by Wilhelm Thiele, 197–202. Sankt Augustin: Asgard-Verlag Hippe, 1990.
Baust, Günter. "Ethische Problemsituationen in der Intensivmedizin der DDR und heute." In *Medizinische Ethik in der DDR: Erfahrungswert oder Altlast?*, edited by Hartmut Bettin and Mariacarla Gadebusch Bondio, 116–26. Lengerich: Pabst Science, 2010.
Beattie, Andrew H. "The Politics of Remembering the GDR: Official and State-Mandated Memory since 1990." In *Remembering the German*

Democratic Republic: Divided Memory in a Unified Germany, edited by David Clarke and Ute Wölfel, 23–34. Basingstoke, UK: Palgrave McMillan, 2011.
Becker, Jurek. *Amanda herzlos*. Frankfurt am Main: Suhrkamp, 1992.
———. *Schlaflose Tage*. Frankfurt am Main: Suhrkamp, 1978.
———. "Die Wiedervereinigung der deutschen Literatur." *German Quarterly* 63, no. 3/4 (1990): 359–66.
Behn, Manfred, ed. *Wirkungsgeschichte von Christa Wolfs "Nachdenken über Christa T."* Königstein: Athenäum, 1978.
Benkert, Otto, and Hanns Hippius, eds. *Kompendium der Psychiatrischen Pharmakotherapie*. 8th edition. Heidelberg: Springer, 2011.
Berg, Sibylle. *Vielen Dank für das Leben*. Berlin: Hanser, 2012. Translated by Ben Knight as *Thank you for This Life* (London: Anthem, 2014).
Berndt, H.-G. "Gedanken zum Inhalt der Vorträge des Kolloquiums 'Ethik und Medizin im Sozialismus'." In *Ethik und Medizin im Sozialismus: Wissenschaftliches Kolloquium des Bereichs Medizin der Ernst-Moritz-Arndt-Universität am 2.10.1974 zu Ehren des 25. Jahrestages der DDR*, edited by Hansgeorg Hüller, 1–6. Greifswald: Ernst-Moritz-Arndt-Universität, 1976.
Berndt, H.-G., and Hans-Georg Hüller. "Zur Gesellschaftsabhängigkeit des ärztlichen Eides." In *Ethik und Medizin im Sozialismus: Wissenschaftliches Kolloquium des Bereichs Medizin der Ernst-Moritz-Arndt-Universität am 2.10.1974 zu Ehren des 25. Jahrestages der DDR*, edited by Hansgeorg Hüller, 40–46. Greifswald: Ernst-Moritz-Arndt-Universität, 1976.
Bettin, Hartmut. "'Deontologija'—eine besondere Seite der Ethik oder die Ethik der anderen Seite?" *Zeitschrift für medizinische Ethik* 58 (2012): 37–50.
Bettin, Hartmut, and Mariacarla Gadebusch Bondio, eds. "An Stelle einer Einleitung: DDR-Medizin—Eine eigene Ethik?" In *Medizinische Ethik in der DDR: Erfahrungswert oder Altlast?*, edited by Hartmut Bettin and Mariacarla Gadebusch Bondio, 7–19. Lengerich: Pabst Science, 2010.
———. *Medizinische Ethik in der DDR: Erfahrungswert oder Altlast?* Lengerich: Pabst Science, 2010.
Bevan, David, ed. *Literature and Sickness*. Amsterdam: Rodopi, 1993.
Bialek, Edward, and Monika Wolting, eds. *Kontinuitäten Brüche Kontroversen: Deutsche Literatur nach dem Mauerfall*. Dresden: Neisse, 2012.
Bieler, Manfred. *Maria Morzek oder Das Kaninchen bin ich*. 1969. Reprint, Munich: dtv, 1990.
Bircken, Margrid. "Lesen und Schreiben als körperliche Erfahrung—Christa Wolfs 'Stadt der Engel oder The Overcoat of Dr. Freud'." In *Christa Wolf im Strom der Erinnerung*, edited by Carsten Gansel, 199–213. Göttingen: V&R unipress, 2014.
Blankenagel, Alexander. "Verfassungsgerichtliche Vergangenheitsbewältigung." *Zeitschrift für Neuere Rechtsgeschichte* 13 (1991): 67–82.
Bleker, Johanna, and Volker Hess, eds. *Die Charité: Geschichte(n) eines Krankenhauses*. Berlin: Akademie Verlag, 2010.

Blumensath, Heinz, and Christel Uebach. *Einführung in die Literaturgeschichte der DDR: Ein Unterrichtsmodell.* Stuttgart: Metzler, 1975.

Boa, Elizabeth. "Labyrinth, Mazes, and Mosaics: Fiction by Christa Wolf, Ingo Schulze, Antje Rávic Strubel, and Jens Sparschuh." In *Debating German Cultural Identity since 1989,* edited by Anne Fuchs, Kathleen James-Chakraborty, and Linda Short, 131–55. Rochester, NY: Camden House, 2011.

Boa, Elizabeth, and Janet Wharton, eds. *Women and the Wende: Social Effects and Cultural Reflections of the German Unification Process.* Amsterdam: Rodopi, 1994.

Böck, Dorothea. "Ich schreibe um herauszufinden warum ich schreiben muss: Frauenliteratur in der DDR zwischen Selbsterfahrung und ästhetischem Experiment." *Feministische Studien I* (1990): 61–74.

Bogdal, Klaus-Michael. "Klimawechsel: Eine kleine Meteorologie der Gegenwartsliteratur." In *Baustelle Gegenwartsliteratur: Die neunziger Jahre,* edited by Andreas Erb, 9–31. Opladen: Westdeutscher Verlag, 1998.

Bohn, Rainer, Knut Hickethier, and Eggo Müller, eds. *Mauer-Show: Das Ende der DDR, die deutsche Einheit und die Medien.* Berlin: edition sigma, 1992.

Bollinger, Stefan, and Fritz Vilmar, eds. *Die DDR war anders: Eine kritische Würdigung ihrer sozialkulturellen Einrichtungen.* Berlin: edition ost im Verlag Das neue Berlin, 2002.

Bönisch, Georg, and Rolf Lamprecht. "'Züge von Menschlichkeit': Generalbundesanwalt Kay Nehm über Amnestie und die Verfolgung von DDR-Spionen." *Der Spiegel,* June 5, 1995, 87–89.

Brasch, Marion, *Ab jetzt ist Ruhe: Roman meiner fabelhaften Familie.* Frankfurt am Main: Fischer, 2012.

Brasch, Thomas. *Vor den Vätern sterben die Söhne.* 1977. Reprint, Frankfurt am Main: Suhrkamp, 2002.

Braun, Volker. *Die hellen Haufen.* Berlin: Suhrkamp, 2011.

———. *Die Übergangsgesellschaft.* Berlin: Henschelverlag, 1987.

———. *Unvollendete Geschichte.* Frankfurt am Main: Suhrkamp, 1990.

Bräunig, Werner. *Ein Kranich am Himmel: Unbekanntes und Bekanntes.* Halle: Mitteldeutscher Verlag, 1981.

———. *Rummelplatz.* Berlin: Aufbau, 2007.

Bredel, Willi. *Die Prüfung.* 1935. Reprint, Berlin: Aufbau, 1946.

Breger, Claudia. "Postmoderne Inszenierungen von Gender in der Literatur: Meinecke, Schmidt, Roes." In *Räume der literarischen Postmoderne: Gender, Performativität, Globalisierung,* edited by Paul Michael Lützeler, 99–125. Studien zur deutschsprachigen Gegenwartsliteratur. Vol. 11. Tübingen: Stauffenburg, 2000.

Brenner, Hildegard, ed. *Nachrichten aus Deutschland: Lyrik Prosa Dramatik. Eine Anthologie der neueren DDR-Literatur.* Reinbek bei Hamburg: Rowohlt, 1967.

Brettschneider, Werner. *Zwischen literarischer Autonomie und Staatsdienst: Die Literatur der DDR.* Berlin: Erich Schmidt, 1972.

Breuer, Ulrich, and Beatrice Sandberg, eds. *Grenzen der Identität und der Fiktionalität: Autobiographisches Schreiben in der deutschsprachigen Gegenwartsliteratur*. Vol. 1. Munich: Iudicium, 2006.
Bridge, Helen. *Women's Writing and Historiography in the GDR*. Oxford: Oxford University Press, 2002.
Brock, Angela. "Producing the 'Socialist Personality'? Socialisation, Education, and the Emergence of New Patterns of Behaviour." In *Power and Society in the GDR, 1961–1979: The 'Normalisation of Rule'?*, edited by Mary Fulbrook, 220–52. New York: Berghahn, 2009.
Brockmann, Stephen. *Literature and German Reunification*. Cambridge: Cambridge University Press, 1999.
Brüns, Elke. "Leibhaftig: Christa Wolfs Gang ins Totenreich." In *Literatur im Krebsgang: Totenbeschwörung und memoria in der deutschsprachigen Literatur nach 1989*, edited by Arne De Winde and Anke Gilleir, 145–58. Amsterdam: Rodopi, 2008.
———. *Nach dem Mauerfall: Eine Literaturgeschichte der Entgrenzung*. Munich: Wilhelm Fink, 2006.
Bruns, Marianne. *Szenenwechsel: Wiedersehen*. 1982. Reprint, Halle: Mitteldeutscher Verlag, 1989.
Brussig, Thomas. *Helden wie wir*. Frankfurt am Main: Fischer, 1995. Translated by John Brownjohn as *Heroes Like Us* (New York: Farrar, Straus & Giroux, 1996).
———. *Leben bis Männer*. Frankfurt am Main: Fischer, 2001.
———. *Wie es leuchtet*. Frankfurt am Main: Fischer, 2004.
Bullivant, Keith. *The Future of German Literature*. Oxford: Berg, 1994.
Burmeister, Brigitte. *Anders oder vom Aufenthalt in der Fremde*. 1988. Reprint, Munich: Luchterhand, 1990.
Butler, Judith. *Bodies that Matter*. New York: Routledge, 1993.
———. "Foucault and the Paradox of Bodily Inscription." *The Journal of Philosophy* 86, no. 11 (1989): 601–7.
———. *Gender Trouble*. 1990. Reprint, New York: Routledge, 1999.
———. *Undoing Gender*. New York: Routledge, 2004.
Byrnes, Deidre. "Writing on the Threshold: Memory, Language, and Identity in Kathrin Schmidt's *Du stirbst nicht*." In *Transitions: Emerging Women Writers in German-Language Literature*, edited by Valerie Heffernan and Gillian Pye. 169–85. Amsterdam: Rodopi, 2013.
Caruth, Cathy, ed. *Trauma: Explorations in Memory*. Baltimore: Johns Hopkins University Press, 1995.
Caspari, Martina. "Im Kern die Krisis: Schuld, Trauer und Neuanfang in Christa Wolfs Erzählung 'Leibhaftig'." *Weimarer Beiträge* 49, no.1 (2003): 135–38.
Childs, David. *The Fall of the GDR*. New York: Routledge, 2014.
Cibulka, Hanns. *Swantow. Die Aufzeichnungen des Andreas Flemming*. Halle: Mitteldeutscher Verlag, 1982.
Clarke, David, and Axel Goodbody, eds. *The Self in Transition: East German Autobiographical Writing Before and After Unification. Essays in Honour of Dennis Tate*. Amsterdam: Rodopi, 2012.

Clarke, David, and Ute Wölfel, eds. *Remembering the German Democratic Republic: Divided Memory in a Unified Germany.* Basingstoke, UK: Palgrave McMillan, 2011.
Clarke, David, and Ute Wölfel. "Remembering the German Democratic Republic in a United Germany." In *Remembering the German Democratic Republic: Divided Memory in a Unified Germany,* edited by David Clarke and Ute Wölfel, 3–22. Basingstoke, UK: Palgrave McMillan, 2011.
Cohen-Pfister, Laurel, and Susanne Vees-Gulani, eds. *Generational Shifts in Contemporary German Culture.* Rochester, NY: Camden House, 2010.
Cölln, Jan, and Franz-Josefl Holznagel, eds. *Positionen der Germanistik in der DDR: Personen—Forschungsfelder—Organisationsformen.* Berlin: Walter de Gruyter, 2012.
Cooke, Paul. *Representing East Germany Since Unification: From Colonization to Nostalgia.* London: Berg, 2005.
Cooke, Paul, and Andrew Plowman, eds. *German Writers and the Politics of Culture: Dealing with the Stasi.* Basingstoke, UK: Palgrave MacMillan, 2003.
Cosentino, Christine. "'Aus Teufels Küche': Gedanken zur Teufelsfigur in der Literatur nach 2000: Christoph Heins *Willenbrock,* Christa Wolfs *Leibhaftig* und Monika Marons *Endmoränen.*" *Germanic Notes and Reviews* 35, no. 2 (2004): 121–27.
———. "Einige Gedanken zu Christa Wolfs *Stadt der Engel oder The Overcoat of Dr. Freud* und Kathrin Schmidts *Du stirbst nicht*: Selbstfindungsanalysen im Gewand der fiktiven Autobiographie." *Glossen* 31, no.1 (2011). http://blogs.dickinson.edu/glossen/archive/christine-cosentino/ http://blogs.dickinson.edu/glossen/archive/christine-cosentino/.
Costabile-Heming, Carol Anne. "Illness as Metaphor: Christa Wolf, the GDR, and Beyond." *Symposium* 64, no. 3 (2010): 202–19.
Crick, Joyce. "Once Again: Illness as Metaphor: Christa Wolf's Nachdenken über Christa T. and Thomas Mann's Der Zauberberg." In *Neue Ansichten: The Reception of Romanticism in the Literature of the GDR,* edited by Howard Gaskill, Karen McPherson, and Andrew Barker, 53–72. Amsterdam: Rodopi, 1990.
Dackweiler, Regina-Maria, and Reinhild Schäfer. "Gewalt, Macht, Geschlecht: Eine Einführung." In *Gewalt-Verhältnisse: Feministische Perspektiven auf Geschlecht und Gewalt,* edited by Regina-Maria Dackweiler and Reinhild Schäfer, 9–26. Frankfurt am Main: Campus, 2002.
Dahlke, Birgit, Martina Langermann, and Thomas Taterka. *LiteraturGesellschaft DDR: Kanonkämpfe und ihre Geschichte(n).* Stuttgart: Metzler, 2000.
"Das Geschäft mit der Krankheit." *Der Spiegel,* March 6, 1972.
"'Das ist russisches Roulette': Schmutzige Geschäfte mit westlichen Pharmakonzernen brachten dem SED-Regime Millionen." *Der Spiegel,* February 4, 1991.
David, Heinz. *"... Es soll das Haus die Charité heißen...".* Hamburg: Akademos Wissenschaftsverlag, 2004.

"DDR verkaufte Menschen für Menschenversuche." *Berliner Kurier*, December 4, 2012. http://www.berliner-kurier.de/kiez-stadt/experimente-ddr-verkaufte-patienten-fuer-menschenversuche,7169128,21035872,view,printVersion.html.

Deiritz, Karl. "Zur Klärung eines Sachverhalts—Literatur und Staatssicherheit." In *Verrat an der Kunst? Rückblicke auf die DDR-Literatur*, edited by Karl Deiritz and Hannes Krauss, 11–17. Berlin: Aufbau, 1993.

Deiritz, Karl, and Hannes Krauss, eds. *Der deutsch-deutsche Literaturstreit oder "Freunde, es spricht sich schlecht mit gebundener Zunge."* Hamburg: Luchterhand, 1991.

Delius, Friedrich Christian. *Die Birnen von Ribbeck*. Reinbek bei Hamburg: Rowohlt, 1991.

Dennis, Mike. "The East German Ministry of State Security and East German Society during the Honecker Era, 1971–1989." In *German Writers and the Politics of Culture: Dealing with the Stasi*, edited by Paul Cooke and Andrew Plowman, 3–24. Basingstoke, UK: Palgrave MacMillan, 2003.

De Silva, Adrian. "Vom Sittenverfall zur Trans*_Homo-Ehe: Ausgewählte juristische Entwicklungen zu Trans* in der Bundesrepublik Deutschland." In *trans*_homo: differenzen, allianzen, widersprüche. differences, alliances, contradictions*, edited by Justin Time and Jannik Franzen, 149–54. Translated as "From Moral Downfall to Trans*_Homo Marriage: Selected Legal Developments on Trans* in the Federal Republic of Germany," 155–60. Berlin: NoNo, 2012.

De Winde, Arne, and Anke Gilleir, eds. *Literatur im Krebsgang: Totenbeschwörung und Memoria in der deutschsprachigen Literatur nach 1989*. Amsterdam: Rodopi, 2008.

Diderot, Denis. "Lettre sur les aveugles à l'usage de ceux qui voient." 1749. Reprint in: *Œuvres completes: Édition critique et annotée, publiée sous la direction de Herbert Dieckmann, Jean Fabre, et Jacques Proust. Avec les soins de Jean Vallot*. Vol. 4. Paris: Hermann, 1978.

"Die Halbwahrheiten über DDR-Menschenversuche." *Zeit Online*, May 17, 2013. http://www.zeit.de/wissen/gesundheit/2013-05/DDR-Medikamentenstudien-Menschenversuche/komplettansicht.

Drescher, Angela, ed. *Dokumentation zu Christa Wolf "Nachdenken über Christa T."* Hamburg: Luchterhand, 1991.

Dröscher, Barbara. *Subjektive Authentizität: Zur Poetik Christa Wolfs zwischen 1964 und 1975*. Würzburg: Königshausen & Neumann, 1993.

Dueck, Cheryl. *Rifts in Time and in the Self: The Female Subject in Two Generations of East German Women Writers*. Amsterdam: Rodopi, 2004.

Durzak, Manfred. "Der Roman der deutschen Wende? Überlegungen zu Thomas Brussigs Buch *Wie es leuchtet*." In *Kontinuitäten Brüche Kontroversen: Deutsche Literatur nach dem Mauerfall*, edited by Edward Bialek and Monika Wolting, 31–44. Dresden: Neisse, 2012.

Ecker, Gisela, ed. *Kein Land in Sicht: Heimat, weiblich?* Munich: Fink, 1997.

Eigler, Friederike. "(Familien-)Geschichte als subversive Genealogie: Kathrin Schmidts *Gunnar-Lennefsen-Expedition*." *Gegenwartsliteratur: Ein germanistisches Jahrbuch/A German Studies Yearbook*. 2 (2003): 262–82.

———. *Gedächtnis und Geschichte in Generationenromanen seit der Wende*. Berlin: Erich Schmidt, 2005.

———. "Rereading Christa Wolf's 'Selbstversuch': Cyborgs and Feminist Critiques of Scientific Discourse." *The German Quarterly* 73, no. 4 (2000): 401–15.

Eke, Norbert Otto, ed. *"Nach der Mauer der Abgrund"? (Wieder-)Annäherungen and die DDR-Literatur*. Amsterdam: Rodopi, 2013.

Elden, Stuart, and Eduardo Mendieta. "Being-With as Making Worlds: The 'Second Coming' of Peter Sloterdijk." In Special issue "The Worlds of Peter Sloterdijk." *Environment and Planning D: Society and Space* 27 (2009): 1–11.

Emmerich, Wolfgang. *Die andere deutsche Literatur: Aufsätze zur Literatur aus der DDR*. Opladen: Westdeutscher Verlag, 1994.

———. Epilogue to *Geschlechtertausch: Drei Geschichten über die Umwandlung der Verhältnisse*, by Sarah Kirsch, Irmtraud Morgner, Christa Wolf, 101–27. Darmstadt: Luchterhand, 1980.

———. "Für eine andere Wahrnehmung der DDR-Literatur: Neue Kontexte, neue Paradigmen, ein neuer Kanon." In *Die andere deutsche Literatur: Aufsätze zur Literatur aus der DDR*, edited by Wolfgang Emmerich, 190–207. Opladen: Westdeutscher Verlag, 1994.

———. *Kleine Literaturgeschichte der DDR. Erweiterte Neuausgabe*. 1996. Reprint, Berlin: Aufbau, 2000.

Erdbrügger, Torsten and Stephan Krause, eds. *Leibesvisitationen: Der Körper als mediales Politikum in den (post)sozialistischen Kulturen und Literaturen*. Heidelberg: Winter, 2014.

Erll, Astrid. *Kollektives Gedächtnis und Erinnerungskulturen: Eine Einführung*. Stuttgart: Metzler, 2005.

———. "Literatur als Medium des kollektiven Gedächtnisses." In *Gedächtniskonzepte der Literaturwissenschaft: Theoretische Grundlegung und Anwendungsperspektiven*, edited by Astrid Erll and Ansgar Nünning, 249–76. Berlin: de Gruyter, 2005.

Ernst, Anna-Sabine. *'Die beste Prophylaxe ist der Sozialismus': Ärzte und medizinische Hochschullehrer in der SBZ/DDR 1945–1961*. Münster: Waxmann, 1997.

Erpenbeck, Jenny. *Aller Tage Abend*. Munich: Albrecht Knaus Verlag, 2012. Translated by Susan Bernofsky as *The End of Days* (New York: New Directions, 2014).

———. *Heimsuchung*. Frankfurt am Main: Eichborn, 2007. Translated by Susan Bernofsky as *Visitation* (New York: New Directions, 2010).

"'Es geht um unsere Ehre.'" *Der Spiegel*, August 26, 1991.

Evers, Marco, Klaus Franke, and Johann Grolle. "Zucht und deutsche Ordnung." *Der Spiegel*, September 27, 1999.

Festge, Otto-Andreas. "Ethische Positionen bei der medizinischen Versorgung behinderter und kranker Kinder in der DDR." In *Medizinische Ethik in der DDR: Erfahrungswert oder Altlast?*, edited by Hartmut Bettin and Mariacarla Gadebusch Bondio, 94–101. Lengerich: Pabst Science, 2010.

Fietz, Kathleen, Kristina Pezzei, and Detlev Schilke. "Ich wusste schnell wieder, wer ich bin: Montagsinterview." *die tageszeitung*, January 4, 2010.

Finch, Helen. "Gender, Identity, and Memory in the Novels of Antje Rávic Strubel." *Women in German Yearbook* 28 (2012): 82–97.

Finlay, Frank. "Literary Debates and the Literary Market since Unification." In *Contemporary German Fiction: Writing in the Berlin Republic*, edited by Stuart Taberner, 21–38. Cambridge: Cambridge University Press, 2007.

Fischer, Gerhard, and David Roberts, eds. *Schreiben nach der Wende: Ein Jahrzehnt deutscher Literatur 1989–1999*. Tübingen: Stauffenburg, 2001.

Fischer, Gerhard, Hans-Joachim Krusch, Hans Modrow, Wolfgang Richter, and Robert Steigerwald, eds. *Gegen den Zeitgeist: Zwei deutsche Staaten in der Geschichte*. Schkeuditz: GNN, 1999.

Fischer, W. "Euthanasie in der Diskussion." In *Ethik und Medizin im Sozialismus: Wissenschaftliches Kolloquium des Bereichs Medizin der Ernst-Moritz-Arndt-Universität am 2.10.1974 zu Ehren des 25. Jahrestages der DDR*, edited by Hansgeorg Hüller, 68–72. Greifswald: Ernst-Moritz-Arndt-Universität, 1976.

Fischer-Kania, Sabine, and Daniel Schäf, eds. *Sprache und Literatur im Spannungsfeld von Politik und Ästhetik. Christa Wolf zum 80. Geburtstag*. Munich: Iudicium, 2011.

Flanagan, Clare, and Stuart Taberner, eds. *1949/1989—Cultural Perspectives on Division and Unity in East and West*. Amsterdam: Rodopi, 2000.

Foucault, Michel. *Discipline and Punish: The Birth of the Prison*. Translated by Alan Sheridan. 1977. Reprint, New York: Vintage Books, 1995.

———. *The History of Sexuality: An Introduction. Vol. 1*. Translated by Robert Hurley. 1978. Reprint, New York: Vintage Books, 1990.

———. "Nietzsche, Genealogy, History." In *The Essential Foucault: Selections from Essential Works of Foucault, 1954–1984*, edited by Paul Rabinow and Nikolas Rose, 351–69. New York: The New Press, 1994.

Fox, Thomas C. "Post-Communist Fantasies: Generational Conflict in Eastern German Literature." In *Generational Shifts in Contemporary German Culture*, edited by Laurel Cohen-Pfister and Susanne Vees-Gulani, 207–24. Rochester, NY: Camden House, 2010.

Franck, Julia. *Lagerfeuer*. Cologne: DuMont, 2003.

———. *Rücken an Rücken*. Frankfurt am Main: Fischer, 2011. Translated by Anthea Bell as *Back to Back* (New York: Grove, 2013).

Franke, Konrad. *Kindlers Literaturgeschichte der Gegenwart: Die Literatur der Deutschen Demokratischen Republik*. Zurich: Kindler, 1974.

———. *Kindlers Literaturgeschichte der Gegenwart: Die Literatur der Deutschen Demokratischen Republik*. Zurich: Kindler, 1971.

Franke, Konrad. *Das Recht im Alltag des Haus- und Betriebsarztes.* Berlin, GDR: Verlag Tribüne, 1980.
Franzen, Jannik. "Störungen der Heteronormativität: Medizinisch-psychologische Forschung und Praxis aus Trans*Perspektive." In *trans*_homo: differenzen, allianzen, widersprüche. differences, alliances, contradictions,* edited by Justin Time and Jannik Franzen, 185–90. Translated as "Disordering Heteronormativity: Medical-Psychological Research and Practice in Trans* Perspectives," 191–95. Berlin: NoNo, 2012.
Frederiksen, Elke P., and Martha Kaarsberg Wallach, eds. *Facing Fascism and Confronting the Past: German Women Writers from Weimar to the Present.* Albany: State University of New York Press, 2000.
Freud, Sigmund. "Konstruktionen in der Analyse." In *Gesammelte Werke: Band 16: Werke aus den Jahren 1932–1939,* edited by Anna Freud, 43–56. London: Imago, 1950. Translated by James Strachey as "Constructions in Analysis." In *The Standard Edition of the Complete Psychological Works of Sigmund Freud. Vol. 23 (1937–1939),* 257–69. London: Hogarth Press/Institute Of Psycho-Analysis, 1964.

———. "Das Unheimliche." In *Studienausgabe: Band IV: Psychologische Schriften,* edited by Alexander Mitscherlich, Angela Richards, and James Strachey, 241–74. Frankfurt am Main: Fischer, 1970. Translated as "The Uncanny." In *Studies in Parapsychology,* edited by Philip Rieff, 19–60. New York: Collier, 1963.

Friedemann, Hedi. "Prävention in der DDR." In *Das Gesundheitswesen der DDR: Aufbruch oder Einbruch. Denkanstöße für eine Neuordnung des Gesundheitswesens in einem deutschen Staat,* edited by Wilhelm Thiele, 246–52. Sankt Augustin: Asgard-Verlag Hippe, 1990.
Fromm, Erich. "Sozialpsychologischer Teil und Erhebungen." In *Studien über Autorität und Familie: Forschungsberichte aus dem Institut für Sozialforschung,* edited by Max Horkheimer, 77–135. Paris: Alcan, 1936.
Fuchs, Anne, Kathleen James-Chakraborty, and Linda Shortt, eds. *Debating German Cultural Identity since 1989.* Rochester, NY: Camden House, 2011.
Fukuyama, Francis. "The end of history?" *The National Interest* 16 (Summer 1989): 3–18.
Fulbrook, Mary. "The Concept of 'Normalisation' and the GDR in Comparative Perspective." In *Power and Society in the GDR, 1961–1979: The 'Normalisation of Rule'?* edited by Mary Fulbrook, 1–30. New York: Berghahn, 2009.

———. *Dissonant Lives: Generations and Violence Through the German Dictatorships.* Oxford: Oxford University Press, 2011.

———."Living through the GDR: History, Life Stories, and Generations in East Germany." In *The GDR Remembered: Representations of the East German State since 1989,* edited by Nick Hodgin and Caroline Pearce, 201–20. Rochester, NY: Camden House, 2011.

———. "'Normalisation' in the GDR in Retrospect: East German Perspectives on their Own Lives." In *Power and Society in the GDR, 1961–1979:*

The 'Normalisation of Rule'? edited by Mary Fulbrook, 278–319. New York: Berghahn, 2009.

———. *The People's State: East German Society from Hitler to Honecker.* New Haven, CT: Yale University Press, 2005.

———, ed. *Power and Society in the GDR, 1961–1979: The 'Normalisation of Rule'?* New York: Berghahn, 2009.

Fulbrook, Mary, and Andrew I. Port. *Becoming East German: Socialist Structures and Sensibilities after Hitler.* New York: Berghahn, 2013.

Gallagher, Kaleen. "The Problem of Shame in Christa Wolf's *Stadt der Engel oder The Overcoat of Dr. Freud.*" *German Life and Letters* 65, no. 3 (July 2012): 378–97.

Galli, Matteo. "Post-Staatliche DDR-Literatur in der Literaturgeschichtsschreibung: Eine Bestandsaufnahme." In *"Nach der Mauer der Abgrund"? (Wieder-)Annäherungen and die DDR-Literatur*, edited by Norbert Otto Eke, 105–18. Amsterdam: Rodopi, 2013.

Gansel, Carsten, ed. *Christa Wolf im Strom der Erinnerung.* Göttingen: V&R unipress, 2014.

Geier, Andrea. "Enteignete Indianer und ausgebeutete Neger: Der Kolonialisierungs-Diskurs in der Literatur nach 1990." In *NachBilder der Wende*, edited by Inge Stephan and Alexandra Tacke, 70–83. Cologne: Böhlau, 2008.

———. "Mediating Immediacy: Historicizing the GDR by Bringing It Back to Life in Postmillennial Works of Fiction." In *Competing Memories of the GDR in Postunification German Culture*, edited by Renate Rechtien and Dennis Tate, 101–13. Rochester, NY: Camden House, 2011.

Geppert, Roswitha. *Die Last, die du nicht trägst.* 1978. Reprint, Halle: Mitteldeutscher Verlag, 1989.

Gerber, Margy, ed. *Proceedings of the International Symposium on the German Democratic Republic.* Washington, DC: University Press of America, 1981.

Gerhard, Ute. "German Women and the Social Costs of Unification." *German Politics and Society* 24 (Winter 1991): 16–33.

Gerstenberger, Katharina. *Writing the New Berlin: The German Capital in Post-Wall Literature.* Rochester, NY: Camden House, 2008.

Gibas, Monika. "'Bonner Ultras', 'Kriegstreiber' und 'Schlotbarone': Die Bundesrepublik als Feindbild der DDR in den fünfziger Jahren." In *Unsere Feinde: Konstruktion des Anderen im Sozialismus*, edited by Silke Satjukow and Rainer Gries, 75–106. Leipzig: Leipziger Universitätsverlag, 2005.

Gieseke, Jens. *Die DDR-Staatssicherheit: Schild und Schwert der Partei.* Bonn: Bundeszentrale für politische Bildung, 2001. Translated by Mary Carlene Forszt as *The GDR State Security: Shield and Sword of the Party* (Berlin: The Federal Commissioner for the Records of the State Security Service of the former German Democratic Republic, 2006).

———. *Die Stasi 1945–1990.* Munich: Pantheon, 2011.

Goethe, Johann Wolfgang von. *Faust: Der Tragödie erster und zweiter Teil. Urfaust*, edited by Erich Trunz. Munich: C. H. Beck, 1984. Translated by David Luke as *Faust: Part One* (Oxford: Oxford University Press, 1987).
Goodbody, Axel, and Dennis Tate, eds. *Geist und Macht: Writers and the State in the GDR*. Amsterdam: Rodopi 1992.
Görlich, Günter. *Eine Anzeige in der Zeitung*. Berlin, GDR: Verlag Neues Leben, 1978.
Götze, Clemens. *Ich werde weiterleben, und richtig gut: Moderne Mythen in der Literatur des 20. Jahrhunderts*. Berlin: Wissenschaftlicher Verlag, 2011.
Granzow, René. *Gehen oder bleiben? Literatur und Schriftsteller der DDR zwischen Ost und West*. Berlin: Frank und Timme, 2008.
Grashoff, Udo. *"In einem Anfall von Depression . . .": Selbsttötungen in der DDR*. Berlin: Christoph Links, 2006.
Grass, Günter. *Ein Schnäppchen namens DDR: Letzte Reden vorm Glockengeläut*. Göttingen: Steidl, 1990.
Gratzik, Paul. *Kohlenkutte*. Berlin: Rotbuch, 1982.
Grau, Günter. "Sozialistische Moral und Homosexualität: Die Politik der SED und das Homosexuellenstrafrecht 1945 bis 1989—ein Rückblick." In *Die Linke und das Laster: Schwule Emanzipation und linke Vorurteile*, edited by Detlef Grumbach, 85–141. Hamburg: Männerschwarm Skript, 1995.
Greiner, Ulrich. "Die deutsche Gesinnungsästhetik." In *Es geht nicht um Christa Wolf: Der Literaturstreit im vereinten Deutschland*, edited by Thomas Anz. 208–16. Frankfurt am Main: Fischer, 1991.
Gröschner, Annett. *Moskauer Eis*. Leipzig: Kiepenheuer, 2000.
———. *Walpurgistag*. Munich: Deutsche Verlagsanstalt, 2011.
Großbölting, Thomas. "Die DDR im vereinten Deutschland," *Aus Politik und Zeitgeschichte* 25–26 (2010): 35–41.
———. "Entbürgerlichte die DDR? Sozialer Bruch und kultureller Wandel in der ostdeutschen Gesellschaft." In *Bürgertum nach 1945*, edited by Manfred Hettling and Bernd Ulrich. 407–32. Hamburg: Hamburger Edition, 2005.
Grumbach, Detlef, ed. *Die Linke und das Laster: Schwule Emanzipation und linke Vorurteile*. Hamburg: Männerschwarm Skript, 1995.
Günther, Ernst. "Das Arztrecht in der DDR und seine Beziehung zur ärztlichen Ethik: Erfahrungen aus dem Umgang mit ärztlichen Fehlleistungen." In *Medizinische Ethik in der DDR: Erfahrungswert oder Altlast?*, edited by Hartmut Bettin and Mariacarla Gadebusch Bondio, 86–93. Lengerich: Pabst Science, 2010.
———. "Patientenschutz und Arzthaftung in der DDR." In *Das Gesundheitswesen der DDR: Aufbruch oder Einbruch. Denkanstöße für eine Neuordnung des Gesundheitswesens in einem deutschen Staat*, edited by Wilhelm Thiele, 161–67. Sankt Augustin: Asgard-Verlag Hippe, 1990.

Haase, Michael. "Christa Wolfs letzter 'Selbstversuch'—Zum Konzept der subjektiven Authentizität in 'Stadt der Engel oder The Overcoat of Dr. Freud.'" In *Christa Wolf im Strom der Erinnerung*, edited by Carsten Gansel, 215–30. Göttingen: V&R unipress, 2014.

Hahn, Susanne. "Ethische Fragen und Problemlösungen des Schwesternberufes im DDR-Gesundheitswesen." In *Medizinische Ethik in der DDR: Erfahrungswert oder Altlast?*, edited by Hartmut Bettin and Mariacarla Gadebusch Bondio, 73–85. Lengerich: Pabst Science, 2010.

Hametner, Michael, and Kerstin Schilling, eds. *"Es genügt nicht die einfache Wahrheit": DDR-Literatur der sechziger Jahre in der Diskussion*. Leipzig: Friedrich-Ebert-Stifung, 1995.

Hartewig, Karin. "'Proben des Abgrunds, über welchem unsere Zivilisation wie eine Brücke schwebt': Der Holocaust in der Publizistik der SBZ/DDR." In *Beschweigen und Bekennen: Die deutsche Nachkriegsgesellschaft und der Holocaust*, edited by Norbert Frei and Sybille Steinbacher, 35–50. Göttingen: Wallstein 2001.

Hartinger, Walfried. *Wechselseitige Wahrnehmung: Heiner Müller und Christa Wolf in der deutschen Kritik—in Ost und West*. Leipzig: Rosa-Luxemburg-Stiftung Sachsen, 2008.

Harych, Horst. "Zur Zukunft der Polikliniken und der ambulanten Versorgung in der DDR," In *Das Gesundheitswesen der DDR: Aufbruch oder Einbruch. Denkanstöße für eine Neuordnung des Gesundheitswesens in einem deutschen Staat*, edited by Wilhelm Thiele, 99–104. Sankt Augustin: Asgard-Verlag Hippe, 1990.

Heffernan, Valerie, and Gillian Pye, eds. *Transitions: Emerging Women Writers in German-Language Literature*. Amsterdam: Rodopi, 2013.

Heidelberger-Leonard, Irene. "Der Literaturstreit—ein Historikerstreit im gesamtdeutschen Kostüm?" In *Der deutsch-deutsche Literaturstreit oder "Freunde, es spricht sich schlecht mit gebundener Zunge,"* edited by Karl Deiritz and Hannes Krauss, 69–77. Hamburg: Luchterhand, 1991.

Heiduczek, Werner. *Tod am Meer*. Halle: Mitteldeutscher Verlag, 1977.

Heilbroner, Robert. "The Triumph of Capitalism." *The New Yorker*, January 23, 1989.

Hein, Christoph. *Der fremde Freund*. Berlin, GDR: Aufbau, 1982. Translated by Krishna Winston as *The Distant Lover* (Munich: Pantheon Books, 1989).

———. *Horns Ende*. Berlin, GDR: Aufbau, 1985.

———. *In seiner frühen Kindheit ein Garten*. Frankfurt am Main: Suhrkamp, 2005.

———. *Weiskerns Nachlass*. Berlin: Suhrkamp, 2011.

Helbig, Holger. "Wandel statt Wende: Wie man den Wenderoman liest/schreibt, während man auf ihn wartet." In *Weiterschreiben: Zur DDR-Literatur nach dem Ende der DDR*, edited by Holger Helbig, Kristin Felsner, Sebastian Horn, and Therese Manz, 75–88. Berlin: Akademie Verlag, 2007.

Helbig, Holger, Kristin Felsner, Sebastian Horn, and Therese Manz, eds. *Weiterschreiben: Zur DDR-Literatur nach dem Ende der DDR*. Berlin: Akademie Verlag, 2007.
Hell, Julia. "Critical Orthodoxies, Old and New, Or The Fantasy of a Pure Voice: Christa Wolf." In *Contentious Memories: Looking Back at the GDR*, edited by Jost Hermand and Marc Silberman, 65–101. New York: Peter Lang, 1998.
———. *Post-Fascist Fantasies: Psychoanalysis, History, and the Literature of East Germany*. Durham, NC: Duke University Press, 1997.
———. "Soft Porn, Kitsch, and Post-Fascist Bodies: The East German Novel of Arrival." *South Atlantic Quarterly* 94, no. 3 (1995): 747–72.
Helmecke, Monika. *Klopfzeichen*. Berlin, GDR: Verlag Neues Leben, 1979.
Henn, Marianne, and Britta Hufeisen, eds. *Frauen: Mitsprechen, Mitschreiben*. Stuttgart: Heinz, 1997.
Henrich, Rolf. *Der vormundschaftliche Staat: Vom Versagen des real existierenden Sozialismus*. Reinbek bei Hamburg: Rowohlt, 1989.
Hensel, Kerstin. *Hallimasch. Erzählungen*. Frankfurt am Main: Luchterhand, 1989.
———. *Im Spinnhaus*. Munich: Luchterhand, 2003.
———. *Lärchenau*. Munich: Luchterhand, 2008.
Hermand, Jost, and Marc Silberman, eds. *Contentious Memories: Looking Back at the GDR*. New York: Peter Lang, 1998.
Herminghouse, Patricia, and Magda Mueller, eds. *Gender and Germanness: Cultural Productions of Nation*. Providence, RI: Berghahn, 1997.
———. "Looking for Germania." In *Gender and Germanness: Cultural Productions of Nation*, edited by Patricia Herminghouse and Magda Mueller, 1–18. Providence, RI: Berghahn, 1997.
Hermsdorf, Klaus. "Regionen deutscher Literatur 1870–1945: Theoretische und typologische Fragen." *Zeitschrift für Germanistik: Neue Folge* 3, no. 1 (1993): 7–17.
Herrn, Rainer. "Ver-körperung des anderen Geschlechts—Transvestitismus und Transsexualität historisch betrachtet." *Aus Politik und Zeitgeschichte* 20/21 (2012): 41–48.
Hess, Volker. "Epilogue." In *Die Charité: Geschichte(n) eines Krankenhauses*, edited by Johanna Bleker and Volker Hess, 243–47. Berlin: Akademie Verlag, 2010.
Hettling, Manfred, and Bernd Ulrich, eds. *Bürgertum nach 1945*. Hamburg: Hamburger Edition, 2005.
Heukenkamp, Ursula. "Ortsgebundenheit: Die DDR-Literatur als Variante des Regionalismus in der deutschen Nachkriegsliteratur." *Weimarer Beiträge* 42 (1996): 30–53.
Heym, Stefan. *Collin*. Munich: Bertelsmann, 1979. Translated as *Collin* (London: Hodder and Stoughton, 1980).
Heymann, Stefan. *Marxismus und Rassenfrage*. Berlin: Dietz, 1948.
Hilzinger, Sonja. Epilogue to *Nachdenken über Christa T.* by Christa Wolf. 211–38. Edited by Sonja Hilzinger. Vol. 2. Munich: Luchterhand, 1999.

Hochhut, Rolf. *Wessis in Weimar: 10 Szenen aus einem besetzten Land.* Munich: dtv, 1993.
Hockerts, Hans Günter. "Grundlinien und soziale Folgen der Sozialpolitik in der DDR." In *Sozialgeschichte der DDR*, edited by Hartmut Kaelble, Jürgen Kocka, and Hartmut Zwahr, 519–44. Stuttgart: Klett Cotta, 1994.
Hodgin, Nick and Caroline Pearce, eds. *The GDR Remembered: Representations of the East German State since 1989.* Rochester, NY: Camden House, 2011.
———. "Introduction." In *The GDR Remembered: Representations of the East German State since 1989*, edited by Nick Hodgin and Caroline Pearce, 1–16. Rochester, NY: Camden House, 2011.
Hoffmann, E. T. A. *Die Bergwerke zu Falun.* 1819. Reprint, Stuttgart: Reclam, 1986.
Hofmann, Ute. "Analyse von Suizidversuchen bei Frauen in Magdeburg." PhD diss., Magdeburg University, 1969.
Hollmer, Heide. "The next generation: Thomas Brussig erzählt Erich Honeckers DDR." In *DDR-Literatur der neunziger Jahre: Sonderband Text + Kritik*, edited by Heinz Ludwig Arnold, 107–21. Munich: edition text + kritik, 2000.
Hörnigk, Frank. "Die Literatur ist zuständig: Über das Verhältnis von Literatur und Politik in der DDR." In *Geist und Macht: Writers and the State in the GDR*, edited by Axel Goodbody and Dennis Tate, 23–34. Amsterdam: Rodopi, 1992.
Hörnigk, Therese. "'. . . aber schreiben kann man dann nicht': Über die Auswirkungen politischer Eingriffe in künstlerische Prozesse." In *Kahlschlag: Das 11. Plenum des ZK der SED 1965. Studien und Dokumente*, edited by Günter Agde, 413–22. Berlin: Aufbau Taschenbuch 1991.
———. *Christa Wolf.* Göttingen: Steidl, 1989.
———. "Ein Buch des Erinnerns, das zum Nachdenken anregte: Christa Wolf's *Nachdenken über Christa T.*" In *Werke und Wirkungen: DDR-Literatur in der Diskussion*, edited by Inge Münz-Koenen, 168–213. Leipzig: Reclam, 1987.
Hüller, Hansgeorg, ed. *Ethik und Medizin im Sozialismus: Wissenschaftliches Kolloquium des Bereichs Medizin der Ernst-Moritz-Arndt-Universität am 2.10.1974 zu Ehren des 25. Jahrestages der DDR.* Greifswald: Ernst-Moritz-Arndt-Universität, 1976.
Hüller, Hans-Georg, H.-G. Berndt, and I. Amon. "Versuch und/oder Erprobung am Menschen." In *Ethik und Medizin im Sozialismus: Wissenschaftliches Kolloquium des Bereichs Medizin der Ernst-Moritz-Arndt-Universität am 2.10.1974 zu Ehren des 25. Jahrestages der DDR*, edited by Hansgeorg Hüller, 46–52. Greifswald: Ernst-Moritz-Arndt-Universität, 1976.
Huntemann, Willi, Malgorzata Klentak-Zablocka, Fabian Lampart, and Thomas Schmidt, eds. *Engagierte Literatur in Wendezeiten.* Würzburg: Königshausen & Neumann, 2003.

Huyssen, Andreas. "Auf den Spuren Ernst Blochs: Nachdenken über Christa Wolf." In *Wirkungsgeschichte von Christa Wolfs "Nachdenken über Christa T.,"* edited by Manfred Behn, 147–55. Königstein: Athenäum, 1978.

Irigaray, Luce. "The Sex Which is Not One." In *The Second Wave: A Reader in Feminist Theory,* edited by Linda Nicholson, 323–29. New York: Routledge, 1997.

Iztueta, Garbine. "Body and Grotesque as Self-Disruption in Kerstin Hensel's Gothic East(ern) German Novel *Lärchenau* (2008)." In *Strategies of Humor in Post-Unification German Literature, Film, and other Media,* edited by Jill E. Twark, 143–64. Newcastle upon Tyne: Cambridge Scholars, 2011.

Jäger, Manfred. *Sozialliteraten: Funktion und Selbstverständnis der Schriftsteller in der DDR.* Düsseldorf: Bertelsmann Universitätsverlag, 1973.

Jagow, Bettina von, and Florian Steger, eds. *Jahrbuch Literatur und Medizin.* Vol. 5. Heidelberg: Universitätsverlag Winter, 2012.

———. *Repräsentationen: Medizin und Ethik in Literatur und Kunst der Moderne.* Heidelberg: Universitätsverlag Winter, 2004.

Jahr, U. "Zur Diagnose und Therapie sogenannter unheilbarer Erkrankungen und ethische Probleme." In *Ethik und Medizin im Sozialismus: Wissenschaftliches Kolloquium des Bereichs Medizin der Ernst-Moritz-Arndt-Universität am 2.10.1974 zu Ehren des 25. Jahrestages der DDR,* edited by Hansgeorg Hüller, 84–89. Greifswald: Ernst-Moritz-Arndt-Universität, 1976.

Janssen-Zimmermann, Antje. "Plädoyer für einen Text—Christa Wolf: 'Was bleibt.'" *neue deutsche literatur* 38, no. 11 (1990): 157–62.

Jarausch, Konrad H. "Die Zukunft der ostdeutschen Vergangenheit—Was wird aus der DDR-Geschichte?" In *DDR-Geschichte vermitteln,* edited by Jens Hüttmann, Ulrich Mählert, and Peer Pasternack, 81–101. Berlin: Metropol, 2004.

Jarausch, Konrad H., and Volker Gransow. *Uniting Germany: Documents and Debates, 1944–1993.* New York: Berghahn, 1994.

Jeremiah, Emily. "Shameful Stories: The Ethics of East German Memory Contests in Fiction by Julia Schoch, Stefan Moster, Antje Rávic Strubel, and Judith Schalansky." In *Ethical Approaches in Contemporary German-language Literature and Culture.* Edinburgh German Yearbook 7, edited by Emily Jeremiah and Frauke Matthes, 65–84. Rochester, NY: Camden House, 2013.

Jeremiah, Emily, and Frauke Matthes, eds. *Ethical Approaches in Contemporary German-language Literature and Culture.* Edinburgh German Yearbook 7. Rochester, NY: Camden House, 2013.

Jessen, Ralph. "'Bildungsbürger', 'Experten', 'Intelligenz': Kontinuität und Wandel der ostdeutschen Bildungsschichten in der Ulbricht-Ära." In *Weimarer Klassik in der Ära Ulbricht,* edited by Lothar Ehrlich and Gunther Mai, 113–34. Cologne: Böhlau, 2000.

Joho, Wolfgang. "Wir begannen nicht im Jahre Null." *neue deutsche literatur* 13, no. 5 (1965): 5–11.

Kacandes, Irene. *Talk Fiction: Literature and the Talk Explosion*. Lincoln: University of Nebraska Press, 2001.
Kaelble, Hartmut, Jürgen Kocka, and Hartmut Zwahr, eds. *Sozialgeschichte der DDR*. Stuttgart: Klett Cotta, 1994.
Kahn, Siegbert. *Antisemitismus und Rassenhetze: Eine Übersicht über ihre Entwicklung in Deutschland*. Berlin: Dietz, 1948.
Käser, Rudolf. "Metaphern der Krankheit: Krebs." In *Lesbarkeit der Kultur: Literaturwissenschaft zwischen Kulturtechnik und Ethnographie*, edited by Gerhard Neumann and Sigrid Weigel, 323–42. Munich: Wilhelm Fink, 2000.
Käser, Rudolf, and Beate Schappach, eds. *Krank geschrieben: Gesundheit und Krankheit im Diskursfeld von Literatur, Geschlecht und Medizin*. Bielefeld: transcript, 2014.
Kaute, Brigitte. "Sprachreflexion in Christa Wolf: *Leibhaftig*." *Studia Neophilologica* 75 (2003): 47–57.
Kirchgäßner, W. "Philosophische Aspekte des Arzt-Patienten-Verhältnisses und die Wirksamkeit der Sprache bei der Festigung dieses Verhältnisses." In *Ethik und Medizin im Sozialismus: Wissenschaftliches Kolloquium des Bereichs Medizin der Ernst-Moritz-Arndt-Universität am 2.10.1974 zu Ehren des 25. Jahrestages der DDR*, edited by Hansgeor Hüller, 21–39. Greifswald: Ernst-Moritz-Arndt-Universität, 1976.
Kirsch, Sarah, Irmtraud Morgner, and Christa Wolf. *Geschlechtertausch: Drei Geschichten über die Umwandlung der Verhältnisse*. Darmstadt: Luchterhand, 1980.
Kleist, Heinrich von. *Herrmannsschlacht*. 1808. Reprint, Stuttgart: Reclam, 2011.
Kleßmann, Christoph. "Konturen einer integrierten Nachkriegsgeschichte." *Aus Politik und Zeitgeschichte* 18/19 (2005): 3–11.
———. "Spaltung und Verflechtung—Ein Konzept zur integrierten Nachkriegsgeschichte 1945 bis 1990." In *Teilung und Integration: Die doppelte deutsche Nachkriegsgeschichte als wissenschaftliches und didaktisches Phänomen*, edited by Christoph Kleßmann and Peter Lautzas, 20–37. Bonn: Bundeszentrale für politische Bildung, 2005.
———. "Zeitgeschichte als wissenschaftliche Aufklärung." *Aus Politik und Zeitgeschichte* 51/52 (2002): 3–13.
Kleßmann, Christoph, and Peter Lautzas, eds. *Teilung und Integration: Die doppelte deutsche Nachkriegsgeschichte als wissenschaftliches und didaktisches Phänomen*. Bonn: Bundeszentrale für politische Bildung, 2005.
Klocke, Sonja. "(Anti-)faschistische Familien und (post-)faschistische Körper—Christa Wolfs *Der geteilte Himmel*." In *Christa Wolf im Strom der Erinnerung*, edited by Carsten Gansel, 69–87. Göttingen: V&R unipress, 2014.
———. "Die frohe Botschaft der Kathrin Schmidt?—Transsexuality, Racism, and Feminist Historiography in *Die Gunnar-Lennefsen-Expedition* (1998)." *Germanistik in Ireland: Jahrbuch der/Yearbook of the Association of Third-Level Teachers of German in Ireland*. 5 (2010): 143–58.

———. "A Woman's Quest for Agency: Kathrin Schmidt, *Du stirbst nicht* (2009)." In *Emerging German Novelists*, edited by Lyn Marven and Stuart Taberner, 228–42. Rochester, NY: Camden House, 2011.
Klöppel, Ulrike. "Geschlechtergrenzen geöffnet?" *Gen-ethischer Informationsdienst* 211 (2012): 35–37.
———. "Medikalisierung 'uneindeutigen' Geschlechts." *Aus Politik und Zeitgeschichte* 20/21 (2012): 28–33.
———. "'Die Verfügung zur Geschlechtsumwandlung von Transsexualisten' im Spiegel der Sexualpolitik der DDR." In *trans*_homo: differenzen, allianzen, widersprüche. differences, alliances, contradictions*, edited by Justin Time and Jannik Franzen, 167–72. Translated as "The 'Ordinance on the Gender Conversion of Transsexualists' as Reflected in the Sexual Politics of the German Democratic Republic," 173–78. Berlin: NoNo, 2012.
———. *XXOXY ungelöst: Hermaphrodismus, Sex und Gender in der deutschen Medizin: Eine historische Studie zur Intersexualität*. Bielefeld: transcript, 2010.
Knopf, Hiltraud, and Ute Fritsche. "Müttersterblichkeit in der DDR." In *Das Gesundheitswesen der DDR: Aufbruch oder Einbruch: Denkanstöße für eine Neuordnung des Gesundheitswesens in einem deutschen Staat*, edited by Wilhelm Thiele, 217–21. Sankt Augustin: Asgard-Verlag Hippe, 1990.
Koch, Lennart. *Ästhetik der Moral bei Christa Wolf und Monika Maron: Der Literaturstreit von der Wende bis zum Ende der neunziger Jahre*. Frankfurt am Main: Peter Lang, 2000.
Kohl, Helmut. "Fernsehansprache von Bundeskanzler Kohl anlässlich des Inkrafttretens der Währungs-, Wirtschafts- und Sozialunion." http://www.helmut-kohl.de/index.php?msg=555.
Köhler, Astrid. *Brückenschläge: DDR-Autoren vor und nach der Wiedervereinigung*. Göttingen: Vandenhoeck & Ruprecht, 2007.
Köhn, Lothar. *Literatur—Geschichte: Beiträge zur deutschen Literatur des 19. und 20. Jahrhunderts*. Münster: LIT, 2000.
Königsdorf, Helga. *Respektloser Umgang*. Berlin, GDR: Aufbau, 1986.
———. *Ungelegener Befund*. Berlin, GDR: Aufbau, 1990.
Körner, Hannelore, and Uwe Körner. "In-vitro-Fertilisation, Embryotransfer und erste 'Retortenkinder' in der DDR." In *Medizinische Ethik in der DDR: Erfahrungswert oder Altlast?*, edited by Hartmut Bettin and Mariacarla Gadebusch Bondio, 127–40. Lengerich: Pabst Science, 2010.
Körner, Uwe, and Hannelore Körner. "Ethische Positionen zum vorgeburtlichen Leben und zur In-vitro-Fertilisation in der DDR." In *Medizinische Ethik in der DDR: Erfahrungswert oder Altlast?*, edited by Hartmut Bettin and Mariacarla Gadebusch Bondio, 141–54. Lengerich: Pabst Science, 2010.
Koskinas, Nikolaos-Ioannis. *"Fremd bin ich eingezogen, fremd ziehe ich wieder aus": Von Kassandra, über Medea, zu Ariadne: Manifestationen der Psyche*

im späten Werk Christa Wolfs. Würzburg: Königshausen & Neumann, 2008.
Kowalczuk, Ilko-Sascha. *Die 101 wichtigsten Fragen: DDR.* Munich: C. H. Beck, 2009.
Krauss, Hannes. "Zonenkindheiten: (Literarische) Rückblicke." In *Weiterschreiben: Zur DDR-Literatur nach dem Ende der DDR*, edited by Holger Helbig, Kristin Felsner, Sebastian Horn, and Therese Manz, 89–101. Berlin: Akademie Verlag 2007.
Krauss, Hannes, and Jochen Vogt. "Staatsdichter, Volkserzieher, Dissidenten?: Entstehung, Untergang und Fortdauer eines Berufsbildes." *Deutschunterricht* 5 (1996): 98–104.
Kroetz, Franz Xaver. *Haus Deutschland: Eine Farce.* Berlin: Rotbuch, 2004.
Kubiczek, André. *Der Genosse, die Prinzessin und ihr lieber Herr Sohn.* Munich: Piper, 2012.
Kuczynski, Jürgen. *"Ein linientreuer Dissident": Memoiren 1945–1989.* Berlin: Aufbau, 1992.
Kuhn, Anna K. "'Eine Königin köpfen ist effektiver als einen König köpfen': The Gender Politics of the Christa Wolf Controversy." In *Women and the Wende: Social Effects and Cultural Reflections of the German Unification Process*, edited by Elizabeth Boa and Janet Wharton, 200–215. Amsterdam: Rodopi, 1994.
———. "Of Trauma, Angels and Healing: Christa Wolf's *Stadt der Engel oder The Overcoat of Dr. Freud.*" *Gegenwartsliteratur: Ein germanistisches Jahrbuch/A German Studies Yearbook.* 10 (2011): 164–85.
Kulawik, Helmut. "Der Suizidversuch: Zur Psychopathologie und Therapie der Suizidalität." PhD diss., Berlin, GDR, 1976.
Küppers, Caroline. "Soziologische Dimension von Geschlecht." *Aus Politik und Zeitgeschichte* 20/21 (2012): 3–8.
Kurz, Paul Konrad. "Besprechung: Wolf, Christa. Leibhaftig." *Stimmen der Zeit* 221, no. 5 (2003): 356–57.
Lammers, Hans-Jörg. *Über die Intersexualität beim Menschen.* Halle: Marhold, 1956.
Langermann, Martina, and Thomas Takerta. "Von der versuchten Verfertigung einer Literaturgesellschaft: Kanon und Norm in der literarischen Kommunikation der DDR." In *LiteraturGesellschaft DDR: Kanonkämpfe und ihre Geschichte(n)*, edited by Birgit Dahlke, Martina Langermann, and Thomas Taterka, 1–32. Stuttgart: Metzler 2000.
Langhoff, Wolfgang. *Die Moorsoldaten.* 1935. Reprint, Berlin: Aufbau 1947.
Laqueur, Thomas. *Auf den Leib geschrieben: Die Inszenierung der Geschlechter von der Antike bis Freud.* Frankfurt am Main: Campus, 1992.
Lehmann, Joachim. "Die Schönheit unseres Lebens: Die Ankunftsliteratur im Spiegel der Literaturkritik." In *"Es genügt nicht die einfache Wahrheit": DDR-Literatur der sechziger Jahre in der Diskussion*, edited by Michael Hametner and Kerstin Schilling, 77–87. Leipzig: Friedrich-Ebert-Stifung, 1995.

Lenin, Vladimir Ilyitsch. "Party Organization and Party Literature" (1905). Marxists Internet Archive, 2001. http://www.marxists.org/archive/lenin/works/1905/nov/13.htm (accessed June 2, 2015).

Lewis, Alison. "'A Difficult Marriage': Marriage and Marital Breakdown in Post-Unification Literature." In *Ossi Wessi*, edited by Donald Backman and Aida Sakalauskaite, 1–23. Newcastle upon Tyne: Cambridge Scholars, 2008.

———. "Reading and Writing the Stasi File: On the Use and Abuses of the File as (Auto)Biography." *German Life and Letters* 56, no. 4 (2003): 377–97.

Lichtenberg, Bernd. "Screenplay *Good Bye Lenin!*" In *Good Bye Lenin! Ein Film von Wolfgang Becker*, edited by Michael Toteberg, 6–133. Berlin: Schwarzkopf & Schwarzkopf, 2003.

Löther, Rolf. "Ethische Aspekte der Beherrschung der Lebensprozesse." In *Ethik und Medizin im Sozialismus: Wissenschaftliches Kolloquium des Bereichs Medizin der Ernst-Moritz-Arndt-Universität am 2.10.1974 zu Ehren des 25. Jahrestages der DDR*, edited by Hansgeorg Hüller, 7–20. Greifswald: Ernst-Moritz-Arndt-Universität, 1976.

Ludwig, Janine, and Mirijam Meuser, eds. *Literatur ohne Land?: Schreibstrategien einer DDR-Literatur im vereinten Deutschland*. Freiburg: Fördergemeinschaft wissenschaftlicher Publikationen von Frauen, 2009.

Luther, Ernst. "Abriss zur Geschichte der medizinischen Ethik in der DDR." In *Medizinische Ethik in der DDR: Erfahrungswert oder Altlast?*, edited by Hartmut Bettin and Mariacarla Gadebusch Bondio, 20–39. Lengerich: Pabst Science, 2010.

Maaz, Hans-Joachim. *Der Gefühlsstau: Ein Psychogramm der DDR*. Berlin: C. H. Beck, 1990.

Magenau, Jörg. *Christa Wolf: Eine Biographie*. Berlin: Kindler, 2002.

Mählert, Ulrich. *Kleine Geschichte der DDR*. Munich: Beck, 2009.

Markgraf Eberhard, and Wieland Otto. "Unfallchirurgie an den Hochschuleinrichtungen der DDR." *Deutsche Gesellschaft für Unfallchirurgie e.V. Mitteilungen und Nachrichten*. Supplement: *Beiträge zur Geschichte der Unfallchirurgie in der DDR* 30 (September 2008): 15–23.

Maron, Monika. *Animal Tristesse*. Frankfurt am Main: Fischer, 1996.

———. *Flugasche*. Frankfurt am Main: Fischer, 1981. Translated by David Marinelli as *Flight of Ashes* (London: Readers International, 1986).

———. "Lebensentwürfe, Zeitenbrüche. Vom Nutzen und Nachteil dunkler Brillen: Wer es sich zu einfach macht beim Rückblick auf seine Geschichte, beraubt sich seiner Biografie." *Süddeutsche Zeitung*. September 13, 2002. Reprint, http://www.historikertag2002.uni-halle.de/artikel/p_47.shtml.

———. *Die Überläuferin*. Frankfurt am Main: Fischer, 1986. Translated by David Marinelli as *The Defector* (London: Readers International, 1988).

Martens, Lorna. *The Promised Land?: Feminist Writing in the German Democratic Republic*. Albany: State University of New York Press, 2001.

Martin, Brigitte. *Nach Freude anstehen*. Berlin, GDR: Der Morgen, 1981.

Martin, Elaine. "Victims or Perpetrators? Literary Responses to Women's Roles in National Socialism." In *Facing Fascism and Confronting the Past: German Women Writers from Weimar to the Present*, edited by Elke P. Frederiksen and Martha Kaarsberg Wallach, 61–82. Albany: State University of New York Press, 2000.

Marven, Lyn, and Stuart Taberner, eds. *Emerging German-Language Novelists of the Twenty-First Century*. Rochester, NY: Camden House, 2011.

Marx, Karl. *Ökonomisch-philosphische Manuskripte aus dem Jahre 1844*, edited by Barbara Zehnpfennig. Hamburg: Felix Meiner, 2005. Edited and translated by Martin Milligan as *Economic and Philosophic Manuscripts of 1844* (Mineola, NY: Dover, 2007).

Mayer, Tamar. "Gender Ironies of Nationalism: Setting the Stage." In *Gender Ironies of Nationalism: Sexing the Nation*, edited by Tamar Mayer, 1–22. London: Routledge, 2000.

———. *Gender Ironies of Nationalism: Sexing the Nation*. London: Routledge, 2000.

McKenzie, John R. P., and Derek Lewis. *The New Germany: Social, Political, and Cultural Challenges of Unification*. Exeter: University of Exeter Press, 1995.

McLaren, Margaret A. *Feminism, Foucault, and Embodied Subjectivity*. Albany: State University of New York Press, 2002.

Mecklinger, Ludwig. *Zur Umsetzung der Gesundheitspolitik im Gesundheits- und Sozialwesen der DDR*. Berlin: Trafo-Verlag Weist, 1998.

Mette, Alexander, Gerhard Misgeld, and Kurt Winter. *Der Arzt in der sozialistischen Gesellschaft*. Berlin, GDR: Akademie Verlag, 1958.

Meyen, Michael. *"Wir haben freier gelebt": Die DDR im kollektiven Gedächtnis der Deutschen*. Bielefeld: transcript, 2013.

Meyer-Gosau, Frauke. "Ritt über den Bodensee. Christa Wolf: *Nachdenken über Christa T.*" In *Verrat an der Kunst? Rückblicke auf die DDR-Literatur*, edited by Karl Deiritz and Hannes Kraus, 132–40. Berlin: Aufbau, 1993.

———. "Den Staat im Leibe. Erzählung: Christa Wolf versucht sich als Exorzistin der alten DDR." *Literaturen* (2002): 84–85.

Millington, Richard. *State, Society and Memories of the Uprising of 17 June 1953 in the GDR*. Basingstoke, UK: Palgrave McMillan, 2014.

Minden, Michael. "Social Hope and the Nightmare of History." *Publications of the English Goethe Society* 80, no. 2/3 (2011): 196–203.

Mittag, Jana, and Arn Sauer. "Geschlechtsidentität und Menschenrechte im internationalen Kontext." *Aus Politik und Zeitgeschichte* 20/21 (2012): 55–62.

Mohr, Reinhard. "Züchter des Übermenschen." *Der Spiegel*, September 6, 1999.

Morgner, Irmtraud. *Amanda: Ein Hexenroman*. Berlin, GDR: Aufbau, 1983.

———. *Leben und Abenteuer der Trobadora Beatriz erzählt von ihrer Spielfrau Laura*. Berlin, GDR: Aufbau 1974. Translated by Jeanette Clausen as *The Life and Adventures of Trobadora Beatrice as Chronicled by Her Minstrel Laura* (Lincoln: U of Nebraska P, 2000).

Morrison, Susan. "The Feminization of the German Democratic Republic in Political Cartoons." *Journal of Popular Culture* 25, no. 4 (1992): 35–51.
Müller, F. "Das Problem der Wahrhaftigkeit zwischen Arzt und Krankem bei unheilbaren Leiden." In *Ethik und Medizin im Sozialismus: Wissenschaftliches Kolloquium des Bereichs Medizin der Ernst-Moritz-Arndt-Universität am 2.10.1974 zu Ehren des 25. Jahrestages der DDR*, edited by Hansgeorg Hüller, 95–104. Greifswald: Ernst-Moritz-Arndt-Universität, 1976.
Müller, Thomas, and Jutta Kahle. "Organisation der Materialwirtschaft im Krankenhaus." In *Das Gesundheitswesen der DDR: Aufbruch oder Einbruch: Denkanstöße für eine Neuordnung des Gesundheitswesens in einem deutschen Staat*, edited by Wilhelm Thiele, 189–91. Sankt Augustin: Asgard-Verlag Hippe, 1990.
Müller-Engbergs, Helmut, ed. *Wer war wer in der DDR?* Berlin: Christoph Links, 2001.
Müntz, Klaus, and Ulrich Wobius. *Das Institut Gatersleben und seine Geschichte: Genetik und Kulturpflanzenforschung in drei politischen Systemen*. Berlin: Springer, 2013.
Muthesius, Sibylle. *Flucht in die Wolken*. Berlin, GDR: Buchverlag Der Morgen, 1981.
Nickel, Hildegard Maria. "Women in the German Democratic Republic and in the New Federal States: Looking Backwards and Forwards." *German Politics and Society* 24 (Winter 1991): 34–52.
Nieraad, Jürgen. "Pronominalstrukturen in realistischer Prosa: Beobachtungen zu Erzählebene und Figurenkonstellation bei Christa Wolf." *Poetica* 10 (1978): 485–506.
Niven, Bill. *Facing the Nazi Past: United Germany and the Legacy of the Third Reich*. London: Routledge, 2002.
Norman, Beret, and Katie Sutton. "'Memory is Always a Story': An Interview with Antje Rávic Strubel." *Women in German Yearbook* 28 (2012): 98–112.
Nusser, Tanja, and Elisabeth Strowick, eds. *Krankheit und Geschlecht: Diskursive Affären zwischen Literatur und Medizin*. Würzburg: Königshausen & Neumann, 2002.
Öhlschläger, Claudia. "*Gender*/Körper, Gedächtnis und Literatur." In *Gedächtniskonzepte der Literaturwissenschaft: Theoretische Grundlegung und Anwendungsperspektiven*, edited by Astrid Erll and Ansgar Nünning, 227–48. Berlin: Walter de Gruyter, 2005.
Öhlschläger, Claudia, and Birgit Wiens, eds. *Körper-Gedächtnis-Schrift: Der Körper als Medium kultureller Erinnerung*. Berlin: Erich Schmidt, 1997.
Opitz, Michael. "Verhängnisvolle Vergangenheit." Büchermarkt. Deutschlandfunk. January 23, 2012. http://www.deutschlandfunk.de/verhaengnisvolle-vergangenheit.700.de.html?dram:article_id=85387.
Orwell, George. *Animal Farm*. 1945. Reprint, New York: Harcourt, Brace and Company, 1946.

———. *Nineteen Eighty-Four*. 1949. Reprint, New York: Alfred A. Knopf, 1992.
Ostner, Ilona, and Eva Schumann. "Steuerung der Familie durch Recht?" Special issue, *Zeitschrift für Familienforschung—Journal of Family Research* (2011): 289–315.
"Patienten für die Industrie." *Der Spiegel*, January 20, 1997.
Paul, Georgina. "'Aber erzählen läßt sich nichts ohne Zeit': Time and Atemporality in Christa Wolf's Subjectively Authentic Narratives." In *The Self in Transition: East German Autobiographical Writing Before and After Unification*, edited by David Clarke and Axel Goodbody, 109–21. Amsterdam: Rodopi, 2012.
Paver, Chloe E. M. "'What we must invent for the sake of the truth': Expiating the Past Through Narrative Invention in Christa Wolf's *Nachdenken über Christa T.*" In *The Short Story: Structure and Element*, edited by William J. Hunter, 103–29. Exeter: Elm Bank, 1996.
Pearce, Caroline. "An Unequal Balance? Memorializing Germany's 'Double Past' since 1990." In *The GDR Remembered: Representations of the East German State since 1989*, edited by Nick Hodgin and Caroline Pearce, 172–98. Rochester, NY: Camden House, 2011.
Peitsch, Helmut. *Nachkriegsliteratur 1945–1989*. Göttingen: V& R unipress, 2009.
Pinfold, Debbie. "'Das Mündel will Vormund sein': The GDR State as Child." *German Life and Letters* 64, no. 2 (2011): 283–304.
Pinkert, Anke. "Pleasures of Fear: Antifascist Myth, Holocaust, and Soft Dissidence in Christa Wolf's *Kindheitsmuster*." *The German Quarterly* 76, no. 1 (2003): 25–37.
———. "Toward a Critical Reparative Practice in Post-1989 German Literature: Christa Wolf's *City of Angels or The Overcoat of Dr. Freud*." In *Memory and Postwar Memorials: Confronting the Violence of the Past*, edited by Marc Silberman and Florence Vatan, 177–96. New York: Palgrave McMillan, 2013.
Pockrandt, Heinz, and Heinz Brunkow. "Zwitter und Scheinzwittertum beim Menschen." *Zentralblatt für Gynäkologie* 78, no. 7 (1956): 927–42.
Poore, Carol. "Illness and the Socialist Personality: Philosophical Debates and Literary Images in the GDR." *Studies in GDR Culture and Society* 6 (1986): 123–35.
Pracht, Erwin. *Einführung in den sozialistischen Realismus*. Berlin, GDR: Dietz, 1975.
Prager, Brad. "The Erection of the Berlin Wall: Thomas Brussig's *Helden wie wir* and the End of East Germany." *The Modern Language Review* 99, no. 4 (2004): 983–98.
Prokop, Otto. "Das zweifelhafte Geschlecht." In *Forensische Medizin*, edited by Otto Prokop and Werner Göhler, 501–3. Berlin, GDR: Verlag Volk und Gesundheit, 1975.
Rabinow, Paul, and Nikolas Rose, eds. *The Essential Foucault: Selections from Essential Works of Foucault, 1954–1984*. New York: The New Press, 1994.

Radbruch, Gustav. "Gesetzliches Unrecht und übergesetzliches Recht." *Süddeutsche Juristenzeitung* (1946): 105–8.
Raddatz, Fritz J. *Traditionen und Tendenzen: Materialien zur Literatur der DDR*. Frankfurt am Main: Suhrkamp, 1972.
Radisch, Iris. "Es gibt zwei deutsche Gegenwartsliteraturen in Ost und West!" In *Schreiben nach der Wende: Ein Jahrzehnt deutscher Literatur 1989–1999*, edited by Gerhard Fischer and David Roberts, 1–14. Tübingen: Stauffenburg, 2007.
Rechtien, Renate. "From *Vergangenheitsbewältigung* to Living with Ghosts: Christa Wolf's *Kindheitsmuster* and *Leibhaftig*." In *The Self in Transition: East German Autobiographical Writing Before and After Unification*, edited by David Clarke and Axel Goodbody, 123–43. Amsterdam: Rodopi, 2012.
———. "The Topography of the Self in Christa Wolf's *Der geteilte Himmel*." *German Life and Letters* 63, no. 4 (2010): 475–89.
Rechtien, Renate, and Dennis Tate, eds. *Competing Memories of the GDR in Postunification German Culture*. Rochester, NY: Camden House, 2011.
Reding, R. "Ärztliche und ethische Probleme bei 'unheilbaren' Erkrankungen." In *Ethik und Medizin im Sozialismus: Wissenschaftliches Kolloquium des Bereichs Medizin der Ernst-Moritz-Arndt-Universität am 2.10.1974 zu Ehren des 25. Jahrestages der DDR*, edited by Hansgeorg Hüller, 89–94. Greifswald: Ernst-Moritz-Arndt-Universität, 1976.
Reich-Ranicki, Marcel. "Christa Wolf's unruhige Elegie." In *Wirkungsgeschichte von Christa Wolfs "Nachdenken über Christa T.,"* edited by Manfred Behn, 59–64. Königstein: Athenäum, 1978.
Reifner, Udo, ed. *Das Recht des Unrechtsstaates: Arbeitsrecht und Staatswissenschaften im Faschismus*. Frankfurt am Main: Campus, 1981.
Reimann, Brigitte. *Ankunft im Alltag*. Berlin, GDR: Verlag Neues Leben, 1961.
———. *Franziska Linkerhand*. Berlin, GDR: Verlag Neues Leben, 1974.
Reimann, Brigitte, and Christa Wolf. *Sei gegrüßt und lebe: Eine Freundschaft in Briefen, 1964–1973*. Berlin: Aufbau, 1993.
Remarque, Erich Maria. *Im Westen nichts Neues*. Berlin: Propylän, 1929. Translated by Arthur Wesley Wheens as *All Quiet on the Western Front* (Boston: Little, Brown and Co., 1929).
Richter-Kuhlmann, Eva A. "Ärzte als inoffizielle Mitarbeiter: Die meisten IM-Ärzte bespitzelten Kollegen." *Deutsches Ärzteblatt* 104, no. 48 (2007): 22.
Ringel, Martina, and Klaus Schneider. "Öffentliches Gesundheits- und Sozialwesen der DDR am Beispiel der Staat Dresden." In *Das Gesundheitswesen der DDR: Aufbruch oder Einbruch: Denkanstöße für eine Neuordnung des Gesundheitswesens in einem deutschen Staat*, edited by Wilhelm Thiele, 69–75. Sankt Augustin: Asgard-Verlag Hippe, 1990.
Rosch, Eleanor. "Cognitive Representation of Semantic Categories." *Journal of Experimental Psychology: General* 104, no. 3 (1975): 192–233.

Rosenberg, Rainer. "Was war DDR-Literatur? Die Diskussion um den Gegenstand in der Literaturwissenschaft der Bundesrepublik Deutschland." *Zeitschrift für Germanistik: Neue Folge* 5, no. 1 (1995): 9–21.
Rosenlöcher, Thomas. *Ostgezeter: Beiträge zur Schimpfkultur*. Frankfurt am Main: Suhrkamp, 1997.
———. *Die Wiederentdeckung des Gehens beim Wandern: Harzreise*. Frankfurt am Main: Suhrkamp, 1991.
Roth, Kersten Sven. "Der Westen als 'Normal Null': Zur Diskurssemantik von 'ostdeutsch' und 'westdeutsch'." In *Diskursmauern: Aktuelle Aspekte der sprachlichen Verhältnisse in Ost und West*, edited by Kersten Sven Roth and Markus Wienen, 69–89. Bremen: Hempen, 2008.
Roth, Kersten Sven, and Markus Wienen, eds. *Diskursmauern: Aktuelle Aspekte der sprachlichen Verhältnisse in Ost und West*. Bremen: Hempen, 2008.
Rücker, Kerstin. "Soziale Netze für Mutter und Kind." In *Das Gesundheitswesen der DDR: Aufbruch oder Einbruch: Denkanstöße für eine Neuordnung des Gesundheitswesens in einem deutschen Staat*, edited by Wilhelm Thiele, 61–68. Sankt Augustin: Asgard-Verlag Hippe, 1990.
"Rückspiegel. Der Spiegel berichtete." *Der Spiegel*, March 17, 1997.
Ruge, Eugen. *In Zeiten des abnehmenden Lichts*. Reinbek bei Hamburg: Rowohlt, 2011. Translated by Anthea Bell as *In Times of Fading Light* (New York: Macmillan, 2013).
Rüther, Günther, ed. *Literatur in der Diktatur: Schreiben im Nationalsozialismus und DDR-Sozialismus*. Paderborn: Schöningh, 1997.
Sabrow, Martin, ed. "Die DDR erinnern." In *Erinnerungsorte der DDR*, edited by Martin Sabrow, 11–27. Munich: C. H. Beck, 2009.
———. *Erinnerungsorte der DDR*. Munich: C. H. Beck, 2009.
Sachs, Nelly. *In den Wohnungen des Todes*. Berlin: Aufbau, 1947.
Sachse, Carola. *Der Hausarbeitstag: Gerechtigkeit und Gleichberechtigung in Ost und West 1939–1994*. Göttingen: Wallstein, 2002.
Sander, Hans-Dietrich. *Geschichte der schönen Literatur in der DDR: Ein Grundriss*. Freiburg: Rombach, 1972.
Satjukow, Silke, and Rainer Gries, eds. *Unsere Feinde: Konstruktion des Anderen im Sozialismus*. Leipzig: Leipziger Universitätsverlag, 2005.
Scarry, Elaine. *The Body in Pain: The Making and Unmaking of the World*. New York: Oxford University Press, 1985.
Schalansky, Judith. *Der Hals der Giraffe*. Berlin: Suhrkamp, 2011. Translated by Shaun Whiteside as *The Giraffe's Neck* (New York: Bloomsbury, 2014).
Scharpe, Ingrid. "Male Privilege and Female Virtue: Gendered Representations of the Two Germanies." *New German Studies* 18, no. 1/2 (1994): 87–106.
Schaumann, Caroline. *Memory Matters: Generational Responses to Germany's Nazi Past in Recent Women's Literature*. Berlin: de Gruyter, 2008.
Schischkin, Alexander Fjodorowitsch. *Grundlagen der marxistischen Ethik*, edited by Reinhold Miller. Berlin, GDR: Dietz, 1965.

Schlaffer, Heinz. *Die kurze Geschichte der deutschen Literatur*. Munich: dtv, 2003.
Schleiermacher, Sabine, and Udo Schagen. "Rekonstruktion und Innovation (1949–1961)." In: *Die Charité: Geschichte(n) eines Krankenhauses*, edited by Johanna Bleker and Volker Hess, 204–42. Berlin: Akademie Verlag, 2010.
Schmidt, Kathrin. *Du stirbst nicht*. Cologne: Kiepenheuer & Witsch, 2009.
———. *Die Gunnar-Lennefsen-Expedition*. 1998. Reprint, Munich: Droemer, 2000.
Schmidt, Thomas. "Über Redeweisen der Literaturwissenschaft, die Zäsur von 1848 und das (un)literarische Engagement der DDR-Literatur." In *Engagierte Literatur in Wendezeiten*, edited by Willi Huntemann, Malgorzata Klentak-Zablocka, Fabian Lampert, and Thomas Schmidt, 49–73. Würzburg: Königshausen & Neumann, 2003.
Schmitt, Hans-Jürgen, ed. *Einführung in Theorie, Geschichte und Funktion der DDR-Literatur*. Stuttgart: Metzler, 1975.
Schmitz, Helmut. "The Return of the Past: Post-Unification Representations of National Socialism: Bernhard Schlink's *Der Vorleser* and Ulla Berkéwics's *Engel sind schwarz und weiß*." In *1949/1989—Cultural Perspectives on Division and Unity in East and West*, edited by Clare Flanagan and Stuart Taberner, 259–76. Amsterdam: Rodopi, 2000.
Schoch, Julia. *Mit der Geschwindigkeit des Sommers*. Munich: Piper, 2009.
Schönborn, Sibylle. "Epochenschwelle 1989—Von der Nachkriegsliteratur zur literarischen Postmoderne: Christa Wolf und Thomas Brussig." In *Sprache und Literatur im Spannungsfeld von Politik und Ästhetik: Christa Wolf zum 80. Geburtstag*, edited by Sabine Fischer-Kania and Daniel Schäf, 11–19. Munich: Iudicium, 2011.
Schönert, Jörg. "Literaturgeschichtsschreibung der DDR und BRD im Vergleich: Am Beispiel von 'Geschichte der Literatur der Deutschen Demokratischen Republik' (Berlin/Ost 1976) und 'Die Literatur der DDR' (München 1983)." In *Positionen der Germanistik in der DDR: Personen—Forschungsfelder—Organisationsformen*, edited by Jan Cölln and Franz-Josef Holznagel, 248–68. Berlin: Walter de Gruyter, 2012.
Schüle Annegret, Thomas Ahbe, and Rainer Gries, eds. *Die DDR aus generationengeschichtlicher Perspektive: Eine Inventur*. Leipzig: Leipziger Universitätsverlag, 2006.
Schulz, Torsten. *Nilowsky*. Stuttgart: Klett-Cotta, 2013.
Schulz, Werner. *Die Untersuchung unnatürlicher Todesfälle*. Berlin, GDR: Ministerium des Innern, 1965.
Schwarz, Peter Paul, and Sebastian Wilde. "'Und doch, und doch . . .'—Transformationen des Utopischen in Christa Wolfs 'Stadt der Engel oder The Overcoat of Dr. Freud.'" In *Christa Wolf im Strom der Erinnerung*, edited by Carsten Gansel, 231–44. Göttingen: V&R unipress, 2014.
Scribner, Charity. "Von 'Leibhaftig' aus zurückblicken: Verleugnung als Trope in Christa Wolfs Schreiben." *Weimarer Beiträge* 50, no. 2 (2004): 212–26.

Sedgwick, Eve. *The Epistomology of the Closet*. Berkeley: University of California Press, 1990.
Seidel, Karl. "Der Suicid im höheren Lebensalter unter sozialpsychatrischem Aspekt." Habilitation, Dresden University, 1967.
Seifert, Ulrike. *Gesundheit staatlich verordnet: Das Arzt-Patienten-Verhältnis im Spiegel sozialistischen Zivilrechtsdenkens in der DDR*. Berlin: Berliner Wissenschafts-Verlag, 2009.
Seiler, Lutz. *Kruso*. Berlin: Suhrkamp, 2014.
Sevin, Dieter. "The Plea for Artistic Freedom in Christa Wolf's "Lesen und Schreiben" and *Nachdenken über Christa T.*: Essay and Fiction as Mutually Supportive Genre Forms." In *Proceedings of the International Symposium on the German Democratic Republic*, edited by Margy Gerber, 45–58. Washington, DC: University Press of America, 1981.
Sharp, Ingrid, and Dagmar Flinspach. "Women in Germany from Division to Unification." In *The New Germany: Social, Political, and Cultural Challenges of Unification*, edited by John R. P. McKenzie and Derek Lewis, 173–95. Exeter: University of Exeter Press, 1995.
Silberman, Marc. "Whose Story Is This? Rewriting the Literary History of the GDR." In *Contentious Memories: Looking Back at the GDR*, edited by Jost Hermand and Marc Silberman, 25–57. New York: Peter Lang, 1998.
Silberman, Marc, and Florence Vatan, eds. *Memory and Postwar Memorials: Confronting the Violence of the Past*. New York: Palgrave McMillan, 2013.
Sillge, Ursula. *Un-Sichtbare Frauen: Lesben und ihre Emanzipation in der DDR*. Berlin: Christoph Links, 1991.
Simonow, Konstantin. *Ich sah das Vernichtungslager*. Berlin: Verlag der Sowjetischen Militärverwaltung in Deutschland, 1946.
Skare, Roswitha. "1989/90: Eine Wende in der deutschen Literaturgeschichte? Tendenzen der neueren Literaturgeschichtsschreibung." In *Wendezeichen? Neue Sichtweisen auf die Literatur der DDR*, edited by Roswitha Skare and Rainer B. Hoppe, 15–43. Amsterdam: Rodopi, 1999.
Skare, Roswitha, and Rainer B. Hoppe, eds. *Wendezeichen? Neue Sichtweisen auf die Literatur der DDR*. Amsterdam: Rodopi, 1999.
Sloterdijk, Peter. "Die Kritische Theorie ist tot: Peter Sloterdijk schreibt an Assheuer und Habermas." *Die Zeit*, September 9, 1999.
———. *Regeln für den Menschenpark*: Ein Antwortschreiben zu Heideggers *Brief über den Humanismus*. Frankfurt am Main: Suhrkamp, 1999. Translated by Mary Varney Rorty as "*Rules for the Human Zoo*: A Response to the *Letter on Humanism*." In special issue "The Worlds of Peter Sloterdijk." *Environment and Planning D: Society and Space* 27 (2009): 12–28.
Soldovieri, Stefan. "Censorship and the Law: The Case of *Das Kaninchen bin ich* (*I am the Rabbit*). In *DEFA: East German Cinema, 1946–1992*, edited by Sean Allan and John Sandfort, 146–63. New York: Berghahn, 1999.

Sontag, Susan. *Illness as Metaphor*. New York: Farrar, Straus and Giroux, 1977.
Spackman, Barbara. *Decadent Genealogies: The Rhetoric of Sickness from Baudelaire to D'Annunzio*. Ithaca, NY: Cornell University Press, 1989.
Stein, Hans. "Gemeinsame Ansätze in Prävention und Gesundheitsförderung müssen weiterentwickelt werden—Einleitung." In *Das Gesundheitswesen der DDR: Aufbruch oder Einbruch: Denkanstöße für eine Neuordnung des Gesundheitswesens in einem deutschen Staat*, edited by Wilhelm Thiele, 243–45. Sankt Augustin: Asgard-Verlag Hippe, 1990.
Stein, Rosemarie. *Die Charité 1945–1992: Ein Mythos von innen*. Berlin: Argon Verlag, 1992.
———. "West-Medikamente in Ost-Berlin korrekt geprüft: Untersuchungsbericht von 1991 erneut aktuell." *Berliner Ärzte: Die offizielle Zeitschrift der Ärztekammer Berlin* 7 (2013): 27–29.
Stephan, Inge. "Medea, meine Schwester? Medea-Texte von Autorinnen im 20. Jahrhundert." In *Frauen: Mitsprechen, Mitschreiben*, edited by Marianne Henn and Britta Hufeisen, 1–23. Stuttgart: Heinz, 1997.
Stephan, Inge, and Alexandra Tacke, eds. *NachBilder der Wende*. Cologne: Böhlau, 2008.
Stewart, Faye. "Queer Elements: The Poetics and Politics of Antje Rávic Strubel's Literary Style." *Women in German Yearbook* 34 (2014): 44–73.
Strubel, Antje Rávic. *Fremd gehen: Ein Nachtstück*. Munich: dtv, 2002.
———. *Sturz der Tage in die Nacht*. Frankfurt am Main: Fischer, 2011.
———. *Tupolew 134*. Munich: C. H. Beck, 2004.
Suckut, Siegfried, ed. *Das Wörterbuch der Staatssicherheit: Definitionen zur politisch-operativen Arbeit*. Berlin: Christoph Links, 2001.
Süß, Sonja. *Politisch mißbraucht? Psychiatrie und Staatssicherheit in der DDR*. Berlin: Christoph Links, 1998.
Sweet, Denis M. "Bodies for Germany, Bodies for Socialism: The German Democratic Republic Devises a Gay (Male) Body." In *Gender and Germanness: Cultural Productions of Nation*, edited by Patricia Hermingshouse and Magda Mueller, 248–62. Providence, RI: Berghahn, 1997.
Taberner, Stuart. *Contemporary German Fiction: Writing the Berlin Republic*. Cambridge: Cambridge University Press, 2007.
———. *German Literature of the 1990s and Beyond: Normalization and the Berlin Republic*. Rochester, NY: Camden House, 2005.
Tanneberger, Stephan. "Ethik in der medizinischen Forschung der DDR." In *Medizinische Ethik in der DDR: Erfahrungswert oder Altlast?*, edited by Hartmut Bettin and Mariacarla Gadebusch Bondio, 40–62. Lengerich: Pabst Science, 2010.
Tanneberger, Stephan, and Hartmut Bettin. "Wortmeldung zum Thema: Arzneimittelprüfung in der DDR." Webpage. Leibniz-Sozietät der Wissenschaften zu Berlin e.V. June 13, 2013. http://leibnizsozietaet.de/meinungsauserung-zum-thema-arzneimittelprufung-in-der-ddr/.
Tate, Dennis. *Shifting Perspectives: East German Autobiographical Narratives Before and After the End of the GDR*. Rochester, NY: Camden House, 2007.

Tellkamp, Uwe. *Der Turm*. Frankfurt am Main: Suhrkamp, 2008. Translated by Mike Mitchell as *The Tower* (London: Allen Lane, 2014).
Thiele, Wilhelm, ed. *Das Gesundheitswesen der DDR: Aufbruch oder Einbruch: Denkanstöße für eine Neuordnung des Gesundheitswesens in einem deutschen Staat*. Sankt Augustin: Asgard-Verlag Hippe, 1990.
———. "Das Gesundheitswesen in einem deutschen Staat—Einigung oder Vereinnahmung?" In *Das Gesundheitswesen der DDR: Aufbruch oder Einbruch: Denkanstöße für eine Neuordnung des Gesundheitswesens in einem deutschen Staat*, edited by Wilhelm Thiele, 11–16. Sankt Augustin: Asgard-Verlag Hippe, 1990.
Thießen, Malte. "Vorsorge als Ordnung des Sozialen: Impfen in der Bundesrepublik und der DDR." *Zeithistorische Forschungen/Studies in Contemporary History* 10, no. 3 (2013): 409–32.
Thietz, Kirsten, ed. *Ende der Selbstverständlichkeit? Die Abschaffung des §218 in der DDR*. Berlin: Basis Druck, 1992.
Thom, Achim, and Genadij Ivanovic Caregorodcev, eds. *Medizin unterm Hakenkreuz*. Berlin, GDR: VEB Verlag Volk und Gesundheit, 1989.
Thom, Wilhelm, and Elfriede Thom. *Rückkehr ins Leben*. 1979. Reprint, Berlin: Verlag Neues Leben, 1991.
Thomas, Merrilyn. "'Aggression in Felt Slippers': Normalisation and the Ideological Struggle in the Context of Détente and *Ostpolitik*." In *Power and Society in the GDR 1961–1979: The "Normalisation of Rule"?*, edited by Mary Fulbrook, 33–51. New York: Berghahn, 2009.
Thompson, Edward Palmer. "History from Below." *Times Literary Supplement*, April 7, 1966: 279–80.
Toellner, Richard. "Medizinische Ethik im Alltag der Hochschule: Erfahrungen aus der Praxis der ärztlichen Ausbildung." In *Ethik in der Medizin: Tagung der Evangelischen Akademie Loccum vom 13. bis 15. Dezember 1985*, edited by Udo Schlaudraff, 17–26. Berlin: Springer, 1987.
———. "Medizinische Ethik in der DDR aus der Sicht des Arbeitskreises Medizinische Ethik-Kommissionen in der BRD." In *Medizinische Ethik in der DDR: Erfahrungswert oder Altlast?*, edited by Hartmut Bettin and Mariacarla Gadebusch Bondio, 63–72. Lengerich: Pabst Science, 2010.
Toteberg, Michael, ed. *Good Bye, Lenin! Ein Film von Wolfgang Becker*. Berlin: Schwarzkopf & Schwarzkopf, 2003.
Twark, Jill. *Humor, Satire, and Identity: Eastern German Literature in the 1990s*. Berlin: de Gruyter. 2007.
———, ed. *Strategies of Humor in Post-Unification German Literature, Film, and other Media*. Newcastle upon Tyne: Cambridge Scholars, 2011.
Verwijs, Rebecca, and Daniel Schäfer. "Der kranke Leib: Seelisch-körperliche Einheit und Medizinkritik in Christa Wolfs Erzählung 'Leibhaftig.'" In *Jahrbuch Literatur und Medizin*. Band V, edited by Bettina von Jagow and Florian Steger, 29–46. Heidelberg: Universitätsverlag Winter, 2012.
Vinke, Hermann, ed. *Akteneinsicht Christa Wolf: Zerrspiegel und Dialog*. Hamburg: Luchterhand, 1993.

Vogt, Jochen. "Langer Abschied von der Nachkriegsliteratur? Ein Kommentar zur letzten westdeutschen Literaturdebatte." In *Der deutsch-deutsche Literaturstreit oder "Freunde, es spricht sich schlecht mit gebundener Zunge,"* edited by Karl Deiritz and Hannes Krauss, 53–68. Hamburg: Luchterhand, 1993.

Völlger, Winfried. *Das Windhahnsyndrom*. Rostock: Hinstorff, 1983.

Vollnhals, Clemens, and Jürgen Weber, eds. *Der Schein der Normalität: Alltag und Herrschaft in der SED-Diktatur*. Munich: Olzog, 2002.

Wagner, Linde. "Polikliniken—ein gesundheitspolitisches Modell." In *Die DDR war anders: Eine kritische Würdigung ihrer sozialkulturellen Einrichtungen*, edited by Stefan Bollinger and Fritz Vilmar, 226–45. Berlin: edition ost im Verlag Das Neue Berlin, 2002.

Walther, Peter. "Einleitung." In *Die dritte Front: Literatur in Brandenburg 1930–1950*, edited by Peter Walther, 7–16. Berlin: Lukas, 2004.

Wander, Maxie, ed. *Guten Morgen, du Schöne*. Darmstadt: Luchterhand, 1978.

———. *Leben wär' eine prima Alternative: Tagebücher und Briefe*, edited by Fred Wander. 1979. Reprint, Munich: dtv, 1994.

———. *Tagebücher und Briefe*. Berlin: Aufbau, 1990.

Warner, Michael. *Fear of a Queer Planet: Queer Politics and Social Theory*. Minneapolis: University of Minnesota Press, 1993.

———. *The Trouble with Normal: Sex, Politics, and the Ethics of Queer Life*. Cambridge, MA: Harvard University Press, 2000.

Webber, Andrew. *Berlin in the Twentieth Century: A Cultural Topography*. Cambridge: Cambridge University Press, 2008.

Weber, Herrmann. *Die DDR 1945–1990*. Munich: Oldenbourg, 2000.

Wedl, Juliette. "Ein Ossi ist ein Ossi ist ein Ossi . . . Regeln der medialen Berichterstattung über 'Ossis' und 'Wessis' in der Wochenzeitung *Die Zeit* seit Mitte der 1990er Jahre." In *Die Ostdeutschen in den Medien: Das Bild von den Anderen nach 1990*, edited by Thomas Ahbe, Rainer Gries, and Wolfgang Schmale, 113–33. 2009. Reprint, Bonn: Bundeszentrale für politische Bildung, 2010.

Wehdeking, Volker. *Generationenwechsel: Intermedialität in der deutschen Gegenwartsliteratur*. Berlin: Erich Schmidt, 2007.

Weigel, Sigrid. *Bilder des kulturellen Gedächtnisses: Beiträge zur Gegenwartsliteratur*. Dülmen-Hiddingsel: tende, 1994.

Weil, Francesca. "Ärzte als inoffizielle Mitarbeiter der Staatssicherheit." *Deutsches Ärzteblatt* 103, no. 23 (2006): A1594–99.

———. "Im Dienste der DDR-Staatssicherheit: Ärzte als inoffizielle Mitarbeiter." *Deutsches Ärzteblatt* 101, no. 48 (2004): A3245–52.

———. *Zielgruppe Ärzteschaft: Ärzte als inoffizielle Mitarbeiter des Ministeriums für Staatssicherheit*. Göttingen: V&R unipress, 2007.

Weisenborn, Günther. *Memorial*. Berlin: Aufbau 1947.

Wenk, Silke. *Versteinerte Weiblichkeit*. Cologne: Böhlau, 1996.

Wiechert, Ernst. *Der Totenwald: Ein Bericht*. 1946. Reprint, Berlin: Union, 1977.

Wierling, Dorothee. "How Do the 1929ers and the 1949ers Differ?" In *Power and Society in the GDR, 1961–1979: The 'Normalisation of Rule'?*, edited by Mary Fulbrook, 204–19. New York: Berghahn, 2009.
Wiesner, Gerd E. "Zur Gesundheitslage der beiden Bevölkerungsteile DDR und BRD—ein Ausdruck sozialer Ungleichheit?" In *Das Gesundheitswesen der DDR: Aufbruch oder Einbruch: Denkanstöße für eine Neuordnung des Gesundheitswesens in einem deutschen Staat*, edited by Wilhelm Thiele, 21–28. Sankt Augustin: Asgard-Verlag Hippe, 1990.
Wilke, Sabine. *Ausgraben und Erinnern: Zur Funktion von Geschichte, Subjekt und geschlechtlicher Identität in den Texten Christa Wolfs*. Würzburg: Königshausen & Neumann, 1993.
Wippermann, Wolfgang. *Dämonisierung durch Vergleich*. Berlin: Rotbuch, 2009.
Wolf, Christa. "Abschied von Phantomen: Zur Sache: Deutschland." (1994) In *Auf dem Weg nach Tabou*, 313–39. Translated by Jan van Heurck as "Parting from Phantoms: On Germany." In *Parting from Phantoms*, 281–303.
———. *Auf dem Weg nach Tabou: Texte 1990–1994*. 1994. Reprint, Munich: dtv, 1996. Translated by Jan van Heurck as *Parting from Phantoms: Selected Writings, 1990–1994* (Chicago: University of Chicago Press, 1997).
———. "Berührung." In *Guten Morgen, du Schöne*, edited by Maxie Wander, 9–20. Darmstadt: Luchterhand, 1978.
———. *Die Dimension des Autors: Essays und Aufsätze: Reden und Gespräche 1959–1985*. Darmstadt: Luchterhand, 1987. Excerpts translated by Jan Van Heurck in *The Author's Dimension: Selected Essays*, edited by Alexander Stephan (New York: Farrar, Strauss and Giroux, 1993); excerpts translated by Hilary Pilkington in *The Fourth Dimension: Interviews with Christa Wolf* (London: Verso, 1988).
———. *Ein Tag im Jahr: 1960–2000*. Munich: Luchterhand 2003. Translated by Lowell A. Bangerter as *One Day a Year: 1960–2000* (New York: Europa Editions, 2007).
———. *Ein Tag im Jahr im neuen Jahrhundert: 2001–2011*, edited by Gerhard Wolf. Berlin: Suhrkamp, 2013.
———. "Forgesetzter Versuch." (1974) In *Die Dimension des Autors*, 339–45.
———. *Der geteilte Himmel*. 1963. Reprint, Munich: dtv, 1973. Translated by Joan Becker as *The Divided Heaven* (Berlin, GDR: Seven Seas Publishers, 1965).
———. "Glauben an Irdisches." (1968) In *Die Dimension des Autors*, 293–322.
———. "Ich bin schon für eine gewisse Maßlosigkeit: Gespräch mit Wilfried F. Schoeller." (1979) In *Die Dimension des Autors*, 865–77. Translated as "I admire a certain lack of restraint: A Conversation with Wilfried F. Schoeller." In *The Fourth Dimension*, 80–89.
———. *Im Dialog*. Hamburg: Luchterhand, 1993.

―――. *Kassandra*. 1983. Reprint, Darmstadt and Neuwied: Luchterhand, 1986. Translated by Jan Van Heurck as *Cassandra: A Novel and Four Essays* (New York: Farrar, Strauss and Giroux, 1984).

―――. *Kein Ort. Nirgends*. Berlin, GDR: Aufbau, 1979. Translated by Jan Van Heurck as *No Place On Earth* (New York: Farrar, Strauss and Giroux, 1982).

―――. *Kindheitsmuster*. 1976. Reprint, Leipzig: Reclam, 1989. Translated by Ursula Molinaro and Hedwig Rappolt as *Patterns of Childhood* (New York: Farrar, Strauss and Giroux, 1980).

―――. "Krankheit und Liebesentzug: Fragen an die psychosomatische Medizin." (1984) In *Die Dimension des Autors*, 727–48. Translated as "Illness and Love Deprivation: Questions for Psychosomatic Medicine." In *The Author's Dimension. Selected Essays*, 69–84.

―――. "Krebs und Gesellschaft." (1991) In *Auf dem Weg nach Tabou*, 115–39. Translated as "Cancer and Society." In *Parting from Phantoms*, 89–108.

―――. *Leibhaftig*. Munich: Luchterhand, 2002. Translated by John S. Barrett as *In the Flesh* (Boston: Verba Mundi/David R. Godine, 2005).

―――. *Lesen und Schreiben: Neue Sammlung*. Darmstadt: Luchterhand, 1980. Portions translated by Joan Becker as *The Reader and The Writer: Essays Sketches Memories* (New York: International Publishers, 1977).

―――. "Lesen und Schreiben." (1968) In *Lesen und Schreiben*, 9–48. Translated as "The Reader and the Writer." In *The Reader and The Writer*, 177–212.

―――. "Literatur als eine Art Flaschenpost." Interview with Christa Wolf. *Börsenblatt für den deutschen Buchhandel* 16 (2002): 7–11.

―――. *Medea: Stimmen*. 1996. Reprint, Munich: dtv, 1998. Translated by John Cullen as *Medea: A Modern Retelling* (New York: Nan A. Talese/Doubleday, 1998).

―――. *Mit anderem Blick*. Frankfurt am Main: Suhrkamp, 2005.

―――. *Moskauer Tagebücher: Wer wir sind und wer wir waren: Reisetagebücher, Texte, Briefe, Dokumente 1957–1989*, edited by Gerhard Wolf. Berlin: Suhrkamp, 2014.

―――. *Nachdenken über Christa T.* 1968. Reprint, Munich: dtv, 1993. Translated by Christopher Middleton as *The Quest for Christa T.* (New York: Delta, 1970).

―――. "Nagelprobe." (1991) In *Auf dem Weg nach Tabou*, 156–69. Translated as "Trial by Nail." In *Parting from Phantoms*, 124–35.

―――. "Projektionsraum Romantik: Gespräch mit Frauke Meyer-Gosau." (1982) In *Die Dimension des Autors*, 878–95. Translated as "Romanticism in Perspective: A Conversation with Frauke Meyer-Gosau." In *The Fourth Dimension*, 90–102.

―――. *Rede, daß ich dich sehe: Essays, Reden, Gespräche*. Berlin: Suhrkamp, 2012.

―――. *Reden im Herbst*. Berlin: Aufbau, 1990.

―――. "Rummelplatz 11. Plenum 1965—Erinnerungsbericht." (1991) In *Auf dem Weg nach Tabou*, 58–70. Translated as "Rummelplatz, the Eleventh Plenum of the Central Committee of the Socialist Unity Party, 1965. A Report from Memory." In *Parting from Phantoms*, 42–53.

———. "Santa Monica, Sonntag, den 27. September 1992." (1992) In *Auf dem Weg nach Tabou*, 232–47. Translated as "Santa Monica, Sunday, September 27, 1992." In *Parting from Phantoms*, 186–98.

———. "Selbstinterview." (1968) In *Lesen und Schreiben*, 51–55. Translated as "Interview with Myself." In *The Reader and The Writer*, 76–80.

———. "Selbstversuch: Traktat zu einem Protokoll." In *Geschlechtertausch: Drei Geschichten über die Umwandlung der Verhältnisse* by Sarah Kirsch, Irmtraud Morgner, and Christa Wolf. Darmstadt: Luchterhand, 1980. 65–100. Translated by Heike Schwarzbauer and Rick Takvorian as "Self-Experiment." In *What Remains & Other Stories*, 197–228 (Chicago: University of Chicago Press, 1993).

———. *Sommerstück*. Frankfurt am Main: Luchterhand, 1989.

———. "Sprache der Wende—Rede auf dem Alexanderplatz." (1989) In *Auf dem Weg nach Tabou*, 11–13. Translated as "The Language of the Turning Point." In *Parting from Phantoms*, 3–5.

———. *Stadt der Engel oder The Overcoat of Dr. Freud*. Berlin: Suhrkamp, 2010. Translated by Damion Searls as *City of Angels Or, The Overcoat Of Dr. Freud* (New York: Farrar, Strauss and Giroux, 2013).

———. *Störfall: Nachrichten eines Tages*. Frankfurt am Main: Luchterhand, 1987. Translated by Heike Schwarzbauer and Rick Takvorian as *Accident: A Day's News* (Chicago: University of Chicago Press, 2001).

———. "Subjektive Authentizität: Gespräch mit Hans Kaufmann." (1973) In *Die Dimension des Autors*, 773–805. Translated as "Subjective Authenticity: A Conversation with Hans Kaufmann." In *The Fourth Dimension*, 17–38.

———. "Unerledigte Widersprüche. Gespräch mit Therese Hörnigk." (1987/1988) In *Reden im Herbst*. Berlin: Aufbau, 1990, 24–68.

———. "Warum schreiben Sie?" (1985) In *Die Dimension des Autors*, 75–76.

———. *Was bleibt*. 1990. Reprint, Munich: Luchterhand, 2001. Translated by Heike Schwarzbauer and Rick Takvorian as "What Remains." In *What Remains & Other Stories*, 231–95. Chicago: University of Chicago Press, 1993.

———. "Die zumutbare Wahrheit: Prosa der Ingeborg Bachmann." (1966) In *Die Dimension des Autors*, 86–100. Translated as "Truth That Can Be Faced—Ingeborg Bachmann's Prose 1966." In *The Reader and The Writer*, 83–96.

———. "Zwischenrede." (1990) In *Auf dem Weg nach Tabou*, 17–22. Translated as "Momentary Interruption." (1990) In *Parting from Phantoms*, 9–13.

Wolf, Gerhard. "Gerhard Wolf zur vierten Reise." In *Moskauer Tagebücher: Wer wir sind und wer wir waren: Reisetagebücher, Texte, Briefe, Dokumente 1957–1989*, Christa Wolf, edited by Gerhard Wolf. 96–99. Berlin: Suhrkamp, 2014.

Wolfram von Eschenbach. *Parzival: Mittelhochdeutsch und Neuhochdeutsch*, edited by Karl Lachmann, translated by Wolfgang Spiewok. Stuttgart: Reclam, 1981.
Wolk, Elisabeth, and Ute Fritsche. "Zur Entwicklung der perinatalen und Säuglingssterblichkeit in der DDR." In *Das Gesundheitswesen der DDR: Aufbruch oder Einbruch: Denkanstöße für eine Neuordnung des Gesundheitswesens in einem deutschen Staat*, edited by Wilhelm Thiele, 222–25. Sankt Augustin: Asgard-Verlag Hippe, 1990.
Wolle, Stefan. *Die heile Welt der Diktatur: Alltag und Herrschaft in der DDR 1971–1989*. Berlin: Christoph Links, 1998.
Wunder, Michael. "Intersexualität: Leben zwischen den Geschlechtern." *Aus Politik und Zeitgeschichte* 20/21 (2012): 34–40.
Yuval-Davis, Nira. *Gender & Nation*. London: Sage, 1997.
Zander, Judith. *Dinge, die wir heute sagten*. Munich: dtv, 2010.

Index

abject: Christa Wolf and her alter ego as, 72, 74, 100; East Germans as, 15–18, 115, 118, 137, 151n25, 163, 176, 188–89; West German medical system as, 125
abjection of the Other: for subject formation for West Germans, 137, 189, 192; for subject formation of the two German states, 15, 51, 68n36, 157; for subject formation within the GDR, 103
abortion, 50–52, 122
adaptation, 42, 48–49, 55–56, 63, 123, 192
Adelson, Leslie, 20–21, 66n10
Adorno, Theodor W., 100
aesthetics of political conviction. *See* Gesinnungsästhetik
Agde, Günter, 29nn48–49
agency: claim to, 21, 38, 49, 64, 74, 106, 129, 165, 168, 194; denying certain individuals, 126, 157, 171, 174; denying patients, 80–81, 85, 118, 156, 184, 189; denying women, 124; in the body, 95; limitations of, 191, 55–56
Ahbe, Thomas, 12, 25n12, 26n19, 26n22, 27n31, 28n38, 29n46, 29n50, 31nn58–60, 33n75, 67n16, 68n38, 69n49, 109n9, 110n19, 110n23, 151n29, 194n1
Amon, I., 142, 153n56, 153n59
Anderson, Edith, 152n33
Ankunftsliteratur, 36, 65–66n5
antifascism, 12–13, 61, 100, 106, 159; founding narratives of, 29n43, 51, 62, 74–75, 98, 106, 189, 194
Anz, Thomas, 31n65
Arbeiteraufstand. *See* Uprising (of June 17, 1953)

Arnim, Achim von, works by: *Des Knaben Wunderhorn*, 105
Arnim, Bettina von, 44
Arnim, Bettina von, works by: *Die Günderode*, 67n19
Arnold, Heinz Ludwig, 18, 32n71
Arrangementgedächtnis, 10–11, 190
Arztethik, 42
Arztvertrag, 101
Assheuer, Thomas, 185n3
Assmann, Aleida, 68n40, 73, 87, 105, 109n15, 111n38, 152n39, 175, 187n20
Assmann, Jan, 12
Atzl, Isabel, 154nn71–72
Aufbauliteratur, 12–13, 20, 54, 65n5, 133, 139, 194
Aufklärungspflicht, 82
"Aufruf für unser Land," 31n61, 34, 65n1

Bachmann, Ingeborg, 105, 111n30, 112n41
Barck, Simone, 9, 28n36, 30n53, 33n75, 69n47
Bathrick, David, 30n51
Bauer, Fritz, 28n41
Bauerkämper, Arnd, 30n57
Bause, Ulrich, 109n13
Baust, Günter, 70n58, 109n10, 109nn12–13
Beattie, Andrew, 28n42, 31n62, 31n64
Becker, Jurek, works by: *Amanda herzlos*, 31n61; *Schlaflose Tage*, 24n10; "Die Wiedervereinigung der deutschen Literatur," 30n53
Becker, Wolfgang, works by: *Good Bye, Lenin!* (film), 23n1
Behn, Manfred, 65n3

Berg, Sibylle, works by: *Vielen Dank für das Leben*, 25n10, 193
Berlin Charité. *See* Charité
Berlin Republic, 10, 149, 157, 184, 189, 192
Berlin Wall. *See* Wall
Berliner Kurier, 152n47
Berndt, H.-G., 70n52, 78, 84, 109n11, 109n18, 110n20, 110n22, 142, 151n30, 153nn55–56, 153n59, 185n4
Betreuungsanordnung, 170–71
Betreuungsverfahren, 170–71, 174, 176
Betreuungsverhältnis, 6, 80–81, 101, 142
Bettin, Hartmut, 25nn12–13, 26n20, 66–67n15, 70nn51–52, 153n53, 169, 185n4, 186n12
Bieler, Manfred, 29n48
Biermann, Wolfgang, 63, 76
binary: of good and evil, 90, 110n24; of life and death, 88; male/female, 22–23, 79, 120, 137; sex and gender, 86, 115, 128, 130–31, 173–74. *See also* dichotomy
binary opposition, 21
bioethics, 156, 158
Bircken, Margrid, 112n47
Blankenagel, Alexander, 28n41
blindness, 8, 116–18, 149n3, 160
Blumensath, Heinz, 30n55
Boa, Elizabeth, 112nn42–43
body: afflicted, 75; ailing, 1, 21–22; of the Christian martyr, 61; collective, 40; communist, 51, 61, 63; of the Communist, 13, 61, 139; desexualized, 50, 63, 139; diseased, 4, 68n33, 87; female, 1–4, 9, 20–22, 80, 125–26, 134; gender-ambiguous, 22, 133; guilty, 61; human, 22, 106; ill, 2, 25n11, 65, 74–75; inscribed, 2, 9, 13, 15, 21, 27n35, 28n35, 54, 63, 82–83, 94, 106, 120, 132–33, 139, 163, 185, 191; intersexual, 9, 20; male, 22, 131; as a mine, 96, 111n40; as mnemonic site, 9, 119; as object of cultural memory, 128; as object of political interest, 25n11; physical reaction of, 37, 180; physicality of, 8; political, 21–22, 105; postfascist, 13, 68n33, 133; pregnant, 51, 119–20, 124, 134; purity of, 53; rebellious, 8, 11, 38, 83, 191; representations of, 2, 8, 22, 119, 186n9; "re-sexualized," 68n33; sexual, 13, 50–51, 133, 139; sexualized, 134; sexually ambiguous, 131; sick, 37, 74; as site of historical experience, 105–6; as site of social experience, 11, 46, 62, 73, 77; socialist, 5, 51; sublime, 13, 61; suffering, 13, 74, 76, 98, 189, 191, 194; as symbolic space, 2; traces on, 8–9, 38, 75, 80, 127, 163; transgender, 2, 4, 9, 20; transsexual, 172; weakened, 106, 168. *See also* symptomatic body
body politic, 9, 21, 46, 73, 77, 82, 106, 120
Bohn, Rainer, 152n44
Bollinger, Stefan, 25n12
Bondio, Mariacarla Gadebusch, 25nn12–13, 26n20, 70nn51–52, 169, 186n12
Bönisch, Georg, 187n28
Brasch, Marion, works by: *Ab jetzt ist Ruhe*, 24–25n10
Brasch, Thomas, works by: *Vor den Vätern sterben die Söhne*, 24–25n10
Braun, Volker, 13
Braun, Volker, works by: *Die hellen Haufen*, 190; *Die Übergangsgesellschaft*, 24–25n10; *Unvollendete Geschichte*, 24–25n10
Bräunig, Werner, works by: *Ein Kranich am Himmel*, 29n48; *Rummelplatz*, 24–25n10, 29n48
Brecht, Bertolt, 100
Bredel, Willi, 12; works by: *Die Prüfung*, 29n43
Breger, Claudia, 150n9
Brenner, Hildegard, 30n52
Brentano, Clemens, works by: *Des Knaben Wunderhorn*, 105

Brettschneider, Werner, 30n55
Bridge, Helen, 28n36, 112n50
Brock, Angela, 26–27n25, 69n43
Brockmann, Stephen, 32n66
Brown Book, 29n50, 69n49
Brunkow, Heinz, 131
Brüns, Elke, 24n9, 31n61, 32n71, 33n79, 109n2, 109n4
Bruns, Marianne, works by: *Szenenwechsel*, 24–25n10
Brussig, Thomas: as post-GDR writer, 3, 19, 192–93
Brussig, Thomas, works by: *Helden wie wir*, 111n33, 136; *Wie es leuchtet*, 3, 20, 31n61, 114–17, 133–37, 143–44, 149, 149n1, 173, 191–93
Bullivant, Keith, 32n66
Burmeister, Brigitte, works by: *Anders oder vom Aufenthalt in der Fremde*, 24–25n10
Butler, Judith, 15, 21–22, 51, 103, 124
Butler, Judith, works by: *Bodies that Matter*, 68n35; "Foucault and the Paradox of Bodily Inscription," 27–28n35; *Gender Trouble*, 21, 33n81, 130; *Undoing Gender*, 123, 130
Byrnes, Deidre, 176, 186n11

cancer, 70n53, 109n12; and breach of doctor-patient confidentiality, 122; combating, 7, 60; in *Nachdenken über Christa T.*, 62–63, 71n63; and *schonende Lüge*, 70n52, 85; in *Sommerstück*, 70n50
capitalism, 15, 56, 96, 165; criticism of, 97, 106, 108, 112n45, 189; as failing, 110n28; GDR as alternative to, 10, 12; lacking faith in, 118; linked with fascism, 101; as norm, 137
Caregorodcev, Genadij Ivanovic, 153n59
Caruth, Cathy, 152n40
Caspari, Martina, 109n1, 113n54
censorship, 29n48, 30n53, 36, 47, 112n44

Central Committee (of the SED), 13, 34, 37, 78, 113n52
Charité, 52–53, 70n53, 109n12, 131, 137, 141, 144, 146–47, 152n45, 153n50, 154n67, 154nn71–72, 160, 162; Medical-Historical Museum of, 147
childbirth, 50, 52–54, 126, 151n27
childcare facilities, 51, 172
Christ-figure, female, 61–62, 64, 105, 113n61
Cibulka, Hanns, works by: *Swantow*, 24–25n10
Clarke, David, 18, 28n40, 31n60, 31n64, 32n68
class, 15, 21, 31nn58–59, 115, 119, 161, 167, 184; difference, 5, 7, 31n59, 78, 112n44; medical, 44; middle, 15, 31n58; progressive, 143; working, 15, 31n58, 43–45, 59, 78, 143
classless society, 7, 86, 127
collaboration: with class enemy, 139; among doctors and nurses, 162, 167, 190; of law and medicine, 186n15; with Nazis, 111n34; with Stasi, 83, 89–90, 103, 106, 121, 141, 145–46, 151n25, 183
colonization as metaphor for German unification, 31n6, 190
concentration camp, 12, 29n43, 98, 127–28, 143, 147, 158, 191
consent of patient, 7, 26n24, 82, 85, 141–42, 171
contamination, 54, 101, 159
contract between doctor and patient. See *Arztvertrag*
Cooke, Paul, 31n61
cooperation: of institutions, 4; patient, 82–83, 85, 87, 125, 169; with Stasi, 72–73, 122
Coper, Helmut, 153n50
Cosentino, Christine, 109n1, 113n56, 187n21
Costabile-Heming, Carol Anne, 109n1, 113n58
Crick, Joyce, 65n2

curriculum for degree programs in medicine, 42, 66n14

Dackweiler, Regina-Maria, 186n7
David, Heinz, 68n41, 147, 154n71–72
De Silva, Adrian, 173, 186n18
death, 4, 78, 85, 105, 128, 165, 172; after unification, 177; as consequence of medical experiments in GDR hospitals, 141; in *Du stirbst nicht*, 173, 177; fight against, 58, 76, 88, 90; in *Good Bye, Lenin!*, 1; in *Lärchenau*, 126, 133, 158, 163–64; in *Leibhaftig*, 104; of mother, 92, 111nn35–36; in *Nachdenken über Christa T.*, 2, 36, 38, 41, 50, 56–57, 60–63, 68n33, 71n62; rescue from, 91; self-inflicted, 102; self-sacrificial, 61
debate on literature. *See Literaturstreit*
Deiritz, Karl, 31–32n65
Delius, Friedrich Christian, works by: *Die Birnen von Ribbek*, 31n61
deontology, socialist, 61; Soviet, 66–67n15
depression, 8; and *Flucht in die Wolken*, 47; in *Nachdenken über Christa T.*, 44–49, 61
dichotomy: angel/devil, 110n24; authenticity/artificiality, 51; challenged, 21, 90, 184; community/individual, 15; dissolution of, 96; East/West, 115, 134; God/devil, 110n24; heaven/hell, 110n24; innocence/experience, 51; lack of sexual body/sexual body, 51; male/female, 79; mind/body, 35, 37–38, 40, 65, 66n9, 75, 87, 93, 95; planned economy/market economy, 15, 51; romantic/realist, 103; socialism/capitalism, 15, 51; solidarity/individualism, 51. *See also* binary
dictatorship: GDR as, 10, 144, 188, 193; model of "two German dictatorships," 16. *See also Diktaturgedächtnis*

Diderot, Denis, works by: "Lettre sur les aveugles à l'usage de ceux qui voient," 150n7
Diktaturgedächtnis, 10–11, 16, 188
doctoral ethics. *See Arztethik*
doctor-patient confidentiality, 7, 120–22, 138, 140, 150n18
doctor-patient relationship, 6, 26n24, 59, 80–82, 85, 109n17, 110n21, 168, 171, 173
doctors: associated with military, 80–81, 167; in capitalist vs. socialist systems, 78, 126; collaboration with nurses, 44, 86, 110n23, 125, 167, 190; in hospitals, 27n31, 44, 126, 141, 146, 167; leaving for the West, 6, 26n22, 53, 133–35, 146; and medical experiments after unification, 115, 157, 160, 162–63; and medical experiments in GDR hospitals, 115, 141–44; reformed education of, 41–44, 66n14, 143, 159; and responsibility towards socialist society, 6, 48, 59, 185n4; and *schonende Lüge*, 57–58, 84–85; socialist, 81, 122, 160; as socialist educators of their patients, 47–48, 59, 67n16; and Stasi, 6, 44, 140, 121, 139; as Stasi IMs, 121–22, 138, 140, 145
Drescher, Angela, 65n3, 66n6
Dröscher, Barbara, 69n48
Dueck, Cheryl, 24n10, 28n37, 65n2
Duldungs- und Befolgungspflicht, 59, 85, 169
Durzak, Manfred, 149n2

Ecker, Gisela, 33n77
Eggert, Heinz, 138
Eigler, Friederike, 129, 150nn9–10, 152n34
Eisler, Hanns, 100
Elden, Stuart, 185n3
Eleventh Plenum (of the Central Committee of the SED), 13, 29n49, 34, 37, 45, 64, 92

Emmerich, Wolfgang, 18, 29–30n51, 30n52, 30n56, 69nn47–48, 65–66n5, 128, 150n11
Erdbrügger, Torsten, 25n11
Erll, Astrid, 32n67, 109n7
Ernst, Anna-Sabine, 26n18, 27n26
Erpenbeck, Jenny, works by: *Aller Tage Abend*, 192; *Heimsuchung*, 24–25n10
ethics, 43–44, 76, 88, 162, 165; Soviet, 61
ethics and ethical standards: in biotechnological research, 27n27, 129, 152n49, 154n68; in GDR and socialist medicine, 6, 9, 25n12, 27n27, 41, 43, 59, 66–67n15, 70n52, 70n58, 110n22, 141–42, 146–47, 152n49, 153n58, 154n68, 159, 160, 162, 169, 194
Ethics Commission: of the GDR, 141; of the Medical Board of Berlin, 141
Ethik in der Medizin, 42
Evers, Marco, 154n73

faith: in liberal democracy, 118; in socialism, 37, 61–63, 65, 104, 140
family: bourgeois notions of, 51, 55, 69n43, 122, 127, 161; challenging traditional and heteronormative notions of, 121, 119, 130, 183; socialist, 51, 122, 172
family relations representing social relations, 13, 51, 54, 100, 102, 127, 148
fascism: as contaminating individuals, 101, 63; linked with capitalism, 100–101, 108, 165; linked with sexuality, 13, 50; victims of, 75, 97–99, 105
Federal Republic of Germany. *See* FRG
feminization: of East Germans and East Germany, 117, 149n3; of the nation, 21
Festge, Otto-Andreas, 66n14, 67n18, 68n41, 110n23, 153n59
Feuchtwanger, Lion, 100
fiction. *See* literature
Fietz, Kathleen, 187n21

Finch, Helen, 184
Finlay, Frank, 31–32n65
Fischer, Gerhard, 24n9, 25n12
Fischer, W., 153n59
Flinspach, Dagmar, 68n38
Fortschrittsgedächtnis, 10–11, 189–90
Foucault, Michel, 5, 27–28n35
Foucault, Michel, works by: *Discipline and Punish*, 25n15, 27–28n35; *The History of Sexuality*, 25n15, 27–28n35, 150n13, 150n15; "Nietzsche, Genealogy, History," 27–28n35, 120
founding narrative: of the FRG, 10, 12, 36, 77; of the GDR, 12, 29n43, 36, 51, 62, 74–75, 77, 99–100, 106, 139, 189
Fox, Thomas C., 32n72
Franck, Julia, works by: *Lagerfeuer*, 24–25n10, 191–92; *Rücken an Rücken*, 24–25n10
Frank, Bruno, 100
Frank, Leonhard, 100
Franke, Klaus, 154n73
Franke, Konrad (German studies scholar), 14, 30n55
Franke, Konrad (lawyer), 47, 68n27
Franzen, Jannik, 172–73
Freud, Sigmund, 47, 76, 111n39, 119, 150n11, 175
Freud, Sigmund, works by: "Konstruktionen in der Analyse," 95–96; "Das Unheimliche," 149n3
FRG: as incorporating GDR, 3, 17, 144; as superior, 10, 28n41, 190, 193; ties to the fascist German past, 12, 14, 36, 69n49, 100
Friedemann, Hedi, 151n27
Fritsche, Ute, 150n22, 151n29, 186n13
Fromm, Erich, 112n49
Fromm, Friedemann, works by: *Weißensee* (film), 24n5
Fukuyama, Francis, 31n59
Fulbrook, Mary, 4, 25n12, 27n30, 27n32, 29nn46–47, 33n75, 67n22, 68nn29–30, 69n43, 77, 150n21, 186n13

Gallagher, Kaleen, 112n42
Galli, Matteo, 33n75
GDR: demise of, 1–3, 19, 34, 65, 73, 76, 104–5, 108, 114, 133, 149, 166, 176, 192; as dictatorship, 10, 16–17, 144, 188, 193; as totalitarian, 10, 12, 28n41, 144; as *Unrechtsstaat*, 10, 28n41, 31n63, 188–89
GDR Society for Medical Care. See *Gesellschaft für Krankenpflege der DDR*
Geier, Andrea, 31n61, 152n44
gender: ambiguity, 22–23, 24n6, 130–31, 133; binary, 21–23, 50, 86, 115, 128, 130–31, 137 173–74, 184; conversion, 135; dimorphism, 130, 137; identity, 131, 134–35, 186n14; reassignment, 135–36; roles, 54–55, 68n32, 129; stereotypes, 135, 174. See also norm
gentle lie. See *schonende Lüge*
Geppert, Roswitha, works by: *Die Last, die du nicht trägst*, 24n10, 66n13
Gerhard, Ute, 150n23
German Democratic Republic. See GDR
Germany: fascist, 34, 38, 100, 143; Nazi, 10, 28n41, 66n9, 75, 96, 99, 107, 144, 149, 191, 194; post-unification, 17, 74–75, 77, 84, 97, 100–101, 108, 114, 118, 122, 125, 128, 133, 140, 148–49, 155, 157–58, 165–66, 170, 172, 174, 178–80, 183–85, 191, 194; unified, 3, 10, 16–17, 19, 73–75, 137, 162, 185, 194
Gerstenberger, Katharina, 24n9, 31n61, 154n71
Gesellschaft für Krankenpflege der DDR, 86
Gesetz über den Mutter- und Kinderschutz und die Rechte der Frau, 51
Gesinnungsästhetik, 17, 32n66
Gibas, Monika, 29n50

Gieseke, Jens, 25n14, 26n21
Goethe, Johann Wolfgang von, works by: *Faust*, 88–89, 110n25
Goodbody, Axel, 18
Görlich, Günter, works by: *Eine Anzeige in der Zeitung*, 24n10, 66n13
Granzow, René, 30n55
Grashoff, Udo, 46, 67n24, 71n61, 102, 104
Grass, Günter, works by: *Ein Schnäppchen namens DDR*, 31n61
Gratzik, Paul, works by: *Kohlenkutte*, 24n10
Grau, Günter, 152n41
Greiner, Ulrich, 17–18, 32n66
Gries, Rainer, 29n46
Grolle, Johann, 154n73
Gröschner, Annett, works by: *Moskauer Eis*, 24–25n10; *Walpurgistag*, 24–25n10
Großbölting, Thomas, 28n40, 110n23
Günderode, Karoline von, 44
Günther, Ernst, 26n18, 27n29, 68n28, 70n52, 109n18, 110n22, 150n19, 153n55
gynecology, 50, 52–53, 125, 151n31

Haase, Michael, 112n47
Hahn, Susanne, 6, 26n24, 27nn31–32, 28n37, 42, 66nn12–13, 67n18, 70n52, 70n59, 78, 90, 109n10, 110nn22–23
Hartewig, Karin, 29n43
Hartinger, Walfried, 65n3, 66n6
Harych, Horst, 151n30
Havemann, Robert, 102
health: as asset of the state, 4–5, 21; as characteristic of the socialist personality, 46; individual and subordinated to the socialist community, 5–7, 78, 81–82, 101, 123, 142, 170; as metaphor for the state of the country, 9, 28n37, 192
health examinations, compulsory, 7; for children and teenagers, 123; during pregnancy, 120, 123–24
Heidelberger-Leonard, Irene, 32n66

Heiduczek, Werner, works by: *Tod am Meer*, 24–25n10
Heilbroner, Robert, 31n59
Hein, Christoph, works by: *Der fremde Freund*, 24–25n10; *Horns Ende*, 24–25n10; *In seiner frühen Kindheit ein Garten*, 190; *Weiskerns Nachlass*, 190
Helbig, Holger, 18, 30n53
Hell, Julia, 12–13, 29n44, 50, 53–54, 61, 66, 68n33, 93–94, 99–100, 133, 139
Helmecke, Monika, works by: *Klopfzeichen*, 24–25n10
Henckel von Donnersmarck, Florian, works by: *Das Leben der Anderen* (film), 24n5
Henrich, Rolf, 70n55
Hensel, Kerstin: as post-GDR writer, 3, 19, 24n8, 32–33n74, 155, 192, 194
Hensel, Kerstin, works by: *Hallimasch*, 32–33n74; *Im Spinnhaus*, 24–25n10; *Lärchenau*, 3, 20, 114–15, 126–28, 131–33, 144–49, 156–64, 184, 191, 193–94
Herminghouse, Patricia, 21
Hermsdorf, Klaus, 32n69
Herrn, Rainer, 33n82
Hess, Volker, 154nn71–72
heteronormativity, 22, 130, 134–36, 171–74
heterosexuality, 16, 22, 172, 174
Heym, Stefan, 12, 24–25n10
Heymann, Stefan, 29n43
Hickethier, Knut, 152n44
hierarchical structures: in FRG hospitals, 125; in GDR hospitals, 81, 85–86, 90, 110n21, 125, 143; in post-unification German society, 16, 31n60; in post-unification hospitals, 167, 184, 35
Hilzinger, Sonja, 50
Historians' Dispute. See *Historikerstreit*
Historikerstreit, 32
Hochhut, Rolf, 31n61

Hockerts, Hans Günter, 26n16, 151n32, 154n64–65
Hoffmann, E. T. A., *Die Bergwerke zu Falun*, 111n40
Hofmann, Michael, 25n12, 67n16, 26n19, 26n22, 27n31, 28n38, 109n9, 110n19, 110n23, 151n29
Holocaust, 29n43, 100, 165
homosexuality, 135, 152n41
Honecker, Erich, 6, 13, 29n49, 45, 78
Hörnigk, Frank, 30n53
Hörnigk, Therese, 39, 65n3, 66n6, 71n62
Hüller, Hans-Georg, 78, 109n11, 109n18, 142, 151n30, 153nn55–56, 153n59, 186n4
Huyssen, Andreas, 70n59

identity: East German, 17, 136, 157; GDR, 12, 70n55; gender, 131, 134–35, 186n14; German cultural, 14; German national, 11, 22; group, 12; post-GDR, 16; sexual, 131, 136; trans, 174; West German, 17
ideology: bourgeois, 44; challenged, 9; confirmed, 9, 60; endangered, 22; Marxist-Leninist, 5, 59–60, 41; medicine influenced by, 70n51, 78, 67n16; GDR, 17, 12, 100; National Socialist, 54, 97, 101; socialist, 63
illness: chronic, 52, 91, 95; combatted by preventative measures, 5, 7, 27n28, 59, 82, 151n27; depictions of, 2, 4, 10, 24–25n10, 35, 83; fatal, 36, 55, 57, 59; as induced by the GDR, 36; leading to insight, 9, 35, 63, 71n64, 76, 87, 91, 93, 95–96, 99, 101–5, 107, 118, 156–57, 176, 181–82; Marxist-Leninist interpretations of, 59; physical, 8–9, 20, 34, 47, 63, 74, 107–8; as protection and retreat, 8, 95–96, 107, 181; psychological, 8–9, 20, 34, 36, 46–48, 63, 74, 108, 140, 171, 186n14; psychosomatic, 2, 34, 38, 48, 99; as punishment, 98;

illness: chronic—*(cont'd)*
  as purification, 53–54, 61, 63,
    74, 76, 101, 105, 113n61; role
    of social factors, 9, 34–35,
    37–38, 42, 59–60, 74, 77,
    95–97, 112n44; romantic, 63,
    111–12n40; signaling socio-
    political crisis, 9, 37, 21–22,
    60, 74, 76, 190; socialism
    as prophylactic against, 47;
    transsexuality as, 186n14
Inoffizielle Mitarbeiter. See Stasi, IMs
  in the medical field
inscription on the body, 9–10, 21,
    27n35, 68n40, 83, 73, 97, 120,
    128, 139, 163–64, 191. *See also*
    body, inscribed
institution for the counseling of
    mothers. *See Mütterberatungsstelle*
institutions: medical, 2–6, 10, 25n12,
    26n22, 36, 41–42, 47, 52, 57,
    59, 65, 77–78, 108, 114–15, 119,
    123, 125, 143, 165–69, 172, 184,
    193–94; network of, 38, 49, 124,
    145, 172; privatized research, 162,
    184; psychiatric, 46, 138, 140,
    195n6; state, 5, 20, 52, 41, 79,
    83, 103, 123, 135, 145, 155, 157,
    172, 185, 191
intelligence agency, 89, 103, 110n27,
    120, 122. *See also* Stasi
intersexuality, 9, 20, 22–23, 27n34,
    129–31, 152n35, 173
Irigaray, Luce, 119, 150n10
Iztueta, Garbine, 32n72, 186n9

Jahr, U., 70n51
Janssen-Zimmermann, Antje, 71n65
Jarausch, Konrad, 28n40, 149n4
Jeremiah, Emily, 187n26

Kacandes, Irene, 73–74, 94, 97, 107,
    109n3, 132, 152n39
Kahle, Jutta, 109n8
Kahlschlag-Plenum. See Eleventh
    Plenum (of the Central Committee
    of the SED)
Kahn, Siegbert, 29n43

Käser, Rudolf, 25n1
Kaute, Brigitte, 109n1
Kirchgäßner, W., 59, 67n16, 70n57,
    112n51, 151n24
Kirsch, Sarah, 128, 152n33
Kleist, Heinrich von, 33n79
Kleßmann, Christoph, 30–31n57
Klocke, Sonja, 65–66n5, 150n8,
    154n75, 186n11, 187n19
Klöppel, Ulrike, 130, 152nn35–36,
    152nn41–43, 173, 186n15
Knopf, Hiltraud, 150n22, 151n29,
    186n13
Koch, Hans, 102, 113n52
Koch, Lennart, 32n68
Kohl, Helmut, 177, 187n22
Köhler, Astrid, 18–20, 24n8,
    33n75
Köhn, Lothar, 68n32
Königsdorf, Helga, works by:
    Respektloser Umgang, 24–25n10;
    Ungelegener Befund, 24–25n10
Körner, Hannelore, 146–47,
    153nn61–62, 154nn68–70,
    154n74
Körner, Uwe, 146–47, 153nn61–62,
    154nn68–70, 154n74
Koskinas, Nikolaos-Ioannis, 109n1
Kowalczuk, Ilko-Sascha, 78, 109n9
Krause, Stephan, 25n11
Krauss, Hannes, 29–30n51,
    31–32n65, 151n2
Kroetz, Franz Xaver, works by: *Haus
    Deutschland*, 31n61
Kubiczek, André, works by: *Der
    Genosse, die Prinzessin und ihr lieber
    Herr Sohn*, 24–25n10
Kuczynski, Jürgen, 29–30n51
Kuhn, Anna K., 32n68, 111n32
Kulawik, Helmut, 67–68n26
Kurz, Paul Konrad, 113n60

Lammers, Hans-Jörg, 130–31
Lamprecht, Rolf, 187n28
Langermann, Martina, 30n53
Langhoff, Wolfgang, works by: *Die
    Moorsoldaten*, 29n43
Laqueur, Thomas, 33n77

law: and doctor-patient confidentiality, 121–22; family, 122; FRG, 7, 121, 135, 155, 171, 183; GDR, 6–7, 27n26, 59, 81–82, 121, 123–24, 135, 146, 172; German Basic, 171; and incapacitation, 171; labor, 82; and lack of persecution of former Stasi officers, 183; and medicine, 49, 59, 169, 185, 186n15, 194; and testing medical products, 141. *See also* abortion; *Arztvertrag*; *Aufklärungspflicht*; *Betreuungsanordnung*; *Betreuungsverfahren*; *Betreuungsverhältnis*; consent of patient; doctor-patient confidentiality; *Duldungs- und Befolgungspflicht*; *Gesetz über den Mutter- und Kinderschutz und die Rechte der Frau*; homosexuality; intersexuality; *Mitwirkungspflicht*; *Offenbarungs- und Informationspflicht*; transsexuality

Law for the Protection of Mothers and Children and the Rights of Women. *See Gesetz über den Mutter- und Kinderschutz und die Rechte der Frau*

Lenin, Wladimir Iljitsch, 5, 21, 45

Lewis, Alison, 31n61, 151n25

Lichtenberg, Bernd, 23n2

literary conventions, 2–3, 8, 19, 134, 148, 185, 194

literature: Austrian, 32n70; Berlin, 24n9; decadent, 150n11; East German, 2–4, 8, 11, 18–20, 23n4, 24n9, 114, 194; Eastern German, 19; fascist, 32n69; GDR, 2, 4, 10–20, 23n4, 24n10, 30n52, 30n55, 32nn69–70, 33n75, 47, 50, 100, 114, 127–28, 194; of the German-speaking countries, 18, 32n70; and Lenin, 45; as a medium of memory, 77; narrating history, 4–5, 20, 65, 185, 192; oppositional, 71n67; pan-German, 14, 32n69, 32n71; political, 17–18, 193; Pop, 32n71; post-GDR, 3–4, 11, 18–19, 23n4, 33n75, 69n46, 114–15, 129, 156, 189, 190–93; socialist, 14, 61; Swiss, 32n70; as venue for societal debates, 18, 28n37, 41, 77; West German, 15–18, 194

literature of arrival. *See Ankunftsliteratur*

literature of socialist construction. *See Aufbauliteratur*

Literaturstreit, 17–18, 31–32n65, 32nn66–67, 72–73, 75, 106

Lokatis, Siegfried, 30n53

Löther, Rolf, 59, 70n57, 151n24

Ludwig, Janine, 18, 30n53

Luther, Ernst, 66n12, 66–67n15

loyal dissident, 14, 29n51, 34, 64, 95, 104, 106

Maaz, Hans-Joachim, 70n55

Maetzig, Kurt, works by: *Das Kaninchen bin ich* (film), 29n48

Magenau, Jörg, 29n48, 32n67, 65n4, 111n36

Mählert, Ulrich, 16

Mann, Heinrich, 100

Mann, Thomas, 100

Markgraf, Eberhard, 66–67n15, 154nn63–64, 154n66

Maron, Monika, 32n68, 117

Maron, Monika, works by: *Animal Triste*, 31n61; *Flugasche*, 24–25n10; "Lebensentwürfe, Zeitenbrüche," 149n5; *Die Überläuferin*, 24–25n10

Martin, Brigitte, works by: *Nach Freude anstehen*, 24–25n10

Martin, Elaine, 66n11

Marx, Karl, 55, 69n45, 70n56, 150n14

Marxism-Leninism, 6, 42, 59

Marxist-Leninist: ideology, 5, 41; interpretations of disease, 59; philosophy, 59; power network, 194; thought, 3–4, 42, 56, 59, 189

Matauschek, Jochen, 109n13

Mattheis, Ruth, 153n50

Mayer, Tamar, 33n80

McLaren, Margaret A., 27–28n35
Mecklinger, Ludwig, 78, 141
media: absence of critical (in the GDR), 9, 14, 17, 64; and Christa Wolf, 17, 72–74, 83–84, 100, 106–7, 183–84; mass, 10–11, 16, 136, 138, 148, 158, 185, 189, 193; West German, 17, 72, 74, 84, 100, 107, 118, 136, 144, 148, 151n25, 153n53, 177, 183–84, 189, 192; and *Wie es leuchtet* (Brussig), 118, 136–37, 144
Medical Board of Berlin, 141, 153n51
medical care relationship. *See Betreuungsverhältnis*
medical discourses, 2–4, 11, 24–25n10, 41, 114, 149
medical education in the GDR, 26n19, 41–44, 66n14, 86, 122, 147, 160; and results, 4, 7, 42, 44, 53, 58, 77–78, 83, 85, 145, 147, 159, 168–72
medical ethics. *See Arztethik*; ethics and ethical standards; *Ethik in der Medizin*
medical experiments: with animal and human cells, 146, 161; in GDR hospitals, 141–43; on human beings, 115, 137, 140–44, 148–49, 152n42, 152n49, 156–57, 161, 163, 193; in Nazi concentration camps, 143, 147. *See also* research
medical institutions. *See* institutions, medical
medical intervention: and lack of patient's consent in the GDR, 7, 80; and patient's consent in the FRG, 7, 26n25, 85
medical system: in the FRG (pre- and post-unification), 9, 78, 119, 124–26, 153, 165–72, 184, 191, 193; in the GDR, 1–5, 8–10, 23, 25nn11–12, 27n26, 27n31, 35–36, 41–42, 47–48, 51–52, 57, 59, 65, 77–85, 87, 108, 110n19, 110n23, 114–15, 119, 121, 123, 125, 127, 137, 143–45, 166–69, 184, 189, 191–94. *See also* doctors, as Stasi IMs; intelligence; Stasi

memory: collective, 10–11, 75, 114, 148–49, 155, 193; communicative, 10; cultural, 1, 12, 20, 24n5, 74–75, 77, 118–19, 128, 149, 155, 184; embodied, 8, 20, 41, 80, 87; historical, 1, 24n5, 155, 164; narrative, 74, 132; suppressed, 76; traumatic, 94, 97
memory of accommodation. *See Arrangementgedächtnis*
memory of progress. *See Fortschrittsgedächtnis*
memory of the GDR as a dictatorship. *See Diktaturgedächtnis*
Mendieta, Eduardo, 185n3
Menschenversuche. See medical experiments
Mette, Alexander, 142
Meuser, Mirijam, 18, 30n53
Meyen, Michael, 28n39
Meyer-Gosau, Frauke, 65n3, 113n54
MfS. See Stasi
Mielke, Erich, 6
Millington, Richard, 67n22
Ministerium für Staatssicherheit. See Stasi
Ministry for State Security. *See* Stasi
Misgeld, Gerhard, 142
Mittag, Jana, 186n14, 186n16
Mitwirkungspflicht, 59, 82–83, 85
Moebius, Ulrich, 153n50
Mohr, Reinhard, 185n3
Morgner, Imtraud, 129
Morgner, Irmtraud, works by: *Amanda: Ein Hexenroman*, 24–25n10; *Leben und Abenteuer der Trobadora Beatriz erzählt von ihrer Spielfrau Laura*, 24–25n10
Morrison, Susan, 31n61
Mueller, Magda, 21
Müller, Eggo, 152n44
Müller, F., 58, 70n52, 70n54
Müller, Heiner, 13
Müller, Thomas, 109n8
Müller-Engbergs, 113n52
Müntz, Klaus, 154n74
Muthesius, Sibylle, 47, 66n13, 67n25
Mütterberatungsstelle, 123, 151

nation, 3, 14–15, 20–22, 30n56, 33n80, 116–17, 121, 191; healthy, 22; troubled, 22–23
National Socialism, 12–13, 28n40, 39, 124, 160
National Socialist, 12, 24, 28n41, 29n50, 42, 54, 112n46, 144
Nazi, 9–10, 12, 34, 39, 53, 66n9, 69n49, 71n64, 97–101, 103, 108, 111n34, 127–28, 141, 143, 147, 153n60, 158–59, 164, 189–91, 194
Nazi Germany. See Germany, Nazi
Nickel, Hildegard Maria, 150n23
Niven, Bill, 28n40
norm: bourgeois, 44, 86, 119, 127; cultural, 5, 17, 165; gender, 22, 55, 136; governing GDR society, 3, 10, 12, 18, 37, 43, 48–49, 52, 82, 84, 101, 106, 157, 169; for health, 22, 166; male, 16, 21–22, 129; political and social, 3, 9, 11, 15, 37, 124, 130, 172; universal, 97; West German, 16, 137
normalization, 123–24
Norman, Beret, 155, 183, 185n2, 187n27
normativity, 16, 118, 130, 137, 144
nostalgia for the East. See *Ostalgie*
Nusser, Tanja, 33n82

Offenbarungs- und Informationspflicht, 59, 85
Öhlschläger, Claudia, 33n77, 109n6
Opitz, Michael, 185n1, 187n25
Orwell, George, 144, 180
Ostalgie, 17, 178, 190
Ostner, Ilona, 150n20
Otto, Wieland, 66–67n15, 154nn63–64, 154n66

paradise: secularized notion of, 65, 71n64, 88–89, 110n25
Party. See SED
patient: consent of, 7, 26n24, 85, 142; and obligation to cooperate, 7, 27n26, 47, 49, 59, 82–85, 123, 169, 171; passive, 48, 81–85, 142, 168–69, 171, 184, 189; rebellious, 47, 120
Paul, Georigna, 122n49
Paver, Chloe E. M., 65n3
Pearce, Caroline, 28n40
Peitsch, Helmut, 29n43, 30n52
Pezzei, Kristina, 187n21
physicians. See doctors
Pinfold, Debbie, 70n55
Pinkert, Anke, 29n43, 113n57, 151n25
Pockrandt, Heinz, 131
Prague Spring (in 1968), 92, 111n33
Prokop, Otto, 131, 152n37, 153n50
psychiatry. See institutions, psychiatric

racism, 29n43, 112n44, 128, 150n15
Radbruch, Gustav, 28n41
Raddatz, Fritz J., 30n55
Radisch, Iris, 18, 32n71, 33n75, 193, 195n5
Rechtien, Renate, 65–66n5, 109n4, 112n41, 113n63
Reding, R., 67n18, 70n51
Reich-Ranicki, Marcel, 36
Reifner, Udo, 28n41
Reimann, Brigitte, 109n12
Reimann, Brigitte, works by: *Ankunft im Alltag*, 65n5; *Franziska Linkerhand*, 24–25n10; *Sei gegrüßt und lebe*, 109n2
Remarque, Erich Maria, 115
research: biomedical, 146, 184; biotechnological, 129; genetic, 3, 20, 146, 148, 157–58, 160–65; on human cells and embryos, 154n68; in human engineering, 145; medical, 35–36, 143, 146–47, 155, 184; medical-historical, 3–4, 36, 52, 59–60, 125, 146, 153n53, 169, 194; pharmaceutical, 3, 20; in response to allegations against GDR medical institutions, 25n12; scientific, 147
Richter-Kuhlmann, Eva A., 150n16
Ringel, Martina, 151n26
Roberts, David, 24n9
Rosch, Eleanor, 27n34

Rosenberg, Rainer, 30n55
Rosenlöcher, Thomas, works by: *Ostgezeter*, 31n61; *Die Wiederentdeckung des Gehens beim Wandern*, 31n61
Roth, Kersten Sven, 16, 31n62
Rücker, Kerstin, 68n39, 150n22, 151n27, 186n13
Ruge Eugen, works by: *In Zeiten des abnehmenden Lichts*, 24–25n10, 190
Rüther, Günther, 32n69

Sabrow, Martin, 10, 28n39, 30n57, 188–89, 190
Sachs, Nelly, works by: *In den Wohnungen des Todes*, 29n43
Sachse, Carola, 68n38
Sander, Hans-Dietrich, 30n55
Sauer, Arn, 186n14, 186n16
Scarry, Elaine, 22, 27n33, 60, 74, 105–6
Schäfer, Daniel, 109n17
Schäfer, Reinhild, 186n7
Schagen, Udo, 26n18, 27n26, 52, 66–67nn14–15, 67nn17–18, 68n41, 110n23, 151n28
Schalansky, Judith, works by: *Der Hals der Giraffe*, 24–25n10, 192, 194n2
Schalk-Golodkowski, 141
Schappach, Beate, 25n11
Scharpe, Ingrid, 31n61
Schaumann, Caroline, 66n11, 112n49
Schilke, Detlev, 187n21
Schischkin, Alexander Fjodorowitsch, 71n61
Schlaffer, Heinz, 32n69
Schleiermacher, Sabine, 26n18, 27n26, 52, 66–67nn14–15, 67nn17–18, 68n41, 110n23, 151n28
Schmidt, Kathrin: as post-GDR writer, 19, 32–33n74, 114, 155, 192–94
Schmidt, Kathrin, works by: *Du stirbst nicht*, 3, 20, 156, 165–78, 184, 187n21, 191, 193; *Die Gunnar-Lennefsen-Expedition*, 3, 20, 32–33n74, 114–15, 118–19, 122–27, 129–31, 138–40, 148–49, 150n8, 150n10, 151n31, 154n75, 167, 173–74, 191, 193–94
Schmidt, Thomas, 30n53
Schmitt, Hans-Jürgen, 30n55
Schmitz, Helmut, 24n9
Schnalke, Thomas, 154nn71–72
Schneider, Klaus, 151n26
Schoch, Julia, works by: *Mit der Geschwindigkeit des Sommers*, 24–25n10
Schönberg, Arnold, 100
schonende Lüge, 57–58, 70n52, 84–85, 110nn21–22
Schönert, Jörg, 30n52
Schulz, Torsten, works by: *Nilowsky*, 24–25n10
Schulz, Werner, 67–68n26
Schulze, Ingo, works by: *Simple Storys*, 24–25n10
Schumann Eva, 150n20
Schwarz, Peter Paul, 111n29
Scribner, Charity, 109n1
secret service. *See* Stasi
SED, 5–6, 10, 12–13, 26n19, 34, 43, 46, 61, 67n25, 78, 102, 104, 113n52, 141, 145, 189
Sedgwick, Eve, 33n76
Seidel, Karl, 67–68n26
Seifert, Ulrike, 26n18, 27n26, 27n29, 47–49, 57, 59, 67nn16–18, 68n28, 70n52, 81–82, 101–2, 109n18, 110n19, 110n23, 112n51, 122–23, 151n24, 153n55, 185n4
Seiler, Lutz, works by: *Kruso*, 24n5
Sevin, Dieter, 65n3
sexuality: accepted by socialist society, 51–52, 134; and *Aufbauliteratur*, 13, 139–40; as category, 15, 115; and fascism, 13, 50, 139; female, 119; as relapse, 68n33; significance of, 148; and violence, 154n67
Sharp, Ingrid, 68n38
shortages in hospitals, 53, 77–78, 127, 141, 189
sickness. *See* illness
Silberman, Marc, 30n55
Simonow, Konstantin, 29n43
Skare, Roswitha, 32n69

Sloterdijk, Peter, 157–65, 185n3
socialism: as alternative to fascism, 10, 39; belief in, 2, 20, 38, 44, 52, 56, 63, 104, 140; as best prophylaxis, 5, 46–47; construction of, 5, 7, 13, 189; democratic, 37; failure of, 16, 31n60, 116, 110n28; humane, 37, 50 63, 73, 92; ideals and values of, 10, 12, 14, 20, 44, 49–50, 53, 58, 61, 63, 65, 72–73, 89–90, 92, 95, 104, 106–8, 160, 164–65, 189–90; real-existing, 14, 19–20, 37–38, 43, 56, 61, 63, 65–66n5, 74, 76, 103–4, 113n56, 133, 172; reform, 53, 64, 136
socialist doctor personality, 42, 145, 160
socialist personality, 26–27nn25–26, 46, 57, 124
Socialist Unity Party. See SED
Soldovieri, Stefan, 29n48
Sontag, Susan, 63
sozialistische Arztpersönlichkeit. See socialist doctor personality
Sozialistische Einheitspartei Deutschlands. See SED
Spackman, Barbara, 65n2
Spiegel, Der, 27n28, 140–41, 142–45, 148, 149n2, 153n51, 153n53, 157–58
Staatssicherheit. See Stasi
Stasi: and admission to medical degree programs, 43; compared to FBI and CIA, 89, 192; and *Diktaturgedächtnis*, 10; employees, 183; in *Die Gunnar-Lennefsen-Expedition* (Schmidt), 120, 122–23, 138–40; in *Helden wie wir* (Brussig), 136; IMs, 121–23, 138, 143, 145, 150n18, 151n25, 187n24; IMs in the medical field, 121–23, 138, 145; in *Lagerfeuer* (Franck), 191–92; in *Lärchenau* (Hensel), 131–33, 145–46; in *Leibhaftig* (Wolf), 76, 103, 108; mediating between physicians and hospitals, 6; mediating between physicians and the SED, 6; in the medical field, 4, 6, 26n22, 44, 115, 121–23, 137–43, 145–46, 193, 195n4; methods, 180, 192, 195n4; monitoring doctors, 146; ongoing influence of, 155–57, 178–80, 183–85; and *operative Legende*, 179, 187n24; in *Stadt der Engel* (Wolf), 89–90, 106–7; Strubel's opinion of, 180–81; in *Sturz der Tage in die Nacht* (Strubel), 156–57, 178–84, 188; and suicide notes of Stasi officers, 104; surveillance by, 4, 14; in *Der Turm* (Tellkamp), 195n4; in *Was bleibt* (Wolf), 64; and West German media, 72, 83, 106, 137–41, 148, 151n25, 193; in *Wie es leuchtet* (Brussig), 143; and *Zersetzung*, 138, 179–80. *See also* doctors, as Stasi IMs; intelligence
Stein, Hans, 26n16
Stein, Rosemarie, 25n12, 153nn50–51, 153n54
Stewart, Faye, 183, 187n29
Stiehler, Volker, 25n12, 26n19, 26n22, 27n31, 28n38, 67n16, 109n9, 110n19, 110n23, 151n29
Stöver, Bernd, 30n57
Strowick, Elisabeth, 33n82
Strubel, Antje Rávic: as post-GDR writer, 19, 155, 192–93
Strubel, Antje Rávic, works by: *Fremd gehen*, 183, 189; *Sturz der Tage in die Nacht*, 3, 20, 69n46, 156–57, 178–84, 188–89, 191–93; *Tupolew 134*, 189
subject formation via abjection of the Other. *See* abjection of the Other
subjective authenticity. *See* Wolf, Christa, and subjective authenticity
Suckut, Siegfried, 187n24
suicide: as anti-socialist behavior, 47, 102; attempt in *Nachdenken über Christa T.* (Wolf), 46; attempt in *Wie es leuchtet* (Brussig), 135; in *Du stirbst nicht* (Schmidt), 174; after June 17, 1953, 46; in *Leibhaftig* (Wolf), 102; among SED party functionaries, 102, 104; *Wende*, 100, 102, 104

Süß, Sonja, 6, 25n12, 26nn22–23, 44, 121, 138, 140, 150nn17–18, 152nn45–46, 154n63
Sutton, Katie, 155, 183, 185n2, 187n27
Sweet, Denis M., 152n41
symptomatic body, 8–11, 20–23, 194; in Christa Wolf's novels, 34–37, 41, 47, 52, 56, 60–62, 65, 74–75, 77, 80, 83, 87, 92–95, 105–7, 139, 189; in *Du stirbst nicht* (Schmidt), 156, 165, 175–76, 178, 185, 191; in *Die Gunnar-Lennefsen-Expedition* (Schmidt), 119, 125, 129, 139, 148, 191; in *In Zeiten des abnehmenden Lichts* (Ruge), 190; in *Kindheitsmuster* (Wolf), 93; in *Lagerfeuer* (Franck), 191; in *Lärchenau* (Hensel), 127–28, 148–49, 156, 185, 191; in *Leibhaftig* (Wolf), 74–75, 77, 80, 83, 87, 92–93, 95, 105–7, 189; in *Nachdenken über Christa T.* (Wolf), 36–37, 41, 47, 52, 56, 60, 62, 65, 93; performance of, 11, 77, 92, 99, 118; in post-GDR novels, 115, 118–19, 125, 127–29, 139, 148–49, 155–57, 165, 175–78, 185, 190–91; prototype of, 9, 22, 27n34, 37; as a socioaesthetic construct, 8–9; in *Stadt der Engel* (Wolf), 107, 189; in *Sturz der Tage in die Nacht* (Strubel), 156–57, 178, 185, 191; in *Wie es leuchtet* (Brussig), 118, 148, 191
symptomatic voice, 91, 94–95, 133

Takerta, Thomas, 30n53
Tanneberger, Stephan, 27n27, 70n59, 141, 143, 152n49, 153n53
Tate, Dennis, 66n6, 69n49, 109n1, 109n5, 112n49, 113n59
transgender, 2, 4, 9, 20, 22–23, 24n6, 27n34
transsexuality, 9, 20, 22–23, 27n34, 133–35, 144, 148–49, 152n42, 172–74, 186nn14–15, 191, 193
trauma: and Christa Wolf, 73, 88, 97, 107, 111n29; demise of GDR and unification as cause for, 73, 95, 97, 111n29, 166, 175–76; in *Du stirbst nicht* (Schmidt), 156, 166, 175–76; in *Lärchenau* (Hensel), 128, 132–33; in *Leibhaftig* (Wolf), 74, 77, 80, 94, 97–98, 111–12n40; in *Nachdenken über Christa T.* (Wolf), 40; narrating, 73–74, 76, 132; in post-GDR literature, 194; as result of Nazi concentration camp, 128; as result of Stasi interference, 132–33, 184; in *Stadt der Engel* (Wolf), 75, 97, 184; in *Sturz der Tage in die Nacht* (Strubel), 184; surfacing on the body, 73, 107. *See also* memory, traumatic
Tellkamp, Uwe, works by: *Der Turm*, 24n5, 24–25n10, 195n4
Thiele, Wilhelm, 151n30
Thießen, Malte, 26n17, 27n26
Thietz, Kirsten, 68n37
Thom, Achim, 153n59
Thom, Elfriede, 66n13
Thom, Wilhelm, 66n13
Thompson, Edward Palmer, 23n3
Toellner, Richard, 142, 152n49, 153n58, 154n68
Twark, Jill, 32n72

Uebach, Christel, 30n55
unconstitutional state. *See Unrechtsstaat*
unification: and allegory of heterosexual couple, 16, 31n61, 149n3; and continued Stasi control, 179, 184; damaging effects of, 68n38, 118, 122, 134, 150n23, 163, 177; and East Germans as underdogs, 192–93; and medical institutions, 7, 125, 156, 167; as "natural" course of history, 15–16, 116; as rape, 16; as result of elections in the GDR in March 1990, 117; rushed, 191; as traumatic rupture, 175, 97; unleashing human experiments, 147, 159, 161, 163. *See also* Germany, post-unification; Germany, unified

Unofficial Informers. *See* Stasi, IMs in the medical field
Unrechtsstaat, 10, 28n41, 31n63, 188–89
Uprising (of June 17, 1953), 28n41, 45–46, 49, 63, 67n22

van der Hart, Onno, 94, 97
van der Kolk, Bessel, 94, 97
Verwijs, Rebecca, 109n17
Viertel, Berthold, 100
Vilmar, Fritz, 25n12
Vinke, Hermann, 113n65
violence: gender-specific, 63, 79, 109n14, 131, 133, 161–62, 186n7; in medical and legal realms, 162, 167, 172, 193; in private realm, 146, 154n67, 159, 161, 163; structural, 97, 108, 133, 191
Vogt, Jochen, 29–30n51
Volksaufstand. *See* Uprising (of June 17, 1953)
Völlger, Winfried, works by: *Das Windhahnsyndrom*, 24–25n10
Vollnhals, Clemens, 28n40

Wagner, Linde, 26n18, 27n32, 109n8, 110n21, 151n29
Wall, 6, 56, 146; building of (in 1961), 6, 13–14, 37, 53, 56, 65n5, 69n48, 96; fall of (in 1989), 1–2, 4, 19, 24n9, 29n48, 39, 64, 71n66, 102, 110n21, 115–16, 126, 136, 148–49, 156, 159, 178–79, 188, 190
Walther, Peter, 32n69
Wander, Maxie, 70n53, 109n12, 110n21
Wander, Maxie, works by: *Leben wär' eine prima Alternative*, 24–25n10, 66n13, 70n53; *Tagebücher und Briefe*, 109n12
Warner, Michael, 186n17
Webber, Andrew, 112n41
Weber, Herrmann, 67n22
Weber, Jürgen, 28n40
Wedl, Juliette, 31n62, 194n1
Wehdeking, Volker, 152n44

Weigel, Helene, 100
Weigel, Sigrid, 8, 20, 27n33, 111n37, 150n12
Weil, Francesca, 25n12, 26n18, 26n23, 67n18, 121, 145, 150nn16–18, 154n63
Weisenborn, Günther, works by: *Memorial*, 29n43
Wende, 4, 15, 100, 102, 104, 116, 135, 143, 148, 166, 194
Wenk, Silke, 33n77
Werfel, Franz, 100
Wiechert, Ernst, works by: *Der Totenwald*, 29n43
Wiens, Birgit, 33n77
Wierling, Dorothee, 29n46
Wiesner, Gerd E., 27n31, 151n29
Winter, Kurt, 142
Wilde, Sebastian, 111n29
Wilke, Sabine, 71n62, 109n14
Wippermann, Wolfgang, 28n40
Wobus, Anna M., 154n74
Wobus, Ulrich, 154n74
Wolf, Christa: as abject, 18, 72, 74, 100; and brief Stasi collaboration, 72–73, 76, 83, 88–90, 106–7, 113n65; criticizing capitalism, 97, 106, 125–26; criticizing conventional medicine and technology, 35, 38, 48, 50, 79, 87, 90; and Eleventh Plenum, 13, 29nn48–49, 37, 66n6, 92; as GDR author, 19; and *Literaturstreit*, 17–18, 32nn67–68, 32n65, 72–73, 75; as loyal dissident, 29n51, 64, 104, 106; observed by the Stasi, 73, 106–7; and protagonists identifying with victims of fascism, 97–99, 108, 112n46, 128; reacting to problems with psychosomatic illness, 34, 36, 55–56, 65n4, 111n36; and *schonende Lüge*, 58, 85; and socialism as only alternative to fascism, 34, 39; and subjective authenticity, 36–37, 42, 44–45, 114, 50. *See also* symptomatic body; symptomatic voice

Wolf, Christa, works by: "Abschied von Phantomen: Zur Sache: Deutschland," 31n59, 72; "Berührung," 68n32, 69n43, 80; *Ein Tag im Jahr: 1960–2000*, 34, 85, 92, 99, 110n22, 111n32, 111n36, 112nn41–42; *Ein Tag im Jahr im neuen Jahrhundert: 2001–2011*, 69n48; *Der geteilte Himmel*, 34–35, 37–39, 65–66n5, 66n6, 68n36, 102; "Glauben an Irdisches," 89, 110n26; "Ich bin schon für eine gewisse Maßlosigkeit," 68n32; *Im Dialog*, 29–30n51, 113n57; *Kassandra*, 24n7, 3, 72, 79, 94, 118; *Kein Ort. Nirgends*, 36; *Kindheitsmuster*, 24n7, 35, 66n9, 71n60, 71n64, 87, 93–94, 99, 101, 109n5, 111n35, 111n39, 112n42, 113n57, 159; "Krankheit und Liebesentzug," 35, 68n29, 81, 90, 99, 151n31, 161; "Krebs und Gesellschaft," 34, 38, 55, 66n7, 78, 110, 125; *Leibhaftig*, 2, 20, 35–37, 72–99, 101–7, 109nn1–2, 109nn4–5, 109n16, 110n22, 111n30, 111n40, 111–12nn40–41, 113n61, 113n63, 120, 125, 133, 156, 165–68, 170, 175, 189–90; "Lesen und Schreiben," 38, 48, 55, 67n20, 68n31, 70n56, 112n47; *Medea: Stimmen*, 31n61, 72, 112n42; *Moskauer Tagebücher*, 30n54, 65n3; *Nachdenken über Christa T.*, 2, 14, 35–64, 65nn2–4, 66n6, 66n8, 67n19, 67n21, 69n42, 69n49, 74, 79, 82, 84, 86, 89, 94, 96, 103, 111n30, 111n40, 124, 192; "Nagelprobe," 113n61; *Rede, daß ich dich sehe*, 66n6; "Rummelplatz 11. Plenum 1965—Erinnerungsbericht," 29n49; "Santa Monica, Sonntag, den 27. September 1992," 31n61; "Selbstversuch: Traktat zu einem Protokoll," 129; *Sommerstück*, 70n50; "Sprache der Wende—Rede auf dem Alexanderplatz," 65n1; *Stadt der Engel oder The Overcoat of Dr. Freud*, 2, 19, 32n67, 35, 72–76, 83–85, 89–91, 97, 100–101, 106–8, 110n24, 110n28, 111n35, 111nn39–40, 112nn41–42, 112n45, 183, 187n21, 189–90; *Störfall: Nachrichten eines Tages*, 35–36, 89, 110n26; "Subjektive Authentizität," 67n20, 69n46, 69n48, 112n48; "Unerledigte Widersprüche," 29n45, 39, 65n4, 66n8, 67n23, 68n31, 69n43, 70n56, 111nn34–35, 112n46, 114; "Warum schreiben Sie?," 67n20; *Was bleibt*, 17, 64, 71nn65–66, 71n68, 83; "Zwischenrede," 71nn67–68

Wolf, Gerhard, 29n49, 65n3
Wölfel, 28n40, 31n60, 31n64, 32n68
Wolfram von Eschenbach, works by: *Parzival*, 150n8
Wolk, Elisabeth, 151n29
Wolle, Stefan, 30n56
Wollweber, Ernst, 6
World War II, 13, 38, 40, 96, 147
Wunder, Michael, 152n35

Yuval-Davis, Nira, 33n78, 33n80

Zander, Judith, works by: *Dinge, die wir heute sagten*, 24–25n10
Zeit, Die, 17, 36, 153, 157, 185n3

www.ingramcontent.com/pod-product-compliance
Lightning Source LLC
Chambersburg PA
CBHW051609230426
43668CB00013B/2041